W9-BMK-528

Introduction to modern France 1500-1640

To Lucien Febvre, in all fidelity

Introduction to modern France 1500-1640

An essay in historical psychology

Robert Mandrou
Directeur des Etudes, Ecole Pratique des Hautes Etudes
Paris

Translated by R. E. Hallmark

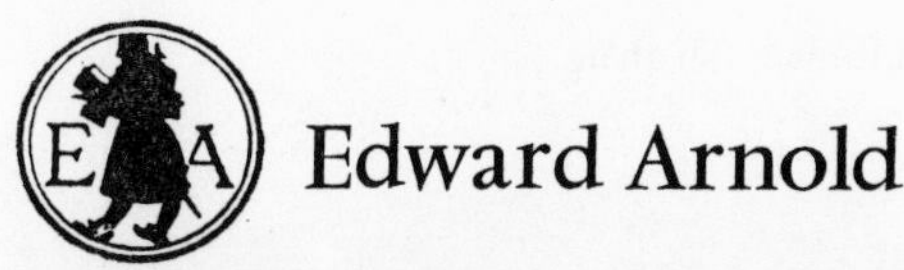

Authorized translation from the French
Introduction à la France moderne; essai de psychologie historique 1500–1640
published by Editions Albin Michel, Paris, in 1961; second edition 1974

This translated edition first published in 1975 by
Edward Arnold (Publishers) Ltd, 25 Hill Street, London W1X 8LL

ISBN: 0 7131 5778 X

Printed in Great Britain by W & J Mackay Limited, Chatham

Contents

List of maps

List of plates

The plates appear as follows: plates **1** and **2** between pages 18 and 19; plates **3** and **4** between pages 50 and 51; plates **5** to **8** between pages 178 and 179 and plates **9** to **12** between pages 210 and 211

1 Malnutrition and Christian charity. The first act of mercy is to feed the hungry. BN, Département des Estampes (Ea 25a, Plate 87).

2 Environment: housing. Research by mathematicians into ways of eliminating the unpleasant effects of smoke. *Théâtre des instruments mathématiques et mécaniques de Jacques Besson Dauphinois, docte mathématicien, avec l'interprétation des figures d'iceluy*, by François Bersald (Lyons 1578). BN Rés. (V, 440, Plate 41).

3 Mental equipment: reckoning. Table for calculating expenditure: an arithmetical table for ready reckoning. BN, Département des Estampes, Rés. (Collection Hennin) (Qb 216, 26, f. 16).

4 Time: an allegorical representation by J. Androuet du Cerceau, *Représentation allégorique du temps*. BN, Département des Estampes (Ed 2b, no. 37).

5 Hunting: an aristocratic privilege. BN, Département des Estampes (Ea 25a, Plate 75 (Aprilus)).

6 A country dance, in *Figures de la Bible: vie pastorale et la fin d'icelle*. BN, Département des Estampes, Rés. (Ed 5g, no. 126).

7 The dream of St Jerome the Ciceronian. St Jerome dreamed that he was suddenly brought before God in judgement and scourged for his attachment to pagan literature: 'Who are you?' 'I am a Christian.' 'You lie, you are not a Christian but a Ciceronian, for where your treasure is, there also is your heart.' BN, Mss latin 920, col. 308 v° (Hours of Louis de Laval); reproduced in Abbé V. Leroquais, *Les Livres d'heures manuscrites de la BN*, Plate 82 (Rés. fol. g. Q63(3)).

8 'The anatomy lesson', frontispiece to *Andreae Vesalii Bruxellensis, scholae medicorum Patavinae professoris, de humani corporis fabrica, libri septem* (Basle 1543). BN, Rés. (f. Ta^{9} 32).

Preface

Writing a book of history is never a mere intellectual amusement, an impression that some have wished to convey about works of literature such as the novel, the short story or the tale. The historian, at work on an ever-perfectible reconstruction of the past, aims to demonstrate, to prove—at the very least to add a stone to the collective construction. And he himself sets his work, and the contribution it makes, within the framework of this long sequence of approximations, of summaries which constitutes historical knowledge.

The present Preface presents no exception to this rule: over a period of some ten years, our efforts of historical research have been directed, in response to Lucien Febvre's appeal, towards the study of collective mentalities? Indeed, this whole volume is an exposition of this effort, its co-ordinates, its methods and its goals. We have perhaps been rash to tread in this domain which, although an instinctive part of any historian's approach, is at the same time an area whose features are as yet ill-defined. Each page of this book, therefore, represents a kind of justification.

We shall therefore content ourselves here with indicating how and why the name of Lucien Febvre will appear so frequently in the pages that follow, and in this way set out our debt and our gratitude to him.

★

Every historian knows how Febvre struggled for half a century to convince his colleagues, his pupils, his friends that they should direct their efforts towards a historical approach open to the new human sciences: economics, sociology, psychology. It was this last that he advocated most fervently towards the end of his life: engrossed by the findings of scholars such as Henri Wallon, Piaget and others, he effectively founded historical psychology,[1] by virtue of some of those combined essays and research programmes, true inspirations to research, which he alone could write, and of which the outstanding example is his great study, 'The reconstruction of affective life in the past: sensibility and history'.[2]

[1] Henri Berr, in the *Synthèse historique*, had also accorded a place to historical psychology: cf. Berr, *Du Scepticisme de Gassendi*, tr. B. Rochot (Paris, 1960), Introduction, p. 19.

[2] 'Comment reconstituer la vie affective d'autrefois? La sensibilité et l'histoire', *Annales d'Histoire sociale* (1941), reprinted in *Combats pour l'histoire* in the rubric 'Alliances et appuis', a programme in itself. A further collected volume, to be published shortly, will reprint Febvre's most important essays on historical psychology.

Since 1938, Febvre had outlined the approach with a firm hand: 'begin by setting out in detail, then by reconstituting for the era under consideration, the mental equipment at the disposal of the men of that era; by a strenuous effort, not only of scholarship but also of imagination, realize again the universe, the whole physical, intellectual and moral universe, within which each of the preceding generations lived and acted.'[3] In short, this book is our first response to Febvre's challenge—but a response which owes to him much of its substance.

An indefatigable scholar, Lucien Febvre was up till his last day engaged in developing study projects and outlines for books. In 1957, while classifying the material he left behind him, we found bundles of papers arranged for an *Introduction to the intellect of the modern Frenchman*: under the main headings were sketched in the broad outlines of the coordinates, so to speak, upon which research was to be based.

Thus we were able to combine our own documentation with that outlined by Febvre: discovering the same methods applied to the same problems of research, we were encouraged in the bold plan of following his outline and bringing it to completion. Febvre's thought and his advice animated the first stage of our work: discovering in his papers new proof that our effort coincided closely with his own, we thought we could do no better than to complete this first attempt at consolidation.

It is of course plain that Lucien Febvre cannot be held responsible in any degree for the present work: neither its imperfections nor the problems of the task we have attempted[4] have escaped us. But what is in question here is enough to justify the enterprise: a study in that area most neglected by history today. 'The historian has not the right to abandon it.'[5]

★

In conclusion, I must extend my warmest thanks to my friend Georges Duby, Professor at the Faculté des Lettres, Aix-en-Provence, whose interest in historical psychology equals my own, and who had the kindness to read this work in proof.

ROBERT MANDROU

[3] *Combats pour l'histoire*, p. 218.

[4] 'At the same time attractive and horribly difficult,' wrote Febvre in the essay quoted above: cf. *Combats pour l'histoire*, p. 229.

[5] *Ibid.*

Preliminary remarks and definitions

If it is quite useful to define the aim of this work in a few lines, it is far more important to assist the reader who is anxious for definition by clarifying certain concepts which will recur time and again, and explaining certain choices which had to be made at the outset.

Our subject is Man—or rather those men who lived in France 'from Columbus to Galileo, from the discovery of the Earth to that of the Heavens', to quote Michelet's splendid phrase; in other words, those who lived at that particularly important stage in the development of the Western world which extends from roughly 1490 to 1650. Our method—which we do not intend to expound dogmatically, since the book as a whole illustrates it—consists in first breaking down this modern civilization into its different constituent elements, and then reassembling it, by observing the lives of the men who embodied and created it. This twofold approach indicates not merely a plan to be followed, but the actual trend of the research. Through it, we are able to achieve the regrouping and hazard the explanations that follow, even though these are only the provisional results of an investigation for which it would be idle to claim completeness—the more so since our presentation of the modern Frenchman has been deliberately devised as an enquiry in the realm of historical psychology, a branch of history which has received so little attention that both methods and models are still to be created.

*

The first term to be defined is 'the modern Frenchman'. Must we specify what kind of man we are dealing with? That period, like every other, had its men of thought and its men of feeling, men who acted upon this earth and others who sought to escape from it into the world beyond; men who created beauty, men of learning, traders and politicians; inventors of machines and creators of

Note. Many of the works referred to in the footnotes are detailed in the Bibliography. In footnotes where this is the case, the name of the author is followed in brackets by the number given to the work in the Bibliography.

abstract systems, who on the basis of a few personal reflections reconstructed the graph of human destiny. It is easy enough for the practitioner of historical biography to take hold of a given human type in the society to which he belongs and which has set its mark upon him, and to study him at leisure. But he runs the risk of forgetting that none of these men is self-sufficient. Each is seen to stand alone, not as an individual but as a character playing his part—a *persona* in the theatrical sense of the word. He personifies one aspect of a single living reality, Man.

To present this synthesis in another way, one could point to the long line of mystics, stretching from the *Ejercitatorio de la vida espiritual* by Garcia Ximenez de Cisneros (which was published, as it happens, in 1500) to the *Traité de l'amour de Dieu* by St François de Sales, and to the *Augustinus*. Alongside them, though within different chronological limits, the list of modern astronomers runs from Copernicus with his *De Revolutionibus*, by way of Tycho Brahé and Kepler to Galileo. Further, one can say that it was not for the same reason that any given important event—for example, the discovery of new lands in the West by Columbus of Genoa in 1492—interested the artist, the master of music composing a motet, the merchant, the officer of the Crown and the philosopher. Yet these men were not strangers one to another: there was part of a whole in each and every one of them. Each man was, in his own way, a synthesis, at the very least a focal point upon which a whole series of influences converged and reacted.

Briefly, these were the triumphant advance made by the recent invention of printing, which quickly spread over the whole of Christendom; the widening of the known world by great geographical discoveries, and of the unknowable worlds by great hypotheses; the development of a humanist mind and of humanist methods, with their critical, positive tendencies; the discovery by the artist of a new way of interpreting and portraying nature; the elaboration of original kinds of religious attitudes; the constitution of great monarchies leading up to the creation of the modern State; and manifestations characteristic of a state of mind and of methods which, in the light of more recent developments, we would readily call 'capitalistic'. All these series of different phenomena, which were roughly concomitant, acted simultaneously upon the inhabitants of a certain number of countries. They produced in them a way of feeling, dispositions and aptitudes which were in marked contrast with those of their predecessors—and of their immediate successors. This was the first flowering of the modern world.[1]

[1] Obviously, we have not overlooked the fact that traditionally in France the 'modern period' covers the three centuries from the beginning of the sixteenth to the end of the eighteenth century. In the present work, we shall consider only the first half of this period without thereby denying the qualification of 'modern' to those who lived after 1650. Our remarks go on to justify adequately this *terminus ad quem*, as also our rejection of any purely numerical division.

From the end of the fifteenth century to the middle of the seventeenth, we see before us a period when various kinds of human activity—intellectual, religious, artistic, political and economic—seem linked together by an exceptionally close bond of interdependence. It is a time when there can clearly be seen in the human consciousness the effects of a lengthy concerted effort, when, in a new environment, 'man rediscovered himself' thanks to Vesalius and Servetus, Martin Luther and John Calvin, Rabelais and Montaigne, who were themselves all differing embodiments of his uneasiness and his restlessness.

To investigate group consciousness over so long a period we shall have to use another ill-defined notion—that of the generation. It is useful provided it is stripped of any automatic numerical formula, such, for example, as the one used by Cournot, who blithely divided each century into three sets of thirty years each (1501–30, 1531–60 and 1561–90) with ten years over to play with; these represented the generations of grandfathers, sons and grandsons.[2] In fact, speaking as historians or sociologists we use the word 'generation' daily in the broadest possible sense, which is how it may be used here. We are justified in speaking of the war and postwar generations given the combination of two factors: a sufficiently large yet coherent group of people, and a series of relatively important events of manifold and of national or worldwide consequence. The events set off in the people a series of chain reactions which, intersecting and intermingling, may well not be uniform but which, different as they are, all proceed from the same mental processes, both conscious and unconscious. They stamp the mind, the heart and the actions of the men of any one generation, provided one bears in mind equally the well-known fact that generations live on in succeeding generations in countless different ways.

★

The next point for clarification: the Frenchman whom we are seeking to recreate was obviously not without roots. He lived in an environment, in a landscape which he had worked in his own way—and which was not the same as those of central Europe, or the mountains and plains of the Mediterranean area. In the general trend towards the assertion of national individuality, the part played by the familiar, everyday setting is surely important, for the French as well as for the Italians or the Germans.

Unfortunately, we are scarcely able to write a lengthy account—or even the kind of description favoured by modern geographers—of the national environment in the sixteenth and seventeenth centuries. If the topography has barely changed—though one hastens to explain that this applies only to coastline, river courses and the mountains which are still wooded—the rest eludes us. On such topics as habitat, economic activities, towns and communications, only the bare

[2] Cournot (135), VIII.

outlines can be gleaned from the sparse evidence of contemporaries.[3]

No longer than is necessary will be spent on the extremely hazy—indeed, contradictory—pictures painted by these laconic eye-witnesses. We shall set the scene without the least hope that it will provide us with all the information on the mentalities of the French in 1600 that a diligent social observer could today derive from it, in comparing a citizen of Limoges with one of Chicago, or a peasant from the Beauce with one from Vaucluse. If we follow *Le Guide des chemins de France* (published in 1552) we switch continually from a joyful land with its fine towns displaying their numerous monuments, its 'recommended' inns and its 'good wines', to 'dangerous roads beset by thieves', as at Luzarches, and the 'devil's highways' between Guérigny and Nevers. The same contrast is to be found in the rare descriptions of the kingdom. Sometimes, one is presented with an idyllic picture of an earthly paradise, a land more prosperous than any other in the world—a myth which has flourished right up to our own times. Thus G. du Vair writes on the eve of the wars of religion: 'there were a great, not to say infinite, number of beautiful cities, large towns and villages, and especially, countless châteaux and beautiful houses which stood resplendent in the midst of countryside better tilled than any other.'[4] At other times, we are told of the huge, dark, and ever-dreaded forests, which hemmed in the cultivated land, advancing right up to the gates of towns and encroaching upon the outskirts of villages. This was no longer the garden of France, but a rugged land over which man had little control. Travellers and pilgrims dreaded roads and paths which ran through the woods, and paid guides very handsomely to lead them and to protect them from brigands and wild beasts. For wild animals too were a continual cause of anxiety everywhere: on his death bed, Bayard's father charged his eldest son to protect the family home from bears.

To go beyond this superficial contrast is to present a regional geography which is not without a great many 'anomalies' (cf. Map 1). It is no surprise to find praise of the fertile plains around Paris, Valois and the Beauce, Goele and Hurepoix, or of the great vineyards of Burgundy, Gaillac, or even of Saint-Pourçain. 'Normal', too, are references to the sterility of La Crau or of the heaths of Brittany, from Nantes to Vannes and from Angers to Rennes. On the other hand, the Beauce was then noted for its rich pasture land, the wines of Dauphiné, Voiron and Chalemont were considered to be of very high quality and the Perche was a fertile region which produced large quantities of cattle, poultry, fruit, cereals and even wild waterfowl.

[3] The art of description, as distinct from that of travel, was not yet born. Even Montaigne, with his sharp mind attuned to observing people and things, describes only the towns on his travels across France, Italy and Germany. The rural landscapes which we would like to 'see' meant nothing to him; he writes: 'so many leagues from such a town to such a town', and that is all.

[4] G. du Vair, *Oeuvres* (1636 edn), p. 2.

The answer is that the French landscape in the sixteenth century reflected a twofold impulse or preoccupation on the part of its inhabitants. On the one hand, there was an abiding concern to produce within the narrow boundaries of a small 'region'—whether politically or topographically defined—all its needs by way of food, clothing and implements; on the other, the growth of trade and of towns had meant that those commodities best promoted by the local soil and climate, the ingenuity of the local inhabitants and transport facilities, made a name for themselves far beyond the traditional boundaries. The history of the great vineyards amply illustrates this second point,[5] but the same applied to local artisan specialities—linen from Brittany, cloth from Berry and the iron-works of Savoy and Lorraine.

However much northern and southern France may still have differed at the end of the sixteenth century,[6] the human texture of the country was the same from the Somme to the Pyrenees and from the Saône to the Atlantic. Everywhere, it was divided into small regional units (*pays*) with their individual characteristics, differing from one another in their shares of natural resources and human development, and in the amount of contact which they enjoyed with their neighbours. They were always able to provide for their own basic needs, hence the admiration of travellers; but at the same time they were locked in a fierce struggle with nature, which was less kind than might appear to a visitor arriving from Hungary or Africa. At the heart of each *pays* lay a town which boasted its monuments, its craftsmen (whose products made a name for themselves at the fairs: for example, kid gloves from Issoudun, and fustians and ribbons from Saint-Maixent), its walls which protected it from the various dangers which beset the open countryside,[7] and, finally, its fairs and markets which attracted merchants from afar and people from the neighbourhood. Charles Estienne counted some 230 towns, mostly modest local capitals like 'Yssoire' or Sézanne, which far outnumbered the famous cities like Lyons with its bank, or Bordeaux with its wines.

★

The human scene in France, so far as we can glimpse it, with its more or less established urban settlements, fertile countryside and often uninhabited mountain regions, was certainly very different from that of the Mediterranean area or of central Europe. All the more reason, therefore, for thinking it unwise to

[5] Cf. the admirable and monumental work by R. Dion, *Histoire de la vigne et du vin en France* (Paris 1959).

[6] To a man like Etienne Dolet, Toulouse and Aquitaine were still barbaric regions, lacking in French culture.

[7] It is difficult to say whether all towns were enclosed by high walls at this time. Certainly, the vast majority of them were: in Normandy people made fun of Coutances with its walls of 'currant-bushes'.

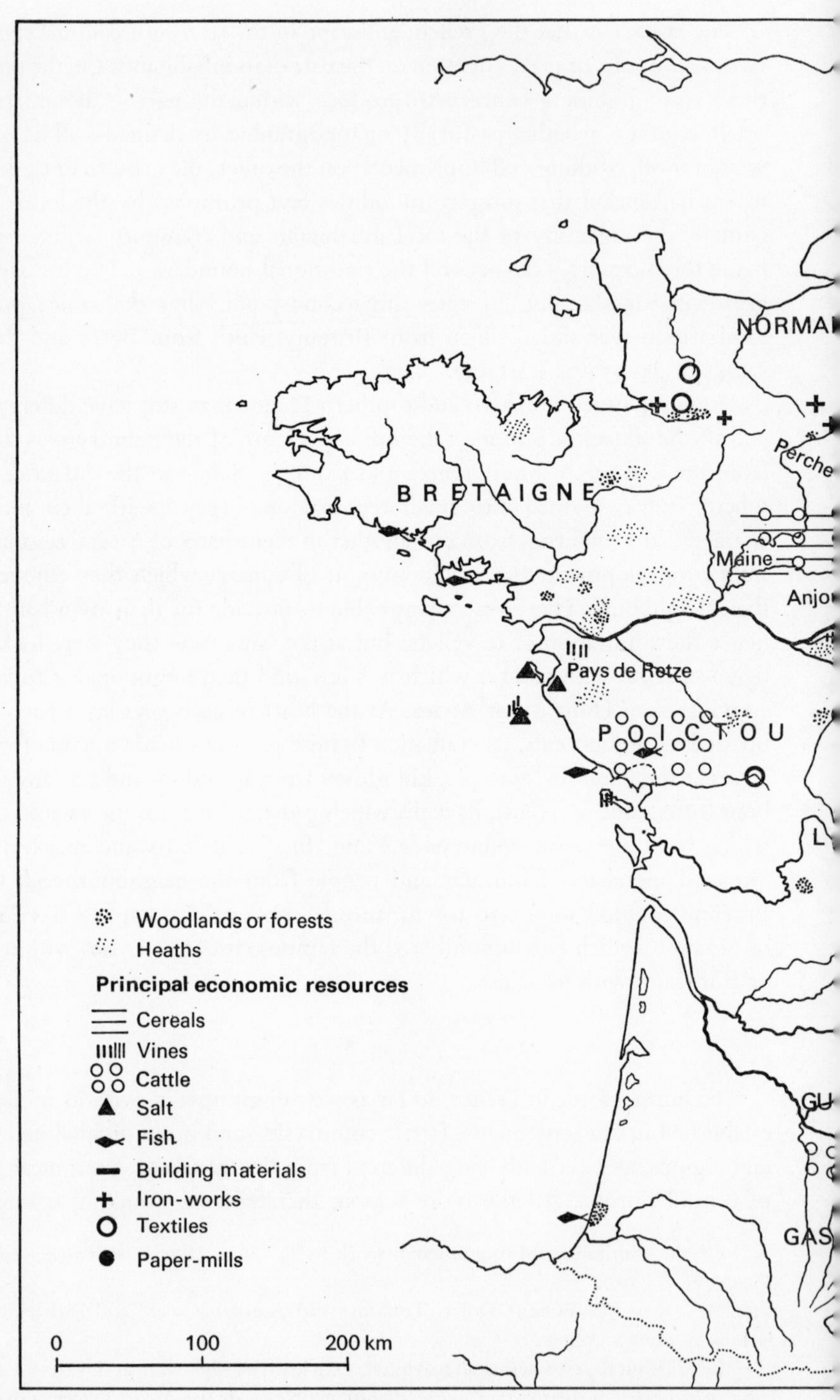

Map 1 The geography of France in the mid-sixteenth century, according to Charles Estienn

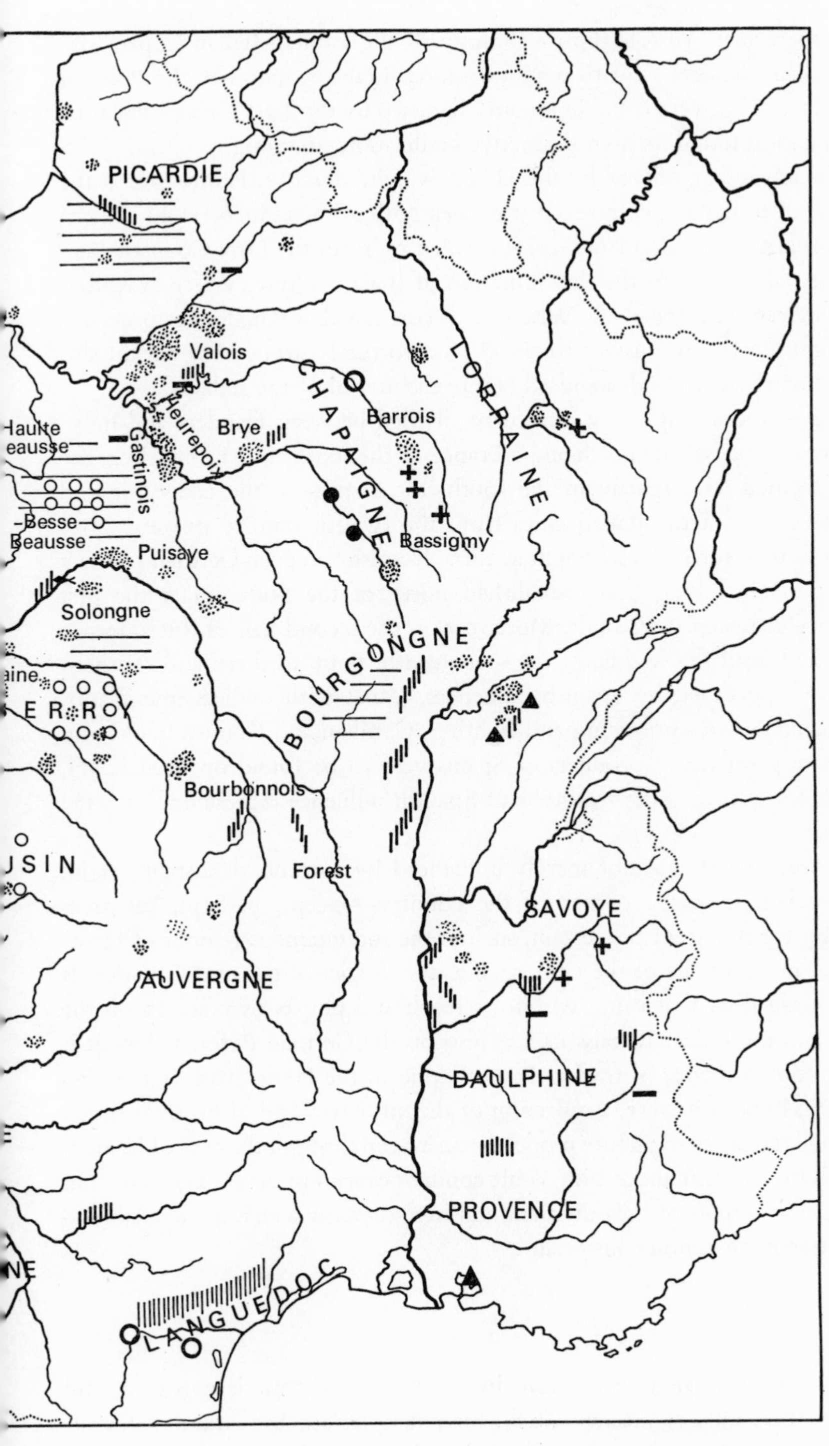

PICARDIE
Valois
Heurepoix
Haulte
eausse
Gastinois
Brye
Barrois
CHAPAIGNE
LORRAINE
Besse
Beausse
Bassigmy
Puisaye
Solongne
BOURGONGNE
aine
ERROY
Bourbonnois
Forest
USIN
SAVOYE
AUVERGNE
DAULPHINE
PROVENCE
NE
LANGUEDOC

attempt to recreate *en bloc* the psychology of the French, Italians, Spaniards, Irish and Rhinelanders—not to mention more distant peoples like the Poles or the Magyars, who were being constantly harassed by the Turks. From this time on, each nation found its own distinctive civilization emerging.

But the advantage offered by this choice is quite obvious. France was at the crossroads of routes and cultures. It was open both to the influences of northern European, not to say Germanic, culture radiating from the Low Countries and the Rhine valley, and to the dissemination of Italian culture, which was itself the Mediterranean *avant-garde*. Where art is concerned, it is no longer necessary to demonstrate this in answer to those who formerly argued for an autochthonous French art of high standard before the arrival of the Italians.

France was, one might say, shared or divided between Flanders and Italy: there was a France of the north and a France of the south. For a long time, the impulse seemed to originate in the south-east, thanks to the economic and artistic precocity of the Italian cities from the twelfth century onwards. But northern Europe formed a school in its turn: Flemish and even German painters and sculptors had long been established north of the Loire when the first Renaissance châteaux were built. Moreover, in the second half of the sixteenth century, and until the middle of the seventeenth, both northern and southern France were pervaded by Spanish influences. What with soldiers, merchants, mountebanks, monks preaching and fighting, Castilian and Flemish books and paintings, a great many products of Spain were to be found on French soil. Consider, for example, the triumphs of Spanish influence represented by 1589 and 1636.

However, France was not merely influenced by currents of distant origin, which reached to every corner of the country—except, perhaps, for areas isolated by the nature of the terrain, such as the mountainous regions of Haut-Limousin, or by the lie of the land, such as the district of the mid-Garonne. It actively grasped all that came within its reach and put its own stamp on the German and the Italian Renaissance, as also on the German Reformation. It is not, therefore, a matter of tracing France alone in the Frenchman, but of discovering in him, as it were, a reflection of the known world of his own times.

We shall try, then, to picture modern man as seen through the eyes of his own day, to think and feel about him as his contemporaries in actual fact did—but using the instruments of measurement and investigation which are available to the mid-twentieth-century historian.

★

Many pictures have already been drawn of the early modern period, and drawn by the hands of masters. Such, for example, are Burckhardt's *Kulturgeschichte*, the hundred or so pages devoted to the sixteenth century by Cournot in his *Considérations*, and especially volume VII of the *Histoire de France*, which Michelet wrote in the middle of the last century. Burckhardt is particularly alive to the external forms of social life, to festivals, cults, and even to politics considered as a social mechanism. Cournot is above all concerned with the march of ideas and events. Michelet is the master, with his wide-ranging grasp, passing from peak to peak, from genius to genius, taking Vesalius, Rabelais, Shakespeare, Montaigne, Cervantes and others and grouping them all around the focus which he created in its entirety: the Renaissance.

We do not intend to follow in their footsteps and add yet another picture of the sixteenth and seventeenth centuries. We have recalled their work simply to indicate once more at the end of these preliminary remarks the particular standpoint of the present work. It is essentially an attempt to recreate and to reconstruct mentalities in an age of radical change, when group psychology was in many ways renewed; an attempt to observe men both at their occupations and in the context of their material civilization, not so as to build up an encyclopedic view but to discover the valid explanations of these attitudes, whether they were new or inherited from the High Middle Ages.

The documentation necessary for such research is vast. Some indication of its general disposition—which inevitably raises many problems of method—must now be given. In fact, it is long familiarity with these attitudes which gives one the prudence necessary to make use of conflicting and disparate evidence. However, if some general principles must be established, one point to be made at the outset is that the evidence of the artist or man of letters must be used with caution: this is equally true of d'Aubigné and Montaigne, and all the more so of Corneille. The artist, whatever his mode of expression, has a gift of second sight, a more refined sensibility than the average man. As a witness, he is at once very good and too good: Ronsard, when obsessed with death or the misfortunes of his country, what it means to have him present! There can be no possibility of ignoring him, but he is to be seen in his true dimensions as a poet. The vast collections of records of criminal proceedings also represent a form of exasperated sensitivity, driven to extremes: here, the *Archives départementales* (series B, G and E) provide us with further evidence for scrutiny, whereby we might discover the elements of truth which lie behind current impressions. The *Archives municipales*, reflecting the day-to-day worries of the townsfolk, form yet another precious source. Even more important are collections of memoirs and the *livres de raison*, an invaluable fund of information, which Lucien Febvre has already exploited in his *Rabelais*: the journals of Gouberville, Claude Haton and Thomas Platter. Then P. de Vigneulles, and later Jean Burel, Pierre de Bessot and many others who commented upon their everyday lives are all highly-prized informants. The travel notes written by lovers of the exotic, the echoes that reach us from the earliest gazettes and broadsheets, and collections of letters, all the opportunities for direct self-expression used by modern man, are now invaluable for our purpose: a description of 'New France' tells us as much about the mother country as it does about Canada, for astonishment and critical observations are highly significant with regard to metropolitan France. Since the use of such material bears little relationship to traditional research, the lacunae will be only too obvious, and we would not think of denying their existence. It would be idle to hope to exhaust all the possibilities offered by the records of criminal proceedings, for example. Perhaps later, given systematic research and team-work, this may be achieved. Meanwhile, let us accept that it was necessary to go ahead and venture on this attempt to make more extensive research possible. May this book be a starting-point.

Part I
Human dimensions

Today it is well known that man changes—physically and psychologically—throughout time and space. The change through space has long been regarded as an acknowledged fact, ever since the exaggerations of Taine or Ratzel. The change through time is a more subtle one, though it is equally clear: a visit to a thirty-year-old film, such as *La Grande illusion*, allows one to perceive immediately—beneath the differences in fashion which strike the eye—how quickly gestures and inflexions change.[1] To counteract the notion, over-popularized by philosophers and men of letters, of an eternal man, never varying in his material and spiritual needs, his passions, and his equal share of common sense, the historian asserts—and proves—human variation and evolution in every sphere. Each civilization, or more accurately each moment of a civilization, sets before us a human being who differs in some degree from his predecessors and his successors, in everything from his nervous equilibrium to his mental equipment. Our first task must be to discern these differences in modern man: to rediscover his reasoning habits, certainly, but also to investigate his bodily techniques, the ways in which the body was used; in other words, to grasp the dimensions of modern man, the nature of his physical, emotional, and intellectual life so far as he himself reveals them to us, and so far as a comparison with more recent and familiar times will allow. Having first obtained this general impression of him, we can then proceed to consider him in his relations with his fellow-men, to see him in his social context, and finally to attempt to assess the contribution made by his various activities to his mental outlook; three approaches designed to capture the full complexity and richness of the subject.

[1] René Clair had already noted this in the *Encyclopédie française* XVIII (1940), pp. 17–88.

Chapter 1
The body: food and environment

Anyone seeking to throw light on the modern mentality must surely consider first the question of food by virtue of the *primum vivere*; for the men of the sixteenth and seventeenth centuries shared with those of earlier times an obsession with daily subsistence. Everyone knows the picture drawn by Taine, so true for the whole of the *ancien régime*: 'The common people resemble a man walking in a lake with the water up to his mouth; the least depression in the bed of the lake, or the smallest wave, and he loses his footing, goes under, and drowns.' A wet year, a late frost, or a July storm could mean anguish and famine for a whole province.

Yet the due recognition of this basic truth has given rise to too narrow a conception of the history of foodstuffs. By stressing the importance of cereals, it has led the few historians concerned with these basic necessities to portray man not only as a great eater of corn, but also as an eater of nothing but corn. Certainly, modern man was mainly concerned with cereals, for experience had shown him how (judged empirically) these were superior to other foodstuffs in terms of their yield in calories. Hence the importance attached throughout the ages to the problems of the production, preservation and use of the precious corn. Hence, also, an anxiety psychosis, which has no equivalent in the psychology of the twentieth-century peasant. It still matters whether the harvest is good or bad, for it affects the pocket; but in former times, in Franche-Comté or in the Beauce, the cry 'is it raining?' was uttered in anguish, for fear of famine. To reserve the land for corn and the corn for men, to protect it from bad weather, fieldmice and thieves—these were economic, technical and above all social problems. It is obvious that anyone who stored corn was speculating on corn. Chauverey said as much in 1574 in a letter to Granvelle, after the Cardinal of Naples had sent him details of a method for storing wheat in the granary for five or six years 'as fine and fresh as the day it is first put there'. Chauverey added: 'If the method is applied, everyone will hoard his corn, and only those in need will sell, so that the poor will have to buy sustenance at the pleasure of the rich.' To the three preoccupations mentioned above a fourth must be added, at least as far as towns were concerned: that of ensuring that corn supplies circulated freely, a problem which was still receiving attention in the eighteenth century under Turgot, and even in the first half of the nineteenth.

Yet whatever may be the importance of a history of cereal prices and markets, or of an evaluation of corn production and consumption, it must also be recognized in the light of present-day dietetic research that it is just as necessary to clarify the question of overall diet. Certainly, the monotony of meals based excessively upon corn is one factor here; but one must equally consider, as far as available evidence will allow, factors such as the very small meat content, and calorie, protein or vitamin deficiency, phenomena which all bring to mind the nutritional deficiencies of the less developed countries. Further, we must look at all the possible repercussions of these various factors on the muscular strength, capacity for work, and vitality of all those subjected to such a diet. Modern man sought with varying degrees of success to balance his diet: this balance, which admitted of chronic or momentary deficiencies, was itself made up of a diet whose components varied, supplementing each other according to the needs of the seasons and especially the inclemencies of the weather. It ensured that the social group was maintained and survived under physiological conditions about which we certainly know very little, but which must be described in as much detail as possible.

The elements of diet

Describing the diet of Canadian Indians with all its peculiarities, a chronicler wrote in 1612, 'no salt, no bread, no wine',[1] which brings us back, at the very outset, to cereals. They were present on every table in the form of bread,[2] gruel or girdle-cakes, and were the basis of the diet for all classes of society. The bourgeois kept some in stock—sacks of corn and flour in his granary, and always a loaf in his breadbin. Nor would anyone have dreamt of locking up at nightfall without first checking that these stocks were safe. The common people in both town and country could not conceive of their daily existence without a quantity of flour. Frequently it would be in the form of bread made from a mixture containing oats or barley, and often from wheat and rye; but in times of famine, it was common to make gruel with pounded chestnuts and acorns. Black or white bread was the staple foodstuff, which, by a very long-standing tradition that had not yet been altered in the modern period, was considered sacred by Church and men alike. To make a cross on a new loaf with the point of a knife before cutting it, or to instil into one's children religious respect for the smallest

[1] 'One of our men . . . lived like them for about six weeks, eating no salt, no bread, and drinking no wine, sleeping on skins on the ground, even in snow.' Lescarbot, *Histoire de la Nouvelle France* (1612; new edn 1866), p. 555.

[2] 'The most necessary of all the foodstuffs that God in His goodness created for man's sustenance,' stated the economic dictionary of Chomel (1718).

crust, amounts to the same thing. 'When I was a small child', writes P. Viret, 'and I heard the bell ringing for going to school, it seemed to be saying what I had had drilled into me: 'Wasted bread means a broken head', and I was quite astonished that it had spoken the truth.'[3]

Corn formed the principal occupation of the peasant, since agriculture as a whole was organized to produce the maximum of cereals, in both the two- and three-field rotations; and for a long time the art of husbandry was directed solely towards increasing the surface areas under cultivation. But it was also the major preoccupation of the townsman: the corn market was never far from the town hall, and was under daily supervision, as were the different trades connected with it—the corn-chandlers and hucksters who purchased grain in the country and transported it to the towns, the oft-detested millers, and especially the bakers, who, exposed to the constant temptation of docking the loaf of a handful of dough, and often threatened with looting, enjoyed little protection against the wrath of the populace. It was the king's responsibility to ensure that the large cities of the time, such as Lyons, Paris and Rouen, were supplied with corn. He bought foreign corn if necessary and carefully fixed the price for each grade of bread; a concern which was never disavowed throughout the whole of this period, nor for long after.

On the one hand, corn was the crop with which peasant empiricism had had the best results—even if yields of five or six to one seem today very mediocre; thus regions where the soil was poor and the climate too wet, such as Brittany, produced wheat, rye, barley and millet. But on the other hand, harvests were barely adequate to provide for the whole population. Everything combined to bring this about: the low yields produced by the agricultural methods used, and especially the unequal distribution, for the landlords—the noble or bourgeois landowners and the Church—deducted their share in kind as soon as it was harvested. The result was a vicious circle. Since corn production was just equal to consumption in an average year, the urgent demand for it could only encourage the peasant to maintain, if not to increase, its production. This diverted him from crops which would have provided the basis for another nutritional balance; and the consumption of cereals was all the greater since there were few complementary products offering a significant calorific yield. The French were to continue to eat great quantities of bread and flour until the agricultural revolution of the eighteenth and nineteenth centuries.[4]

[3] P. Viret, *Office des morts* (1552), p. 71; quoted in *P. Viret d'après lui-même* (Lausanne 1911), p. 4.

[4] Many attempts have been made to estimate his daily ration, from Messance in his *Recherches sur la population* (1756) to Labrousse in *La Crise de l'économie française à la veille de la Révolution* (1944), p. xxiv. Cf. the following quotation from Messance, p. 286: 'the head of a family who is responsible for keeping and feeding a wife and three children is presumed to consume, in the course of a year, the amount of 15 *setiers* (Paris measure), on the basis of 3 *setiers* per head. This assessment is far too generous. . . .'

The lower classes normally ate vegetables with their bread—the 'pot herbs' from their garden, turnips, broad beans, lentils, peas, cabbages, leeks, onions or sorrel, which they boiled or prepared more elaborately, using animal fats or walnut or rape-seed oil. In all, this does not offer a great deal of variety. Naturally, the various plants discovered in America, tomatoes, haricot beans, aubergines and potatoes, were not available; but neither were many kinds of vegetables, less common than those mentioned above, which were grown by monks in their kitchen gardens, or by botanists who were interested in rare plants, nor some, such as melons, artichokes, cauliflowers, rhubarb or chicory, which had been occasionally imported from the East during the Middle Ages. Sop with vegetables, this was the poor man's dish—a good thick soup, which filled the stomach and gave the impression of being nourishing. Take, for instance, this recipe from 1650, which is to be found in a 'manual for the relief of the poor':

> Fill with water a cooking-pot or cauldron which holds exactly five bucketfuls and add to it 25 pounds of bread, broken small, plus, on meat days, seven *quarterons* of animal fat or, on fast-days, seven *quarterons* of butter; four *litrons* of peas or broad beans with herbs or a half-bushel of turnips or cabbages, leeks or onions, or other pot-herbs, plus salt in proportion, costing 14 *sous* or thereabouts. The lot, cooked down to four bucketfuls, will be enough for a hundred people and is to be served out with a ladle holding one bowlful.[5]

These common vegetables, grown by the peasant in his garden, or bought in the market for a few pence, thus had their place on every table, served with the usual seasoning—parsley and chervil.

On the other hand, butcher's meat and game were eaten less frequently. For the peasantry and likewise for the humbler classes in the towns, meat was an exceptional dish served only a few times a year, and certainly not every Sunday, despite the legendary vow of Henri IV. This low rate of meat consumption is adequately explained by the poor methods of rearing stock, with grazing taking place surreptitiously in the corn fields, and on the heaths and commons. Only towns had butchers' shops, and they found supplies erratic—almost as irregular as those for the sea and freshwater fish market. No doubt the peasant could keep a little poultry, or a pig, over and above what he provided for his lord; but the scarcity of salt, at any rate in areas far from the sea or the salt-pans of Franche-Comté and Lorraine, generally made curing impossible. Very often, peasant households had none to season their daily stock-pot; and resorting to trade with the formidable dealers in contraband salt was not without its dangers. Without exaggerating, it might even be suggested that the humbler classes in town and country would have found it difficult to make any restrictions in their diet during Lent. Deliveries of fresh fish, of cod, and fresh, smoked or salted

[5] BN, Mss, *fonds français*, 21,802, f. 81.

herring were too irregular.[6] Of course, eggs were the great standby; but in fact, for the really poor, Lent lasted the whole year round. The more well-to-do in town and country laid in private stocks. Their salting-tub would contain pork, and sometimes also game, as well as the animal fats, especially beef fats, which were indispensable for cooking. But all meat was very expensive, as were the other animal products, milk, butter and cheese. They were almost luxury items and were never squandered. At the carefully-organized banquets held to celebrate one or other of the great festivals, the greatest skill went into the economical handling of the roasts: they were preceded by boiled meats, designed to 'take away the worst of the hunger'. Fine cuts of game, in particular, were always appreciated, but the very excesses of praise lavished upon them allows one to suppose how rare they were. There is no doubt that meat was not the daily rule, even in high society: Louis XIV was to scandalize those who witnessed his gargantuan repasts.[7]

The consumption of 'sweets' varied similarly from social group to social group. Wild fruit, of course, was available to all, and the peasantry ate the bilberries, blackberries, raspberries, morello cherries, sour apples and other fruits which grew in the woods. Together with acorns, for which in bad years men would compete with their livestock, these poor fruits represented one of the invaluable resources of the common woodlands. But the bourgeois in the towns had fruit from their orchards or from the market and these they often kept throughout the winter by drying or preserving. Apricots, medlars, peaches, plums, grapes, cherries, almonds, and a hundred widely acknowledged varieties of apples and pears, often served with rose-water, make quite a long list. There were in addition the pastries, made with sugar,[8] still a rare commodity, or with honey, which would normally round off a well-organized meal. These were made (to return to it once again) from pure wheaten flour—not from rye, barley or acorns. Such choice dishes were never to be found on the tables of the poor except on special occasions, perhaps twice or three times in the year, when meat was also on the menu.

The list we have just compiled could give a false impression: that almost the same variety of foodstuffs was available then as we have today, for all that was missing, in fact, were the exotic commodities from America or the tropics. These began to make their appearance in Europe during this period. It should be emphasized once more that the difference between the fare of the poor

[6] Sea or freshwater fish formed only a small proportion of the food eaten. Poor salting and slow transport accounted for the many complaints about herrings being 'bad and unfit for human consumption'.

[7] Some German historians, in particular Schmoller at the end of the last century, noted a very high consumption of meat in the towns of medieval Germany. The file is open.

[8] There was not enough honey for it alone to replace sugar in the making of sweets, and, depending upon the region and its local recipes, many substitutes were used—e.g. *cidre cuit* in Normandy.

peasant or urban journeyman and that of the nobleman or the bourgeois was more than simply a question of quantity—and of quality. Year in, year out, the poor would dine only on vegetable produce, the barest essentials for survival, which just kept them from death's door: bread and flour formed practically the whole of their diet. Nor did the richest enjoy every day the fine and wide choice of animal and vegetable commodities which we have mentioned. The town market no doubt offered all of them for sale, especially the Paris market, about which we have more information;[9] but frugality was the general rule. If there is a period in history when diet was dominated by cereals, with wheat becoming more and more important at the expense of the others, it was indeed the modern period, and this trend in fact persisted until the nineteenth century, when Maurizio became concerned by the monopoly that wheat held.[10]

It is much more difficult to show how the different dishes which complemented the cereal diet were prepared. Vegetables and meats were then cooked in fats, oils and spices. The spices, such as pepper, cinnamon and ginger, exotic commodities imported from the East, were used sparingly by the townsfolk. They were invariably stockpiled and were included among the supplies that the bourgeois kept in his larder, like his corn and salt provisions; and they were also given as presents. But they were a standard commodity for one section of society alone. This was not the case with fats and oils, which were both used even when rancid—indeed, especially when rancid, because the family pot thereby acquired more taste. Thus Fazy de Rame sold 'old' lard,[11] and in 1502 he used the last of a goatskin bottle of olive oil, which had been sent to him five years before, to feast his lawyer. But it is not possible to draw a map indicating the prevalent usage of lard or beef fats, olive oil, nut oil, or hempseed oil. Butter would seem to have been used far less then for cooking than now, while the use of olive oil would seem to have been much more widespread and important than it is today. However, these are no more than generalizations for which insufficient supporting evidence can be found. No cookery books in the proper sense of the word were written, at any rate in France,[12] before the middle of the seventeenth century: treatises of the *De re cibaria* type were studies by doctors, whose principal concern was to classify foodstuffs according to their utility for the human organism, or their qualities judged according to the medical criteria of the age, such as the three subdivisions of the human body: spirits, humours and solids, the hot and the wet, and so on.

[9] According to Scaliger, the small provincial town market often did little business. For he notes at Chambéry: 'Never have I seen so fine and so big a market anywhere as there, nor so many peasants. Everything is there in plenty.'

[10] Maurizio (75), *passim*.

[11] De Manteyer (44), I, p. 82.

[12] Here again, the Mediterranean countries were precursors: cf. the *Libro de cucina* from the fourteenth century, quoted by I. Origo, *Le Marchand de Prato* (Paris 1959), of which there is also an English version, *The merchant of Prato* (London 1957).

Plate 1 Malnutrition and Christian charity. The first act of mercy is to feed the hungry.

NOVVM ET CERTVM INVENTVM, CONSTRVENDIS
LOCO QVAMVIS HVMILI CAMINIS, À QVIBVS ET
SOLIS RADII, ET VENTORVM FLATVS, ITA ARCENTVR
VT IN CVBICVLIS, FVMO, NVLLVS OFFENDATVR-

Plate 2 Environment: housing. Research by mathematicians into ways of eliminating the unpleasant effects of smoke.

Drink

It proves impossible, therefore, to determine the regions where the different basic cooking elements were used. The same difficulty is encountered in trying to classify drinking habits on a regional basis.[13] In this respect, as in many others, France was a meeting-point for traditions, a land where the drinking patterns of three major areas met and intermingled: the wine of the Mediterranean area; beer, then considered to be the drink *par excellence* of northern Europe and especially of England; and cider, of which the Normans and the Biscayans are supposed to have held the monopoly in the fifteenth century. As everyone knows, the vine had reached all the provinces, and the inhabitants of Normandy appreciated wine just as much as those of Provence. Though Normandy without any doubt grew more apple trees than many other provinces by the end of the sixteenth century, cider and perry were made everywhere: for example, Brie made a perry which was considered very poor. Only beer—or the Gallic ale—could be located with any great certainty, and considered as the drink of the Flemings and other peoples of the north and north-east. Fery de Guyon pulled a face when drinking it for the first time during his travels in the north.[14]

Between these three drinks (or perhaps we should say four, so as to include plain water, which everyone drank) there existed a hierarchy and, as in the case of foodstuffs, a kind of social distribution. As far as drinking habits are concerned, we normally accept the traditional image of the Frenchman as a wine-drinker from the time when the Phocaeans first brought the vine to Marseilles and succeeded in acclimatizing the plant in the country. All the usual associations spring to mind—the pride of the producer, who drank his own wine, irrespective of its quality, in the Alps as in Burgundy; the pride of the bourgeois, whose cellar was as well-stocked as his granary; the inhabitant of Lyons who owned a small vineyard in Beaujolais, and the Parisian who made his wine at Montmartre or Argenteuil. In fact, the same was true for drink as for corn; in the one case it was black bread versus white, in the other, good wine, cider or perry, versus water. Vauban, on a visit to Vézelay at the end of the seventeenth century, still maintained that some peasants drank wine only three times a year. The rest of the time they drank water or the inferior drinks which were kept in the great households for the common labourers—*petit cidre* or *vins verds*. In contrast, better-furnished tables more commonly carried both the drinks that were also sold in taverns—cider and wine, but especially wine. Though some doctors,

[13] We have deliberately refrained from using in this context the well-worn but over-ambitious expressions 'butter, oil or wine civilizations'.

[14] Beer was not, of course, at that time the café drink which it eventually became in the nineteenth and twentieth centuries in France. Besides, there is a good reason why it was not widely drunk: it used up corn and barley, which were better employed for other purposes. In times of shortage, legislation prohibiting brewing was often called for and enforced.

notably from Normandy,[15] maintained that wine represented a grave danger to health, bringing dropsy, dysentery or fever upon anyone who over-indulged, and doing so in an extremely insidious fashion, since this 'gentle, pleasant enemy' ruined its devotees without their realizing it, though the same doctors attributed to cider the valuable property of ensuring long life more than any other drink, there is no doubt that wine was preferred, both in the 'wine taverns', and at home.

Gaudeamus, let's make good cheer,
Let's drink down the wine and leave the beer,

as they sang in Amiens in 1600.

This preference does not call for lengthy explanations. However much the devotees of cider in the late sixteenth century might try to make the most of its different types, or expound the virtues of the tens of different varieties of apples that the lord of Gouberville made known in Normandy, cider could not hold its own in competition with vintages that more than a thousand years of viticulture had established and made known throughout Europe. The composition of the wine-cellars of bourgeois merchants or the urban or religious communities provides us with a map of the wine industry (cf. map 2) which is quite different from the one that we are familiar with today. The 'French' wines —that is, those from Ile-de-France—were invariably considered to be of high quality, and their vineyards, Montmartre, Argenteuil and Dammartin, were quoted far beyond the Paris area. This is also the case with the red and white wines of Orléans, reputed to be among the very best. Next came those of Gascony and Aunis, Anjou and the Soissons region, Champagne—the still, not the sparkling wine—and Auxerrois. Yet the first prize was held by Burgundy, and in particular by Beaune, whose wines were at a premium everywhere. The picture is completed by the imported wines, of which there were only a few, the most important being malmsey, the port of the day.

All town halls kept impressive stocks of wine in their cellars. For not only was it a nourishing beverage, or thought to be so; it was also the drink for official receptions, and even the prisoners in their cells had a right to a ration on festive occasions. Above all, apart from the general distributions which marked the happy occasion of some Royal Entry, when an Orléans *clairet* was served to the ladies, and a rich red Beaune to the gentlemen, these fine wines were carefully preserved, according to a tradition inherited from the Middle Ages, to be presented as gifts. A cask of Beaune wine made a royal present: when, following his appointment as governor of Normandy by François I, the Duke of Alençon made his entry into Rouen, he was presented with three casks of Beaune wine, 'of which two were *clairets* and one white' (20 August 1516). Wine, whether a vintage of quality matured in the wood for several years or the modest local variety, was indeed the drink which prevailed.

[15] Le Paulmier (61), *passim*.

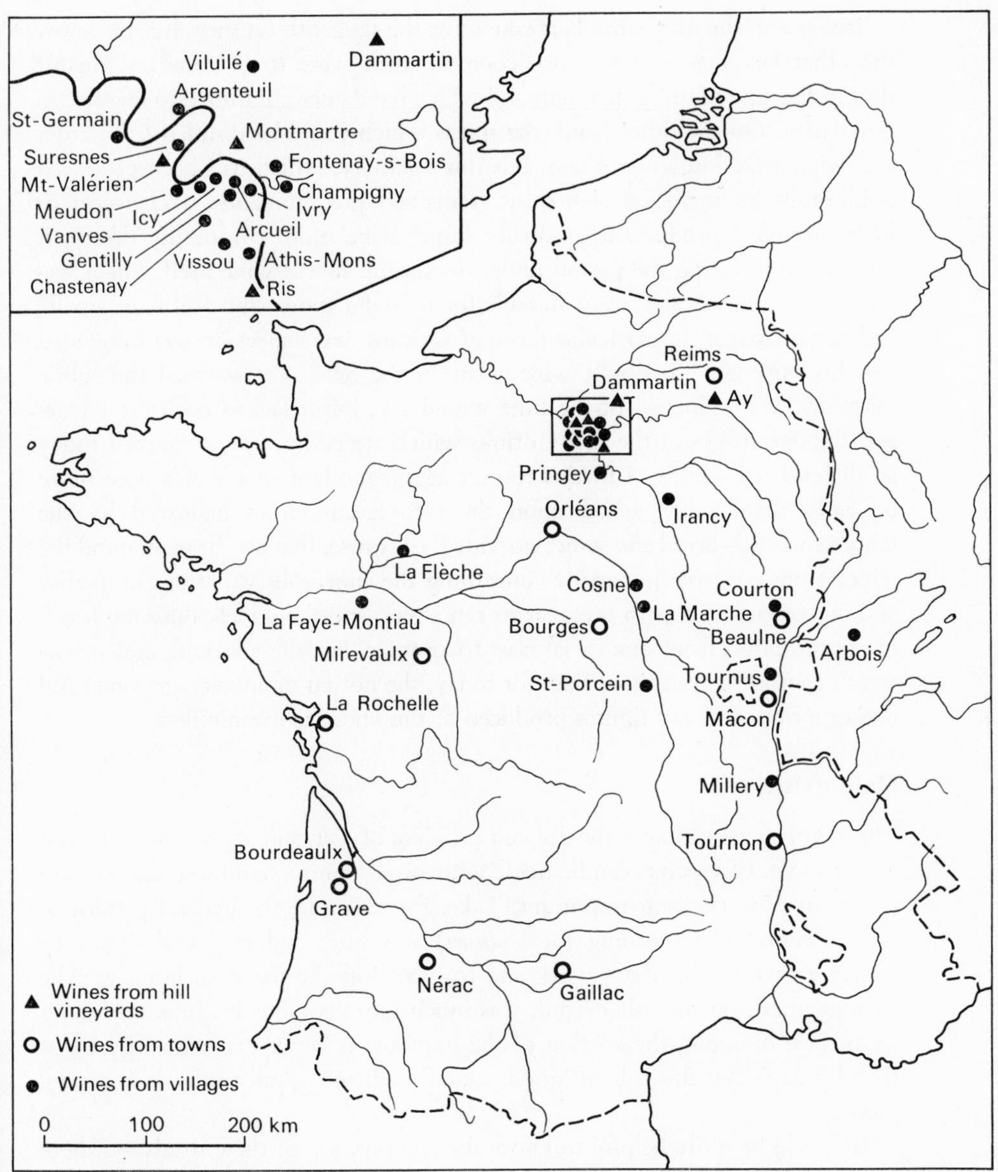

Map 2 The great vineyards of France in the sixteenth century, according to Etienne Dolet, *Commentarium linguae latinae* II.

It was also the only stimulant taken, for the sixteenth century did not know the other beverages—coffee, tea, cocoa—which were to become fashionable during the Age of Enlightenment and which have since continued to increase in popularity. On the other hand, the spirits which could be distilled from cider and wine were known to them, but this *aqua vitæ*, which had been produced assiduously by medieval alchemists, remained predominantly a chemical or pharmaceutical product. It gradually came to be more commonly drunk, it would seem, during the period under discussion. It was wine itself which was regarded as the cordial 'most suitable for reviving those who feel faint or ill', and certain wines, in particular those of Orléans, were specially recommended for this purpose. No doubt wine went to the head—or warmed the subtle humours, as the doctors of the time would say; but it lacked both the virtues and the drawbacks of the many drinks which are commonly consumed today at all levels of society.[16] In this respect again, modern man's diet was, more typically than today, based upon the two commodities hallowed by the Christian faith—bread and wine; provided, of course, that one bears in mind the reservations we have just made concerning the enormous variations in quality and ingredients that both these terms can cover, and the widely differing levels of consumption from one social class to another. For the sixteenth and seventeenth centuries, even more than for today, the notion of an average total food consumption, and any figures produced to this end, are meaningless.

Malnutrition

This involves returning to the difficult problem of diet, and approaching it from a new angle. Few points can be made with any certainty, and those that can are in our opinion the least important. Take, for example, the general pattern of eating habits. The morning meal (*disner*) was brief and frugal, designed to sustain a man for his day's work and to 'ward off the pangs of hunger'. The evening meal, on the other hand, was much more copious because, according to medical opinion, 'the coction of the humours is better performed by night than by day'. But this rule of 'good, sound medicine' is only valid as a general guide.

It would be more helpful to know the composition of these meals, but here again we must be content with the most widely differing accounts. We are shown only the extremes—either gigantic feasts worthy of Gargantua, or the privations that led to physiological disorders. We have many descriptions of the former—the banquets and great feasts organized for kings, emperors and princes, which have come down to posterity as models of culinary ostentation. At the banquet of the Order of the Golden Fleece in Utrecht in January 1546, five courses were served, amounting to a huge array of soups, meats, assorted

[16] On the dearth of stimulants, cf. Part III, ch. 18.

venisons, side-dishes, pâtés of all kinds, preserves, fruit jellies, cheese and so forth, all washed down with white wines and *clairets* and preceded by malmsey. Here, by way of example, are details, according to the accounts of John of Vandenesse:

> *First course:* Beef and mutton, ham and tongue, soup, calf's head, venison with turnips, strained peas, roast veal, hot swan, gosling, turkey, veal pâté, udder pâté and side-dishes.
>
> *Second course:* Breast of veal, roast sausages, tripe, cutlets, venison stew, hot venison pâté, roast pheasant, roast capon, plover, heron, partridge pâté, roast spring chicken, pigeon and side-dishes.
>
> *Third course:* Peacock, partridge, teal, fox, pork jelly, hot pigeon pâté, cold heron pâté, blancmange (white savoury sauce), clear (aspic) jelly, roast duck, roast drake, joint of mutton and side-dishes.
>
> *Fourth course:* Cold turkey pâté, cold venison pâté, hare pâté, partridge pâté, heron pâté, boar's head, cold swan, bustard, crane, pheasant pâté.
>
> *Fifth course:* Three varieties of jelly, three varieties of dried fruit, three varieties of preserves, a *castreling* (form of nougat), a flan, a tart, raw and cooked pears, aniseed, medlars, chestnuts, cheese. When everything had been cleared away, except the tablecloths, wafers and biscuits were served with white and red hippocras. The meal was preceded by dry toasts and malmsey.

A real orgy, even assuming that each guest took only a small helping of each of the five courses.

It is difficult to find descriptions of more normal meals. *Livres de raison* record only those feasts which gathered together the whole family, in the widest sense of the word, to celebrate the important religious festivals. These too were exceptional occasions, as were the great feasts of the religious communities. In 1618, the Chapter of Dole provided a supper for sixteen people, and for this purpose bought quantities of roebuck and mutton, three partridges, two turkeys, eight quails, two leverets, seven chickens, fourteen pigeons, larding fat, preserves, capers, olives, three pigeon and venison pâtés, pastries, biscuits, artichokes, cherries, pears, plums and hazelnuts; a huge feast, but one based upon standard commodities.

In contrast to these great agapes, whence the guests could depart well and truly protected from gnawing hunger pains for a day or two, we find only echoes of the daily hardships of the greater part of the population, with its black bread, vegetables and water. A Parisian document of the seventeenth century reveals the dangers of being over-generous where charity was concerned, and thereby stripping the surrounding countryside of its agricultural workers. Though long, the text is worth quoting in full.

> By admitting paupers coming in from the fields to the workhouse, one is depriving the countryside of workers to till the land and of farmhands who

> are so desperately needed to take the cattle to pasture, because if such persons, irrespective of age or sex, are assured of shelter in Paris, where every day they will receive soup, bread which can be called white by comparison with theirs, meat and wine for doing nothing, as is customarily given to the poor who are growing old, one can easily believe that they will not stay on the land, where they are obliged to work from morning till night and have only a piece of black bread and water to drink, thinking themselves very lucky if, once or twice a year, they have a little bacon rind to rub their bread with, and never a drop of wine. . . .[17]

Doubtless this is a picture of the feeding conditions of the most poverty-stricken day-labourers who, landless and often homeless, wandered the countryside the year round in search of work, food and shelter. Here again, our knowledge is virtually limited to the extremes.

★

At all events, these do allow us to make some reasonably valid assertions. Firstly, one can point to the fluctuations in the pattern of eating; for without any doubt it was normal for all social classes to alternate between frugality and feasting. A consequence of the general insecurity where food was concerned, this oscillation imposed itself as a rite, some signs of which can still be found today. The festivals of the fraternities or the Entries in the towns and those of the harvest, grape-harvest or Saint Martin's Day in the country were always occasions for fine living for a few hours at least—and with innumerable variations in the form it took, of course. But these huge feasts, after which a man had to live on bread and water for months on end, provided compensation, however meagre, for ill-fortune and were appreciated for that reason; the very precariousness of existence explained them. The virtue of thrift, of making one's resources spread evenly over a given period, cannot be conceived of without a certain margin of supply. *Mutatis mutandis*, all those who went hungry between 1940 and 1945 will understand how they felt. One other factor to be taken into account in explaining these 'orgies' is the ever-present dangers threatening the granary; what was the good of laying up large stocks if brigands or soldiers might come along the next day and carry them off?

It seems equally obvious that there was as yet no great refinement in their diet. The pâtés, meats and side-dishes of even the most ostentatious banquets do not seem to have called for elaborate preparation. One would be tempted to speak of gluttony, were it not for the need to consider the cold which sorely tried them in winter and justified their eating rather more than we do. Nevertheless, it would seem that this was not the age of the gourmet, and one has to await the beginning of the seventeenth century to hear of the *rue aux Ours* in

[17] BN, Mss, *fonds français*, 21.803, 234.

Paris,[18] and until the eighteenth to find the same Chapter of Dole ordering (in 1756) the following menu for a reception for the Archbishop of Besançon: 'bisque d'écrevisse, potage à la reine, grenouilles à la poulette, truites grillées, anguilles en serpentin, filets de brochet, carpes du Doubs avec coulis d'écrevisse, tourte de laitances de carpes', and so on.[19]

The third point, which calls for much detailed research, is the lack of balance in this cereal-based diet; in other words, the chronic ailments which excesses and deficiencies inflicted upon the body.

Such notions as the predominance of starches, lack of proteins and vitamin deficiency, which are the ABC of modern dietetics, are surely equally applicable to a study of the diet of three centuries ago.[20] To begin with, it should be noted that the great discoverers experienced directly one such deficiency disease—scurvy. Yet this ailment met with on long sea-voyages was not new: the lack of fresh food in winter, in particular in mountain regions, had meant that mild forms of it were prevalent. Thus seamen and explorers easily found remedies for it when the disease became more acute. But this diet involves many other deficiencies. It could account for the many deformities at an early age—the knock-knees, gnarled limbs, and toothless gums which we find in 'everyday' iconography, by which we mean illustrations which do not depict the great of this world, who were better fed and safe from these deficiencies. The effects of chronic malnutrition, as we know, are not to be calculated only in numbers of calories. Light could be shed on this point by the research of the medical profession into the deficiencies present in the inhabitants of the less developed countries. The doctors of this early period have left us good descriptions of common chronic ailments, which they attributed to a given drink or a pernicious humour. A systematic comparison of contemporary studies on Africa or south-east Asia, and the investigations into famine between 1940 and 1944 which European medicine undertook but over-hastily abandoned, with the medical findings of the modern period ought to bear fruit. The field is wide open for a historian interested in the basic conditions of material life.

[18] 'We normally made as good cheer there as one could in the famous *rue aux Ours*,' wrote Lescarbot in 1612 (*Histoire de la Nouvelle France*, p. 554). But Estienne (345) had already mentioned ten or so good eating-houses across France.

[19] Translator's note: to preserve the air of *haute cuisine*, the text of this menu has been deliberately left in French. The items mentioned are crayfish bisque, chicken soup, frogs' legs with allemande sauce, grilled trout, whole eels, fillets of pike, Doubs carp with crayfish sauce, and soft roe of carp flan.

[20] It would be very tempting to include a few graphs at this point—e.g. the breakdown of a typical menu into proteins, carbohydrates, etc. This is scarcely possible except in very specific cases—for example, for seamen whose food supplies are known. There is, however, one article from abroad which is worthy of mention—Mario Novelli's study of the Spinola family of Genoa, entitled 'Bilanci alimentari in Liguria all' inizio del seicento' in the *Revista Internazionale di Science Economiche e Commerciali* 1 (1955).

Nevertheless the major preoccupation of modern man was to avoid hunger (cf. Plate 1). This obsession, which a few good meals a year could not dispel, is reflected even in place names and personal names: *Bramefaim* ('Howl-for-hunger'), *Marche tourte* ('March-pie'), *Tue tourte* ('Kill [gobble]-the-pie'). Such picturesque names as these bear laconic witness to this universal obsession whose psychological implications it is difficult to appreciate fully. There is no doubt, for example, that one of the main advantages that popular opinion ascribed to the privileged classes of this world was the freedom from such preoccupations. Early in the seventeenth century, when France witnessed the spread of the Rosicrucian brotherhood, about which much was said in ignorance of the facts, it was popularly rumoured that its members were safe from such ills. 'They are not subject to hunger, thirst, old age, illness or any other discomfort,' stated the *Mercure français*.[21] In contrast, we know only too well how famine could ravage whole provinces, how the failure of some crop could crowd the roads with people searching for food of even the most elementary kind. This involved not just individuals, but whole sections of the population: 'public necessity' was the term used in countless documents. Some writers even describe a certain hunger disease—a frenzy which drove men to cannibalism, so common a feature of the Middle Ages[22] and also of the period under discussion: 'That wretchedness which is rightly called frenzy, in so far as nature is broken down, bodies waste away, senses are alienated and wits distracted, so that not only do people turn savage, but they are driven to such fury that no person can look upon another without evil intent.'[23]

Physiological deficiency wasted away the body, drained it of strength and vigour, and paved the way for epidemics. No less serious and important were its psychological repercussions, for it inured the heart to terror and anguish. Doubtless, one cannot lay to its account all the popular disturbances of the age, the peasant *jacqueries* and urban revolts. Many other factors, social, economic and in particular fiscal, may have intervened to trigger them off. It is quite certain, however, that this daily fear for the morrow lay behind the individual and collective panics, the 'rabid terrors' mentioned in many documents. The effect of this chronic malnutrition was to produce in man the mentality of the hunted with its superstitions, its sudden outbursts of anger and its hypersensitivity. Other ages, with their different economic and social contexts, may know other forms of fear and terror; this is so today. But the first and most striking feature of this modern civilization was the obsession with starving to death, an obsession which varied in intensity according to locality and class, being stronger in the country than in the town, rare among the upper classes and well-fed

[21] Volume for the year 1624, p. 380.

[22] Cf. in particular on this point, for central Europe, F. Curschmann, *Hungersnöte im Mittelalter* (Leipzig 1900).

[23] Lescarbot, *Histoire de la Nouvelle France*, p. 196.

fighting men, and constant among the lower classes. In this respect, moreover, the modern period was merely a continuation of the Middle Ages.

Environment: clothing

Nor was there any fundamental change from the Middle Ages to the modern period as regards the equally vital battle against the inclemencies of the weather, against a climate which was so very changeable and only too often hostile to man. Clothing and accommodation, where again the more lavish displays are better known than the humble norm, were still for most people forms of protection; it is in this capacity that they are primarily to be thought of, however fascinating may seem the evolution of princely dwellings like the *châteaux* of the Loire, and changes of fashion such as medieval porches and miniatures already reveal to us.[24] Certainly the two aspects are not absolutely distinct: the growing fashion for short clothes for men and underlinen in the fourteenth century is not insignificant. But on the other hand, it is quite clear that the extravagant fashions of the fifteenth century in the style of Isabella of Bavaria relate only to a very small minority. Indeed this was largely a financial matter, for resistance to fashion stemmed from the high price of elaborately-ornamented clothing. For the peasantry and the urban middle classes at least, a fashionable suit of clothes represented a real capital asset and normally lasted a lifetime. *A fortiori*, the evolution of the ordinary dwelling was not determined by that of the castle, as it descended from its lofty hill-top site in the sixteenth century to become a hunting lodge and summer residence. What we shall endeavour to assess is just how effective was the protection which clothing and housing afforded against cold and bad weather.

At the risk of gross oversimplification, we shall not here consider the contribution made by dress, in all its necessary variety, to the social spectacle; nor shall we consider national or regional aspects which marked a fashion or a collective tradition.

Clothing was certainly a means of protection, above all against the cold. In winter, everyone put on one or two additional garments, but specially-designed summer clothes in lightweight materials, such as we wear today, did not exist. Thus protection from heat, whatever may have been the risks—of sunstroke, for instance—did not present any great problem. But the cold had to be fought both indoors and out, as we shall see—hence, in the first place, the importance of clothes which reached down to the ankles. In the Middle Ages, all except the peasantry wore long, full gowns with many folds, a fact which throws light upon a whole mode of behaviour. The way a man walked to avoid tripping over the many folds, the way he held his arms well away from his body to be

[24] We shall, however, be returning in chs. 2 and 3 of Part II to the subject of clothes and buildings as indications of social distinctions.

able to extricate his hands more easily and hold up the drooping folds was determined by it. Inevitably, he moved slowly and took long strides. A man wearing shorter clothes, brought in to the waist, had a livelier step and an ease of gesture which was denied by the more cumbersome apparel. Such freedom of gesture was undoubtedly influential, but as yet we have no means of assessing this.

Peasants and the lower classes of towns and villages, who had to walk a good deal and to work with their hands, had thus always worn short clothes—a shirt, commonly worn since the fourteenth century, and breeches, and over these a tunic (*cotte*) or doublet, garments which were brought in to the waist and did not impede movement. On top, at least in winter, they wore a short cloak with a wide collar, and on their feet clogs, hose, or sometimes boots; the whole essentially a working outfit. The wardrobe of women of the lower classes comprised longer garments—a smock (*chemise à femme*), a tunic (*cotte*) or gown sometimes worn tight across the bust, and a second gown over the top, often called simply an 'over-gown' (*robe de dessus*), all of which came down to the knee. Perrette, the farmer's wife in La Fontaine, was thus 'dressed in short clothes'. The shirts and smocks were of linen or hemp, and the gowns, doublets and mantles of wool.

The wardrobe of the well-to-do classes, although basically similar, obviously had more refinements. Shirts might be of silk or very fine linen, and the parts which showed, trimmed with lace. The nobility and the bourgeoisie no longer wore the medieval tunic shaped like an overall which continued to be the dress of the poor, but a short, very close-fitting doublet which was fastened to their trunk hose and worn under a long cloak, which protected it whilst also covering the whole body like a long cape. The ladies wore smocks, under- and over-gowns, which reached down to the ground but allowed their 'under-linen' to be seen, and over their gowns a *chaperon*, a kind of hooded cloak which fastened under the chin with a clasp and covered the whole outfit.

The quality of cloths and hides, the standard of the tailoring and the impressiveness of the wardrobe thus sufficed to distinguish one mode of dress from another. Against the bite of the cold, both rich and poor put on additional layers of clothing, the distinction lying in the quality of the finish. Against rain and snow, all had to rely on these gowns and cloaks which were by no means waterproof and were set to dry in the chimney corner on returning home. Was this adequate protection? Looked at from today's standpoint, when we put on extra clothes to go out, it might seem so. But modern man was cold even in his own home. Consequently, he was always heavily clothed, because the cold assailed him even indoors, and because his resistance was low, as is the case with all who are undernourished.

Sartorial refinement was thus aimed not so much at providing better protection, a factor necessarily limited by the restricted range of materials available even to the rich, as at originality in colour and cut. The fourteenth century saw the fantasies of Charles VII's contemporaries. Later Italy took over and led the fashion in such refinements, and was still their source in the sixteenth century. Brantôme, describing a beautiful lady, would clothe her 'in Italian fashion' or even 'in the style of Siena'. Similarly furs, jewels and perfumes were luxury items limited to those in high society: between 1500 and 1550 there was a flourishing trade in Burgundian jewellery and perfumes from Italy and Spain for use in the small world of the court. Even for the courtiers, however, the high price of all qualities of cloth meant that clothes were durable goods which could be worn for a lifetime, and which were bequeathed to one or another of the children by name. The wardrobe of a noble lady or of a rich bourgeois was a capital asset which was included in the marriage contract or probate inventory. Generally, it comprised two complete outfits per season which would be brought out year after year. How meticulously Marot described his elegant bourgeoise —'a bodice of pure blue, laced with yellow . . . cuffs of bright scarlet, a gown of perse, full and open . . . black hose, small pattens, white underlinen, a tufted sash, an oval-shaped hood . . . small ear-locks in her hair, and sparkling eyes.'[25] These were the stylish fantasies of a small minority.

Environment: living accommodation

It was while travelling through Baden that Montaigne came across 'the pleasant warmth' of the 'stove', that small, well-heated room found in the German-speaking countries. He observes that, 'whereas we put on our warm, furred dressing-gowns when we enter the house, they, on the contrary, strip down to their doublets, and even go bareheaded in the 'stove', then dress warmly to go back into the open air.'[26] Houses were uncomfortable, essentially because they afforded little protection. More accurately, let us say that, while they were reasonably proof against damp, rain and snow, they did little to keep out the cold, and this was as true of the most splendid châteaux as of the wattle and daub huts.

Whatever the house, the main room continued to be the one where the whole family spent as much time as possible, often with its animals. There it was more or less warm. This was the hall (*salle*) which contained the huge, well-appointed fireplace, and was also called the kitchen: once, when the lord of Gouberville was ill, he had to stay in bed for a few days, unable to get up; but he records with satisfaction the day when he 'went down to the kitchen again'. In Vivarais, it was known as the *chauffoir*—the room were everyone could take his place under or in front of the mantelpiece and cook in the heat of the fire on one side, while feeling the cold on the other. The huge fireplaces neither retained the heat

[25] Marot goes on to say that she would have tempted St Francis of Paule.
[26] Montaigne (346), I, visit to Baden.

nor radiated it out into the room, but the communal hall was certainly the most welcoming room in the house. It was there that the evenings were spent around the hearth and that guests were received, with furniture brought in specially for the occasion.

Everything was organized to satisfy this overwhelming concern to conserve heat by every possible means. We need not mention the building materials themselves—the walls of local stone or of dried mud protected by panels of timber.[27] However, there is no doubt that heat conservation was behind the abiding preference for thatched roofs, despite the fire risks which led municipal authorities to forbid their use, within urban areas at least. Hence, also, the small size of apertures—the narrow windows, well-protected by shutters or oilcloths, or glazed (in the case of the better houses). Even in broad daylight rooms were dark, and oil lamps had to be used for reading as soon as the light started to fade. The presence of numerous mats and carpets in every room is likewise to be explained by their value as insulation. A warm, carpeted room was the privilege of the rich—or of the well-to-do, at least. For carpets, the poor substituted a layer of foliage, quite an appreciable[28] means of insulation which even people of rank did not scorn on occasion. Yet, despite so many precautions, houses were still icy. To avoid the worst, parents took very young children into bed with them in the winter.[29] It was also common to have several adults sleeping in one vast four-poster, insulated from the rest of the room by curtains to keep in the warm, humid, stuffy air they breathed.

Lucky too was the man who could decently heat his hall, and who had enough wood to do so. Some regions, such as the towns in the Somme Valley, Abbeville, Amiens, and Péronne, had supplies of peat. Others even had mined coal, notably around St Étienne. Nowhere in France, however, was coal in general use, as it was in England at the same period, with the result that both town and country used wood from the forests for heating. This was expensive, for transport was difficult and costly, and subject to formidable hazards. In January 1646, Paris suffered from 'a shortage of wood, there being not a single log in Paris. For the river having been low all summer, and having frozen over

[27] These buildings were often far from solidly built. In 1636, a bourgeois of Le Puy expressed his astonishment at a house falling down one evening when there was neither wind nor rain! 'On St Crispin's Day, without wind or rain, one wall . . . collapsed completely, which caused the roofs and floors and furniture all to fall in a heap and be destroyed, and by great misfortune all the inhabitants were killed.' Jacmon (32), p. 104.

[28] Ronsard (112), *Amours*, CLXVII:

Go, child, and with plundering hand
Reap the mosaic blooms of verdant spring,
Then, generously strewing all the house,
Spread me a dappled carpet, deep and rich.

[29] The lord of Louvencourt did not forget this childhood memory and quotes it in his *Amours*. Cf. L. Lorgnier, *La Vie amiénoise* (Paris 1942), p. 56.

the day after Christmas, the wood only came from the fields around and cost twice the normal price.'[30]

Inside these houses—which seem so inhospitable to us, and which were not divided up into different rooms, each with a specific function, since they consisted only of the hall and bedrooms (the dining-room being generally adopted only in the eighteenth century)—luxury thus lay in the furnishings, and not in the comfort of air-conditioning. The peasantry had basic furniture: chests, which held anything and everything, and could be easily carried off on the back of man or beast to the nearest forest when soldiers or brigands were reported nearby; kitchen utensils, a spinning wheel, a table, and a few benches. In contrast, kings and princes displayed in their apartments dressers laden with gold plate, and hung their walls with thick carpets imported from the East. The wealth of the nobility or bourgeoisie was measured equally in pewter and silver plate, or in linen, especially the bed-linen carefully piled in chests in the hall; in small mirrors set in expensive frames; or in some copper or wrought-iron clock (at least from 1530–1540); later, paintings and ancestral portraits gradually made their appearance as decorations. But of all these different items, only the carpets and hangings covering floors and walls and screening windows could help in the comfort of the interior. Such help, while not negligible, did not amount to very much.

It is no surprise, therefore, to see these people constantly abroad, their faces to the wind. Even in town they lived away from their homes, meeting in one another's houses or in the tavern, because they needed to move from place to place. Before the techniques of domestic heating that we know today were introduced, they had no other means of escaping the rigours of winter than to flee to the south, and, in fact, this was what so intelligent and rich a man as Desbarreaux, a councillor of the *Parlement*, managed to do in the seventeenth century. Bayle tells us that 'he took pleasure in changing his residence according to the season . . . above all, he would go in search of the sun on the coast of Provence during the winter, and spend the three months of this unpleasant season in Marseilles.'[31]

Thus, even in the towns modern man was strictly at the mercy of climatic conditions, and there was little he could do about it. Cold, high winds, storms and heatwaves had a strong hold over him and constantly made his life uncomfortable, to an extent which we today would find very difficult to imagine. He enjoyed neither stable temperature, nor good, cheerful lighting, nor any practical form of ventilation.[32] The effect of this was all the more harmful to his physical balance and even to his health since (back we come to it) in the main he was undernourished and thus, primarily, susceptible to cold, as everyone

[30] D'Ormesson, *Mémoires* I, p. 344.

[31] Bayle, *Dictionnaire critique*, 'Desbarreaux'.

[32] This was a major preoccupation of the times: cf. Plate 2.

knows. The lack of fresh air and light was not without its importance either, though people counteracted this by going out as much as possible and by, as it were, living outside, in the open air; though this again meant that they could not avoid the cold for at least three months of the year. Hunger and cold, these were the two outstanding material factors of human life at that period. It is fortunate that only exceptionally did they coincide, for then they resulted in disaster and annihilation.

Chapter 2
The body: health, diseases and 'population'

It becomes more difficult when one tries to go beyond such purely material data and form some idea of what we would today understand by the state of the population's health. Obviously, no statistics are available; but the main reason is that here, even more than in the topics already discussed, complex notions are involved—the notions reflecting or replacing science in which the people of those times were steeped.

For them, their body and their very existence were perceptible only in the context of their outward activity, in the gestures which expressed physical or emotional activity, in everything which gave life some degree of human flavour. All that physiology has revealed to us over the last century and a half about the functioning of the human animal, whereby the body incessantly assimilates molecules of allied matter, whilst rejecting all that has become heterogeneous—all this was unknown to both Vesalius and Rabelais. Knowledge of the human body was confined to morphology, to the discovery of forms which culminated in the Anatomy Lesson. But organic life itself, so to speak, did not exist: medical treatises abounded in considerations on the combinations and conflicts of the 'elements' of air, fire and water inside the body, phenomena which the doctors themselves maintained to be all-explanatory. This belief in addition accounts for the almost total lack of curiosity displayed by the average cultured man with regard to knowing and investigating how his body really functioned.

Illness was thus considered as a foreign element which lodged in the body of the sick person and had to be expelled, a concept which was partly magical, for it was plausible to exorcize an affliction from an organism which had been unjustifiably invaded.

The therapeutics of the last century, which used physico-chemical methods to impose a cure upon a 'patient' who 'underwent' treatment long retained this vocabulary, the burdensome inheritance of an obsolete view of medicine. Though alien matter, disease was none the less subtle matter. Wind and humours explain the part attributed, perhaps under the influence of the Stoic humanist tradition, to the 'passions of the soul', which bred their own particular diseases.

Envy gave rise to insomnia and jaundice, sloth to languor and lethargy, and melancholy to even worse: *affectus frequentes contemptique morbum faciunt*. . . . Finally, disease and illness could be identified with sin, the work of the Devil —and hence possession by him; it could be the suffering necessary for the redemption of the sinner, for Christian tradition did not have to wait for Claudel to give some meaning to the anguish of pain. In this case there was no other remedy save faith and grace.

Thus, it ought at least to be easy to define the healthy, 'normal' man, even if this is a completely negative definition to which a Dr Knock would certainly take exception; in fact, merely 'a person not suffering from any disease'. However, because of their lack of preoccupation with matters of physiology, doctors and surgeons were scarcely concerned to define the 'normal' functioning of the body. To Rabelais, good health meant little more than good humour, whereas we would like so much more information on the subject—information on height and weight, muscular strength and endurance, and even on how much riding, walking and other physical exercise was engaged in. The physical mechanisms would equally be of importance in defining the behaviour of the 'normal' man—the relative daily use of the sitting, lying and standing positions, the proportion of rest to exercise and so on. Here, evidence is so scarce that it is unusable.[1] Similarly, it is meaningless to talk of hygiene or health preservation in the sixteenth century. If Montaigne recommended bathing, it was because of the evil odours given off by accumulated filth;[2] otherwise, almost the only recommendation to be found everywhere which could approximate to a rule of hygiene was to avoid the evil, damp, cold and, as Pierre de l'Estoile called it, the tainted air of the towns in autumn, for it bred contagion. But this already brings us back to the battle against disease.

It also means that the other side of the picture is exaggerated. For whereas we have no evidence upon which to base a description of the man in good health, his weight and complexion, we do on the other hand have a vast amount of medical literature which all conveys an undeniable fact: namely, that disease was rife, that the whole population was in a state of chronic morbidity, and above all that medicine was helpless in the face of even the most common ailments. Prescriptions for avoiding plague, in the form of carefully-printed pamphlets, circulated rapidly from one end of Europe to the other, so great was the fear of contagion, and so unreliable did the many proposed remedies reveal

[1] Where can one, in fact, find any reliable information which will allow us to determine such straightforward details as height and weight? There were no recruiting boards and few medical reports. Painting and sculpture are not sure guides, despite all the deductions one is tempted to make from Callot, for example. But at best these would only be pointers to morphology: knock knees, contorted bodies, goitres or pox-ridden faces and so on. Until research teams have systematically combed the lesser-known texts for all the evidence, however slight, we must confess our ignorance.

[2] *Essays* II, 37.

themselves to be in the face of the scourges which regularly accompanied famine and war. Thus one can further understand the constant appearance, alongside medical treatments learnedly justified in good Sorbonne Latin, of the most widely differing superstitious practices, practices which often seemed to those who used them no less effective than the advice offered by the Faculty. Such prescriptions, methods of treatment and public safety regulations provide us ultimately not so much with a description of the diseases, already familiar to the people of the day, as with the remedies to be applied to them. As a result, medicine today is hesitant when it comes to identifying the countless fevers and the terrible plagues, only too often treated as *cholera morbi*, which periodically ravaged town and country.

Diseases

What were the ailments which preyed upon people in those days and which they habitually dreaded? To answer this question, we must be guided by contemporary accounts, which carry decisive weight, while at the same time trying to deduce from these often very detailed descriptions the exact nature of the diseases in question. Thus, while most of them were treated as fevers or agues, and *livres de raison* and memoirs[3] are filled with references to the appropriately 'numbered' versions of them—the tertian, quartan, double quartan agues—it is obvious that these cover a very wide range of diseases. Moreover, there were few diseases which were not considered contagious, as we can see in the following quotation, taken from a memorialist whose medical geography is not without interest: 'We blame leprosy on the Jews, phthisis on the English, scrofula on the Spaniards, goitre on the people of Savoy, the pox on the Indians and scurvy on Northerners.'[4] So goitre was contagious!

However, an order of precedence of sorts can easily be drawn up. Plague, though itself a generic term almost to the same extent as fever, headed the list, along with the other parasitic diseases such as typhus, purpura fever (also called 'army fever') and the sweating sickness. Next came the nutritional diseases resulting from deficiencies or lack of a balanced diet; and these were followed by the scourge which ravaged western Europe in the sixteenth century, causing great alarm at the time—syphilis.

Plague and typhus usually accompanied famine and war. The constant connection between them was invariably noted by contemporaries, who particularly dreaded germ-carriers—the vagabonds and the destitute who were always on the move during the great crises. Were fleas and lice recognized to be carriers

[3] Take, for example, this extract from the memoirs of the Marquis de Beauvais Nangis (10), p. 117: 'Upon my arrival, I felt very ill; the quartan ague took hold of me and I returned to Paris, where I remained, suffering from the quartan, double quartan, triple quartan, continual quartan ague. So melancholic was I. . . .'

[4] BN, Mss, *fonds français*, 21,730, 153.

of infection? This is by no means certain, even though useful precautions were often taken in this respect: at Paris, in 1596, the heads and faces of all vagabonds were ordered to be shaved;[5] while in 1638, the same city prohibited the selling and peddling of old clothes, 'second-hand clothes, linen and other poor-quality chattels'.[6] But mostly the atmosphere was blamed for spreading disease, in particular between seasons, when it was warm and moist and when sudden, sharp changes in temperature were common. 'Plague is a poisonous atmospheric vapour which attacks the heart; it occurs when the weather is changeable, being now hot, now cold, now clear and now overcast . . . when vermin abound on the earth, when a warm wind lasts into autumn, when worms and smallpox torment small children.'[7] Once contagion broke out, nothing could stop it. Epidemics which started at the end of winter usually lasted until the heat of summer, at which point, in the plains of the south, they handed over to another parasitic disease, in this case one whose geographical boundaries were narrower —malaria. Plague and purpura fever despatched their victims quickly, especially in the towns with their narrow streets and closely-packed houses. There, epidemics always took the greatest toll,[8] and a plague-stricken town was condemned to months of isolation. Just as each infected house was placed under seal and entrusted to the watchful supervision of neighbours, so too the whole town was shut in upon itself, and its inhabitants refused permission to move elsewhere—the only exception being the country houses to which the rich bourgeois usually withdrew as soon as the first cases were certified, to return only when the period of quarantine was comfortably over.

In 1629, plague ravaged Le Puy from May to the end of August, claiming in all some thousands of victims; the worst months were July and August, when between 100 and 160 people died each day. In 1630, at Pinerolo, then occupied by French troops, plague killed nine out of every ten inhabitants and more than 500 French soldiers.[9] The virulence of these epidemics is doubtless to be explained by the poor general condition of bodies whose resistance to attack had been weakened by famine. But the crowded conditions in the cities, with their tiny, narrow streets, and the general lack of proper means of refuse disposal—it was quite common to find townspeople forbidden, at the height of contagion, to spread straw in the streets for making compost—greatly helped to spread disease. In vain did towns close their gates to vagrants suspected of carrying the 'bubos', or villages unceremoniously expel them; all conditions favoured contagion.

[5] BN, Mss, *fonds français*, 21,630, 45.

[6] *Ibid.*, 55.

[7] 'Brief indication of how to recognize when is the dangerous time for catching plague' in *Le Livre de raison de Boisvert* (Tamizey de Larroque (38)).

[8] Here again, a few sound, carefully-compiled monographs would give us a clearer picture. Cf. my account of the plague at Uelzen, *Annales E.S.C.* 1 (1959).

[9] Souvigny (31), I, p. 240.

Plagues and fevers were a permanent element of the mental climate in which men existed from generation to generation.

Important too were the nutritional diseases which we find so difficult to identify. How many different disorders must have gone unspecified under such names as diarrhoea, or dysentery,[10] complaints which were intractable enough even to cause death. However, included in this category are the mariners' scurvy, clearly diagnosed by its contemporaries and treated with relative ease, as we have already seen. Similarly, there was the bread disease, ergotism, which reappeared a few years ago at Pont-Saint-Esprit, a dreadful ailment, but one which is easy to combat at the cost of a little hardship.[11] Lastly, gout, the disease of the over-nourished and consequently affecting only a small section of the population, was greatly feared: it was regarded as the worst of the rheumatic afflictions and the most intolerable of sufferings, because it immobilized its victims. But it was so very much less common than fevers—or even than the ill-identified nutritional diseases caused by some chronic deficiency. The most clear-cut of these was scrofula, better known because of the wonder-working intervention of the kings of France. Strumous adenitis is typical of diseases caused by malnutrition, the best remedy for it—apart from the cleanliness necessitated by the open neck-wounds which are quick to become purulent—being a richer diet, in particular one with a higher meat content. But adenitis, if neglected, could become tubercular and the small wounds could develop into a disease which took a very long time to cure. In France, from the time of the High Middle Ages, the sick readily sought the aid of the king, who on the occasion of the great feast-days wielded miraculous powers, identical with those of a saint, by laying his finger on the forehead of the patient and reciting a ritual formula promising him that he would be cured. This rite and its popularity form the subject of an admirable study by Marc Bloch.[12]

However, all these were traditional ailments which had been common in the Middle Ages too. Joinville and the crusades of St Louis had had to contend with scurvy; the same is true of plague and fevers. Popular imagination was much more vividly caught at the beginning of the modern period by the lightning spread of the 'disease of Naples'—syphilis. A matter for discretion by the end of the seventeenth century, and thereafter long treated in the greatest secrecy (until modern antibiotics made it harmless), syphilis was so virulent when it first appeared in Europe that the dismay of contemporaries is readily explained. It

[10] There was one straightforward version of it—grape-harvest dysentery. Cf. Souvigny (31), I, p. 78.

[11] One document recounts, for example, how 'our two parishes have been greatly upset by a fog which appeared on Ascension Day and tainted the rye so that those who ate bread made from it became intoxicated, their limbs were stiff, and they were seized by continual trembling'. (BN, Mss, Nv, *fonds français*, 21, 644, 267.)

[12] Bloch (201).

covered its early victims in putrid sores, purulent tumours and huge, ulcerated lesions, and transformed them into repulsive monsters. Eaten away as they were by the disease, they certainly could not dream of hiding it, as it was to become easier to do in the nineteenth century. Brought back from Italy at the beginning of the sixteenth century by the soldiers of François I—and, so tradition has it, by the king himself—the pox speedily established itself throughout the land. By the 1550s it was among the leading preoccupations of the medical profession, and 'to cure the pox' formed the main chapter of treatises on contagious diseases. No doubt doctors quickly found remedies with a salts of mercury base sufficiently effective for Rabelais to be able to make jokes about it by dedicating his *Gargantua* to his friends, the 'most esteemed and poxy fellows'. But not everyone laughed with Rabelais. This import from America made loose gallantry a hazardous pastime for centuries, and, soon after the voyages of Christopher Columbus, added yet another physiological disorder to those that modern man had inherited from former times.

There were some small compensations. Leprosy, which throughout the Middle Ages wrought as much havoc as the plague—and above all burdened the healthy population with a great army of sick who were slow to die and who had to be isolated in lazar-houses—seemed to be on the wane. During the sixteenth century, Amiens allowed to lapse its custom of making all new burghers who settled in the town provide a certificate to the effect that 'they came of good families and were born in legal wedlock, and not of fathers or mothers suspected of or suffering from the disease of leprosy'. However, this laxity proved to have its drawbacks and in 1574 it was decided to revert to the former, more prudent practice.

Yet another compensation was the apparently low incidence of tuberculosis and, in all probability, of cancer. References are indeed to be found to 'pulmonary' diseases, 'pleurisies', 'asthmas' and 'phthisis', affecting young and old alike and even proving fatal. But 'diseases of the lungs' and 'tightness of the chest', which resulted in the spitting of blood and incessant coughing, were not common ailments like those already mentioned. *A fortiori*, cancer, another disease difficult to identify,[13] would seem to have been even rarer. Nor was there much alcoholism, for spirits were not yet sufficiently commonly drunk. (Indeed, they were hardly used for cleaning wounds, even though these were in all circumstances an open invitation to death.)

Mental illnesses must be dealt with separately, for they pose even greater problems. Everyone whose talk deviated from the normal or was unorthodox risked being considered possessed of the Devil. This takes us into the complex

[13] Du Fossé, in his memoirs on the gentlemen of Port-Royal, mentions what is perhaps a case of it: 'The disease which attacked him was first an inflammation affecting his legs, which became so acute that terrible incisions had to be made and practically the whole of the main leg-bone was removed and proved to be completely carious' (du Fossé (5), p. 367).

world of Satan's henchmen, who, moreover, knew mixtures and potions capable of luring those under their influence away to artificial paradises. This form of derangement cannot strictly be considered a disease—despite the fact that magic was quite commonly practised. Consequently, the only people regarded as simply 'mad' were the 'innocents', 'the poor lunatics' 'bereft of their senses' as they were referred to, who wandered through towns and villages, mumbling abuse to all they met. Free to go where they pleased and often treated charitably to a cloak (for it was common to see these simpletons wandering about very lightly dressed) or to a bowl of soup, they would doubtless fit the title of village idiots which is still bestowed upon the simple-minded today. This was certainly a far less common affliction than it is today, when alcoholism sees to it that psychiatric wards are not short of patients.

Remedies and medicines

This brief sketch of the common diseases does not give a clear idea of the utter desolation of those struck down by illness and helpless to fight it. We read, for example, of a good bourgeois of Paris, afflicted with a paralysis of the tongue, and very worried about his fate: 'Each of my friends was kind enough to bring along all those of his acquaintance who had some skill in these matters. I was bled underneath the tongue, I took the English drops, I tried spirit of hartshorn, essence of viper's powder, aniseed tincture, extract of lime blossom, vulneraries and several other remedies which, in each case, they claimed to be specifically for my own ailment. But, far from being relieved by them, the paralysis steadily worsened.'[14] No doubt the fact that this ailment was less common and less well-known than plague explains his resorting to consult anyone, whether medically qualified or not; but for several reasons this explanation is only partly valid.

For treatment, each man according to his means could call upon doctors and surgeons, who were properly organized into guilds and held the appropriate diplomas conferred upon them by the university and guilds. But the medicine taught in the university was still that of Hippocrates and Galen, regurgitated time and again and applied to diseases diagnosed according to an empirical tradition. The enduringly great doctors of the time are those bold pragmatists who, following their own experience, went beyond the lessons of the schools in order to perfect their own methods empirically. Such a man was Ambroise Paré, who applied himself to the new field of 'wounds made by arquebuses and other firearms'. But for every doctor or surgeon endowed with the capacity to deduce from observation, how many others were content to apply their set lessons and to follow Hippocrates! Moreover, there were a few rare disciples of Paracelsus and the German mystics, in quest of the secret of life, who indulged

[14] *Ibid.*, p. 490.

in abstruse research prompted by secret spell-books, in which alchemy loomed large. Their role was not important, despite the prestige they enjoyed, notably in some of the large cities such as Paris and Strasburg.

The essential fact conditioning medical practice was the ineffectiveness of therapy. Even for so common a disease as plague, the best remedy was flight, so inadequate seemed the prescriptions tried by the doctors.[15] Thus remedies admitted by the most diverse popular traditions, even including countless superstitious practices preserved for us by the early almanacs and the *livres de raison*, were generally regarded as being on a par with the most authoritative medical advice.[16] M. du Fossé, whose case we have just quoted, accepted all the remedies suggested by his friends and tried them one after the other with equal trustfulness. So also one finds the inhabitants of a town in the grip of an epidemic resorting simultaneously to the preparation of 'fumigations' which were certainly effective (one contained, for example, six pounds of sulphur, four pounds of antimony, etc.), and to such devotional exercises as attendance at the sprinkling of Holy Water three times in three parishes on a single Sunday.

In the sphere of officially-licensed medicine, the range of medicaments available was very varied. For plague alone, the list of preventives and curatives proposed by treatises on the subject stretched over tens of pages.[17] Apart from the universal use of blood-letting and purging, which were supposed to dispose of all evil humours, two methods of treatment seemed to predominate: pharmacology and the use of thermal springs. Pharmacy rested on the combination of the simple properties of vegetable and mineral substances; hence the infinite variety of remedies proposed for any given disease. The addition of a few more mint leaves or three more grains of cinnamon made a new remedy to swell the already long list. Most medicaments came in the form of liquids in which herbs or powders had been macerated or boiled: vinegar to which was added rue, mint, rosemary and lavender was considered a good protection against plague; a mixture of new cider and syrup of roses was good for the consumptive, while one of cider and absinth was believed to rid children of worms and help the digestion of their parents. Some, it is true, maintained that good wine, 'that September liquor', drunk according to nature's demands, was a sovereign remedy against all illnesses. Besides such potions, there were tablets made from

[15] Let us quote one example from many. At Mâcon in 1630, 'most of the population is dying of hunger and plague, which has meant that the great majority of the inhabitants of the town have been obliged to retire to the country to avoid a worse evil' (AD, Saône-et-Loire, Series B, 1067).

[16] One should not be led astray by the scientific, or indeed mathematical, terms in which these are couched. If Laurent Joubert in his *Erreurs populaires* (94) recommends that male babies be fed every three hours and females every four, it is because the uneven number is the male number and the even, the female.

[17] From the fifteenth century, many medical manuscripts, both in French and Latin, were in circulation.

different powders: plague could be warded off with pills containing sulphur, viper's troche, diarrhodon and so on. The same disease could equally be combated with fumigations, in which houses and people were liberally steeped.[18] To begin with, such preparations contained the 'simples', whose properties had been recognized from the earliest times, and the spices imported from the Indian Ocean and the Far East through Mediterranean traders. During the seventeenth century, the pharmaceutical arsenal was enriched by the discoveries made by missionaries in the New World: thus quinine 'which cures without fail the quartan or tertian ague', was first used for medical purposes in the 1650s and fetched exorbitant prices. Such progress, though empirical, was none the less considerable.

The inadequate properties of careful mixtures of herbs and mineral powders were supplemented by the effects of thermal springs. These were praised by doctors and apothecaries in such fulsome terms as will surprise anyone who has been led to believe that Mme de Sévigné pioneered the field. Long before—and in all the provinces—mineral springs had been located and recommended for an impressive list of ailments. On the boundaries of Burgundy, near Moulins, there were medicinal springs 'containing some measure of vitriol and sulphur', which were recommended for colic, palsies, retention of urine, stomach pains, jaundice and so on.[19]

The enthusiasm for the properties of these mineral waters was a logical development of medical theories which admitted of the conflict between humours and liquids within the human body. But Italy may also have helped to create the fashion for taking the waters: at Amiens in 1560, and at Mâcon in 1606, we hear of Italians selling in the market a 'mineral oil, otherwise called naphtha', which was recommended for cold humours.

Certainly, these medicaments did not enjoy much greater prestige than the practices recommended by popular tradition, otherwise the latter would not have been so scrupulously preserved in memoirs. No doubt the importance of

[18] A manuscript prescription distinguishes between the common fumigation and that used by people of quality (BN, Mss, *nouveau fonds français*, 21,630, f. 212 *et seq.*). Chemicals which are to be used to make the common fumigation: sulphur, 6 lb; resin, 6; antimony, 4; yellow arsenic, 4; cinnabar, 3; litharge, 4; asafoetida, 3; cumin, 4; euphorbium, 4; ginger, 4; bran, 57. Chemicals which must be used to make a more refined fumigation for persons of quality.... Incense, 4 lb; benzoin, 2; storax, 5; myrrh, 4; cinnamon, 4; nutmeg, 2; aniseed, 6; Florentine iris, 6; laudanum, 2; cloves, 1; bran, 64.... One can remain in this fumigation for a good half-hour, but in the former, no longer than the time it takes to say a *paternoster*.

[19] Forges-les-Eaux, in Normandy, found someone to sing its praises as early as 1573: *Recueil de la vertu de la fontaine médécinale de S. Eloy, dicte de Jouvence, trouvé au pays de Bray, au village de Forges, par M. de Verrenes, chevalier des deux ordres de Sa Majesté, l'an 1573. Mis en lumière par Maistre Pierre de Grousset, appotiquaire de Monseigneur le Prince, selon les effects qu'il en a recogneu, depuis dix ans en ça, pour y avoir pensé et médicamenté de plusieurs sortes de maladies depuis ledit temps* (Paris, Pierre Vitray, 1607). The diseases treated there included gallstones, calculi and gravel, stomach pains and diseases of the brain.

what was at stake justified the precision and fancifulness of the details of such practices: curing an adder's bite by applying to the wound the blood of a newly-killed hen, washing children on Good Friday to preserve them from scabies, and passing three times through the flames of the firebrands on the first Sunday in Lent to ward off colic were some of the many remedies resting on an empirical tradition with strong magical undertones, bordering on religious practices —though regarded as superstitious even by some contemporaries, such as Paré or Montaigne. Natural and even blatantly superstitious practices were therefore rife. The second category, long tolerated by the Church, was much more important than the first. In addition to gestures and acts performed on the occasion of Church festivals, such as those we have just quoted, it included many prayers, invocations and orisons which figured in everyone's repertoire and which invoked miraculous powers of the saints, or of Christ Himself. Sometimes couched in Latin[20]—hence possibly the work of clerks—such texts made up a kind of medical compendium which the sick always had ready to hand. The Church did not repudiate such texts and practices until late in the seventeenth century, and then with great discretion, for prayers for medical purposes had been said by priests since the time of the primitive Church.

Provided that members of the clergy were in agreement, there could be no objection, at least in the Catholic Church, to a request that exorcisms and prayers be used to drive illness from men (and even from animals). However, especially in the seventeenth century, the participation of the Church seems to have been a condition of the execution—and of the success—of such rites. Thus there were ultimately three methods of treatment open to the sick, which we have distinguished for the sake of analysis, but which could more or less be combined or in any case implemented consecutively or simultaneously by the same person.

In addition to these methods, there remained surgery, either at the hand of the barber-surgeon, who did not hold university diplomas but was acknowledged to be competent to perform at least a bleeding, or of the master-surgeon, whose university qualifications were on a par with those of his fellow physicians. The surgeon treated wounds, deformities from birth (removing superfluous fingers or replacing a missing arm was for Ambroise Paré his primary job), or accidental deformities (hernias, wounds, ulcers, gangrene). He was also a physician, his manual skills serving only to complete the cure when normal medical treatment was inadequate. Thus the *Introduction ou Entrée pour parvenir à la vraye cognois-*

[20] To stop a haemorrhage, recite '*Sanguis Christi maneat in te sicut Christus fecit in se*'. To cure toothache, recite the prayer of St Apollonia: '*Beata Apollonia grave tormentum pro Domino sustinuit. Primo, tiranni exruerunt dentes ejus cum multis afariis. Et cum esset in illo tormento grave ad Dominum Jesum Christum. Et quicumque nomen suum devote invocaret, malum in dentibus non sentiret. Versus. Ora pro nobis, beata Apollonia, ut digni efficiamur promissionibus Christi. Amen.*' The two remedies are given in L. Guilbert, *Nouveau recueil de registres domestiques* (Limoges 1895), pp. 288–9.

sance de la chirurgie, by the same Ambroise Paré, was a medical treatise; it did not dwell on surgical techniques but examined diseases, faculties and humours. Both medicine and surgery were baulked by the huge gaps in anatomical and physiological knowledge, which only later centuries were very gradually to tackle. This explains why so skilful a surgeon as Paré spent the best years of his life on the battlefield, where his services were necessarily most appreciated, operating on the wounded, cauterizing wounds with a hot iron or boiling oil, removing bullets or splinters, and amputating gangrenous limbs.

The inefficacy of these remedies was particularly felt during epidemics. To combat contagion even the smallest towns had acquired, since the twelfth and thirteenth centuries, a whole apparatus of defence by which they endeavoured to make up for medical inadequacies.[21] Each community had its hospital, which made it possible for the sick to be isolated, at least in the early stages. In the sixteenth century, France boasted more than a thousand hospitals (*hôtels-Dieu*) and almost as many lazar-houses, though the latter were gradually being converted to other uses at this time (cf. map 3). Usually run by regulars, these medieval foundations had functioned to everyone's satisfaction for centuries, but the economic revolution of the sixteenth century dealt a hard blow to the administration of their temporalities. Many were in jeopardy at the beginning of the next century: because they lacked the necessary revenues, they refused to take in patients, and under Henri IV a royal commission held a long inquiry into their situation. A few years later, Vincent de Paul was to increase the number of new foundations.

These hospitals were the home of the sick—and of the old and needy. But in addition urban communities had an impressive array of regulations which were invariably revived whenever an epidemic threatened. These measures were often extremely harsh, since they involved evacuating all contaminated dwellings, expelling beggars and suspects, destroying stray animals, closing the markets and the lawcourts, prohibiting certain kinds of business activities (for example, cobbling), placing those who were cured in quarantine outside the town and compelling the sick still undergoing treatment to wear special clothes which could be seen from a distance.

These measures, which were aimed at isolating the sick, invariably proved ineffective in their own way: the hospitals, soon overflowing with patients, rapidly became the chief foci of infection and helped to spread the disease—all the more so since they were usually situated in the centre of the old town. Other precautions taken by one town against another, such as placing the infected town in quarantine, leaving goods for delivery to it in some open place outside the walls for days on end, and prohibiting trade and travel, did not prove much more successful.

[21] What was the extent of this inadequacy in the view of the average man? Cf. Montaigne, *Essays* II, ch. 37, devoted almost entirely to doctors and medicine.

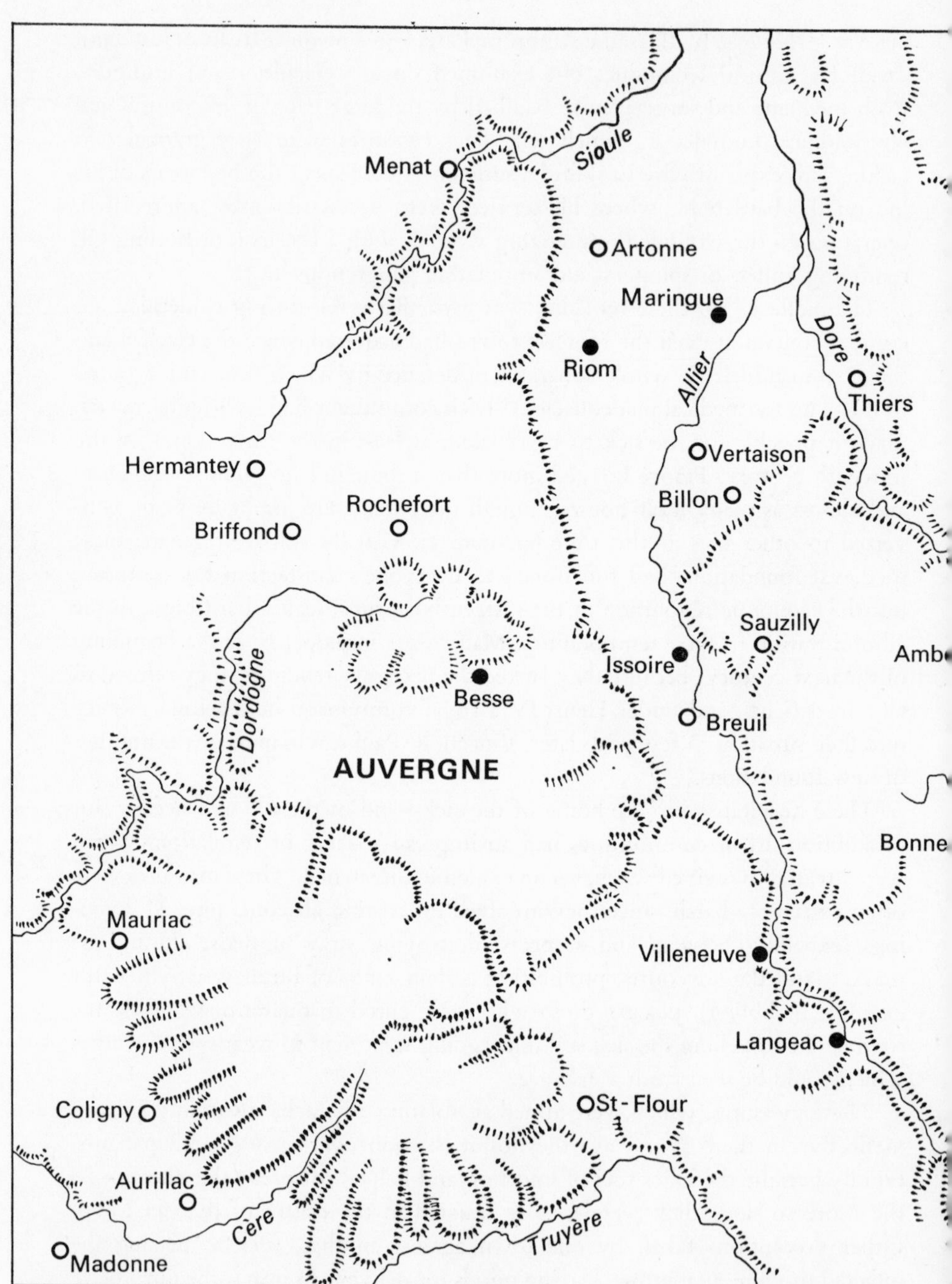

Map 3 Hospital resources in Lyonnais and the Auvergne.

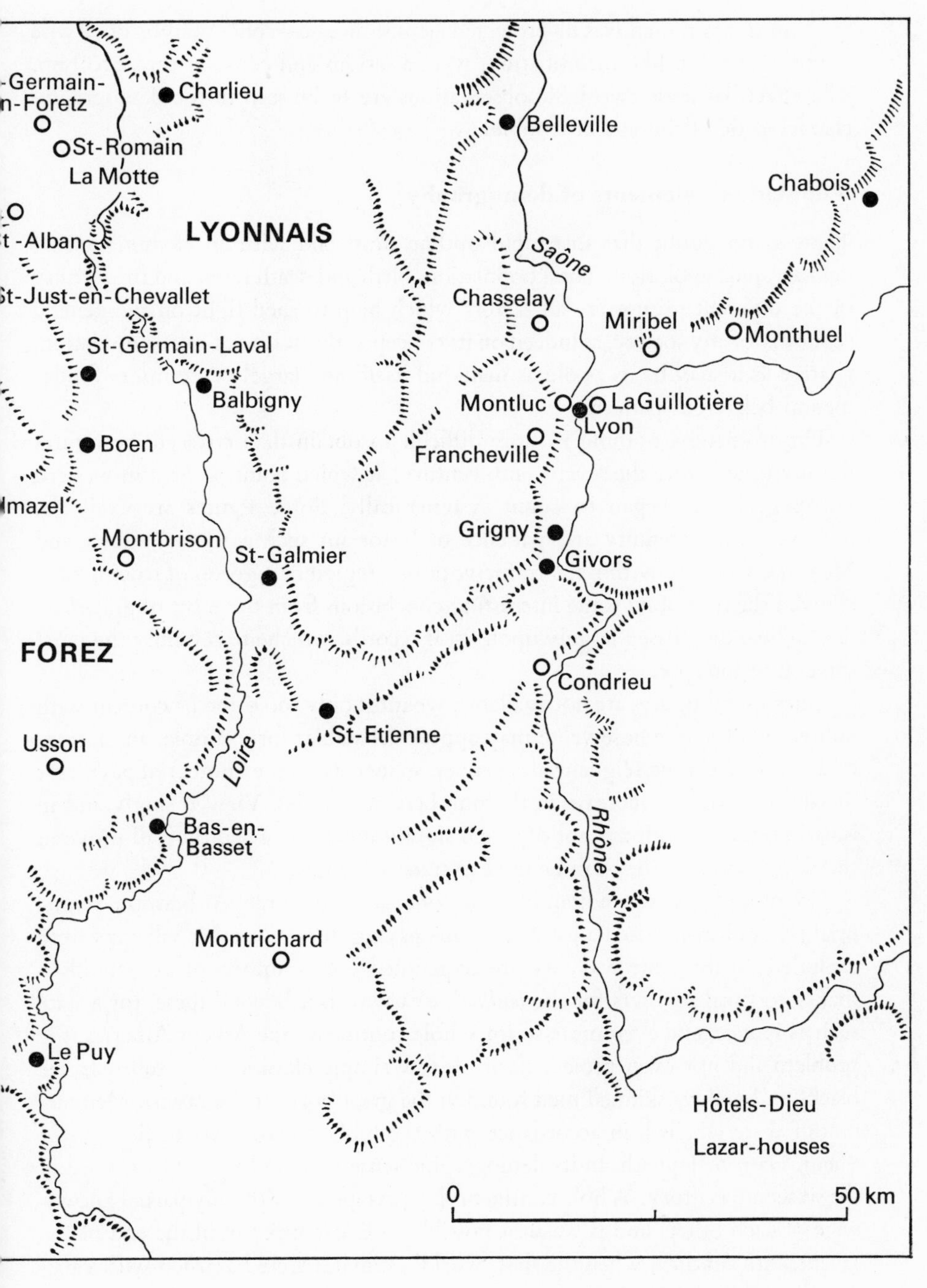

-Germain-
n-Foretz
Charlieu
St-Romain
La Motte
t -Alban
LYONNAIS
St-Just-en-Chevallet
St-Germain-Laval
Balbigny
Boen
lmazel
Montbrison
St-Galmier
FOREZ
Usson
Loire
Bas-en-
Basset
Montrichard
Le Puy
St-Etienne
Belleville
Saône
Chasselay
Miribel
Monthuel
Chabois
Montluc
Lyon
La Guillotière
Francheville
Grigny
Givors
Condrieu
Rhône
Hôtels-Dieu
Lazar-houses
0
50 km

Thus modern man was ill-protected against disease—contagious or otherwise—and epidemics, like malnutrition, were a serious and constant threat to him. The effects of these two basic observations are to be seen in the demography characteristic of this age of troubles.

'Population': elements of demography

There is no doubt that this rapid outline must end with an examination of demographic evolution. Total population, birth and death rates, and the fertility of the different groups are all factors which help to shed light on the general economy of any society, as indeed on its concepts: the notion of over-population, relative as it may be, is as old as mankind itself, and largely determines fundamental behaviour patterns.

Unfortunately, nothing is more difficult to obtain than consecutive figures for any time before the seventeenth century, at which point, at least in western Europe, scholars began to count systematically. Some figures are available, however: the ingenuity and patience of historians such as Lot, Goubert and Meuvret, working within the framework of a region or a group of towns, have allowed them to draw some interesting conclusions from the most fragmentary data. These they based largely upon fiscal records, which are certainly the most difficult to interpret.

Since useful figures are not available, we must only too often be content with indirect evidence, whose value may appear debatable: for example, an increase or decrease in certain seigneurial revenues, an increase in the number of payments of sales-tax, and an increase in the numbers of notaries. Viewed singly and in isolation, these trends are not of much significance; but when they all move in the same direction they can be used to trace a change.

Counting heads was not among the concepts of the time. At best, the seignorial rent-roll comprised a list of peasants paying dues, but other villagers were excluded. In the same way, we are acquainted with numbers of households—thanks to fiscal registers for the *bailliage* or town. But beyond these, for a state such as France, and even more so for whole continents like Asia or America, the problem did not even present itself. A few simple classifications sufficed: the black- and yellow-skinned men found in the great ports of the eastern Mediterranean were labelled, in accordance with the biblical classification, the sons of Shem, Ham or Japheth. In its demographic sense mankind was only a word in the sixteenth century. Whole continents lay juxtaposed with only partial knowledge of each other; and it was not possible to know more until the end of the seventeenth century, when the first 'world' estimates were hazarded with varying degrees of success.[22]

Nevertheless, the sixteenth and seventeenth centuries witnessed sizable

[22] For example, in 1661, Riccioli attributed to America a population of 300 millions.

population movements. Many left for America, of course, and many more succumbed to the attraction of central and southern Italy. The 'shoulder to shoulder' conditions of Flanders and Italy contrasted with the empty or virtually empty spaces of some mountain areas. These movements and contrasts made no great impression upon the contemporaries of Rabelais or Montaigne, and the problems which they raised were foreign to them. Each man regarded himself as a member of a great mystical body: his Church; of a political unit, which was not yet called the State; and above all of a community, be it town or village, which did not count its inhabitants because it knew them personally and placed them in the social hierarchy, which was all that was necessary to their daily existence.

Even more understandably, therefore, they felt no need to analyse the structure of any given group. Males and females, young and old were merely the subjects of brief—or picturesque—references. The same applied to the duration of life: the high mortality rate lends credibility to myths of centenarians, which were all the more easily acceptable since the virtual lack of official registration allowed all manner of fantasies. Sometimes these were coloured by vanity: Thomas Platter, who became a widower at the age of 73, remarried immediately and was not a little proud of having had six children by this second marriage.

Many estimates have been made, among them those of Braudel for the Mediterranean area as a whole, those of Roupnel whose skilful deductions are based on a district by district count of the households of Dijon, those of Goubert, who has patiently taken a census of his Beauvaisis. All these figures suggest that France had a population of 16 millions at the end of the sixteenth century—in fact, a high density of population if one bears in mind the low yield of the land under cultivation, which covered a much smaller area than in the eighteenth and nineteenth centuries. France was a very crowded country[23] despite the uninhabited areas of, in particular, the Massif Central. But it is scarcely possible to state with accuracy anything more than the total.

Beyond this, one has to be content with a comparison of the deductions drawn from the general conditions of food and health, which we have just examined, with the more solid statistics available for periods immediately following, and resting on the same demographic characteristics. The most obvious feature is the brevity of life—perhaps twenty years—a result of the

[23] Lescarbot, who was anxious to find inhabitants for New France, observed that this 'over-crowding' had slowed down the birth-rate (despite the repressive laws of 1557). At least, this was his impression. 'In the early centuries when virginity was reprehensible, seeing that God had commanded men and women to increase and multiply, and to fill the earth. But when it was filled, this love grew marvellously cold, and children began to be a burden to their fathers and mothers, so that many spurned them and very often brought about their deaths' (*Histoire de la Nouvelle France*, p. 634).

high death-rate which, as always, affected the weakest first—that is to say, the children.

A man's life is wretchedly short, said Pascal, who wanted to reckon it from the age of reason. This accounts for their marrying at such an early age, as also for the many widows of fifteen or even younger who were to be found in all the towns. Equally, it explains the prestige of the 'greybeards', who by passing the age of forty had shown that their constitution was able to stand up to any test, and the place of honour which was reserved for the old in a society where it was so common to die young. Obviously, these are only generalizations which cannot compare with the sound statistics on the average age of first marriages which can be drawn today from official registration records.

Compensating for the high death-rate, there seems generally to have been a high birth-rate, even if births did seem a burden, at least in the towns. In the middle of the sixteenth century, there was concern in Paris over the number of abortions taking place, despite fierce repressive measures which normally involved the death sentence for women and girls convicted of having 'concealed their pregnancy' and 'killed the fruit of their womb'.[24]

However, the most decisive feature of this demography would seem to be its mobility, its spasmodic nature. An epidemic, and *a fortiori* a series of epidemics, ruined a region or a town and the population was reduced by a quarter, sometimes even by half. But this gap was soon filled, both by movements into the area of new inhabitants from neighbouring provinces, and by births; thus the harvests of death and the new buds of life make the available data fluctuate violently.[25] Religious fervour also added to this instability in the course of the sixteenth century: a glance at the influx of Protestant refugees into Geneva between 1549 and 1560 is enough to convince one of this. At no time, therefore, could one speak of a stable population.

Finally, it seems quite certain that such mobility in human life implied a certain contempt for that life. These sudden fluctuations in population affecting all age-groups, the movements from place to place, and the high birth-rate meant that the individual was not considered the valuable creature that he is in the twentieth century, when, except in war-time, miracles are performed each day to save or prolong human lives. The readiness with which murder was committed[26] in all classes of society is, moreover, the best proof of this.

[24] At the end of the seventeenth century, Bayle (*Dictionnaire*, 'Patin') maintained that matters had only worsened since 1557. For his part, Henri Estienne observed that only women in service died as a result of this harsh law.

[25] As an example of these fluctuations, cf. Roupnel's study of the households of Dijon, where he gives the following figures: *1572*, 3198 households; *1580*, 3591; *1602*, 3029; *1626*, 3984; *1653*, 4007 (Roupnel (155)).

[26] Cardan (290) calmly recounts an attempted murder which closely concerned him: '*Tentatis, ut audivi, abortivis medicamentis frustra, ortus sum anno MDI, VIII cal. octobris*'.

Chapter 3
The mind: senses, sensations, emotions, passions

It is no easier to assess modern man's mind than his body, again for many reasons. Principally, it is because there is inherent in the subject an element of confusion which there can be no question of eliminating completely. To separate the emotional from the rational in the approved manner of our philosophers is a temptation better resisted. For the contemporaries of Ronsard or Malherbe, this is not a necessary distinction, and it would be dangerous to impose it upon them: the least sensation which we would maintain to be objective, such as the colour of a flower, or the shape of a piece of furniture, was emotionally charged. The only legitimate method of approach here is to underline this fusion of the emotional and the rational until Descartes and probably beyond, and to progress from the simple to the complex; from the sensations to the attitudes dictated by the abstractions of speech and the printed word—a lengthy exploration of mental equipment which it is difficult to determine in this eventful period, when it was being renewed to a large extent.

To begin with, then, we shall examine senses and sensations as and where we find evidence of them—especially in the works of the poets, who were endowed with a sensibility which was perhaps no keener than that of the average man but which expressed itself more readily. Ronsard and his companions of the Pléiade, together with Marot and D'Aubigné, will momentarily be our guides to capture the sensory tonality of the first century of modern times. This is not without risks, of course, but these must be taken since other sources, in particular the memorialists, have little to offer by way of the immediate recording of sensations, or basic, spontaneous information on their feelings.

This investigation of the 'five senses of nature' is not without its surprises either—at least if one sets them starkly beside those of the twentieth century. The development and use of the different sense organs was not the same as ours —far from it.[1] The order of their importance was not the same, for sight, which

[1] Readers of *Rabelais et le problème de l'incroyance au XVIième siècle* (final chapters) are certainly aware of this. But the discoveries made by Lucien Febvre have not yet become part of the common knowledge of the average man of culture.

is dominant today, stood in third position, a long way behind hearing and touch. The eye, which organizes, classifies and orders, was not the favourite organ of a period which preferred to listen—with all the disturbing imprecision which this abiding preference involved.[2] Obviously, the sense organs were the same as our own, and even, very probably, sharper and more practised in those times of continual violence, when constant vigilance was necessary and a traveller never crossed a moor or a forest without once or twice climbing a tall tree to scan the countryside and to see that there was no band of brigands on the prowl. However, it was hearing rather than sight which stimulated the imagination, while touch was likewise infinitely more important than sight.

Primacy of hearing and touch

In this, the modern period prolonged an essential characteristic of medieval civilization, though somewhat paradoxically, since the ever-increasing number of printed books showed the growing popularity of reading. Yet information was still principally imparted by word of mouth: even the great of this world listened more than they read. They were surrounded by counsellors who spoke with them, instructed them orally and read to them. In the administrative assemblies, the counsellors of kings and princes quite naturally often held the title of 'auditors',[3] while during the long evenings in the humblest country cottage, it was story-telling which continued to provide food for thought and to fire the imagination. Moreover, even the enthusiastic readers, the humanists, were accustomed to doing so aloud—thus *hearing* the text before them.

The first reason for this primacy was a religious one: it was the Word of God that was the supreme authority of the Church. Faith itself was a matter of hearing. The prophets in the centuries before Christ were ever crying: 'Hear ye!' 'They do not hear!' 'They will not hear!' God worked through the Word which he had made known for all men to hear, a point admirably expressed by Luther in his Commentary on the Epistle to the Hebrews:[4] 'If you ask a Christian what action makes him worthy of the name of Christian, he can make no other reply than this: the hearing of the Word of God, that is to say, the Faith (*Auditum verbi Dei, id est fidem*).' And Luther adds: '*Ideo solae aures sunt organa Christiani hominis, quia non ex ullius membri operibus, sed de fide justificatur, et Christianus judicatur.*' Thus the ears alone were the organs for a Christian—which conferred a special dignity upon them.

[2] One might note in passing that in the eighteenth century sight was still poorly considered. Diderot wrote in the *Lettre sur les sourds et muets:* 'I found that of all the senses, sight was the most superficial'; and Buffon says of touch: 'This is the reliable sense, the touchstone and measure of all the others' (*Histoire naturelle*, 'Homme').

[3] The term has been retained in the twentieth century, when reports are more often written than presented orally—e.g. *auditeurs* in the *Conseil d'État*.

[4] Martin Luther, *Commentaire sur l'Epître aux Hébreux*, ed. Ficker, pp. 105–6.

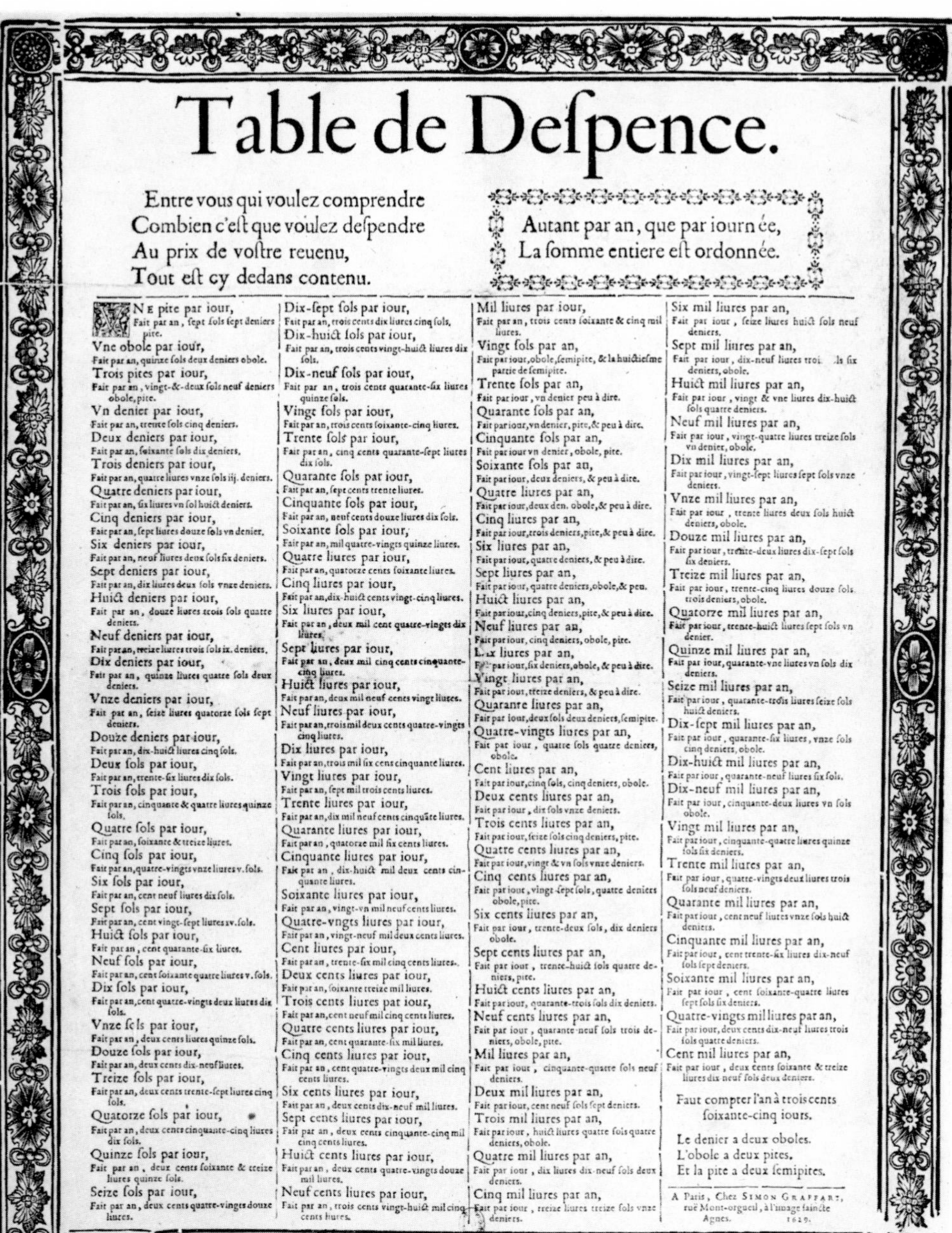

Table de Deſpence.

Entre vous qui voulez comprendre
Combien c'eſt que voulez deſpendre
Au prix de voſtre reuenu,
Tout eſt cy dedans contenu.

Autant par an, que par iournée,
La ſomme entiere eſt ordonnée.

VNE pite par iour,
Fait par an, ſept ſols ſept deniers pite.

Vne obole par iour,
Fait par an, quinze ſols deux deniers obole.

Trois pites par iour,
Fait par an, vingt-&-deux ſols neuf deniers obole, pite.

Vn denier par iour,
Fait par an, trente ſols cinq deniers.

Deux deniers par iour,
Fait par an, ſoixante ſols dix deniers.

Trois deniers par iour,
Fait par an, quatre liures vnze ſols iij. deniers.

Quatre deniers par iour,
Fait par an, ſix liures vn ſol huict deniers.

Cinq deniers par iour,
Fait par an, ſept liures douze ſols vn denier.

Six deniers par iour,
Fait par an, neuf liures deux ſols ſix deniers.

Sept deniers par iour,
Fait par an, dix liures deux ſols vnze deniers.

Huict deniers par iour,
Fait par an, douze liures trois ſols quatre deniers.

Neuf deniers par iour,
Fait par an, treize liures trois ſols ix. deniers.

Dix deniers par iour,
Fait par an, quinze liures quatre ſols deux deniers.

Vnze deniers par iour,
Fait par an, ſeize liures quatorze ſols ſept deniers.

Douze deniers par iour,
Fait par an, dix-huict liures cinq ſols.

Deux ſols par iour,
Fait par an, trente-ſix liures dix ſols.

Trois ſols par iour,
Fait par an, cinquante & quatre liures quinze ſols.

Quatre ſols par iour,
Fait par an, ſoixante & treize liures.

Cinq ſols par iour,
Fait par an, quatre-vingts vnze liures v. ſols.

Six ſols par iour,
Fait par an, cent neuf liures dix ſols.

Sept ſols par iour,
Fait par an, cent vingt-ſept liures xv. ſols.

Huict ſols par iour,
Fait par an, cent quarante-ſix liures.

Neuf ſols par iour,
Fait par an, cent ſoixante quatre liures v. ſols.

Dix ſols par iour,
Fait par an, cent quatre-vingts deux liures dix ſols.

Vnze ſols par iour,
Fait par an, deux cents liures quinze ſols.

Douze ſols par iour,
Fait par an, deux cents dix-neuf liures.

Treize ſols par iour,
Fait par an, deux cents trente-ſept liures cinq ſols.

Quatorze ſols par iour,
Fait par an, deux cents cinquante-cinq liures dix ſols.

Quinze ſols par iour,
Fait par an, deux cents ſoixante & treize liures quinze ſols.

Seize ſols par iour,
Fait par an, deux cents quatre-vingts douze liures.

Dix-ſept ſols par iour,
Fait par an, trois cents dix liures cinq ſols.

Dix-huict ſols par iour,
Fait par an, trois cents vingt-huict liures dix ſols.

Dix-neuf ſols par iour,
Fait par an, trois cents quarante-ſix liures quinze ſols.

Vingt ſols par iour,
Fait par an, trois cents ſoixante-cinq liures.

Trente ſols par iour,
Fait par an, cinq cents quarante-ſept liures dix ſols.

Quarante ſols par iour,
Fait par an, ſept cents trente liures.

Cinquante ſols par iour,
Fait par an, neuf cents douze liures dix ſols.

Soixante ſols par iour,
Fait par an, mil quatre-vingts quinze liures.

Quatre liures par iour,
Fait par an, quatorze cents ſoixante liures.

Cinq liures par iour,
Fait par an, dix-huict cents vingt-cinq liures.

Six liures par iour,
Fait par an, deux mil cent quatre-vingts dix liures.

Sept liures par iour,
Fait par an, deux mil cinq cents cinquante-cinq liures.

Huict liures par iour,
Fait par an, deux mil neuf cents vingt liures.

Neuf liures par iour,
Fait par an, trois mil deux cents quatre-vingts cinq liures.

Dix liures par iour,
Fait par an, trois mil ſix cens cinquante liures.

Vingt liures par iour,
Fait par an, ſept mil trois cents liures.

Trente liures par iour,
Fait par an, dix mil neuf cents cinquãte liures.

Quarante liures par iour,
Fait par an, quatorze mil ſix cents liures.

Cinquante liures par iour,
Fait par an, dix-huict mil deux cents cinquante liures.

Soixante liures par iour,
Fait par an, vingt-vn mil neuf cents liures.

Quatre-vngts liures par iour,
Fait par an, vingt-neuf mil deux cents liures.

Cent liures par iour,
Fait par an, trente-ſix mil cinq cents liures.

Deux cents liures par iour,
Fait par an, ſoixante treize mil liures.

Trois cents liures par iour,
Fait par an, cent neuf mil cinq cents liures.

Quatre cents liures par iour,
Fait par an, cent quarante-ſix mil liures.

Cinq cents liures par iour,
Fait par an, cent quatre-vingts deux mil cinq cents liures.

Six cents liures par iour,
Fait par an, deux cents dix-neuf mil liures.

Sept cents liures par iour,
Fait par an, deux cents cinquante-cinq mil cinq cents liures.

Huict cents liures par iour,
Fait par an, deux cents quatre-vingts douze mil liures.

Neuf cents liures par iour,
Fait par an, trois cents vingt-huict mil cinq cents liures.

Mil liures par iour,
Fait par an, trois cents ſoixante & cinq mil liures.

Vingt ſols par an,
Fait par iour, obole, ſemipite, & la huictieſme partie de ſemipite.

Trente ſols par an,
Fait par iour, vn denier peu à dire.

Quarante ſols par an,
Fait par iour, vn denier, pite, & peu à dire.

Cinquante ſols par an,
Fait par iour vn denier, obole, pite.

Soixante ſols par an,
Fait par iour, deux deniers, & peu à dire.

Quatre liures par an,
Fait par iour, deux den. obole, & peu à dire.

Cinq liures par an,
Fait par iour, trois deniers, pite, & peu à dire.

Six liures par an,
Fait par iour, quatre deniers, & peu à dire.

Sept liures par an,
Fait par iour, quatre deniers, obole, & peu.

Huict liures par an,
Fait par iour, cinq deniers, pite, & peu à dire.

Neuf liures par an,
Fait par iour, cinq deniers, obole, pite.

Dix liures par an,
Fait par iour, ſix deniers, obole, & peu à dire.

Vingt liures par an,
Fait par iour, treize deniers, & peu à dire.

Quarante liures par an,
Fait par iour, deux ſols deux deniers, ſemipite.

Quatre-vingts liures par an,
Fait par iour, quatre ſols quatre deniers, obole.

Cent liures par an,
Fait par iour, cinq ſols, cinq deniers, obole.

Deux cents liures par an,
Fait par iour, dix ſols vnze deniers.

Trois cents liures par an,
Fait par iour, ſeize ſols cinq deniers, pite.

Quatre cents liures par an,
Fait par iour, vingt & vn ſols vnze deniers.

Cinq cents liures par an,
Fait par iour, vingt-ſept ſols, quatre deniers obole, pite.

Six cents liures par an,
Fait par iour, trente-deux ſols, dix deniers obole.

Sept cents liures par an,
Fait par iour, trente-huict ſols quatre deniers, pite.

Huict cents liures par an,
Fait par iour, quarante-trois ſols dix deniers.

Neuf cents liures par an,
Fait par iour, quarante-neuf ſols trois deniers, obole, pite.

Mil liures par an,
Fait par iour, cinquante-quatre ſols neuf deniers.

Deux mil liures par an,
Fait par iour, cent neuf ſols ſept deniers.

Trois mil liures par an,
Fait par iour, huict liures quatre ſols quatre deniers, obole.

Quatre mil liures par an,
Fait par iour, dix liures dix-neuf ſols deux deniers.

Cinq mil liures par an,
Fait par iour, treize liures treize ſols vnze deniers.

Six mil liures par an,
Fait par iour, ſeize liures huict ſols neuf deniers.

Sept mil liures par an,
Fait par iour, dix-neuf liures trois ſols ſix deniers, obole.

Huict mil liures par an,
Fait par iour, vingt & vne liures dix-huict ſols quatre deniers.

Neuf mil liures par an,
Fait par iour, vingt-quatre liures treize ſols vn denier, obole.

Dix mil liures par an,
Fait par iour, vingt-ſept liures ſept ſols vnze deniers.

Vnze mil liures par an,
Fait par iour, trente liures deux ſols huict deniers, obole.

Douze mil liures par an,
Fait par iour, trente-deux liures dix-ſept ſols ſix deniers.

Treize mil liures par an,
Fait par iour, trente-cinq liures douze ſols trois deniers, obole.

Quatorze mil liures par an,
Fait par iour, trente-huict liures ſept ſols vn denier.

Quinze mil liures par an,
Fait par iour, quarante-vne liures vn ſols dix deniers.

Seize mil liures par an,
Fait par iour, quarante-trois liures ſeize ſols huict deniers.

Dix-ſept mil liures par an,
Fait par iour, quarante-ſix liures, vnze ſols cinq deniers, obole.

Dix-huict mil liures par an,
Fait par iour, quarante-neuf liures ſix ſols.

Dix-neuf mil liures par an,
Fait par iour, cinquante-deux liures vn ſols obole.

Vingt mil liures par an,
Fait par iour, cinquante-quatre liures quinze ſols ſix deniers.

Trente mil liures par an,
Fait par iour, quatre-vingts deux liures trois ſols neuf deniers.

Quarante mil liures par an,
Fait par iour, cent neuf liures vnze ſols huict deniers.

Cinquante mil liures par an,
Fait par iour, cent trente-ſix liures dix-neuf ſols ſept deniers.

Soixante mil liures par an,
Fait par iour, cent ſoixante-quatre liures ſept ſols ſix deniers.

Quatre-vingts mil liures par an,
Fait par iour, deux cents dix-neuf liures trois ſols quatre deniers.

Cent mil liures par an,
Fait par iour, deux cents ſoixante & treize liures dix-neuf ſols deux deniers.

Faut compter l'an à trois cents ſoixante-cinq iours.

Le denier a deux oboles.
L'obole a deux pites.
Et la pite a deux ſemipites.

A Paris, Chez SIMON GRAFFART, ruë Mont-orgueil, à l'image ſaincte Agnes. 1629.

Plate 3 Mental equipment: reckoning. Table for calculating expenditure: an arithmetical table for ready reckoning.

Plate 4 Time: an allegorical representation by Jacques Androuet du Cerceau.

However, added to what one might call this doctrinal preference was the fact that hearing was more subtly sensitive than the other faculties—as far as one can judge from the poets, who were all men of sound rather than of sight. The sounds of running brooks and songs of birds constantly recur in the works of Marot and Ronsard; Marot's little *chansons*, which abound in magpies, linnets and goldfinches, never refer to their plumage, but rather to their gay warbling—the linnets' songs and the magpies' chatter and, in the depths of the forest, 'the most hideous calls and howls of dangerous beasts'.[5] Du Bellay seeks to sing the praises of the source of the Loire in the following terms:

> Pour saluer de joyeuses aubades
> Celle qui t'a, et tes filles liquides
> Deïfié de ce bruyt éternel.[6]

Ronsard conjures up the sea and its watery inhabitants, but does not adorn them with attractive shapes or colours. It was a sound which the presence of these marine creatures brought to mind:

> Et par les palais humides
> Hucha les soeurs néréides
> Qui ronflaient au bruit des flots.[7]

When he wished to delight the King or his patroness there was no better way than to appeal to hearing. For example:

> Notre Roi,
> Duquel la divine oreille
> Humera cette merveille.[8]

and elsewhere:

> Il faut que j'aille tanter
> L'oreille de Marguerite
> Et dans son palais chanter.[9]

This brings us to vocal and instrumental music. In Ronsard we find the harp, the lyre and the lute recurring time and again—and even flutes and trumpets. More often than noise or thunder, it was music which was celebrated—and universally appreciated, for, as Ronsard says in a preface to a collection of *chansons*, it uplifts all well-born souls: 'he, Sire, who hears a gentle harmony of

[5] Cf. Marot's *Temple de Cupido*, *Eglogue au roy*, *Elégie II*, etc.; Du Bellay's *L'Olive* ed. Chamard, I, 29, 45, 114, 121; II, 37, 59; Ronsard, *Odes* I, 63; II ,69; III, 72; III, 77; IV, 16, 133.

[6] To greet with joyous morning-song,
Her who both thy nymphs and thee
Hath deified with this eternal roar.

[7] And thro' the watery palaces
Did to the nereid sisters sound the call,
Whose snoring rose in rhythm with the waves.

[8] Our king,
Whose ear divine
This wonder will absorb

[9] Now must I go to tempt
The ear of Marguerite,
And in her palace sing.

instruments, or the sweetness of the natural voice, and does not rejoice at it, is not moved by it and does not thrill from head to foot at the sound as if sweetly enraptured and in some way transported out of himself, it is a sure sign that his soul is deformed, vicious and depraved, and one must beware of him.'[10] Music was valued so highly that a man such as Cardan had among his servants two young musicians whose sole duty was to play to him. It brought harmony to all, and introduced order into their feelings and their troubles. Composed, regulated, ordered in its sequence and its expression of alternating sentiments, a piece of music was no doubt for them something soothing, something of which they never tired.[11] As Sancho Panza said to the duchess, who was disturbed at hearing the distant sound of an orchestra in the forest, 'Where there is music, Madam, there could be no mischief.' '*Musica me juvat*,' said Cardan, and this was virtually the motto of this period which was so captivated by the art.

Touch came immediately after hearing, again possibly on religious grounds, since there was such a thing as a sacred touch—that of the saint who cured the sick by the miraculous laying-on of hands.

The poets were constantly touching and feeling—and also licking,[12] 'greedily' (*goulûment*), to use the word which often comes from their pens. Ronsard can again be used to illustrate this point:

Que de coral, que de lys, que de roses . . .
Tastay je lors entre deux maniments. . . .[13]

To depict a well-turned leg, he does not strive to suggest its shape by using ready comparisons, or by launching into physical description; it is enough to indicate that it begs to be touched:

. . . la jambe de bon tour
Pleine de chair tout à l'entour
Que volontiers on tâterait.[14]

[10] Preface addressed to Charles IX introducing *Le Mellange de chansons tant de vieux autheurs que des modernes* (Paris 1572).

[11] In Rabelais's Fifth Book, ch. 21, Quint Essence even cured the sick with song. J. B. Porta's *Magia Naturalis* also includes a chapter on music therapy, '*De lyra et multis quibusdam ejus proprietatibus*' (Porta (298), XX, ch. 7).

[12] Ronsard, *Odes à du Bellay* I, 9:

Et pour licher la gloire douce
Qui emmielle ton renom.
(And to lick the honeyed glory
Which sweetens thy renown.)

[13] *Amours*, ed. Blanchemain, I, 106:

What coral and what lilies, what roses . . .
I tasted then between two movements. . . .

[14] *Ibid.* II, 403:

. . . the shapely leg
Whose full round flesh
Would so delight the touch.

Until the eighteenth century at least, touch remained one of the master senses. It checked and confirmed what sight could only bring to one's notice. It verified perception, giving solidity to the impressions provided by other senses, which were not as reliable. Here is still further confirmation of the subordinate role played by sight in the life of modern man, whose first instinct was to listen. One has only to recall the tragedy of Ronsard's deafness.

The secondary role of sight

As well as its musicians, the age no doubt had its painters—and even its draughtsmen, if only Leonardo da Vinci. However, such people as da Vinci, Dürer, Holbein and the rest were rather exceptional. In fact, it is quite clear that the contemporaries of these imaginative geniuses were not used to seeing, depicting or describing shapes. Erasmus did not draw; not once did he 'doodle' in the margins of his books. Marguerite de Navarre and Brantôme, both well placed to observe the great people of their day, did not describe them: of all the kings, emperors and popes that they knew we have not a single living silhouette before us. Rabelais too gave life to his characters through their words: during the storm, it is Frère Jean who talks while the rigging groans and the mast comes crashing down. However, modern man was alive to vividly-contrasted colours. The flowers mentioned by the poets are few in number, but their colours are distinct: the rose, the lily, the carnation (which is usually red) and, less frequently, the violet. The livery worn by the sergeants on festive occasions was commonly made in bright colours, which struck the eye and bore a whole symbolism, about which little is known.[15]

The fact that hitherto no one has investigated these colours and their poetic usage[16] means that we must be discreet in our brief remarks upon the palettes of the various poets. In Ronsard, besides the flowers already mentioned, we find ebony, vermilion and crimson, which is not a red, but a superlative, equally applicable to blue and brown. In du Bellay's *Olive*, half a dozen basic colours recur—gold in superabundance, black and white (with their variants—whitening, etc.) and red, with its train of vermilion, coral and rich ruby—while blue or violet and their shades are not mentioned. On the other hand, du Bellay uses a whole range of precious stones which act as colour images: a shapely foot displays 'five gems' which are its nails; the lips are of coral, the teeth, well-set pearls, clear or crystalline, and the neck is of porphyry; bright emeralds, fine rubies, pearls and sapphires make up his repertoire. D'Aubigné's resources are greater, and include crimson red. The 'black pools' and wild flowers, such as

[15] Green was the colour of fools—L'Estoile indicates in August 1589 that, upon the death of Henri III, the common people of Paris wore green for mourning, to show their joy.

[16] As has been done for the Latin language in a noted thesis: J. André, *Étude sur les termes de couleur dans la langue latine* (Paris 1949).

the marigold and the columbine, represent acquisitions for the poetic palette at the end of the century.

Is there any connexion between this enrichment and the effort undoubtedly made at the end of the century and in the next to improve vision? There is no doubt that there was an improvement, albeit a modest one: windows were fitted with clear-glass panes, spectacles provided for weak eyes, and rooms equipped with better lighting, all of which contributed towards the same end. Alongside these improvements, which affected the rich first, and which were elements of comfort, one should include the optical instruments and lenses which made it possible to observe the heavens, as well as the microscopic. Galileo's telescope and the first microscope lenses were instruments of scientific progress, but with them longer and better trained vision came into play. This marked the beginning of the promotion of sight, which was obviously closely dependent on the rise of modern science.

*

Whereas today smell and taste are relatively unimportant by comparison with the other three senses, the men of the sixteenth century were extremely susceptible to scents and perfumes—as also to sweets. The terms 'sweet' and 'sweets' were in constant use—as were 'sugar' and 'honey'—and gave rise to countless metaphors. For Ronsard, a kiss was not a contact; it was not connected with touch, but with scent:

Quand de ta lèvre à demi close
Je sens ton haleine de rose. . . .[17]

On another occasion, to Cassandra, he adds:

Nymphe aux beaux yeux
Qui souffles de ta bouche
Une Arabie à qui près en approuche
Pour déraciner mon esmoy
Cent mille baisers donne moy.[18]

To modern man, scent was something positive, the *cause* of a transformation rather than an effect, for humours and wind played the same important part in the animal and vegetable kingdoms as they did in human nature.

[17] *Odes*, ed. Blanchemain, I, 124:

When from thy half-closed lips
Rose-scented breath I smell. . . .

[18] *Amours*, ed. Blanchemain, II, 431:

Nymph with the beauteous eyes
Whose mouth breathes out a scent
Of Araby to him who would draw nigh
To tear out the sorrow from my breast
A hundred thousand kisses give to me.

Yet neither smell nor taste created artistic forms, at least, not before Brillat-Savarin, and one is tempted to wonder whether this fact explains their inferior status.

Thus thought was enveloped in an atmosphere which was more confused than ours: smell and taste, the most affective of the senses, were much more developed than they are with us. These, along with hearing, weighed heavily in favour of the emotional rather than the rational. It is not surprising that for long after this the senses, together with the whole imaginative world which was nourished by them, were considered as leading only to error and falsehood. Malebranche still maintained that they were given to us for the preservation of the body, as instruments of our instincts, 'and not to learn the truth'.

The men of those difficult times thus lived close to nature, which they touched, listened to and drank in from close quarters; but they reacted violently to the impressions they received. For these well-attuned, alert affective senses were matched by a very keen and spontaneous sensibility, which seemed to be carried to extremes by its own impulses, as also by the uncertainty fostered by the very imprecision of their knowledge of the outside world, which was assumed to be hostile in many of its manifestations. Simple natural contrasts such as day and night, cold and warmth, gave rise to emotions charged with supernatural symbols, with anthropomorphic or occult explanations, which in their turn served only to amplify the immediate reaction produced by the sensations. Added to this essentially affective sensory apparatus were the distortions produced by an easily-exasperated sensibility, which was only too ready to plunge into the fathomless depths of the imaginary.

Contrasts and violent reactions

For centuries still to come, night was dreaded for itself. Nocturnal darkness was the realm of fear everywhere, in both town and country—even in Paris, where the watch had more rounds than in any other town. From curfew to the opening of the gates, the town, with all its lights and fires extinguished, shrank fearfully into darkness. A gang of mischievous lads could easily make a whole district howl in terror: solitary women would be left to scream by their neighbours; children would see in their waking dreams all the werewolves which they had read about in story-books; young and old alike, filled with anxiety, would long for the return of daylight, bringing liberation from the dreaded danger 'that walketh in darkness'. The same terror prevailed in the countryside where night also meant hostility, as Racan vividly reveals:

> Les coqs ne chantent point, j'entends aucun bruit. . . .
> Maint fantôme hideux couvert de corps sans corps,
> Visite en liberté la demeure des morts.
> Je saute à bas du lit et ne vois rien paraître
> Que l'ombre de la nuit dont la noire pâleur

Peint les champs et les prés d'une même couleur
Et cette obscurité qui tout le monde enserre. . . .[19]

Night was the realm of darkness—and consequently also of ghosts and hell-hounds: the Spirit of Evil was at home there, just as the reassuring light was the province of a God of goodness. On moonless nights the Devil's spouses flew off to the sabbath on their broomsticks; but even when witches were not abroad, any manner of evil encounter was possible. As Ronsard writes:

La nuit des fantômes volans
Claquetans leurs becs violans
En sifflant mon âme espovantent.[20]

The light which pierced the darkness and freed objects from its grip, etching distinct forms and picking out faces with bold clarity, was the same light that so many painters from Rembrandt to La Tour, delighting in contrasts of light and shade, loved to depict.

The contrast of night and day was the most important of those which haunted the troubled imaginations of the times, for it contained their ignorance. Any inexplicable phenomenon—a comet, eclipse, or freakish animal—instantly became a manifestation of evil, an omen of disaster against which there could be no defence. Cardan, the scholar who was so often ill, awoke one morning to see the sun shining through cracks in the shutters and dust dancing in its rays. He fled panic-stricken in his nightshirt, thinking that he had seen some monster snapping off heads with its teeth. On another night (in 1557), he felt his bed shake, but managed to drop off to sleep again. The next morning a servant brought word that on the previous day his son had contracted an unsatisfactory marriage. The bed's shaking had been a miraculous warning from his familiar spirit.

It is on the emotional plane, therefore, that we must first reckon with this world (which today we call supernatural) with its population of demons and grotesque, imaginary creatures: a world crawling with horned devils who, with goat's ears pricked, prance about on their hairy legs, brandishing their hooks; a realm in which werewolves roam, appearing in two different places at the

[19] Racan, *Bergeries* I, i:

No cocks crow and not a sound is heard. . . .
Many a hideous ghost whose flesh is yet not flesh
Roaming unhindered in the halls of Death.
I leap down from my bed, but nothing see
Beyond the gloom of night whose lustre dim
Bathes in monotone the fields and glades,
And world-embracing black obscurity.

[20] At night, the flying phantoms,
Champing ferocious jaws,
Do by their whistling terrify my soul.

same time, in one as a beast, in the other as a human being; sometimes lycanthropic devils, but always dreadful to behold, ever menacing—in fact, exactly as the painters and sculptors of the time of Hieronymus Bosch and Breughel the Elder imagined them to be. This was an imaginary world of exceptional immediacy. It produced fear and nightmares such as are caused by primeval terror; and no doubt it appeared more teeming and oppressive than the images of a heavenly paradise or even than earth itself, which every man could explore peacefully and familiarly in broad daylight.

Temperaments made hypersensitive by the constant interplay of these daily contrasts often revealed a pronounced liking for spectacles and events involving death. Here again a gulf separates us from these very recent times, for we would regard as cruel such collective delight at the sight of torture or a public execution. To dice with death was not in the least extraordinary: if a joust or tournament resulted in a death, this was no cause for lamentation. Such an event received only the briefest mention in the journal of a bourgeois of Paris (in 1515): 'On Monday 14 February jousting began in front of the Hotel des Tournelles. It was of a very high standard, and a nobleman was killed by a blow from a lance.' A century later, Monconys crossed Holland and greatly admired the houses, meadows and trees that he saw, adding, 'and along the roads there are many magnificent gibbets'. Such macabre admiration is nothing; more significant were the crowds gathering to watch torture, or a well-staged execution. In 1571 at Provins, the executioner, making his debut in the profession, bungled a straightforward decapitation and had to face his victim, then the crowd of aggrieved spectators. At Metz in 1500, three thousand people gathered on the ice of a lake in midwinter to see the drowning of two women who had beaten a lad to death with a stick. In 1510, Philippe de Vigneulles recounts how all his fellow-citizens assembled to watch the execution of a counterfeiter condemned to be boiled in oil. The whole town was present, so much so that 'one couldn't move one's feet' in the square. The unfortunate wretch was thrown head-first into the great cauldron full of boiling oil.

However, once this moment of intense emotion was over, the greatest criminals were not forgotten. At the beginning of the seventeenth century, at any rate, small-time pedlars often had in their packs slim pamphlets relating the crimes of the now-repentant wretch, set to a well-known tune:

Diligemment examiné
Le siège m'a tost condamné
D'estre pendu et mis en cendre
Avecque la quille de bois
Afin qu'un chacun pust apprendre
Qu'il faut mieux révérer les Croix.[21]

[21] 'Music on a condemned man' (Aldendorf, an alleged Protestant, who had broken a crucifix at Lyons), 'to the tune of *Adieu dédaigneuse beauté*', published at Lyons in 1627

Although these doleful ballads, strictly moral in tone, invariably ended with the invocation of some saint, if not of Christ Himself or the Trinity, their immediate effect was surely to perpetuate the memory of famous crimes and their authors, thus fostering this collective taste for violence.[22]

In such instances, cruelty came very close to utter insensitivity, and in this emotional attitude to death as a public spectacle we again find the same low value being placed upon human life as we saw in connexion with disease.

But death or execution was the most extreme case of all. In their anxiety when confronted by the outside world, by an impenetrable nature which it was still impossible to interpret, the people of the sixteenth and seventeenth centuries were ever aggressive towards their fellow-men. When discussion or argument became overheated, it soon led to blows. At Laon in 1611, the inhabitants of the suburbs and villages had to be forbidden to carry arquebuses between sunset and dawn, 'to prevent the inhabitants in future from killing each other over the slightest tiffs!'[23] Peasant characteristics? Men of law, even those belonging to the *Parlements*, the highest judicial assemblies in the land, were not above such behaviour. Even if firearms were not involved, they would come to blows in the midst of a sitting, to repay a heated remark or settle some dispute over precedence or the sharing out of *douceurs*.[24]

Emotions and passions

Behind these outbursts of temper—violent though they may have been—and at a much deeper level, we find men of strong emotions. The rebirth of classical letters did not succeed in imposing the ancient terminology and the usual classification of virtues and vices. 'Passion' was not equivalent to 'vice', for these 'powerful emotions' of the soul seemed to a large extent to derive from mechanical phenomena which were capable of producing great acts. The wise and happy man would 'turn to good use' his passions, and employ them to some profitable

---

(AN, *fonds Rondonneau,* AD III, 2, 188). The extract quoted forms the sixth of seven verses.

After thorough examination
The bench did soon condemn me
To be hanged and burnt to ashes
Upon the wooden stake
That every man might thereby learn
To show more reverence for crucifixes.

[22] This cruel taste for corporal punishment lasted for a long time. Even in the nineteenth century, executions drew huge crowds, as L. Chevalier noted in his *Classes laborieuses et classes dangereuses pendant la première moitié du XIXe siècle* (Paris 1959).

[23] AD, Aisne, B, 227, quoted in the printed catalogue, p. 31.

[24] As happened at Pau in 1637 (AD, Basses Pyrénées, B, 4538), and at Rouen in 1642 (BN, Mss, *fonds français*, 18939, f. 2).

end, since, after all, he could not help but have them. He would have had to be God, or else reduced to the state of a lifeless statue, to have avoided passions —a concept which was both mechanistic and voluntaristic, since only through willpower could man escape their grip.

Yet his willpower had to be all the stronger because these passions developed in time with and in proportion to his emotions. To hate one's neighbour was at least to be readily disposed to thrash him soundly—or, if social position demanded restraint, to pay others to perform the work of vengeance; or again, to call on one's children to do so. In 1646, a consul of Le Puy came to grips with a tax-collector of the same town over a consular election: first, words were exchanged—'Fool, ignoramus', 'little boy'; finally the tax-collector sent for his children, and addressed them as follows: 'I have reared mastiffs which bark and do not bite. I shall disinherit you if you do not kill Royet [his adversary].' His wishes were carried out by his heirs.[25]

If the impulses were not curbed, therefore, the machinery of passion could run amok, as was apparent in every sphere of emotional activity, but especially in the realm of love.[26] Long before the masterpieces of Racine and Corneille portrayed them so incomparably, the conflicts of love and duty had been carried to their direst extremes. Pierre de l'Estoile bewailed the 'foolish passions of young ladies' which led them to pine away into the grave. 'Mademoiselle Marie de Baillon, my niece, who was about 20 years old, died in this town of Paris, in the house of Monsieur X, where she had been placed to prevent her marrying a gentleman with whom she was so infatuated that, having found a way of meeting him and speaking to him, she died of love 24 hours later.'[27]

The usual solution in such love affairs thwarted on social grounds—and one, moreover, which was much to be preferred to death—was abduction followed by a hasty marriage a few miles away. All well and good if the young widow —or single girl—was in agreement, and a party to it; the whole affair takes on an air of musical comedy. But it is much more remarkable to see girls carried off against their will and fighting tooth and nail to resist their intending abductors. D'Ormesson tells of a second attempt made by M. de Charmoy on the person of Mademoiselle de Saint-Croix, who had taken refuge following the first alarm in the convent of the *filles Dieu* in the rue Saint-Denis.

> Charmoy, in his madness, resolved to carry off the girl. To this end, at one o'clock on the night of the feast of Our Lady he came with Saint-Ange and five men. They blasted open one door . . . and went up to the girl's room, but she had fled from it with a nun into a wood loft. Finding her there they dragged her from it by force, though she wore only a shift. She clung to a ladder, but they pulled her away so that she struck her head

[25] BN, Mss, *fonds français*, 18342, f. 95.

[26] Quite apart from the love or vanity of the courtiers, as Bussy describes it.

[27] *De L'Estoile* (2), 6th December 1593.

> on the floor. She threw herself at their legs to stop them taking her. They rained blows upon her with sticks and spurs, and struck her arms to make her release her hold. They dragged her stark naked into the garden and tried to lift her over the wall, but she clung to the ladder and the wall. They pulled her by the hair, but still they could not succeed in their design. Finally they tied her on the back of one of their number, but when he tried to climb the ladder two rungs broke. In the meantime, however, the alarm-bell was ringing. . . .[28]

A common enough scene, apparently, since the thugs used in these operations were so experienced that they took precautions against possible knife-thrusts. 'She struck at her abductors with a knife, but they were wearing strong buff jerkins.'[29]

Another equally violent passion, and one closely connected with this frenzy of unrequited love, was jealousy, which also claimed many victims. The *crime passionnel* was very common, though not so much was made of it as today (the first news sheets, at the beginning of the seventeenth century, were much more concerned with political information than anything else). Doubtless it was punished more severely than today, when so many extenuating circumstances intervene to moderate sentences, but repressive measures were not very effective.

Can one go further, and assert that these forms of uncontrollable passion were more common than mere lechery? A systematic investigation of the whole range of available evidence would be necessary before one could be sure. Ronsard and some of the other poets can be used to support both cases.[30] However, the contribution of one great traveller who admired the natives of New France points very strongly to libertinage: 'But today most [women] prefer to use their breasts as inducements to dalliance; and, wishing to enjoy themselves, they send their children off into the country, where they are perhaps farmed out or given to depraved nurses whose corruption and evil disposition they suck together with their milk.'[31] Nevertheless, this century and a half of modern France seems to have been distinguished by exasperated passion rather than sophisticated pleasures.

Were the same excesses to be found in other spheres of activity? Certainly, if the term 'religious passion' can be used of the Leaguers and the Protestants taking part in the civil wars at the end of the sixteenth century. Similarly, the nobleman's sense of honour and the ardour with which the old nobility defended their threatened social position come under the same heading. Not that we propose to catalogue all the passions current at the time—honour, love, friendship and so on; in any case, a full list of these would no doubt be provided by

[28] D'Ormesson, *Mémoires* I, p. 471.

[29] Dubuisson-Aubenay, *Mémoires* I, p. 46.

[30] 'When I right greedily devour
This white breast round as an apple,' sings one of them.

[31] Lescarbot, *Histoire de la Nouvelle France*, p. 631.

Pibrac's quatrains, those pompous, cautionary verses written in lifeless doggerel which were recopied in dozens of *livres de raison* under the title 'Advice to children'. Using the best available criterion, the passions of love, we have indicated this state of passionate exasperation; and this, in its turn, provides further evidence of the predominance of the emotional over the rational.

Chapter 4
The mind: mental equipment and fundamental attitudes

The expression 'mental equipment' has become a part of the common heritage of all historians. It is almost twenty years since it was suggested by Lucien Febvre[1] in his *Problème de l'incroyance*, and it has been adopted to denote the basic furniture of the mind, that apparatus which the historian ought to recreate for each period and each civilization before making any attempt to grasp its conceptual efforts, its collective thought processes and the movement of ideas. Just as we could not conceive of studying architecture or the art of weaving in some distant period without first describing the techniques available to the artisan of the time, so we must reconstruct the mental resources at the disposal of professional intellectuals and laymen for analysing, describing and explaining the world, men and God. This involves, in the first instance, reconstructing a vocabulary and its usage, studying a language which was a vehicle for thoughts and feelings; equally, it involves reconstructing man's environment as it appeared to him—all complex questions in the case of an age in which the national languages fought their way to the fore in competition with Latin and the local dialects, and when the current notions of the world were upset by the voyages of exploration and the discoveries of Copernicus and Galileo.

The spoken and written languages

In his *Rabelais*, Lucien Febvre set out to show that the French in the sixteenth century, given their jerky syntax and a vocabulary lacking in abstract philosophical terms, did not have the necessary linguistic tools to be able to formulate the concepts of unbelief.[2] These often subtle observations obviously do not exhaust the problem of the linguistic equipment of the time, but merely illuminate a particular question which was well-defined at the outset.

In the period under discussion the question of language was indeed singularly complex. In the sixteenth century the French had at their disposal not one, but

[1] And almost thirty years since he imposed its use in the *Encyclopédie française*, I.

[2] Febvre (284), pp. 384 ff.

four languages—an abundance which was not so much a sign of wealth as of wholesale mutation. At the time, this constituted a formidable handicap for men, hampered as they were by their rival tongues and impeded by the neologisms of one or other of them. In fact, their problem was twofold, for there were two refined languages, Latin and literary French, and at the same time two groups of dialects, one relating to the north and the other to the south. Despite its convenience as a means of international communication, the Latin used by clerks and scholars was becoming less common at the moment when the different nations of Europe were building up and codifying their respective languages. Brunot has already shrewdly noted how the efforts of the humanists to promote Ciceronian Latin in its purest form helped to stiffen 'classical' Latin into an inflexible dead language. The other living forms of Latin, that of the Church, of doctors and of other scholars,[3] were thus cut off from their source of fresh life-blood—and condemned indirectly, in their turn, by the progress of the vernacular. From Ambroise Paré to Descartes the same trend continued. Despite all protests—by the Faculty of Medicine in the former case and by fellow scientists in the latter—Latin was abandoned in favour of the beautiful language of France. Only the Catholic Church (and the University which was part of it) obstinately remained loyal to Latin, partly as a reaction against the Protestants, who had been concerned in every country to make the Word available to the faithful and had translated the Bible, Luther of course being amongst the first to do so.

But in everyday life the dialects in general use had replaced low Latin as long ago as the High Middle Ages. At the beginning of the modern period, the *oil* and *oc* dialects continued to be all the more widely used, since the literary language could only win acceptance among the lower classes—especially the peasantry—through the medium of the printed word. These dialects were composed wholly of concrete terms, even more so than French if this were possible, and were virtually the professional jargons of men of the soil, who needed nothing more than the picturesque vocabulary of their implements and of the fruits of nature.

Yet definite progress was made by the literary language, as a result of a long succession of different causes. These included, as well as works like the *Défense et illustration*, the royal ordinance of François I, imposing the use of French in the law courts and choosing the moment to codify the practice of royal officials;

[3] Rou, in his *Mémoires*, jeered at both the Latin of the philosophers, the *entia rationis* of his Aristotle, and that of the doctors, who defined opium '*in eo virtus dormitiva cujus est natura sensus assoupire*' (Rou (9), I, p. 24). But Descartes gives an even clearer indication of the extent of this long-term break: 'If I write in French, which is the language of my country, rather than in Latin, the language of my tutors, it is because I hope that those who rely solely upon pure natural reason will be better judges of my views than those who only believe in the writings of Antiquity.'

and especially the development of printing itself.[4] Publishing works written in French and translations[5] led to the inevitable research with a view to systematizing spelling and syntax. The quirks of the spoken word were gradually accommodated—though over a very long period, of course, since the process of fixing the literary language continued until the nineteenth century—by a system of regulation accepted by typographers and editors, and often instigated by them (notably by Geoffroy Tory and Robert Estienne) and then taken in hand in the next century, in the time of Malherbe, by Ménage and Vaugelas and the French Academy from its foundation. 'Against the glaring errors committed in the provinces or by the dregs of Paris', the *Remarques* of Vaugelas codified good usage (that of the Court and of reputable authors) and the literary language. This no longer had any reason to be envious of Latin and in 1648 replaced it for the purposes of diplomacy.

This language now spread at the same rate as the ability to read, itself the instrument of communication and self-education.[6] There can be no doubt of this. The men of the modern period eagerly devoured the printed word, which revealed new thoughts and new worlds to them. From the fifteenth century onwards they learned to read it and to recognize its rapidly standardized type instead of script. Even in the humble dwellings of artisans—just as in the homes of the cultured—a place was made near the dresser or the mantelpiece in the living-room for the *Holy Bible*, and the *Quatre fils Aymon*, *Oger le Danois*, *Mélusine*, the *Calendrier des Bergers*, the *Golden Legend*, or the *Roman de la Rose*. Unfortunately it is difficult to set limits to the knowledge of reading, although it would again seem to be necessary to distinguish between town and country. As early as the fifteenth century, towns such as Rouen possessed a municipal library, where books were laid out at the disposal of the inhabitants. When the *échevins* took up office, they swore not to misappropriate any of them,[7] and in 1619 works were still chained to the tables where they were read. Equally, many probate inventories allow one to establish that merchants and lawyers, doctors and artisans had private libraries, which were often well stocked. But apart from in the towns, where religious fervour could not fail to kindle a taste for reading and to promote the spread of the language, it is very difficult to establish anything.

We know, of course, along with Brunot, that the roads of the eighteenth century, the railways of the nineteenth and, finally, compulsory primary educa-

[4] On this question, cf. Febvre and Martin (286), pp. 477 ff. We shall have cause to return to this point later.

[5] For example, Amyot's language with its reduplication: 'his home and his property', 'his might and his army'.

[6] In previous centuries, the spread of French had been dependent upon the extension of royal power. This is particularly clear in the south in the fifteenth century: cf. Brun (131).

[7] To all appearances, a book was regarded as having something mysterious, some occult power about it.

tion were necessary for the French language to complete its conquest of France. The beginning of the modern period was an essential stage in this progression —a stage when a language which was still in many respects deficient, whose vocabulary was wholly concrete and pleonastic—and whose syntax was woolly, confusing planes and perspectives, was only beginning to be accepted by its speakers. There is no need to dwell on these deficiencies,[8] which can be measured negatively by the additions made in following centuries. The philosophical and scientific languages were built up gradually from Descartes and Fermat to Condillac and Lavoisier. In these spheres the only original stock was scholastic jargon, the legacy of the medieval Schools, with all its limitations—and its usage narrowly restricted to clerks; in other words, an instrument of formal logic, devoid of any other value.

Another point worth noting is that the progress of the vernaculars throughout Europe was apparent to travellers and merchants, who recommended all to learn foreign languages. Everywhere it was said that Latin was dying and that it was imperative to learn the language of one's neighbours. Montaigne and Rabelais recommended, in particular, Italian, while in the mid-seventeenth century Savary, the model merchant, wanted young people destined for a career in commerce to be taught, after arithmetic and book-keeping, 'the Italian, Spanish and German languages, which are essential for those who wish to trade abroad'. Here it was for business purposes; for Montaigne it was to become acquainted with the manners and customs of other countries. Obviously, foreign languages did not appear yet as the languages of culture. At most it was a question of making oneself understood in order to live comfortably in the manner of the host country and to do business. Moreover, neither philosophical German nor commercial English had yet been formulated. Both at home and abroad, scholars and men of letters had at their disposal idioms open only to the concrete terms of everyday life.

On the other hand, all thought develops within notions which have existed for centuries as premises without any significant change. If it is true that in the twentieth century each great material discovery entails the elaboration of a new spatial framework, of a new geometry, then this is one of the great innovations of our own day in which many such revolutions have taken place. In former times, space, time and natural environment did not appear to vary in this way, and their very stability imposed apparently immutable limitations on everyone.

[8] Lucien Febvre, following F. Brunot, has dealt conclusively with this question, and it would be pointless to cover the ground again. Anyone who is familiar with Vaugelas, for example, can recognize the cogency of his case: cf. the discussion on *esclavage* and *esclavitude*.

That the adoption of French was a slow process cannot be disputed, but evidence which would help in ascertaining its stages is rare. One good example is provided by the account-book of the church of Fournes (Aude), which was written in pure *oc* dialect until 1572, then interspersed with Gallicisms until 1596, after which it was written in good French. Cf. J. Anglade, *Notice sur un livre de comptes* (Montpellier 1900). But this is only one example.

Yet with the modern period horizons began to widen. As we know, first came the discovery of the earth, then of the heavens. In 1460 Nicholas of Cusa had already speculated learnedly on the incompleteness of the ancient world: if the Roman Emperor was called master of the world, it was a misuse of language. Yet we must be careful. America, the Pacific Ocean, and the flora and fauna of the new lands were not instantly present in everyone's mind. Doubtless, a man who continued to spend his whole life in a very limited setting, a mountain canton or a village in the plain, and never saw the wide open spaces or the sea stretching into infinity, did not have the same capacity for imagining the new expanses as did the traveller or merchant who was brought into daily contact with all parts of the world, and whose notion of space was progressively enlarged until it encompassed the whole planet.

These great vistas of space, time and natural environment thus presented obvious disparities. If it is true that the voyages of discovery, by making possible the deduction that the earth was round, upset a notion of the world, then we must try to give an account of this upheaval, to see perhaps even incompatible and contradictory notions existing side by side; but at the same time to see what was the immediate, everyday notion of space (cf. Map 4).

Space and time

Both are mental constructions, efforts of man based upon his movements. Space is places remembered, hence, primarily, the familiar world within which a man's activities take place. This is not so apparent today, when map-reading and travel are so common, but it was a very real feature in former times. Space was always measured in terms of the human body—the foot, the pace, the cubit—then of its movements—a forest which took three days to cross, a field which took three days to plough, three days' this, three days' that. All these were measured in terms of traditional country life within the narrow boundaries of an estate.

But it is important to realize that beyond, so great was the unknown that there was no further place for intermediate measurement. Letters sent from one end of France did not reach the other, nor did they arrive from one shore of the Mediterranean to the other.[9] Not only were such immensities too difficult to measure; they also offered no element of regularity: with messengers crossing land on horseback and ships at the mercy of the winds at sea, there could be no certainty about the distance between Paris and Madrid or Rome. Beyond a man's own familiar canton, where every road, house and tree was known to him and where all the common measurements were used, there were only the immeasurable expanses of the new world, and only those who had had

[9] Cf. Braudel (349), pp. 310 ff., which describes all possible measurements of the Mediterranean area.

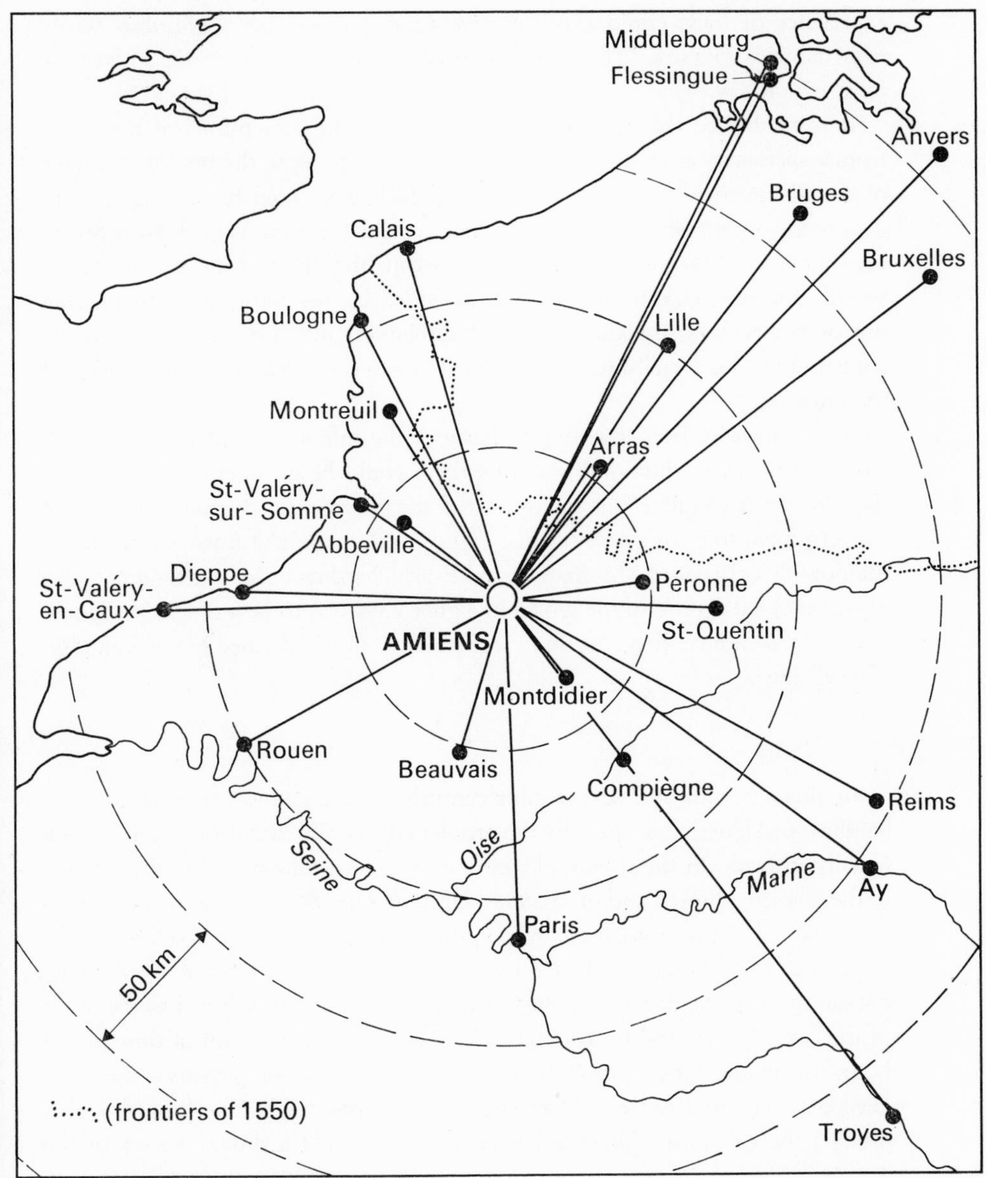

Map 4 The contemporary notion of space: the business connections of a minor merchant of Amiens (late sixteenth century).

experience of these could avoid exaggeration. Christopher Columbus wrote from Jamaica in 1503, 'The world is small; I say the world is not so large as most people say.'[10]

If some lacked the opportunity to learn the true dimensions of the globe from experience, at least it was possible for them to sense the new importance of the ill-measured distances. The terms which were used for a long time to denote the distant lands where Europeans settled—the New World, New Spain, New France—illustrate a new method of estimating distance and the size of the world. An even clearer indication is provided by the artist, who by making use of perspective introduced a third dimension into his paintings, thereby contributing—as a well-known repercussion—to the spread of a wider view of the universe.[11]

A few decades later, the awful silence of the infinity of outer space was to trouble Pascal's meditations, and here there could be no question of adapting the already inadequate human terrestrial measurements. By the standards of modern man, to cross a country like France or the whole of Europe remained a memorable experience. (Montaigne and Esprinchard recorded the stages of such a journey.) To go round the world in eighty days was to be a fine achievement in the nineteenth century. Nothing seemed very clearly defined beyond a radius of one league.

★

In the sixteenth and seventeenth centuries, the conquest of time was not handicapped like that of space by the problem of infinite extension, but it proved equally difficult. In the towns, clocks or watchmen announced the time, while in the country, church and monastery bells rang out across the fields. Yet everyone retained expressions used by country-folk accustomed to following the sun's course. Although he had a clock in his house, the lord of Gouberville constantly used the phrases 'about sunrise' or 'at sunset' or referred to the flight of the 'woodcocks' and to 'cock-crow'.[12] He reckoned duration of time not in hours or mathematical subdivisions of the hour, but in prayers—'the time needed to say an *Ave* or a *Miserere* or two *paternosters*'.[13] The 'hours' which divided the day into eight equal parts were no doubt a distant legacy of the

[10] Letter to Queen Isabella, in F. de Navarette, *Coleccion de los viages y descubrimientos . . .* (Madrid 1858), I, p. 300.

[11] Technically, the introduction of perspective into representational art was more than that, of course; but it did also involve this extension.

[12] Viret, *Exposition de la foy chrestienne* (Geneva, T. Rivery, 1564), p. 179. 'Soldiers, in particular German soldiers, normally take cocks with them when they go to war, to serve as clocks for them at night.'

[13] In Hainault, the popular expression 'un *avé*', is still employed today to mean a brief moment.

monastic life with its rhythm of pious exercises. Accuracy in assessing the time spent at a job or the time of day was not yet an intellectual requirement or a need of daily life. Gargantua says quite naturally: 'Never do I make myself a slave to time.'[14]

Medieval clocks and clepsydras, which had been used for centuries, were delicate instruments which easily went wrong. The big town clock had to have a clock-keeper in constant attendance to wind up the weights and to supervise its movement and chimes (if it did not have to be chimed by hand). In any case, all these fine medieval mechanisms, which were the pride of towns, belfries and cathedrals, merely sounded the hour. When Montaigne crossed Bavaria he reported as a curiosity the clock at Landsberg which struck the quarters, 'and it is said that the Nuremberg clock strikes the minutes'. Water or sand clepsydras were unreliable; 'the water ones,' writes Scaliger, 'are less durable but more reliable, because sand sometimes banks up or becomes so damp that it will not always flow; water flows perpetually where there is the smallest hole, but it evaporates and more has to be added. . . . Finely crushed enamel is better than sand.' Precision clockmaking was born only in the mid-seventeenth century, when on 16 June 1657 Huyghens presented to the States of Holland the first clock which measured time by the regular oscillations of its pendulum. The first pendulum-clocks appeared in France between 1660 and 1665.

The quarter-hours and hours dividing up the day were subject to daily correction, for all clocks were altered to agree with the sun at midday—a simple but necessary check in view of the state of technical progress. Beyond these divisions, the degree of imprecision was as great. Certainly, for the rural population, the year constituted a rhythmic succession of weeks, thanks to Sunday rest, and of seasons with their cycle of tasks. There were the short ploughing days from the Feast of Saint Remigius to the first Sunday in Lent, and then the longer days of Lent itself.[15] The Sundays, called by the first words of the appropriate introit, were not dates but names—*Quasimodo*, *Cantate Domino*, *Reminiscere*. The Sundays of the great festivals also had a common name which was sometimes translated from the Latin: Whit Sunday was 'Rose Easter' (from *pascha rosata*), Palm Sunday, 'Flower Easter'; while the second Sunday after Easter was the 'Sunday of the White Cloths'. Only monasteries and *échevinages* had perpetual calendars, by which the date of Easter was calculated each year and the new calendar established, to be announced from the pulpit, Sunday by Sunday, month by month; while the years themselves began either on 1st January, 25th December or 25th March, in accordance with group preference. Doubtless, the reform of the calendar by Pope Gregory XIII in 1582 drew the attention of the intellectually inquisitive to the difficulties of the solar calendar,

[14] For many, time still remained an allegory. Cf. Plate 4.

[15] Rabelais, wishing to date his arrival in Touraine, spoke of 'when the cicadas begin to grow hoarse'—i.e. towards the middle of September (Lefranc, *Rabelais*, I, 15).

which this reform established in detail as the basis of the official calendar of the Roman Church. The polemics aroused by the application of the measure which recouped ten days at one fell swoop (in France, by a decree of 3rd November 1582, it was decided to pass straight from 9th to 20th December) no doubt gave informed opinion a more accurate idea of the calendar. It is striking to see the *premier échevin* of Rouen begin an address to his colleagues on 3rd January 1643 with the following highly technical reference: 'Gentlemen, although we see the whole universe revolving in its customary way, and night following day, and day night, and the sun in completing its full course lighting our hemisphere for 182 days, 15 hours and one minute, and spending as long in the other hemisphere. . . .'[16] Such concern for precision is touching and smacks of newly-acquired knowledge and of a recent preoccupation with such matters.

Time was not the precious commodity which it is today, even though human life is now much longer. This apparent paradox cannot be reduced, as has been believed, to a mere difference in religious concepts, for the eternity promised to modern man still awaits many of our contemporaries. The progress made in mathematics,[17] in clockmaking and, above all, in means of communication are a far better explanation. Yet it is important to emphasize that indifference and imprecision went hand in hand: approximation was still the general rule.

Natural environment

The French of the sixteenth and seventeenth centuries were brought into direct contact with nature much more than we are, and as part of everyday life. We do not have to envisage from the start a cosmogony whose general lines would in any case be very difficult to define, for we are not dealing with an environment which was perceived scientifically and mastered technically. Of these two terms which characterize contact with nature in the twentieth century, the second would be the more applicable to the modern period, though there is no standard of comparison between the two. The natural environment, at once a source of assistance and of dread, was to be mastered in a daily struggle carried on by an unarmed man, a struggle first to know and to understand. This was why in the Middle Ages some had already devoted so much time to inquiring into the hidden significance of creatures in numerous Bestiaries and Lapidaries. Lacking even the most summary of classifications, Renaissance man was, as it were, lost and deprived of a guide. 'I imagine man,' writes Montaigne, 'looking around himself at the infinite number of objects, plants, animals and metals; I do not know where to have him begin his investigation.'[18]

Thus man's surroundings beset him and pressed in upon him on all sides.

[16] *Archives municipales de Rouen*, A, 25; *Inventaires* I (Rouen 1887), p. 323.

[17] Cf. Montaigne, *Essays* II, 37. Cf. also the table of expenditure in Plate 3.

[18] Numbers themselves still retained their symbolical value in the sixteenth century: even and odd, 3, 7, etc.

The plentiful fauna gave the countryside the appearance of an earthly paradise, so teeming was it with wild life. Everywhere, from Provence to Normandy, it was necessary to hold *battues* (known as *huées*) to protect livestock from the boars, wolves and foxes which roamed in packs. Wolves and boars entered villages. The boars 'holed up' near the houses, played with the domestic pigs and ate apples in the gardens. The lord of Gouberville killed several in his. Similarly, at night he caught dozens of starlings in his dovecote, where they came to eat his pigeons' corn. 'After supper, we covered the pigeon-house with sheets and caught three bushelfuls of starlings.' Both wild and domestic animals were readily considered to be relatives of man, and a whole complex of sentimental attitudes stemmed from their haunting presence. Men enjoyed imitating animals and discovering in themselves physical or moral features which were characteristic of the animals and plants around them. This is certainly the origin of the countless family names drawn from the vegetable and animal kingdoms—Loiseau (*l'oiseau:* the bird), Mouton (sheep), Lelièvre (*le lièvre:* the hare), Lehoux (*le houx:* the holly), Duchesne (*du chesne:* of the oak), Durosier (*du rosier:* of the rose-bush). From the friendly familiarity with which dogs were treated to the crime of bestiality, so often mentioned in legal records, the range of domestic promiscuity was virtually that of a fraternity.

But the nature that met their eyes was not enough. They distorted it in their imagination and added to it a disordered world of freakish, terrifying monsters. Ambroise Paré describes in the same breath rare and, as it were, exotic animals, like the crocodile which M. de la Vernade brought back from Cairo to Paris via Venice in 1517,[19] and land and sea monsters, conjured up with gusto and portrayed complete with their mysterious horns and their respective habits: sea-camels, many-headed serpents and beasts part-human, part-animal—in fact the complete menagerie in which Breughel and Callot delighted. This was the imaginary world which haunted the dreams—and sometimes the daydreams—of children and adults.

Implied in this are two strongly-contrasted attitudes. On the one hand we find a fear of the unknown and of the 'unnatural'; but on the other—and here again the very imprecision of knowledge left unlimited scope for the emotions—there is apparent an innocent love of nature, of mother earth, for example, and the riches which she supported or held concealed within her. The water of rivers and lakes, the forests where hunted game took refuge and where man could easily lose himself, belonged to all, and were common benefits. So too were the plants of grasslands and wastes whose properties were well-known—woundwort, marsh bedstraw which was used against hydrophobia, and the thorn-apple with is narcotic properties. The rhythm of the seasons—and even of irregularities, such as an early spring in mid-winter or hoar-frost in the middle of May—and plant life, too, enchanted them, from the first flowers to the

[19] Bourrilly (1), p. 44.

richest harvests. To a certain extent they lived in time with this rhythm and relished the successes with a kind of innocent eagerness.

To impose order upon this natural environment was not yet their whole-hearted concern. It was the seventeenth century at its height which set about creating gardens, planting eagerly and methodically. The previous century was concerned with building, and was content to situate its *châteaux* in the heart of woods full of game, as Anne de Montmorency did during his retirement. A century later, the great Condé was to work with Le Nôtre to bring order and symmetry into this same forest of Chantilly. In the sixteenth century, to master nature was to domesticate animals. A taste for animal violence, over which the horseman had to show his mastery each day, was an essential part of their feeling for life. Hunting, where horses reared before a jump or before the larger animals which turned on them, provided riders with an ever-welcome opportunity to test their equestrian skills and to show off their energy in mastering their mounts in a particularly daring trial. For those who could take part in it, deer hunting was the master passion, an occasion when a brave man could revel in his own superiority.

Thus the natural environment was not so much a field for thought, a basis for intellectual speculation and technical transformation, as a constituent of activity. It was thought, and especially felt, to be the point of application of daily activities—a world which was simultaneously hostile and fraternal, a hard and mysterious world for man. Whatever progress may have been made in the natural sciences at that time, when nomenclature became more precise, there is no doubt that the cosmos was even less a sphere of mental activity for modern man than the notions of time and space.

Conclusion to Part I

We shall not try to hide the great degree of artificiality present in the approach that we have tentatively followed in Part I. To grasp the dimensions of man as an isolated individual is always to deform him, to separate him from more complex human realities. The precariousness of material life or chronic malnutrition cannot be understood without reference to techniques of agricultural production, or to the systems by which land revenues were distributed. So too, the predominance of the emotional or the diffusion of languages are factors of civilization which involve a whole social hierarchy, the complete organization of human relationships. Vaugelas and Ménage are excellent witnesses to this fact.

We can quote one final proof, which as it were epitomizes the inadequacy of this initial attempt to reconstruct the Frenchman who lived in the early modern period; namely the difficulty that we must admit we find in giving a straightforward description of the educational models of the times. Information about the way in which the young were brought up, minds were equipped, and bodies and characters moulded would surely be the best mirror of the human dimensions we have hitherto explored.[1]

It is of course easy enough to glean many individual educational features from the *livres de raison*, so often intended for the instruction of future generations, or to use Montaigne or Rabelais, the master-pedagogues revered by literary history, or the experience of the Jesuit or Oratorian colleges, to reconstruct more than one educational—and especially instructional—method. In any case, everyone knows that sixteenth-century colleges, notably those attended by Montaigne and Rabelais, were squalid prisons, where the humanities were taught by the cane. Everyone is familiar with the contrast drawn by Montaigne between 'a trained mind and a very full mind', and with the 'modest programme' which the young Gargantua diligently followed in acquiring the ideal education conceived by his creator, Master François Rabelais. Equally famous is the

[1] As has recently been attempted for the bourgeoisie and the nobility. Cf. Ariès (144).

humanist teaching of the Jesuit colleges where good table manners and the art of horsemanship had their place alongside intellectual exercises in Latin, mathematics and geography.

Of course, it is not without interest to see the scholastic instruction of the medieval colleges, built in the shadow of the great Faculties of Law, Theology and Medicine, give way at the end of the sixteenth century to new forms of education which were both more liberal and more open to the new sciences;[2] nor is it unimportant to see the Oratorians, when they first opened their establishments at the beginning of the seventeenth century, choose to teach in French, and to teach children how to read in French, and not in Latin as had been the custom with all their predecessors.

Yet all these educational methods together cannot provide us with sufficient material for reconstruction. In the first place, they concern only adolescents (or older children) from the age of seven or eight to twenty at least, and deal essentially with formal education; whereas psychologists and paediatricians have taught us over the last half-century the importance of early education, from the cradle to the initial age of reason when children go to school.[3] In the second place, these colleges and their teachers were destined to educate only a very small minority of young people, at most the children of the nobility and bourgeoisie.

We certainly know very little about the early stages of their upbringing. Medical works devote a few lines—or at most a few pages—to feeding the newborn child or to the choice of a nurse, who was to be 'gay, cheerful, sober, chaste, clean, gentle, diligent and neither melancholy nor drunken'. Sometimes, too, they instruct on how to swaddle babies. This does not amount to much.

But even when we come to children of college age we have to consider what sections of society these establishments catered for. Certainly the children of peasants, whether of day-labourers or husbandmen, never had any schooling other than in the parish catechism classes, where the village priest had them faltering through the Gospel truths and reciting and singing from memory some of the church hymns until they went off to work in the fields. A precocious apprenticeship indeed! On the other hand, in the towns we have a clearer picture of communities eager to set up the colleges necessary to educate the sons of Gentlemen of the Robe and merchants, for whom the liberal arts were a necessary preparation for their father's profession. About 1640 there was not a town in France which did not have at least one college. The more important towns had several, each competing with the others to attract the lucrative custom of the rich bourgeoisie and great noble families. Sometimes the *échevins* undertook to pay the fees of poor children—the sons of artisans employed in

[2] Cf. de Dainville (281).

[3] Not to mention the fact that moralists and pedagogues were concerned with boys, and only mentioned girls in passing.

small urban crafts—and also themselves ensured the payment of the principal's salary, for if the latter were not well paid, he would leave, abandoning town and college. But as a general rule this education, which combined some aspects of our primary and secondary education, was reserved for the upper classes, for whom it was either a professional necessity or a social obligation.[4] Thus instruction and education were unequally meted out according to the resources and requirements of parents, and ranged from the moral lessons of the catechism classes to the humanist education of the Jesuits and the Protestant academies, and on to the higher education of the universities.

Undoubtedly, this was essentially a social problem. If it is true that medieval schools and universities were being transformed, and that apprenticeship, that almost universal method of training in the Middle Ages, was waning,[5] then the new methods of education must be considered in the social context within which they were taking shape. It is time to pass on to the second stage of our inquiry and to consider the social groups; in other words, to redefine, according to his human environment, the average man hitherto portrayed.

[4] As street battles between students, and also the solemn theatrical occasions of the Jesuit colleges, illustrate.

[5] As Ariès (144) has clearly shown.

Part II
The social context

It has so often been stated and restated that the sixteenth century saw the assertion of individualism that it is doubtless worthwhile to stress the strength of tradition—that is to say, of the forces of constraint and solidarity. The most individualistic of modern men, the Protestant who left his village and his country to break for ever with Catholic tradition, remained part of a group. As a French refugee at Geneva or Strasburg, he exchanged his native town for another which was basically no different from it. He continued to belong to a trade or profession, and indeed to a social class for, noble or commoner, he kept his original status even in his new country.

An agent at once for constraint and solidarity, it was in the latter capacity that the social environment always made its greatest impact, even in the sixteenth century. Firstly, this was because of the general insecurity: everywhere the social climate continued to be dominated by war, by sporadic internal disturbances and conflicts with foreign powers, which ravaged whole provinces. The artistic achievements of the sixteenth century lead us to forget its miseries. Like those before it, it was a period of long internal and external upheavals, in the midst of which the solidarity of the group, from the tiny rural hamlet to the much larger urban community, was indispensable. Yet all tradition is also built upon more or less vehement reactions; however, systematic negation had not yet come into being even in the time of Luther and Montaigne. Custom continued to exert a powerful influence, preserving and transmitting the countless experiences of ancestors within a closed system, when any outside initiative or innovation was automatically repelled—until some higher authority imposed its adoption. And if it is true that the Reformed Church, even more than Catholicism (which had itself already been concerned with the salvation of each individual) made man face God by himself, making him responsible for his actions while at the same time predestined, nevertheless mass conversion appeared far preferable to individual conversion. This was the meaning of *cujus regio, eius religio* in Luther's own country.

A similar form of constraint, which today we would call totalitarian, and a similar conformism were to be found on many other levels within the village community. A neighbour's fine harvest or thriving livestock were dangerous signs of success, which could indicate magical practices. Apart from the lord and his representative, no-one was allowed to be richer than the other members of the community. In this respect, witchcraft certainly remained, as in the Middle Ages, a formidably effective weapon in the hands of peasant communities.

Though they continued to exert a great influence on the individual, the social groups displayed a certain instability. This is not to say that latent nomadism can be considered the most important feature of this unstable society. There is no doubt that the vast majority of the population of France in the sixteenth and seventeenth centuries was settled and firmly attached to the land or a town. Even the 'vagabonds' were only rarely committed to roaming the roads for the whole of their lives: at the first opportunity—perhaps when a village was burnt down by soldiers and left empty, or when hospitality was extended by a monastery or an alms-house—they readily settled down. But the taste for migration was not completely dead. Mountain regions, where agricultural activity did not last as long as in the plains and was less of a tie, formed reserves of seasonal migrants: the inhabitants of the Cévennes and Provence worked as grape-harvesters, the Cantalous went as far afield as Spain to work on the harvest; and also peoples like the Swiss, the Corsicans and the Sardinians formed reserves of mercenaries for neighbouring powers. But this affected townsmen as well as peasants: the companies of players who went from town to town at the beginning of the seventeenth century, living out the *Roman comique*, often recruited young people who were not recognized artists but were attracted by travel for its own sake. This was the case with the young Théophile de Viau, son of a respectable barrister in the *Parlement* of Toulouse, who joined an undistinguished company as its poet. These brief trials of restive adolescents and annual migrations of rural groups in search of supplementary earnings were largely an escape from the constraining social environment which closely circumscribed everyday human activities with a web of tradition.[1]

*

To define the different forces for solidarity and their hold over everyday life, and over the modern mentality, is thus to measure the generally acknowledged growth of individualism. It means recognizing the influence of the different social groups, from the family to the nation, in the formation of the individual conscience. It also means examining factors which are very variable, and seeing them in the proper historical perspective.

Firstly, we need not consider the question of race. Although the racial prob-

[1] On nomadism, cf. Part III, ch. 17.

lem began to pose itself during the same period for the Spanish, Portuguese and Dutch in their distant colonies, it was foreign to France, with one exception which was religious rather than racial: the Jews. Having been expelled from France at the end of the fourteenth century, the Jews were present in large numbers in the borderlands (Alsace and Lorraine) and the enclaves (Avignon). They were tolerated at Metz when the town became French in 1599. So too were the Portuguese Marranos who settled in Bordeaux and in some towns in the Midi. At Montpellier, Thomas Platter mentions a large colony of them which was not held in high regard: their name was an insult, and during the Carnival effigies of the most prominent among them were paraded round the streets before being handed over to the public executioner. They could not hold the office of consul. Yet they dressed as Christians and some, he says, went so far as to call themselves Catholics, even Protestants. Traditional religious anti-semitism no doubt persisted, to judge from the following lines of Ronsard:

> Je n'ayme point les Juifs: ils ont mis en la Croix
> Ce Christ, ce Messias, qui noz péchez efface,
> Des prophètes occis ensanglanté la place,
> Murmuré contre Dieu qui leur donna des lois.[2]

Socially, this feeling was of no great significance, since in fact there were no Jewish communities in existence on French soil at the time.[3] Only one was French in language and culture, namely that of the Comtat-Venaissin, which the Constituent Assembly united with France in 1791, by annexing this papal territory.

However, the modern period saw undermined the most stable force for social solidarity that western Europe had ever known. For more than a thousand years the Catholic religion had provided an overriding pattern of existence for the whole population, from birth to death. The Reformation, by offering men a choice which brought in its wake a whole series of doubts and disputes, divided first towns and then villages—though in the latter case with more difficulty and at a later date. It shook the political structures themselves when the country was torn by civil wars. Thus, this socio-religious pattern survived—unbelief and especially atheism were not current at this time, as Febvre and Pintard have shown—and all remained Christians, either Catholics or Protestants according to their confession; but many Frenchmen did not hesitate, in the hour of persecution, to leave their belongings, home and family to ensure

[2] *Sonnet des pièces retranchées*, ed. Blanchemain, I, p. 418:

> I like not the Jews: they nailed to the Cross
> The Christ, the Messiah, who paid for our sins,
> They murdered the prophets, bathed the earth with their blood
> And murmured 'gainst God who had given them their laws.

[3] However, the Portuguese Jews in Bordeaux were subject to persecution, so that the Crown was led to grant them letters of protection on two occasions (1550 and 1574).

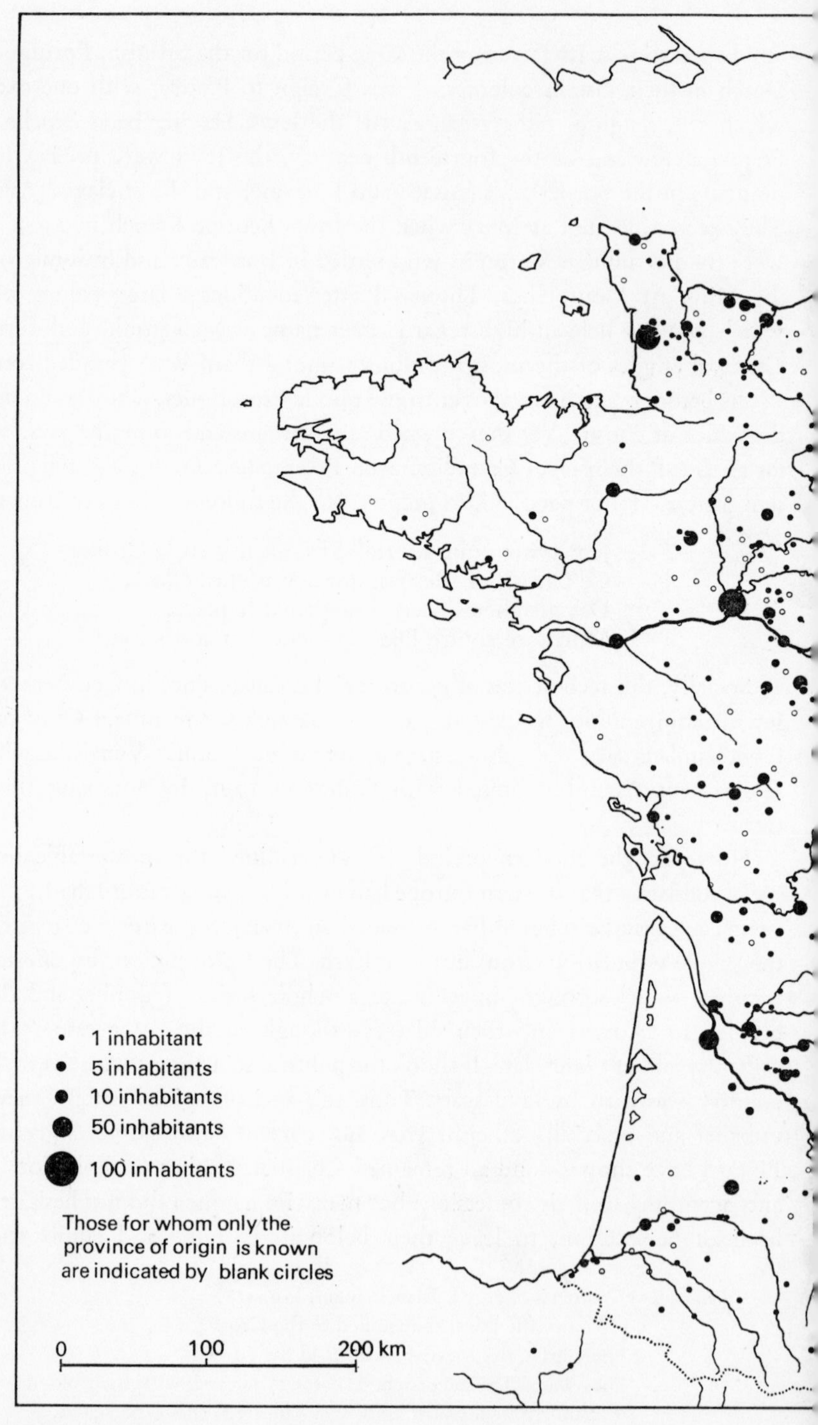

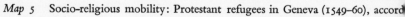

Map 5 Socio-religious mobility: Protestant refugees in Geneva (1549–60), accord

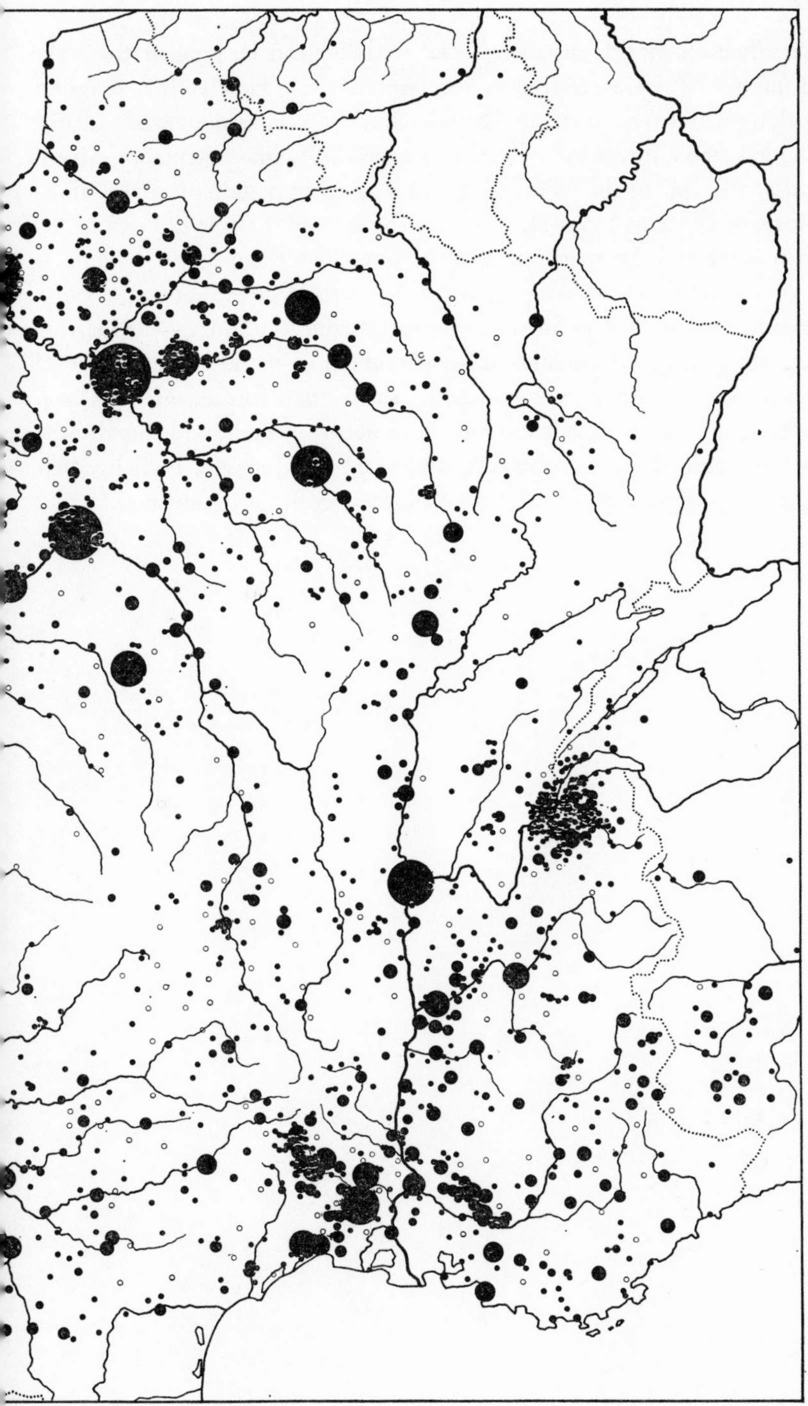

endorf.

their own salvation. In this instance, social mobility can be gauged from the reactions provoked by a religious crisis (see Map 5). Finally, this religious framework ceased to be such an absolute force for constraint and became one of the less stable forces for solidarity; just as the political structure which, ill-defined at the end of the Middle Ages and again impaired, after the 'absolutist' efforts of François I and Henri II, by the bloody wars at the end of the sixteenth century and the rebellions which prolonged them at the beginning of the seventeenth, was following the reverse pattern of development.

As a result, the basic forces for solidarity were reduced to three—the married couple and the family, which ensured the perpetuation of the species; the local environment, some town or village parish which often formed life's horizon for those people who were sedentary and too deeply rooted; and, finally, the groups which from that time onwards comprised social classes, both by their way of life, their organization and, above all, their group consciousness.

Chapter 5
Basic forces for solidarity: the married couple and the family

The family, the primary cell of social life (since it receives man at birth) is more clearly defined today than it was in the sixteenth century. Now it obviously comprises primarily a man, his wife and their children, and is legally defined, albeit loosely. On the other hand, in the time of Calvin or of Descartes, the family was still a large domestic community which included a wide kinship by blood and marriage (not to mention godparents) as well as the nuclear family of the spouses and their children. Within its ranks the strength of blood ties was constantly asserted, especially in matters of justice, including the practice of the vendetta, that private brand of justice exercised through family solidarity almost throughout France, and not only on certain Mediterranean islands.

The nuclear family, which thus remained firmly established amidst a wider kinship, was both hallowed by the Catholic Church, which made marriage one of its sacraments, and protected by the secular authorities, which prosecuted in the criminal courts for adultery, incest and immorality. Although these 'evils' met with heavy legal penalties,[1] and doubtless an equal measure of disapproval in the common morality of the time, they were none the less rife, despite laws and repressive measures. In addition to the lawful family, which was the normal unit, we must try to envisage these marginal activities which formed its counterpart, as it were, and cannot be regarded as negligible.

Marriage and the lawful family

The *livres de raison* contain many accounts of family events: baptisms, to which both near and more distant relatives were invited; funerals, which likewise brought together blood and marriage relations and often the *échevins* in full dress; and especially weddings, which always occasioned big celebrations. Reading these often picturesque accounts, one is tempted to paint a rather

[1] Some were of the opinion that extra-Christian unions ought equally to be proscribed and punished by death at the stake: marriage between a Christian and a Jewess or Saracen woman 'is not contrary to nature, but, nevertheless, in the judgement and sight of our faith, it is held and reputed to be so'.

idyllic picture of family life. Weddings in particular were always marked by great noisy revelry, especially if the bride was a widow, when they ended in a charivari. Drinking, shouting, jests in what we would consider to be bad taste (for example, the *garçonnade* in Burgundy) and even the coarsest practical jokes all had a place in the celebrations. Sometimes these resulted in legal proceedings:

> Guillebert Dumortier is also alleged to have been invited to the wedding feast of the child of Michel Dael, in the parish of Halluin. Seeing the table laid and most of the guests seated, he took it upon himself to make a present to the company of some veal in two dishes, in which he had concealed two frogs, commonly called *raines*. When the said dishes were opened, the frogs jumped out on to the tables and on to the food, causing an uproar in which everything is said to have been overturned, to the great displeasure of the petitioner.[2]

These great family feasts, however, should not deceive us as to the real nature of the 'marriage bond'.

It is doubtless no misrepresentation to assert the predominance of the joint family over the nuclear family.[3] Many points concerning marriage itself, paternal authority and the part played by widows in inheritances justify this conclusion.

The qualities demanded of a wife were essentially those which made a good housekeeper. Beauty and an affectionate nature counted for less than the expected conjugal virtues—goodness and a practical turn of mind. Henri de Campion, for example, observed of a young lady who had the desirable qualities for marriage:

> she is reasonably beautiful, of handsome and noble stature, and of marvellous gentleness; her goodness is unparallelled, her conduct good, her virtue untarnished, and her mind discerning. She bore neither in her face nor in her character the liveliness that beguiles most men. . . .[4]

Moreover the marked discrepancies in age between husband and wife which were so common, and which were virtually sought after by families to ensure the success of the operation—precisely on the domestic plane—could only encourage this tendency. At the age of twenty-four, André Tiraqueau, a barrister at Fontenay le Comte, married a girl of twelve. Guillaume Budé, at thirty-eight, chose one of fifteen. Even in royal families marriage was approached rationally. As sensitive a woman as Marguerite de Navarre married a man she certainly did not love, yet she served him faithfully.

Thus marriage tended primarily to ensure prosperity—or at least to maintain the patrimony. This is also shown by the way in which inheritances were

[2] AD, Nord, B, 1817: *Inventaire imprimé*, III, 308.

[3] Even if a trend towards the latter is apparent during the period under discussion, at least in the ruling classes. Cf. Ariès (144).

[4] De Campion (4), p. 213.

settled and by the efforts made in all circles to maintain land inheritances intact and to compensate for the privileges which this gave to the eldest, so as to avoid dispute or fragmentation. In the Middle Ages, Provence, where Roman law prevailed, saw some most remarkable institutions, contracts of *affrairamentum* which made it possible not only for sons-in-law but even for complete strangers to be brought into the management of the estate in order to preserve its unity.[5] These contracts later disappeared but the same concern persisted in other ways. While the legal aspect of such arrangements is not unfamiliar, we do not know enough about their practical application to be able to judge their effectiveness. Doubtless this preoccupation with the patrimony seems completely justified on political or social grounds in the case of the aristocracy, as also for the peasantry, where the land for cultivation could not be allowed to drop below a certain minimum area. But there seems to be no doubt that this concept of a 'landed' patrimony also actuated townspeople, whose fortunes lay largely in movable wealth. Quite apart from business premises, such as the artisan's workshop, it is certain that to a townsman, a patrimony which did not include some property both inside and outside the town limits was virtually inconceivable. Doubtless only the urban lower classes, consisting of guild journeymen and of all kinds of poorly-paid workers, could ignore such preoccupations.

The same conclusion might be drawn from the maintenance of the authority of the father, a veritable *pater familias*. Etienne Pasquier deals with this point at length in his letters. For example, he refuses to accept that children should marry without parental consent, a practice which certain monks were trying to legitimize. 'I cannot believe that when headstrong youth has no other guide than inordinate passion, God has any part in it. . . . I wish that without glossing over the subject, a good, stable law be instituted, whereby a marriage between children which parents have not sealed with their authority be declared null and void.'[6] Nor could there be any question of choosing a career—or even a religious vocation—without paternal advice: 'A child cannot take religious vows without the express consent of his father and mother.' Legal proceedings must be taken against such a vocation: 'A lord has right of pursuit against his villeins even to the ends of the earth. And shall we not have this right over the children in our midst?'[7]

Here Pasquier is defending parental rights, but elsewhere he writes: 'By natural law, a wife must bow to her husband's will.' It is undoubtedly true that supreme authority in such matters and in many others lay with the father, in

[5] R. Aubenas, 'Le contrat d'*affrairamentum* dans le droit provençal du moyen âge', *Revue historique du droit* (1933), p. 478; and 'La famille dans l'ancienne Provence', *Annales d'histoire économique et sociale* (1936), pp. 523–40.

[6] E. Pasquier, *Lettres* (Lyons 1607), III, letter 1; cf. also Rabelais (321).

[7] *Ibid.*, XI, letter 9.

complete accordance with Roman law. In fact, the wife became head of the family only when she was widowed, as often happened in this period of incessant wars and disorders, given also the marked difference in age between the two partners. The young widow, merry or not, then held a real delegation of paternal authority. She administered her husband's fortune, managed his business affairs and ruled his children with all the authority of the dead father. On this point there can be no doubt that the prescriptions of Roman law were exceeded. But it is clear that this custom was established to safeguard the patrimony from the threat involved in the premature loss of the head of the family.

Are such domestic preoccupations sufficient to explain the insistence with which the worthy memorialists recall conjugal friendship, as Montaigne liked to describe it: 'A good marriage, if there be one, rejects the companionship and conditions of love, and tries to imitate those of friendship. It is an agreeable partnership in life, full of constancy, trust and an infinite number of useful and reliable services and mutual obligations.'[8] A good marriage—if there be one. Montaigne was sceptical, for he maintained when speaking of friendship in another chapter that woman was incapable of achieving the firm steadfastness of this relationship. In fact, no-one seemed to expect from marriage anything more than an association where the wife 'discreet, polite, unflinching in her loyalty', in the words of Antoine Héroët, was subservient to her husband.

It was, of course, the total subservience of an inferior. Secluded in the home, thrown back upon menial tasks and the children, and engrossed in the small world of the family, women were certainly able to find a release in the religious activity of the century, in the Reformation and Counter-Reformation.[9] Many married women who would otherwise have had to spend their lives fretting under restraint were thus able to escape their domestic slavery through reading the Gospels and the practice of prayer and of charitable works. The Catholic revival at the beginning of the seventeenth century was to a large extent the work of women, as was also the first blaze of Calvinism from 1540 to 1560. But for those who were thus able to find compensation for their inferior status in a more intense religious life, there were others who were content to take it out on their families. As one memorialist in the middle of the seventeenth century puts it:

> In our age, there is no longer a Socrates to endure the bad temper of Xanthippe. Out of a hundred men, barely two would be found who could suffer patiently their wives' moods. This incompatibility of will is the cause of the many unhappy marriages, separations, divorces, poisonings and murders which make martyrs of the wretched, ill-matched couples in this world, and condemn them to suffer hell-pains in the next.[10]

For not only was the legal wife kept on the fringe of active life, confined within the domestic environment and treated as the first of the women servants

[8] *Essays* III, 5; cf. also I, 28 and 30.
[9] Cf. my article in *Annales E.S.C.* (1958), p. 4.
[10] Souvigny (31), III, p. 85.

—so much so that, as Pasquier himself recommended, it was a good thing to gratify one of her whims from time to time, so that she did not think that she had been relegated to their level; she was regarded above all as a friend, not a sweetheart, as the housekeeper, the lady of the house, but not as the beloved, if we take Luther's words as being valid for the whole of western Europe. 'One can love a wench, yes; but one's lawful wife—ach!'

Casual relationships: passing love affairs

In his letters, Pasquier gives 'love affairs' a place alongside marriage. For, he says, 'there is no woman, however beautiful, to whom a man is not indifferent once they have slept together for a year.'[11]

Alongside lawful wedlock, entered into for life and for the perpetuation of the species, common morality, if not the law of the time, was thus quite tolerant of casual love affairs, though rather unequally so. While men, the sex really inclined to polygamy, were treated indulgently, married women were viewed more strictly, and adultery on their part was punished by death—unless they were pregnant! Even the unmarried mother was shown no mercy, since all attempts to 'conceal' or, what was worse, to destroy her offspring were proscribed by law.

Generally speaking, there is no doubt that these brief liaisons were not considered in husbands as a sign of marital infidelity. Antoine Héroët, describing the platonic love of his *Parfaite Amye*, that idealized friendship with ecstatic overtones, says with delicate simplicity:

Or s'il advient quelquefois en la vie
Que l'âme étant en tel état ravie,
Les corps voisins comme morts délaissés
D'amour et non d'autre chose pressés,
Sans y penser se mettent à leur aise
Que la main touche et que la bouche baise,
Cela n'est pas pour déshonneur compté;
C'est un instinct de naïve bonté . . . .

And further adds:

Pris le plaisir, plus ne leur en souvient.[12]

[11] E. Pasquier, *Lettres* I, letter 9.

[12] Héroët (115), *La Parfaite Amye* I, p. 33:

But, if it should sometimes happen in life
That while the soul is in such a state enraptured,
Their bodies side by side left as dead,
By love and naught else incited,
Should without thinking seek their comfort,
That the hand should touch, and the lips kiss,
This is not as dishonour counted;
It is an impulse of natural kindness . . . .
The pleasure taken, they give it no more thought.

However, extra-marital adventures were not always so ethereal. In the smallest town in the kingdom the inconstant husband had at his disposal 'women of easy virtue', who were a public scandal and of whom the champions of morality could never completely rid the towns, despite all the measures taken to intern them. At Le Puy, in 1644, we find that 'Master Claude Spert de Volhac, abbot of Saint Pierre la Tour, moved to pity and seeking to prevent the disorder, scandal and miseries which were caused day and night in the town and its suburbs by public and clandestine harlots, to this end acquired a house and garden round which he had a high wall built, affording complete security. . . . and had the public harlots interned in it.'[13] This female population was very numerous, and, though doubtless not so well organized or set up as today, it was growing to the extent of forming a veritable hierarchy. Henri Estienne clearly indicates this in the article *cortisana* in his French-Italian Dictionary: 'we cannot dispense with this Italian word for referring to a harlot of standing. . . . And many people wrongly imagine that courtesan can properly be used of any whore, however much of a hussy she may be. There is as much difference between a courtesan and a mere whore as between a small shop-keeper and a great merchant.'

There is no doubt that in their efforts to protect the institution of marriage the Church and public authorities in practice lacked the necessary weapons. The repression of adultery, though certainly severe, proved no more effective than such legal threats normally are. Collective measures taken against prostitutes and those who harboured them, and involving imprisonment or expulsion from the towns, yielded no greater success. One has only to note the regularity with which the ordinances concerning them were renewed.[14]

These extra-marital associations, whether of an established or merely casual nature, could produce many illegitimate children. While we know how persons of rank solved the problem,[15] making room for their natural children in their own legal families, so that their bastards were soon endowed with fiefs and private incomes, it is difficult to say what the common practice was. Frequent cases of infanticide dealt with by the criminal courts indicate one solution. Another lay in the adoptions which we find mentioned in *livres de raison*—children who were found in the Church porch, taken in by a sacristan and

[13] Jacmon (32), p. 213.

[14] Thus in the case of Paris, 19th July 1619, 17th September 1644, etc., 'It is forbidden for anyone to harbour or receive into their homes any immoral persons. . . . All harlots are ordered to leave the town and suburbs of Paris within twenty-four hours.' Note also how many men were found guilty 'of having been found at night in a brothel with a whore even though they were married'—which leads one to believe that the reputation of Calvin in Geneva with regard to zealous supervision of morals has been largely exaggerated.

[15] And even the lesser nobility: with the lord of Gouberville lived his natural sister, Guillemette, and her brother Symonnet. Gouberville gave his half-sister in marriage, and his uncle, a priest, helped to pay for the wedding.

borne off as quickly as possible to a wet-nurse. But in this period when the lower classes lived so near to poverty, unmarried mothers were not necessarily the only ones to abandon their children. Lawfully married couples might well abandon the latest-born children of a large family, and such cases are not infrequently mentioned in legal records. Vincent de Paul was the first to be concerned to offer the destitute and wretched girls and women of Paris the expedient of a home for foundlings. From its foundation it took in at least one child every day, and was soon taking many more.[16]

At the beginning of the modern period the family was a social unit which was changing in character. In the towns it was closer to the nuclear family of today, whereas in the country the older pattern of the joint family still persisted. But this changing social unit was also seriously threatened—much more so than the *laudatores temporis acti* believe, misled as they are by the long campaign denouncing the evils of more recent legislation like the *Code civil* and the divorce laws. To the men of the time marriage represented far more an establishment, in the economic sense of the word, than a creation of affection. Conjugal, sexual and emotional factors could scarcely harmonize in a society where civil and religious imperatives weighed heavily on everyday life to ensure that the primacy of the family was respected. Thus the family was solely an instrument for ensuring the preservation of both the patrimony and the species. It was a non-egalitarian relationship, since it established male superiority, the ideal of the hierarchical society thus being reproduced within the basic social cell—and not without risks, as we have seen.

[16] Léon Lallemand, *Histoire des enfants abandonnés et délaissés* (Paris 1885). In the eighteenth century, the figure sometimes reached 7,000 a year.

Chapter 6
Basic forces for solidarity: the parish

Beyond the family and the home, which formed the immediate framework, both material and moral, for everyday life, lay the social group of the parish, which was obviously a much more effective force than its twentieth-century counterpart.

There were, of course, links between home and parish, for the priest attended every important moment in life—birth, baptism, marriage and death. In this capacity the parish can already be seen as the guarantor of family stability. However, it was not only a religious but also a legal institution: its role was sanctioned by law, which endowed the parishioners, its members, with certain prerogatives and obligations. It constituted both an electoral ward (for the appointment of municipalities), and an administrative and fiscal area.

The civil and religious life of the parish is doubtless comparatively little known. The priests of the sixteenth and even of the seventeenth centuries have left no full accounts of their difficult lives among their parishioners. The *agence générale du clergé*, which provides, especially for the eighteenth century, so many documents on the active parish life of the times, was not established until 1579, and the habit of corresponding with it spread only during the following century. Furthermore, the acts of the Council of Trent, which pronounced on the participation of laymen in the fabric of the Church and in the administration of the wealth of the parish community,[1] did not become generally applied until late in the seventeenth century, and it was again the eighteenth which derived most benefit from them. The laity doubtless did not await the authorization of Trent to participate in parish administration. Since the thirteenth century they had shared in the upkeep and the daily life of the Church, despite the prohibitions of the Lateran Council which maintained that all things sacred were the prerogative of the clergy alone. Thus, despite the obvious paradox, one can justifiably say that the specifically religious side of parish life was more active in the century of the *philosophes* than at the beginning of the modern period.

[1] Participation which had long been demanded, in particular in the States-General, e.g. at Orléans in 1560.

But the role of the parish as a social unit is as evident in one period as in the other. All who lived within its boundaries were automatically reckoned as parishioners, from the mere fact of their residence; and if it is true that the parish meeting did not yet involve the kind of collective guidance of the community's spiritual life which it became at the end of the seventeenth century, the parish was nevertheless alive in the form of the Sunday gathering for mass, when for a long time the priest—or his deputy—communed with his flock. It is as well to recall here that the lower clergy, at least the country clergy, were very close to the peasantry, since they were recruited from amongst its ranks. For this very reason they could not help but bring the faithful into their religious lives, all the more so when the parish was served by a mere layman, deputizing for a non-resident parish priest. Mere deputies or titular incumbents were thus in charge of the community, and at the end of the Middle Ages there could be no question of their exercising despotic rule over it. Sacristans and churchwardens had long acted at their side as spokesmen for the tiny parish society, where everyone knew his neighbour and communal life was a weekly reality.

However, there is no doubt that the most clear-cut distinction existed between town and country in this respect, a distinction not only in observances, which do not concern us for the moment, but also in the integrality of the unit. The country parish was the unit of population and work, perpetuated through the centuries under its ecclesiastical title; it was also the extent of the known world for the most sedentary of the peasants, that is to say the property owners. The town parish, on the other hand, was a district community, one among several which together made up the larger community of the town. The latter engulfed the tiny parish and, without lessening its religious importance, certainly diminished its standing as a civil unit.[2]

The country parish and the village

The traditional view, according to which the present-day commune was based upon the parish of former times, is not altogether accurate. In fact, the pattern of present-day communes represents[3]—at least for certain regions—a redistribution of territory which sometimes involved abandoning parish boundaries as

[2] The Reformation seriously disrupted this structure, which was at once civil and religious. In country parishes, notably in the Cévennes, the whole community was converted and the problem was solved. In the towns it was different, hence the quandary in which municipal authorities found themselves, faced with an insoluble problem: the solution of creating Protestant parishes without a territorial basis seemed unattainable; to move the unconverted in the case of the wholesale conversion of a parish seemed simpler. During the whole period 1560–1685, the problem was discussed and debated without a solution ever emerging. Let it be said again that we are here considering the parish as a territorial and civil unit.

[3] As it can be observed, by careful scrutiny, on the map published in the *Annales E.S.C.* 3 (1958) with a commentary by G. Duby.

they were laid down in the Middle Ages. At the end of the seventeenth century, Vauban counted approximately 36,000 parishes—that is to say, one fifth more than today, while the total area was then smaller. The country parish at that period remained in part what it originally had been—a unit of work and cultivation. Whether the steeple around which the community gathered belonged to a village, a lord's chapel, a monastery or even a roadside alms-house, the unit remained the same. In most cases, allowing for some reorganization caused, in particular, by the Hundred Years' War, the parish and the peasant community were indistinguishable. The parish was the group of peasants jointly engaged in cultivating an area of land and living a life of close interdependence.[4]

Thus along with communal worship one must include as one of the most important features of the parish scene the customary practices of joint agricultural work. The techniques of ploughing (with the swing plough) and harvesting (with the sickle), and others which presupposed complicated and expensive equipment (the mill, the wine-press or even the oven), necessitated all kinds of joint activity. Cooperation and the use of the lord's equipment thus combined with the inevitable consequences of the way plots were distributed over unenclosed stretches of terrain across much of the country (in the northern half, at least); and above all with the system of maintaining huge, undivided expanses as common land administered by a council of heads of families. Agrarian individualism was not yet a reality, even in relatively sparsely populated regions, where the remote places and small hamlets did not live in the kind of isolation which became so common in the nineteenth century. Meetings were held, sometimes in the church itself after mass (or on Sunday afternoon) sometimes at the mill, whose vast outbuildings could always accommodate a meeting of the male villagers, and sometimes also in the tavern: meetings when, in the presence of the priest and of the lord's representative, decisions were taken on the dates of the corn and grape harvests, the allocation of water for irrigation, and the saying of prayers for rain or for ending frosts; when also loans of draught animals for ploughing of for transport purposes were arranged. It was there that the whole of the daily round was planned in time with the seasons, by means of these general decisions and friendly agreements between neighbours which involved fewer people. But also they had to decide the allotment of seignorial, ecclesiastical and royal taxes, of which the assessment and rate were not so admirably fixed as our own percentages and schedules. The tithe was mostly levied in the fields, while the harvest was still in swathes on the ground; the lords' dues in kind were collected at the mill or the wine-press; while cash levies were even more difficult to settle because of collective solidarity in face of the lord's steward and farmers of the royal *taille*. Often a peasant, a mere layman, bearing the title of *syndic*, represented the community; he was head of the

[4] As a precaution, however, royal commands were addressed 'to the members of the community and other inhabitants of the parish'.

village and trusted by everyone. Finally, the fact that many of the joint operations of country life were accompanied by religious ceremonies, traces of which are still to be found in the countryside today (masses to celebrate the grape-harvest for example) served to emphasize further the predominance of collective activity within the parish. The intervention of religion sanctified the most solemn moments of the communal life, through the words of a priest who was simultaneously the representative of God and a peasant among peasants, very often a product of the same community, and a faithful everyday companion.

But the parish was equally a unit of defence against all the dangers that beset the peasant community, primarily against the external hazards constituted by brigands and soldiers. Vagabonds who lay hidden in the woods, whence they emerged when driven by hunger, soldiers who roamed the frontier provinces, moving from one set of quarters to another during the long winters, and all kinds of looters—these were enemies against which the parishioners defended themselves as best they could. Since the Middle Ages it was traditional to try to fortify the village itself, or if not the village, then some other refuge, which might be the old castle if it was still standing (until the application of Richelieu's edicts) or possibly the church itself. In the fourteenth and fifteenth centuries, during the Hundred Years' War, many an old castle or church was thus 'restored' by peasant communities. As soon as the alarm was given, everyone repaired there with his coffer and his livestock—at the risk of losing life and belongings in the fire if the soldiers set the church alight. However effective these defensive measures may have been, the perpetual alarms of these troubled times (eastern France scarcely ceased to live under threat, from the time of the sporadic campaigns of Charles V to the wholesale devastation of the Thirty Years' War) made up a basic element of parish solidarity. As seignorial protection was a thing of the distant past, and royal protection was non-existent, for the necessary troops entrusted with defence against foreign powers were virtually as dangerous as the invaders, peasant communities could only count upon themselves to limit their losses by ensuring the safety of a few pieces of furniture and their livestock. The lookout on the medieval keep was now replaced by a peasant posted in the church tower to watch the roads, ready to sound the alarm. The need for security remained the same and only the community acting together could meet it.

In addition, there were the struggles against seignorial oppression. Doubtless the disasters of the fourteenth and fifteenth centuries enabled those who survived plagues, wars and *jacqueries* to obtain improved conditions from their lords. But the price rise throughout the sixteenth century and the consequent pressure on the part of the nobility, who were anxious to maintain their standard of living in the face of the rising bourgeoisie, soon resulted in a re-awakening of tension—which increased in the seventeenth century when the slackening pace of American trade made this social crisis all the more acute. Doubtless the peasant revolts which occurred in the context of the Wars of Religion during the second half of the sixteenth century, and especially movements such as the *Nu-pieds* of Normandy in 1639, were not mere replicas of the *jacqueries* of the fourteenth century. But they all stemmed from the same atmosphere of revolt endemic throughout the *ancien régime*. At the very core of this perpetual rebelliousness are to be found both a religious element and a sense of group solidarity. This sense of a kind of rural communism, which found expression in the maintenance of undivided common lands (ponds and streams, woods and wastes) and in naïve, evangelistic dictums, was a permanent feature of the peasant mentality. Everyone knows the most famous of such dictums: 'When Adam delved and Eve span, who was then the gentleman?'

Certainly these sporadic uprisings occurred after much brooding over hatred and oppression, which bred resentment and a thirst for vengeance. But this state of mind retained a religious tonality, a kind of Christianity of the poor propagated orally during long evenings at home, and in the course of parish meetings when the steward came to lay down the law or when some burly husbandman, delegated to levy a portion of the taxes, was too forthright in his demands. One day, these often hated figures would find themselves confronted by the whole parish in league.

Village solidarity also found expression in the more agreeable circumstances of the solemn festivals—the great revelry occasioned by the corn or grape harvests, the celebrations held with neighbouring villages to mark parish festivals in the name of the patron saint of each church—or again, the rough encounters when the individual or team contests constituted an evocation, if not an imitation, of aristocratic tournaments, as well as a sporting activity of seemingly unlimited brutality. Take, for example, the bouts which the comte de Souvigny witnessed in Lower Brittany in 1626 and describes at length:

> The inhabitants of five or six parishes were gathered in their own camps, led by the man who was ready to wrestle. He then advanced half-way to face his counterpart and at close quarters they exchanged courtesies, saying how great an honour it was to face someone who was so highly thought of. The other replied appropriately, and with a handshake both promised not to use any underhanded means or illegal holds. . . . They drew ten or twelve paces apart and then, half-crouching, slowly closed in to come to grips, each attempting to catch his opponent in the fall known as the Breton fall, which some managed to do. In the event of the winner being able to throw the loser down on his back, all his fellow-villagers rushed out before him with oboes, to crown him as a token of victory. In other cases the contest was so determined that the champions gasped for breath and were covered in blood. . . .[5]

Finally, the French peasantry could demonstrate their solidarity in opposition to the townsman. This feeling no doubt existed, especially in communities

[5] Souvigny (31) I, p. 155.

which lay near a conurbation. Contact between villein and townsman varied in frequency according to distance and topography. However, only the scorn of the townspeople for the peasantry found expression.[6]

Despite the attraction that towns held for the peasantry, the continual mingling and extensive depletion of country populations contaminated by urban epidemics, and the trade in foodstuffs, there is no doubt that town life and the town parish represented a different world and a different set of loyalties.

The town parish

Sixteenth-century towns were not of course big conurbations: Paris, the capital city, already appeared to be of colossal size, yet it had only 300,000 inhabitants (in round figures, for greater precision is scarcely possible here);[7] while Lyons ranked as a second capital and a very big city with less than 100,000, and average-sized towns such as Rheims or Bourges were agglomerations of some 10,000 people. But however small they were, they were divided into several parishes. According as accidents of endowment and foundations determined each district had its church or chapel, and formed a subdivision within a much more important whole. This initial feature would itself be enough to make the urban parish environment distinctive. Even if the population of some parishes was not much greater than that of a rural community, the citizen readily felt that he belonged both to his parish and to the great city with which he was familiar, and which displayed human faces in such numbers and of such diversity as would have been inconceivable in the country setting. This dual allegiance thus necessitated entirely different human relationships and an entirely different notion of the world.

In fact, the urban parish was itself a much more varied world. Whilst the rural community only confronted peasant with peasant[8]—except, of course, for the lord of the manor and his servants—in the town, the same street, and often the same house, brought into daily contact the great bourgeois banker or merchant, the journeyman carpenter and the artisan cobbler. All were immersed in the same urban environment, but while the one was tied to his workshop, the other had correspondents throughout Europe, travelled and visited foreign countries. In the same church nave, very different social groups rubbed shoulders, their dissimilarities extending to their modes of dress, and especially their ways of life.

At the same time, each citizen through his guild—or his fraternity, the

[6] The *Bourgeois de Paris* writes in 1524 that an incendiary 'was the ugliest villein that ever was seen' (Bourrilly (1), p. 163, n. 1).

[7] For the end of the seventeenth century, calculations based on numbers of households suggest 400,000.

[8] Even in the case of the village peasant-artisan.

'professional parish'—was directly connected with other inhabitants of the town, who lived in other districts which were sometimes a long way from his own. And when on Sunday he strolled round the ramparts with his friends, looking down from their height at the flat countryside, left defenceless against brigandage, and out at the distant hamlets which were so often burnt down, he inevitably felt the security of being protected by strong, fortified walls, which were well maintained and guarded. Thus, within the small district community, several different layers of solidarity were superimposed, constituting so many extensions to the basic social and territorial group formed by the parish ir both town and country.

District festivals—of which our street fairs are a distant reminiscence—bear witness, however, to the strength of parish ties. In his *Mémoires*, Claude Haton gives a full account of the way in which Corpus Christi was celebrated each summer at Provins, parish by parish during the octave. The streets were hung with tapestries and the houses decorated; sports and games were played in groups of from twelve to twenty, the men playing *soulle* and draughts, and the women skittles; then all ate supper together. And he concludes: 'if the weather is fine and clear, they set up the tables in the streets . . . in full view of any passers-by who care to look—and in this way, they maintain peace, concord and friendship with one another—which is indeed most praiseworthy, for at these gatherings the poor are received as well as the rich, if they care to attend.'[9] The atmosphere of the village, where everyone knew everyone else, is thus rediscovered within even the largest of cities.

However, the parish formed part of a political organism which had a certain autonomy, and parochialism existed on the scale of both the parish and the town. In 1575, the mayor of Amiens was proud to have acquired two swans, which he installed on the town moat. In 1625, when the same town received with great pomp the Queen Mother, who was escorting the queen of England, it asked as a favour 'that the preface to the edict of reinstatement of this town might be corrected or revoked, as being prejudicial to the honour of its inhabitants; that the *premier échevin* might in future have the title of mayor . . . .'[10] The care with which the dress of the *échevins* is described and discussed in municipal debates and the generous salaries paid by towns to their employees, from the doctor to the clerks of the courts, bear witness to the vitality of these feelings of civic pride. At Rouen in 1516, the '*grenetier*' *du sel* received 85 *livres*, the clock-keeper 30, and the gate-keeper 12. At Amiens, whenever an *échevin* attended a funeral, he was afterwards entertained in the best 'pastry-shop' in town. Inter-city rivalries provide further evidence of the same feelings: the people of Rouen maintained that the royal loans they had raised were not repaid, unlike those of Paris . . . but 'if Rouen and Normandy should be lost, so should Paris also . . . .' The royal towns had long since acquired such municipal autonomy

[9] Haton (7), II, p. 612. [10] AM, Amiens, BB 61, f. 191.

that they attracted people from the neighbourhood, and their prestige extended to all their inhabitants.

But there was another collective feeling in which the townsman shared—that of security. The town was a stronghold, and behind its walls lay an oasis of peace amid the dangers which constantly beset the countryside around. Doubtless its walls were not totally impregnable. As centres of culture and of easy living, towns attracted armies, and to sack a large town was as glorious an achievement as to defeat an opposing army. But the bourgeois were able to defend themselves, to take up arms and man the artillery. Amiens had had its companies of archers in the fourteenth century, and in the sixteenth it had its *harquebusiers* as well. They all trained on Sundays, here by parishes, there in mixed units. Arms practice was carried out in small companies of about thirty or fifty, under the direction of masters of the battle-axe or the sword. The rich bourgeois had their armour at home, which they maintained with care. Finally, the town itself was responsible for the artillery, heavy equipment which often had to be obtained from a distance. In 1536 Amiens sent 'to the iron-works in the Beauvaisis for some iron cannon-balls', and in 1577 the king borrowed 20 *milliers* of gunpowder from the town of Amiens to besiege La Charité. The security of the well-guarded town, with its own trained bourgeois militia capable of defending it against all comers, was a valuable asset, and explains the sometimes aggressive parochialism in certain towns during the Wars of Religion.

The economic and social advantages by which the citizen benefited also lay outside the sphere of the town parish. Not every district had the facilities enjoyed by any street today.[11] But each town provided at the community's expense a surgeon, doctor, hospital and midwife, together with a whole range of equipment, scales, mills and so on, which was used by all the trades. The clock, which tolled the hours from the belfry, was itself part of a common heritage to which the townspeople was still proudly attached. Since the Middle Ages, towns had vied with each other to have the finest clocks and the most ornate belfries. Thus the townsman belonged to two equally well-established communities—on the one hand to his parish, and on the other to the town as a whole.

However, he also knew something of the world beyond his own district and the town limits. Often he travelled; but in any case his eyes were open on a wider world. The most stay-at-home of the town merchants had their agents: the merchants of Amiens were represented in Bremen, Antwerp, Middelburg and in Spain. They bought and forwarded from one market to another, without the goods concerned ever coming inland: after being trans-shipped at Saint Valéry, Caen or Rouen, they were re-dispatched to their final purchaser. But traders were not the only group involved. We read of two apothecaries of

[11] In many towns, streets were open sewers: at Amiens, in 1570, a woman was convicted of 'having thrown a potful of water and filth through her window into the street, without shouting "Mind the water"'.

Amiens in 1582, A. Accard and J. de Haudicourt, who, when examined as to their qualifications, claimed to have studied and served their apprenticeship in Paris, Bordeaux, Rouen, Lyons, Orléans, Tours and Mantes. Not to mention the vagabonds, cheapjacks and others who slipped into a town and lived there as best they could in houses of ill repute. An edict of 1609 indicates the permanent presence in Amiens of idlers and vagabonds 'both from this kingdom and from foreign countries, such as Dutchmen, Irish or Scots. . . .'

The townsman felt privileged, especially on festive occasions when, to celebrate the announcement of a peace-treaty or a solemn Entry, wine-casks were broached in all the squares, the whole town was decked with triumphal arches and *tableaux*, and everyone was out in the streets, making merry and dancing round bonfires. But such festivities were exceptional. From day to day the townsmen frequented the taverns and inns, which were theoretically reserved for travellers staying overnight in the town, but in fact welcomed all customers.[12] Occasionally, they also had the opportunity of enjoying the plays that itinerant players put on in the evening on their makeshift stage; or again, once or twice a year, with great solemnity the local college, especially Jesuit colleges from about 1570, mounted a large-scale theatrical production of the life of a Christian martyr, or some deed of ancient mythology, an event which would long be talked about all over the town. A certain urbanity thus characterized town life, which nevertheless contained a large element of debauchery, to judge from the many complaints made by the devout, and countless decisions taken by the bailiffs responsible for keeping order. We read, for example, of a band of revellers at Mâcon in 1625 which called itself the 'Joyful Band', adopted a leader, nicknamed the prince, and a livery, 'and perpetrates many shameful debauches by day and by night in inns, taverns and private houses, where they take or meet harlots and loose women, and spend the night with them, which could result in murders and mishaps.'[13]

Thus, between his parish and his town, the townsman of the sixteenth century found himself incorporated in an entity which was, at all events, a centre of culture. Monuments, like the clock-tower and the cathedral, festivals and celebrations of all kinds and relations with the world outside gave each city its own distinct stamp and pronounced originality, which the country-dweller could not even imagine. For centuries, northern and southern France had stood in contrast by reason of their towns, which were more crowded and animated in the

[12] Edicts and ordinances frequently reminded innkeepers of their duty. A typical example from Forcalquier in 1619 reads: 'To remedy the disorders and great debauchery common in this town, it is once again forbidden for all the landlords, tavern-keepers and innkeepers of Forcalquier to admit any inhabitants of the town to eat, drink or play cards, and all inhabitants are forbidden to frequent and patronize the aforesaid inns.' AD, Basses-Alpes, B, 818.

[13] AD, Saône-et-Loire, B, 1642.

Mediterranean area than in the plains of the Paris basin. Already, Paris and Lyons had amongst their populations an important group of artists, who lived amid their fellow-citizens, enlivened the festivals and helped to adorn the locality.

Finally, urban society lived in constant turmoil, in a climate of financial and social difficulties which greatly helped to inform group consciousness. Administered by its *échevins*, the town was answerable to the king and his representatives, officials who were difficult to get on with and who had to be gratified with endless gifts—'petits pots de vin'.[14] Royal claims in one form or another were more onerous. A royal Entry was a financial catastrophe from which a town suffered for many months after. The king's needs of fresh money were even more costly, for these compulsory loans were always repaid very slowly and with difficulty. Even the States-General, which were so often summoned in the sixteenth century, were an expensive item for urban communities, which had to pay the travel and subsistence expenses of their delegates for the duration of a session. Lastly, in order to defend themselves, towns went to great expense to maintain representatives at court who ensured that they were protected, or spared supplementary taxation, or exempted from a particular tax which would have been especially harmful to their trade. A town like Rouen was bled white at the beginning of the reign of François I. On 9th May 1515, the king asked the States of Normandy for 127,609 *livres tournois*, of which the town had to pay its share plus a gift of 10,000 *livres* from the town itself. There followed another demand in August (717,000 *livres* from the States), and a further gift of 10,000 *livres* in May 1516. In August, the joyful Entry of the duke of Alençon took place and a new levy was raised from the States (720,000 *livres*). In 1519 and 1520, the 'gift' of 10,000 *livres* was repeated. When Henri II came to Rouen in October 1550, the coffers were empty; but if the king 'were not received in great honour and triumph, harm could result from it for the inhabitants, and the king's displeasure', for 'in the cities of Paris, Lyons, Troyes and others, his Majesty was received and made his Entry in very great honour'. Rouen could do no less and so the cost was divided proportionately among the 140 richest and most obviously solvent citizens, of whom 74 were compelled to participate in the Entry as 'pages of honour'—and compelled by 'confiscation of their goods' if necessary. On 5th October 1550, the *échevins* and pages of honour came smiling before the king to present him with 'a gold statue of Minerva holding an olive branch', which signified strength, peace and wisdom, and to offer the Queen 'a gold statue of the virgin Astraea, weighing 13 *marcs*'. The constable received two huge vases in silver-gilt, and the duchess of Valentinois two great bowls and two large ewers in silver-gilt. The situation was the same in the time of Henri IV and Louis XIII. Exploited and ill-used by the royal authority, which saw in them an inexhaustible financial reserve, the

[14] Often taking the form, literally, of wine. A bailiff taking up office received a cask of good Burgundy or Bordeaux. There are numerous examples of this at Amiens.

towns never ceased to run into debt and to make every sacrifice to meet the demands made upon them—until the winds of rebellion began to blow. If a disturbance broke out in one district, and some royal agent, a poll-tax collector or exciseman for instance, was manhandled by the angry crowd, it was not uncommon to see the *Parlement* itself side with the rioters, at least by refraining from bringing those responsible to justice, and even by joining the revolt, as at Rouen in 1639. Urban riots were not all of this kind, as we shall see in a moment; but this was quite a common occurrence in both the sixteenth and seventeenth centuries. Thus the town, founded back in the Middle Ages with the benefits of important collective privileges, still kept these privileges in part, and prolonged its resistance to being subordinated to the State, which had not, as yet, the means to take its place where administration and above all the organization of economic life and international trade were concerned. However, royal pressure relentlessly increased in the time of François I, Henri II and Richelieu.

Today, we call urban life hectic: speed and jolting transport seem to be the keynote. In the case of medieval and early modern towns, we should rather talk of the intensity of life: contact with others and the wholesale confrontation of problems of national importance were the ingredients of everyday life—as also were the many social contrasts which gave rise to class solidarity. For convenience of presentation, we have chosen to deal with these separately.

Chapter 7
Basic forces for solidarity: orders and social classes

The personal and territorial bonds of vassalage and seignory, established in the High Middle Ages, and the territorial links of the parish had been the firmest binding forces of medieval society. From the Middle Ages onwards, these gave way more and more to relationships which were formed, not between the orders, but between social groups. In the sixteenth and seventeenth centuries, the pace of this evolutionary process quickened, pushing into the background the older ties, which can thereafter be justifiably considered as survivals, while the connections between groups gradually became the bases of the firmest social relationships. Noblemen, bourgeois, peasants and urban lower classes felt a close bond of solidarity within their own ranks, and very soon in opposition to other groups—which justifies our using the expression 'social classes'.

Without any doubt, the term is controversial: for the last half century, one school of historical thought, while not caring to admit how far its pseudo-positivist attitude reflects staunch political conservatism, has maintained that this 'Marxist' terminology—and its corollary, the concept of class struggle—should not be used with reference to any period before the nineteenth century. Idealizing the image of the *ancien régime* as a refuge from and a consolation for the miseries of the contemporary scene, it purports to define its social relationships within the double framework of altogether satisfactory legal definitions—those of the orders, and of a paternalism which, it declares, was perfectly legitimate in a hierarchical society: the lord protected his peasants, the king his loyal towns and his good bourgeois, and the guild master his journeymen.

This legal and paternalistic pattern is no more successful in giving a true picture of the social solidarities of the time than would be some para-Marxist interpretation, which attempted to make the guild journeymen and village day-labourers correspond to the industrial and rural proletariat of the nineteenth century. There are two reasons for this: firstly, by the modern period the orders no longer had the social importance that the strictest jurists ascribed to them; secondly, the main social groups—the traditional nobility, the merchant bourgeoisie and the peasantry—displayed almost all the distinctive features of 'class' in the strictest historical sense of the word, with or without class consciousness.

There is no doubt that in the sixteenth century the orders or 'estates' no longer had the social importance which they may have had in the twelfth or thirteenth centuries. The kings of France had long beeen aware of this, even if they did regularly summon the States-General and address themselves according to ritual to the clergy, the nobility and the Third Estate. The last of these, unwieldy as it was, was sub-divided into groups—bourgeois, merchants and husbandmen, at least. As one jurist striving to define the orders at the beginning of the seventeenth century declared:[1]

> as for the king's subjects, they are divided according to orders, estates or individual occupations. Some are dedicated particularly to the service of God, others to bearing arms in defence of the State, and others still to feeding it and to maintaining it through the arts of peace. These are our three orders or States-General of France, the clergy, the nobility and the Third Estate. But each of these orders is further subdivided into subordinate categories or lesser orders: in the Third Estate, which is the largest, there are several orders, namely men of letters, financiers, merchants, artisans, husbandmen and manual workers, most of which however are mere occupations rather than established orders.

This is plainly to recall the former tripartite division of society, and to recognize that it was no longer wholly valid. The subdivision of the Third Estate into important, quite distinct—and even opposing—groups is only too obvious: the bourgeoisie alone ranged from the small money lenders operating in the suburbs to the ambitious and cumbersome world of the *offices*, which was to become the *noblesse de robe* in the seventeenth century. But the nobility was no less diverse: nobles of ancient extraction, who claimed to be descended from the Crusaders, did not consider as true nobles those who through the favour of royal letters or the grant of a post were added to their ranks overnight. The clergy too, which by its recruitment, its regular assemblies and its hierarchy, maintaining constant contact within its ranks, genuinely constituted one body, was no more an order than the others. Moreover, it was a long time since it had seen 'a shepherd's son raised above kings'. The division into upper and lower clergy reflected within its ranks the most deeply-rooted social antagonism of the time. The nobility monopolized the benefices and the high ecclesiastical offices, even if improper appointments continued to provoke outcries, while country benefices and even those in small towns had to depend on chance local vocations. The clergy of a Church which, according to its first principles, was egalitarian, was itself subject to the dominant social cleavage. We must not be surprised occasionally to find parish priests leading a peasant insurrection, as at Blanzac near Angoulême in 1636.[2]

[1] Loyseau (161), Preface, para. 7.

[2] An example mentioned by Porchnev (179), p. 654: 'twelve or fifteen groups led by their parish priests.'

The medieval social pattern—in any case in a rather idealized form—of entirely self-contained estates, hierarchically juxtaposed, whereby the peasant did not compare himself to the lord nor the artisan to the knight, but each remained where God had placed him 'invested with the dignity of his estate', was no longer of any great significance. Assuredly, it took a long time for both individuals and groups to become aware of their common interests and of their solidarity in the face of other individuals and groups. To trace the history of the first regrouping within the orders, or even from one order to another—in the case of the clergy—would involve our turning back to the heart of the Middle Ages, as far as the eleventh and twelfth centuries.

Furthermore, the different groups had not attained a clear state of self-awareness by the period under discussion, if only because former distinctions persisted under the influence of the jurists. In the sixteenth century, the word *bourgeois* still meant the medieval townsman, determined by virtue of his place in the town; but equally, the term was already applied to the businessmen who grew rich in commerce or banking as distinct from the lesser people of the guilds or the small shopkeepers, whose trade did not yield the same profits. Similarly, while noblemen were still feudal knights-at-arms, descendants of a companion of St Louis or of Louis XII, they were also the landowners, whether proprietors of small estates which barely provided them with a living, or lords of large domains. The economic definitions upon which we base our present-day social distinctions were thus not as decisive at that time.

However, it was indeed the protracted economic development of the sixteenth and seventeenth centuries which caused the feelings of antagonism and solidarity, which can justifiably be termed class feelings, to break out on a large scale. The growth of international commerce, the stimulus given to the monetary economy by the influx of precious metals from America, speeded up a process which had already become apparent during the last three centuries of the Middle Ages: the enriching of the merchant bourgeoisie, and especially of the financiers, the progress of the towns and the lesser headway made by the rural nobility, then the ruinous effects of war and the diverting of bourgeois fortunes into purchasing ancestral estates at auction and obtaining easy titles of nobility—all these factors, basic to the social and economic history of the sixteenth century, constituted the fabric of a decisive transformation. At that time, two ideals of life were in daily confrontation, the one fostered by literature of a former age, 'stuffed with honour' and well represented by the old French epics, which held pride of place in all the nobles' libraries, the other finding even in the rebirth of antiquity the inspiration for a completely different notion of the world, of men and their activities; while the ravages of war and the economic difficulties of the period 1620–40 explain in a sense the retarded self-awareness of the lower classes, whose emotions frequently led them to acts of rebellion which were far more complex than a simple struggle between rich and poor.

The economic evolution here acted as a psychological catalyst. One has only to recall in this respect the misery of the many nobles, ruined and sometimes wounded in the Wars of Religion, to whom Henri IV had to render assistance throughout his reign by giving them positions of authority in abbeys, or granting them pensions out of the revenues of charitable institutions,[3] to understand their bitterness when confronted with the impertinent success of the bourgeoisie. The awakening of this consciousness—without which there is no question of class—is no less evident than the differences in standards and ways of life on which these social solidarities were based. Thus one memorialist could write in the middle of the seventeenth century: 'The Bourgeois, the Husbandman, the Soldier and the Merchant all have different notions of the same thing; and what one does without scruple, the other would not wish to enter his thoughts under any circumstances.'[4]

With the modern period, the class which had ruled for five centuries, though perilously for three of them, saw its domination irretrievably slip from its grasp. Undermined in its social, though not in its material, prerogatives, it turned to fight, resisting on all fronts, struggling against the insidious invasion of the recently ennobled, and against the unwarranted assimilation of the *noblesse de robe*. It clung desperately to its privileges, the last vestige of the seignorial régime, and fought royal authority while at the same time proclaiming its loyalty and requesting royal aid. Thus the modern period saw a social crisis on an unprecedented scale—which continued until the Revolution.

The traditional nobility

By gaily idealizing the noble past of knighthood, contemporaries had no difficulty in describing the evolution which was being accomplished before their eyes. In 1576—admittedly, in the midst of the religious wars—Haton writes:

> In days gone by, the noblemen of France acquired this title of nobility and their privileges from kings and princes because of their virtues and the good service which they rendered to the same kings and princes and to their homeland, France. They were devout, faithful, Catholic, supporters of the Church, wise, prudent, gentle, benign and clement towards their subjects and other. . . . The noblemen who once were gentlemen of virtue are now plunderers and murderers, heretics, infidels, irreverent, idolaters, insane, cruel, proud, arrogant, pillagers of other people's property, sacrilegious, oppressors of the people. . . .[5]

[3] Cf. *Archives nationales*, the sadly incomplete dossiers (numbered V7) of the *Chambre de la charité chrétienne*, instituted to organize such aid.

[4] L.M.D.L.F., *Mémoires et réflexions sur les principaux événements du règne de Louis XIV* (Rotterdam, 1717), p. 14.

[5] Haton (7), II, pp. 854–5; we must add, however, that he specifies: 'I am referring only to the wicked, who in number exceed the good and virtuous by more than three quarters.'

Despite its excesses this hyperbolical lament expresses the disillusionment of the commoner.

Of the ancient legal definition of nobility, thanks to which the order could be quite clearly defined in the fourteenth century, not a great deal remained. The right to receive knighthood, and the practice of doing so, had lapsed. The right to have free or noble military fiefs without special permission remained, but in fact it was undermined by the practice of discreet ennoblement, by the purchasing of noble estates. Undoubtedly, the memory of martial chivalry still persisted: the nobles were soldiers, the first in the land. But if they no longer responded to the royal summons of the feudal levy—as was shown on many occasions, notably in 1575 and 1635—it was partly because they had lost their sense of military duty, and partly because the monarchy had taken to raising professional armies, of which the nobility could still form the cadres, but which no longer constituted a feudal army as in the past. What remained of their military role, therefore, was principally the relics—trophies in châteaux, tales and legends of ancestral battles, glorious genealogies, and even the sense of personal honour. Jousting, duelling, and the taste that persisted for small-scale spoliative skirmishing and for rebellion against royal authority can also be said to stem from the same tradition, but they reflected other pressures too, in the first case, social and in the second, economic.

However, of their military function there still remained the associated administrative prerogatives. On a noble estate, the lord dispensed justice through a judge acting as his representative. He levied feudal dues, which were still considerable in so far as they remained payments in kind; though these were, so to speak, affixed to the land and were likewise collected as an ordinary ground rent by the bourgeoisie, when the property happened to pass into the hands of commoners—a factor which in a way helped to blur the very definition of noble rank.

Finally, if as a result of persistent pressure by the monarchy the definitions concerning their military and administrative functions were no longer operative, those concerning their rights, of minor importance in the thirteenth century, but vitally important three centuries later, still applied. Some already called these the privileges of the nobility. Thus they had their own civil and criminal law: laws of inheritance, whereby in almost all provinces the estate remained intact in the hands of the first-born son; and criminal law which exempted the noble from being hanged. And above all they were exempted from permanent royal taxation, that is to say, primarily, from the *taille*. This was no doubt the most noticeable outward sign of nobility, the one which, together with the prohibition of 'derogation', which applied to rural pursuits as well as commerce and expressed the notion contained in the formula 'to live like a nobleman', most clearly indicated the line separating the nobleman from the commoner. These were the strongest bonds of unity within the class.

Thus the nobility was a privileged, ruling class and it intended to remain so.

Its domination, which was expressed daily in countless different ways, from the church pew to the seignorial court, was sustained by notions in part mythical, as for example the racial concept: the nobleman was above the commoner because he was of a different blood; he was well-born. In the sixteenth century, the expression 'free and well-born' was no doubt also used to describe the humanists, those who were steeped in the humanities, but the idea of blue blood still held favour. Then again, the nobility looked back nostalgically to its military role. Whether one had great ancestors or not, war was the solution to material difficulties. The pay and plunder it brought in had long been—especially in the fourteenth and fifteenth centuries—an easy remedy for financial embarrassment. To take up arms again, in whatever cause, was a persistent ambition, and one which found many opportunities for satisfaction throughout this period. The seignorial institution, which remained more dynamic in some places than in others, formed the basis of this hegemony. It is true that we have no documents describing the relations between the château and the village community (or even the place of the nobility in urban localities). Masters and villeins met each Sunday at Mass in the parish church, where the lord had his place reserved in the front row and often in the choir. Both ranks came continually into contact the whole year round, the one feeding the other, paying dues and *banalités*, cursing game and pigeons, and grumbling about the steward and the miller, the judge and the lawyer, all of them tiresome agents of the lord in the rural community. As regards its economic basis, the social power of the nobility remained rooted in the land.

However, the new era opened with a general crisis in seignorial revenues—a crisis affecting revenues more than seignorial authority itself, for if the structure of the latter did not undergo any sudden upheavals, such a crisis affected all the nobility's resources. For example, their judicial rights were no longer profitable. The lord had to pay his judge, not in land, but in money, and even if he compelled his tenants to help him by means of *douceurs*, he could not escape assuming at least part of the cost. Moreover, on many estates the income from fines and confiscations was no longer adequate to pay for the minor law officers—the jailer and the executioner—not to mention food for the prisoners. Big, important actions, like the series of witchcraft trials when whole villages were prosecuted, were needed for the seignorial court to show a profit. But very often it did not prosecute, all the more so as royal justice was providing stiff competition, quickly winning over local officials and taking over cases even before the appeal, which was becoming more and more the general rule. In the legal sphere, the noble was losing both money and prestige.

In a more general way, the modern period placed the landowners in an extremely difficult economic situation. On the one hand, the price rise, though it also affected natural produce and thereby increased revenues, was much more marked in the case of the goods made by the town artisans, so that the increase in income was far outweighed by the increase in expenditure. On the other hand, as a result of the half century or more of the Italian Wars, from Charles VIII to Henri II, the class as a whole had acquired a taste for luxury, for sumptuous decor and an easy life in which sport, gaming, artists and women played a big part. This stimulus to spending without real compensation for it would alone be enough to explain the seriousness of the crisis within this group, which at that very moment became aware of the increasing wealth of the merchant bourgeoisie. It is therefore not surprising to see, six months after the death of Henri II, 1,500 French soldiers and gentlemen leave for Sicily in the service of the King of Spain; nor to see the younger sons of noble families throw themselves into a military career with great enthusiasm—for there was scarcely any other way open to them of prospering—while their elder brothers, who were heirs to the estate, refused to serve when the anachronistic levy was summoned, in order to stay on their land to keep a careful watch on its returns. Nor again is it surprising to see the order of the nobility in 1614 so bitterly demanding the maintenance of its privileges and the restoration of its challenged pre-eminence.

The extent of the crisis (the progressive dispossession of the ruling class) can be gauged from the efforts made in every possible direction to consolidate wealth. For centuries, the accumulation of ecclesiastical *commendams* had been one means readily employed.[6] Institutionalized by the 1516 Concordat, this practice continued to operate almost exclusively to the advantage of the nobility. Marriage to a well-endowed heiress, the daughter of a *partisan* or 'tax-farmer', was also a common practice, which appreciably strengthened their financial position.[7] Some nobles became pettifoggers, and like moneylenders went through suits lasting for years over a few *livres*.[8] The most artful joined the king's retinue and—from the fourteenth century onwards, but especially in the sixteenth—tried to obtain from their service at court pensions, endowments or gratuities which would supplement their land revenues. Moreover, all were ready to take up arms when the monarchy presumed to impose a State tax upon them. During the period of the great popular uprisings at the beginning of the seventeenth

[6] In fact, nobles grabbed desperately at benefices. The Cardinal de Guise and the Duc de Nevers went to law over the conferment of a priory. Eventually, the cardinal hurled himself on the duke, whereupon they began to fight in earnest and had to be separated.

[7] Memorialists noted this somewhat bitterly in the seventeenth century. Cf. for example Dubuisson-Aubenay: 'On Saturday 1st February, 1648, the Chevalier de Chemerault married the daughter of Tabouret, a tax-farmer, a man of very humble extraction, who gives him 100,000 crowns in cash, and expectations of a further 200,000 *livres*' (Dubuisson-Aubenay (3), I, p. 7).

[8] A good example of this from the south-east in 1638: 'Never has one seen a gentleman worth 5,000 or 6,000 *livres* a year be a more cunning defender at law of his own cause than the sieur de Pierregrosse. For, over 25 crowns that he owes them, on good and just grounds, he has kept two illiterate peasants, his creditors, continually in litigation since 1633, and has compelled them in that time to undergo four *instances* and as many *sentences*.' AD, Drôme, B, 48 (printed catalogue p. 14).

century, this was one of the most frequent causes of unrest among the nobility. Last of all—and here the position of the younger generation is a clear indication—it was common in the early seventeenth century to find the younger sons of good families plainly resorting to fraudulent means of making money. This was a frequent occurrence in Paris, where it claimed many victims and provoked many lawsuits, so much so that in 1624 the *Parlement* forbade loans to be made, with or without security, to these young noblemen who had no other means of livelihood than to exploit their family name: 'prohibits all people, of whatever status, rank or condition they may be, to lend money to the children of good families, even though they claim to be of age, and even if they submit their birth certificates to those who make the loans to them; to all merchants, goldsmiths, jewellers and others. . . .'[9]

The diversity of means employed by the traditional nobility to adjust their steadily worsening economic situation must not deceive us as to one fact: there was no diffusion or contamination. Nobles who married a financier's daughter did not thereby derogate or become *bourgeois*. Those who pawned family jewels with a goldsmith did not lose their rank because of these dubious transactions. Quite the reverse. In face of the rising bourgeoisie, the old nobility closed its ranks, struggling against this invasion and withdrawing into itself. Throughout the seventeenth century, a long defensive action continued to be fought, tending to make a veritable caste of the order. At the beginning of the century, when a jurist like Charles Loyseau studied with so much confusing detail the means used by commoners to become noble, he helped the nobility to become aware of a threat which had steadily grown in the sixteenth century. In theory, says Loyseau, there should be no ennoblement without the prince's consent, but commoners have many means at their disposal. By purchasing a noble estate, a fief, they can surreptitiously become the new master of a village. Alternatively, they can serve at a lord's side for some years, and then one day brazenly claim this service as a basis for exemption from the *taille*, which amounts to tacit ennoblement. The official methods were no less important. Appointment to certain high positions—constable, chancellor, superintendent of finances, great chamberlain, grand falconer, grand almoner, etc.—or the conferment by the king of letters of nobility, duly registered in return for certain compensation, were the two most normal procedures. Doubtless, such new members of the nobility were always considered as upstarts, who had to spend some time ridding themselves of their commoner's stigma. G. Budé claims in fact that a family elevated to the nobility by letters patent was really only regarded as noble in the third generation. But at the end of the sixteenth century, the reactions of the nobility went further than to impose a period of quarantine. The traditional nobility demanded of the king that these practices should cease, and at the same time it called for the old orders of knighthood, especially that of Saint-Michel,

[9] *Archives nationales*, AD, III, 29, 78.

to be restored to honour, to re-establish the bonds of vassalage of the early nobility, with its illusory freedom from plebeian pollution.

Doubtless these demands, this defensive reaction by the nobility, did not meet with satisfaction until the time of Colbert,[10] and then only partially. The monarchy, ill-used by its rebellious nobility in the second half of the sixteenth century, and often threatened by it early in the seventeenth, did not adopt all its points of view. The king never forsook the practice of conferring nobility by letters, which allowed him to distribute much-prized honours, and he continued to encourage the formation of a new category of nobility, the *noblesse de robe*, alongside the *noblesse d'épée*. Finally, and above all, he imposed submission to royal authority upon this discontented, turbulent class, which was all the more of a nuisance in that it was no longer useful: this was the aim behind the prohibition of duelling, and the dismantling of castles. Increasingly as time went on, and according to royal design, only the seignorial régime maintained the social domination of the nobility: which is to say that it was maintained with difficulty, and under many a challenge and threat in the unstable and constantly uncomfortable state which continued until the end of the eighteenth century.

The bourgeoisie or bourgeoisies

To define the bourgeoisie is a very difficult task. Beyond the medieval criterion—the inhabitant of a town, duly enrolled on the registers of citizenship (*bourgeoisie*) a definition which was certainly out of date by the period under discussion[11]—there is no perceptible basis for precise definition. The main reason for this lies in the variety of ways of growing rich in this century of Spanish America. Finance, trade, royal or urban offices, or even land-holdings were all avenues to success which could take a man into the ranks of the bourgeoisie, even if the *nouveaux riches* had to acquire the bourgeois way of life and the particular mentality of the class. For to be a bourgeois was first and foremost to share in a way of life which differed from that of both the lower classes and of the aristocrat by descent. Its essential feature, as I see it, was a certain security in the face of the hazards common to all human life, particularly in troubled times such as those: the security of the well-stocked granary, of the property-owner snugly ensconced in his own house, the security of the citizen behind the town walls, effectively surrounded by his fellow-citizens. Further, the bourgeois did little work with his hands. Even if he was a merchant or a manufacturer, he was not a manual worker. And to be a bourgeois was, in addition, to share in a mentality,

[10] Think, for example, of the revision of titles, the subject of many pronouncements in the *Conseil royal*, and of the restoration of the orders of chivalry.

[11] However, according to Loyseau those who were not to be classed as bourgeois were 'the nobility: even when they reside in town, they are not styled bourgeois', and 'the base persons of the humbler classes'; the term was rightly applied to 'those inhabitants who share in the honours of the city, and have a voice in its assemblies'.

a way of thinking, which comprised its virtues—forethought, thrift, a sense of profit and expenditure—and also a taste for luxury. Later on, in the full spate of Western capitalism, the bourgeois way of life and mentality may well have revealed other, somewhat different features.

Defining the bourgeoisie is difficult for another reason, namely that it comprised a diverse social group with divergent interests. It reveals many of the characteristics of a ruling class, in particular its economic power, which was steadily consolidated throughout the sixteenth century. Yet a large section of the group desired only to escape from their condition and become noble—in the traditional manner, if possible, through service to the king or through positions in the legal profession, which became a second category of nobility at the beginning of the seventeenth century. Thus, they did not form a caste. Modern society offered its members many individual opportunities to desert and renounce their humble origins, to the profound discontent of the traditional nobility in the period under discussion. The time had not yet come for the protests by the *noblesse de robe* when their ranks were in turn threatened by similar invasions. But until the stiffening resistance and major clashes of the eighteenth century, social interpenetration remained the general rule in the early modern period. Thus the bourgeoisie, lying between the lower classes, which were a source of new recruits at each demographic upheaval or social crisis, and the nobility, to which it aspired, was the least distinctive of the social categories within a shifting society. No doubt one is justified in tentatively distinguishing the 'upper Third Estate', dominated by the *noblesse de robe* and composed mainly of financiers, international merchants and tax-farmers, from the middle and lower bourgeoisie made up of small-scale dealers, well-to-do artisans, 'small tax-farmers' and second-rank merchants, all of whom were distinguishable from the lower classes as being men of undoubted substance, though not of great wealth. Nevertheless, the most important feature of the class remained this twofold escape, this double 'feudalization'—the elevation to the ranks of the traditional ruling class, and the creation of a second category of nobility, the *noblesse de robe*, which immediately detached itself from the 'upper Third Estate'.

At the beginning of the modern period, the bourgeoisie, as defined above, was the most active and enterprising of all sections of French society. At the heart of the kingdom, it engaged in all the essential activities and controlled almost all the sources of wealth. In the first instance promoting production and trade, it headed the industries created by the monarchy to secure certain monopolies—arms, artillery, foundries, gunpowder and shipbuilding. It was in charge of the first public transport undertakings, the iron, gold and silver mines, and also obviously managed the bulk of the textile industry (silk, tapestries and woollens), wax and paper manufacturing, and so on. Likewise the bourgeoisie controlled finance, not only banking, which backed international commerce in Lyons and Paris, but also public finance through the royal officials entrusted with the direct administration of the king's revenues—the *trésoriers généraux*, *receveurs généraux et particuliers*, *receveurs des domaines*, *receveurs des tailles*—and through the *partisans* and tax-farmers who levied certain taxes in place of the monarchy, and made huge profits from their services.[12] A *trésorier de l'épargne* could quietly amass an outrageous fortune, like the famous Puget in the reign of Henri IV. Under the orders of these great financiers, a milling horde of under-farmers and sundry henchmen shared with profit in the exploitation of public funds. Finally, the bourgeoisie was in possession of an increasing proportion of land. As the crisis in aristocratic revenues grew more acute, the town bourgeoisie, ever eager to acquire real estate, took over. The acquisition of a country estate remained the basis for noble rank. But this did not prevent the bourgeois from also buying an office at some time before or afterwards. More often than not, families gained entry to the parliamentary world once they were equipped with the social authority that an estate conferred upon them. But there were many, notably at Dijon, who were content to cultivate their estates, which proved the soundest of propositions from the time when the decline in trade adversely affected movable wealth. The bourgeois, moreover, did not consider his land an unproductive possession. He preserved or re-established the feudal dues, in particular payments in kind, rents which increased in value as prices rose. Immediately after the civil wars, the bourgeoisie set about restoring estates, as demanded by Henri IV and Sully, and extolled by Olivier de Serres. In Burgundy,[13] round Dijon, they bought vineyards and investigated the quality of the different wines of Chambertin and Chenove: a slow process of classification and improvement which resulted, in the eighteenth century, in the recognition of the great vintage wines which are still made today.

In a France swept by trade currents stronger than any medieval period had known, where the growing influence of money was strongly felt—as Jean Bodin and so many others recorded—the bourgeoisie thus occupied a prominent place in the material life of the country. By the same token, since it controlled the sources of wealth, it occupied the corridors of power. It held the offices in the civil service and the administration of justice—from the local courts to the provincial and Paris *Parlements*—and even some of the important positions and high dignities at the king's side. Moreover all these positions purchased from the king became hereditary in the early seventeenth century. As the culmination of a lengthy evolutionary process, the edict of Henri IV in 1604, in the temporary

[12] D'Ormesson often recalls these scandalous fortunes. In 1645, he writes 'being ashamed to see that Lambert died worth 4 millions and more and childless; that Ragois left prodigious wealth; that Galand died leaving 12 millions without the king taking a share, for which every man would have given him his blessing; that it was odious that those who administered the country's finances should grow so prodigiously rich.'

[13] Burgundy is merely one example. The same was true of Ile-de-France, Poitou etc.: cf. Venard (84); Raveau (180).

and revocable form of a nine-year lease, sealed the establishment of a judicial plutocracy in France. The *paulette* sanctioned the purchasability or, as Savaron called it, the simony of offices. Since the fifteenth century, provosts and clerks of the court had been leasing their functions. Despite many protests, especially from the States-General, the sale of offices became an established practice, and was legalized under François I, figuring among the fiscal resources of the monarchy under the *bureau des parties casuelles* (set up in 1522). The high cost attached to the procedures involved (resignation and royal assent) explains the zeal, described by Rabelais, with which lessees sought to recover their stake at the expense of their feudal dependants and taxpayers.

With the *paulette*—officially the *annuel*, or *droit annuel* which exempted the owners of offices from resigning and eliminated the need for royal nomination and solicitations by courtiers[14]—office holders gained complete independence with regard to the king. They no longer needed to prepare themselves seriously for their duties, since they were assured of obtaining by inheritance 'what they ought to acquire by their learning'. The price of offices rose immediately, a good indication of the way the bourgeoisie favoured hereditary posts. The position of councillor in the *Parlement* of Brittany, worth 16,000 *livres* in 1604, rose to 40,000 by 1609. Even the first presidencies, which did not come under the *paulette* and continued to be filled by royal appointments, increased in value in the same proportion. The trend persisted for a long time, since a first presidency in the *Parlement* of Rouen, which was sold for 150,000 *livres* in 1610, was estimated by Colbert at twice that figure in 1665.

The rush for offices is no doubt to be explained by the need to find investments in a time of economic difficulties; but an additional factor was the desire for social advancement, which was fostered by the monarchy for obvious financial reasons. The more offices it created, the more candidates there were. 'If ever a king of France,' writes Loyseau, 'wished to appropriate the wealth of his subjects . . . he need only create many offices; they will all race each other to the king with their purses; anyone without money will sell his land; anyone without enough land will sell himself . . . and will consent to be a slave to become an office holder.'[15] Through the offices, the bourgeoisie administered the country.

Though rich and powerful, and experienced in business and in the administration of the kingdom, the bourgeoisie nevertheless remained dominated by the nobility. It did not even attempt to appropriate political power, but was content

[14] These solicitations were by no means disinterested: they were well rewarded and allowed the creation of personal clienteles. Henri IV is said to have wanted to avoid a return to this practice when he instituted the *annuel*: 'Having observed that, when MM. de Guise were in favour, because they had been able to have all the vacant offices given to their own dependants, they had thereby acquired such influence among the office holders that they knew them better than the king; and that this was what had most helped them in promoting the League.'

[15] Loyseau (163), III, ch. 2.

to serve, though its zeal in doing so fluctuated, it is true. Even during the *Fronde*, the monarchy was more afraid of the nobility than of the *Parlementaires*. The bourgeoisie did not (yet) attack the monarchy, except in a sporadic, restricted manner. The bourgeois revolts, which were at first submerged in the main current of the religious wars but became more clearly characterized in the 1630s, never amounted to anything more than passing, short-lived uprisings, mostly prompted by the misappropriation of loans by the king when in financial straits. *Rentiers* holding *rentes sur l'Hôtel de ville* were incensed when some reduction in their bonds brutally deprived them of part of their resources.[16] Often, in provincial towns the bourgeoisie and lower classes united in a cause for a time, under the impulse of a common fiscal hatred of some royal agent; but the impulse died down like a fit of temper in a few days. At Troyes in 1627, Dijon in 1630 (the *Lanturlu*), Aix-en-Provence in 1631, Toulouse in 1632, Bordeaux and Agen in 1635, and Rouen in 1639, the disturbances were never prolonged. They did not link up with other towns, nor even assume the threatening proportions of a rustic rebellion.[17] During the *Fronde* itself, the *Parlementaires* who set the tone and spoke in the name of the very bourgeoisie to which they considered they no longer belonged, shrank from prolonged uprisings which would endanger the system of monarchy, and not merely call into question the problem of *rentes* or that of the *intendants*. But thirty-five years earlier, when the *Parlement* of Paris was in conflict with Marie de' Medici in 1615, the pattern was already established—the firmest of remonstrances, followed by a token rebellion, and then a return to favour.

The principal explanation of this political impotence is psychological: the inefficacy and fruitlessness of the opposition of the bourgeoisie stemmed from the fact that it had less of a sense of solidarity than any other class. Class consciousness was awakened within it under the threat of looting, when the urban lower classes rose up against all who had houses of their own.[18] But, following the example of the *noblesse de robe*, with the *Parlementaires* leading the field, the bourgeoisie above all fostered a mentality of escape to noble rank. A bourgeois who was rich, intelligent and active was not satisfied to remain a bourgeois, but wanted to

[16] A common enough scene, which Omer Talon recounts dispassionately in his *Mémoires* (I, p. 241, in the La Haye edition of 1732): 'On March 24th of this year [1638], the Council [*Direction*] met at the Chancellor's in the usual way, to deal with the payment of the *rentes sur l'Hôtel de Ville*, about which several individual complaints had been made. At the end of the Council, some of the investors, seeing that they were to receive no satisfaction, made an uproar in the Chancellor's apartments, hurling insults and threats. . . .'

[17] Cf. Porchnev (179) and Roupnel (181), quoted above; cf. also the evidence of Bigot de Monville for Normandy.

[18] Social uneasiness in the towns was extensive enough for a mere influx of the poor in time of famine to arouse fear. Haton notes at Troyes in 1573 that 'the more well-to-do began to live in fear of a popular uprising and revolt against them on the part of these paupers.'

join the nobility and renounce his original status as a commoner. The bourgeoisie was a diverse collection of rivalries and instabilities, which set at its head the hybrid group of 'social half-breeds', the *noblesse de robe*, great and small—those who thought that they had escaped the inferior condition of commoner, and had been the first to put an end to their anxieties by becoming royal officials. The spirit behind this was downright renegade in so far as the bourgeois[19] based his fortune on work, thrift and the art of making his profits multiply, while the ideal of the nobleman remained that of an idle, extravagant life, since to 'live like a nobleman' amounted to considering work as dishonourable and wretched. This renegade spirit, which explains the ease with which the monarchy always quashed the 'remonstrances' of the *Parlementaires* in the sixteenth and seventeenth centuries, also accounts for the confusion inherent in social conflicts, in the frequent revolts when, as at Rouen in 1639, the *Parlementaires* let the lower classes have their head and refused even to quell them, while shortly afterwards they meted out savage punishment; or when nobles and bourgeois found themselves at times allies and at others enemies, without any constant ever emerging, not even the classic factor of the struggle of the rich against the poor.

The rural and urban lower classes

The lower classes of town and country made up the manpower of French society. The term proletariat is unsuitable in this context; it is anachronistic and would give a wrong impression, since it acquired a precise connotation in the nineteenth century which bears no relation to the conditions of the earlier period. *Menu peuple* or 'humble classes' was the expression of the times, which did not always distinguish townsmen from peasantry. It is true that a famine sufficed to see towns invaded by a wave of peasants falling back upon the sustenance of the town granaries. Moreover, there was constant interchange between the journeymen of the town crafts, vagabonds and dreaded brigands. Often, contemporary writers used terms such as 'the common people' and 'the poor' to include all the cast-offs of society; the equating of the 'working classes' with 'dangerous classes' did not hold good only for the nineteenth century.[20]

However, the peasantry formed a well-defined social group, at once by its parish environment, by its subjection to the seignorial regime and by its traditions; though even within the framework of the rural community pronounced differences in ways of life were appearing. Everywhere, though more especially near large towns where landlords found supervision easier, the village was dominated by the husbandmen who were responsible for levying the lord's dues and administering the lord's equipment. Often, indeed, such prominent members

[19] After the period in question and the *Fronde*, the *noblesse de robe* became more clearly detached from the bourgeoisie, to form a social class which in part found its own ideology in certain aspects of Jansenism: cf. Goldmann (335).

[20] Cf. Chevalier, *Classes laborieuses et classes dangereuses*.

of the group might become the target of the frequent revolts directed against the château and royal officials. But equally a deeper solidarity acted in their favour in these rebellions, which were the most common manifestation of the oppression under which the peasant masses laboured. In the *Croquants* and *Nu-pieds*, countrymen had a very old tradition, handed down orally for centuries. The *Jacqueries* of 1358 and the terrors of the fifteenth century remained in the collective memory as a call to new uprisings, to which contemporary chronicles constantly refer. Though submerged in the civil wars in the second half of the sixteenth century, these became surprisingly frequent during the next fifty years.[21] Attacking royal tax-collectors, châteaux and the king's armies too—without stirring far from their own familiar stretch of countryside—the insurgents, sometimes incited by their priests, sometimes by noblemen, ravaged and laid waste to the vicinity, made for the neighbouring town, and sometimes shut themselves up in it in order to be better able to defend themselves. But these peasant uprisings no more endangered the established order than the urban revolts. Lescarbot describes them as follows in 1612:

> I might say that the *menu peuple* is a strange animal. And I remember in this connection the war of the *croquants*, amongst whom I found myself once in my life, at Querci. It was the strangest sight in the world, that rabble in clogs, on account of which they were called *croquants*, as their clogs, which were studded at toe and heel, went 'croc' with each step. The mob was all at sixes and sevens, everyone being leader, some armed with bill-hooks attached to poles, others with rusty old swords, and so on. . . .[22]

Systematic study of these violent peasant demonstrations is only just beginning, despite the amount of material available. Even though accounts in *livres de raison*, the correspondence of the *intendants* and the judgments and investigations found in legal records rarely give us the peasant's point of view, a study of these continual revolts should allow their character to be defined. Porchnev's book on popular uprisings from 1623 to 1648 already enables one to assert that the peasant mobs were often helped and guided by members of other social groups, in particular by noblemen intent upon protecting their feudal dependants against royal taxation. But the peasants' anger was as often turned against the châteaux. These sudden, brutal and short-lived outbursts were the manifestation of old and abiding feelings of resentment, which built up gradually under silent subjection to the lord and his representatives, who were often more detestable than their master himself, and under a lasting hatred of the rough soldiery which was so quick to plunder and to seize everything in accordance with the custom mentioned by Montaigne: 'to punish, even with death, those who obstinately

[21] Cf. Porchnev (179), of which a French translation was published in 1963 by the *Centre de recherches historiques*.

[22] Lescarbot, *Histoire de la Nouvelle France* (1866 edn) p. 493.

persist in defending a place which by the rules of warfare cannot be held. Otherwise, in the hope of impunity, there is not a henhouse which would not hold up an army.'[23]

★

The urban lower classes present a more varied spectacle, and their behaviour is less reminiscent of the classic dialectic between master and slave. Small-time artisans pursuing their trades in the shadow of the cathedral, journeymen and apprentices belonging to guilds and fraternities, cheapjacks such as water-carriers, waferers and stallkeepers formed social groups within the dual setting of the town and their trades. They too belonged to the *menu peuple* but led less restricted lives than the peasantry. The men of the mechanical trades played a leading role in the Reformation from the middle of the sixteenth century onwards. Reading the Bible and the countless printed pamphlets and placards which were distributed from door to door and posted on walls, artisans shared in this religious fervour long before the peasantry—and because of it the social preoccupations which they had already revealed in the thirteenth, fourteenth and fifteenth centuries were pushed into the background for some fifty years.

However, here again savage riots directed against royal officials and royal justice, as also against the rich bourgeoisie, reveal an urban climate of social fear similar enough to the state of tension in the countryside. 'To loot the homes of the bourgeoisie' was ever a possibility in these outbursts, hence the discretion of the rich in sometimes allowing events to take their course, though somewhat uneasily, so quick were the rebels to turn against them. The time of the League saw all kinds of disorders masquerading behind religious motives, but the period immediately following saw the reappearance of these revolts due to poverty and taxation, of the kind contemporaries recalled in terror. It was so easy, as they said repeatedly, to incite rebellion. Take the following document, written in Marseilles in 1640:

> The disturbance was promoted by those who fomented unrest on two plausible pretexts: the first was the shortage of corn, and that the bakers were without bread, which was an easy way of upsetting the temper of the populace; the second, that the bakers and corn-merchants would not accept 'doubloons', which has also caused commotions in Marseilles several times already.[24]

★

To the bourgeois writers who have left us information on these reticent lower classes, and even to law officers, there was no clear-cut distinction,[25] it is

[23] Montaigne, *Essays* I, 15.

[24] *BN*, Mss, *Nouveau fonds français*, 18976, f. 475.

[25] Except, perhaps, for the matter of residence; vagrants could not give an address.

true, between the lower class of journeymen and artisans, and the lawless rabble of thieves and 'paupers' who periodically had to be expelled from the towns into the open countryside. Thus the object of institutions like the *aumône générale* in Lyons was to assist beggars and to provide labour for those trades which needed it. They brought up orphans and retrieved from amongst the beggars arrested at the town gates or in the markets the young for whom work could be found. This floating urban population of paupers, beggars and layabouts was an imposing one: in 1534 an attempted census of people requiring assistance in Lyons yielded 7,000 proud poor in feeble health and 675 beggars and children of beggars. In 1586, the same town opened workshops to provide them with work and feed them, and 4,772 men and women were enrolled, receiving soup in the morning and a few pence at the day's end.

In times of famine their numbers were swelled by the many vagabonds and even peasants who descended upon the towns hoping to find a welcome. As long as stocks held out charity was liberally distributed, but only too often the *échevins* were obliged to close the gates and drive from the town these insanitary[26] crowds that clogged the streets. In fact, the vagabonds, beggars and thieves who controlled the highways and forests around Paris and Rouen, and were masters of the streets after nightfall, terrorizing the defenceless inhabitants, were indistinguishable from the *menu peuple* in the eyes of the bourgeois—at least in times of revolt.

There is no doubt that large cities like Paris, Lyons and Rouen had within their walls a large population of outlaws who took advantage of the almost total inefficacy of the urban police. In 1634, Omer Talon complained dolefully: 'The city of Paris . . . is full of thieves and there is now far less security than there was during the civil wars, when, although the lawlessness of the soldiers and even the state of hostilities made anything permissible, merchandise arrived in Paris with far less hindrance and law and order were enforced far better than they are now.'[27] Certainly, there can be no question of looking for any kind of class-consciousness within this asocial group. However, through its involvement with the urban and rural lower classes, it helped to blur the group consciousness of the latter, who were strongly motivated, in imitation, to observe an hierarchical code of honour which would distinguish them from the rabble.

Orders or classes? Both categories were currently effective. I did not set out to give a fuller description of them here, for they are in any case sufficiently

[26] As Haton notes in 1573: 'they so completely filled the town of Provins with lice that the inhabitants would not have dared to sit on the stall seats or any others in the streets. . . . The barn of the Priory of St Agnoul, in which many of these paupers sought shelter at night because of the hay it contained, was so ridden with lice and fleas that anyone remaining in there long enough to recite the *Ave Maria* would have found his legs and clothes covered in them.'

[27] O. Talon, *Mémoires* I, 71.

familiar to us all, but merely to underline their essential characteristics. The most conscious of the classes was an order, the second in the land—the nobility. Yet in many respects, the popular masses and the bourgeoisie, gradually better moulded and growing in self-awareness, were proclaiming themselves more and more as classes.

Chapter 8
Threatened forces for solidarity: the State, the monarchy and the Church

At the summit of the social edifice, above the subordinate units of the family and the parish, the monarchy constituted the political framework on a national scale and ensured the administrative structure in the form of provinces, *bailliages* (and *sénéchaussés*) and *prévotés*.

As the supreme authority, held in ever greater respect despite frequent clashes, it enjoyed the protection of the Catholic Church, its ally,[1] which crowned its Most Christian Kings, ascribed to them a privileged place within its ranks—above a priest and almost the equal of a bishop—and acknowledged their miraculous powers to cure scrofula. Since the distant ages when the immediate descendants of Hugh Capet had had to struggle to impose their authority on the petty lords of the Ile-de-France and the Hurepoix, the monarchy had not ceased to strengthen and extend its power, and this steady advance resulted at the end of the fifteenth century in the successors of St Louis and Philip the Fair being the undisputed masters of one of the largest domains in Europe. The gradual emergence of national feeling amid wars and foreign occupations had acted in their favour, as also the legal scholarship of the *juristes*, who culled from Roman law the principles of public authority: the king was emperor in his realm and he appeared to be even more respected and heeded than the emperor of the German Holy Roman Empire.

As the culmination of this consolidation of royal authority, patiently pursued for five centuries, there emerged the prospect of absolute monarchy, such as François I perhaps dreamed of during the early years of his reign, between 1515 and 1525: a prospect which would include reinforcing the ties between the government and local administration, improving the yield of royal taxation and setting up a large, strong and permanent army. But by the mid-sixteenth century, there was no longer any possibility of this fine slowly-wrought structure. The learned theory of the divine right of kings was violently contested in

[1] This alliance was both a mystical bond and a very precise legal pact which found its final form in the Concordat of Bologna (1516).

the thick of the civil wars. Two kings were assassinated by subjects convinced that tyrants could not continue to rule. Royal sovereignty was flouted by Churchmen who only a short time ago had most helped to sanctify it: one faith, one law, one king, the traditional formula which had so long been the basis of that authority, no longer had any meaning in a divided France. With great difficulty, Henri IV was able to restore peace by compelling recognition of the religious division of the French and imposing that precarious agreement, the Edict of Nantes. The most fragile political structure,[2] and the slowest to win control, thus found itself threatened and belaboured for long decades of unrest and revolts, which added to the chronic inadequacies of a State ill-equipped to ensure the administration of a territory so vast by the standards of sixteenth century communications. For religious disunity was obviously not the only cause of the weakness of royal authority, as many contemporaries believed and said.

The religious schism certainly rocked everyday life to its very foundations. The disintegration of the parish wherever nonconformity became established was an event whose psychological repercussions are difficult to gauge. Two groups were created, rapidly becoming hostile to each other, or at any rate 'competing', both eager to win converts. *A fortiori*, when it was families that were split, the neophytes of the new faith stirred up all kinds of scandals and rivalries around themselves. In all communities, Protestants and Catholics deepened their faith in the light of the contradictions they were concerned to answer. To speak of moral and theological discussions is perhaps going too far in the case of the Sunday confrontations, upon which documentary evidence is unfortunately lacking. The learned debates and diplomatic attempts at reconciliation have left many traces, but these tell us nothing of the atmosphere prevailing in parishes divided into two communities, each of which was eager to assert the primacy of its respective creed. Nevertheless, this was one of the underlying realities of the Reformation.

The king and royal authority

At that time the king was not, as we are tempted to imagine by comparison with twentieth-century monarchs, a Head of State, a cog in the constitutional mechanism. He was the sovereign and, more profoundly, the guarantor of prosperity, the palladium of the nation. It was he who, by virtue of the royal blood that flowed in his veins, was the support of his subjects, ensured their success in war and their cultural achievements. Royalty was a mystical concept.

In the French monarchy, the king was supreme. When a town had to receive a prince of the blood, the *échevins* deliberated at length upon the honours to be

[2] Bearing in mind the disappearance (politically speaking) of the great fiefs. The last of these, Burgundy, struck its colours at the end of the fifteenth century.

rendered to him. Some were to be reserved for the king alone.[3] The king also wielded formidable power, against which all were helpless—as long proved true: to fall on one's knees before him and put up with his moods was everyone's lot. Here again, the reactions of the towns are significant. Was the king pleased with them, or not? This was a matter for fate to decide. Yet once the bourgeois were in the presence of royal officials, however high-ranking, they resisted and argued, speaking their minds and invoking the public interest—which was often that of their town. Furthermore, the king was the sole repository of authority, so that if he left his kingdom—or *a fortiori*, if he was taken prisoner like François I at Pavia—the people were uneasy. The sovereign well realized this when, in proclaiming the transference of power to his mother, he emphasized his express wish to see his decision respected; 'and that he wanted her to be obeyed'.

In fact, the 1791 Constituent Assembly formalized these accepted principles with due legal stringency when it proclaimed royalty as 'indivisible' and 'hereditary within the reigning family in the male line, in order of primogeniture, with the perpetual exclusion of women and their descendants'. For this hereditary principle—a fact before it was legally established—was one of the conditioning factors of royal power. If it is true that the Capetians had originally been elected, there was no longer any trace of selection except in the coronation service (*sacre*). At Rheims, even until the eighteenth century, two bishops raised the one to be anointed and showed him to all present, asking the people if it accepted him as king; after which the archbishop of Rheims received the customary oath from the monarch, and recited the following prayer: 'Multiply, great God, Thy gifts and blessings on Thy servant whom in humble devotion we all elect to the kingdom.'

Once the original election was forgotten, the other principles (primogeniture, exclusion of female lines and of women themselves, with regencies in the case of minority) were gradually determined during the Middle Ages and were firmly established by the beginning of the sixteenth century. Only the procedure in the case of a minority remained in doubt and the *Parlement* of Paris took advantage of this to play a decisive role in such difficult circumstances. But regency never affected the succession itself.[4]

However, from the elective origins of the monarchy, from references culled

[3] The court and court service equally reflected this supremacy. It needed the wit of Montaigne to criticize it. 'I have never been able to imagine that it was an appreciable comfort in an intelligent man's life to have twenty men supervising his close-stool; or that the services of a man worth 10,000 *livres* a year, or who has taken Casale or defended Siena, should be more convenient and acceptable to him than those of a good valet' (*Essays* I, 42).

[4] Heredity was so well accepted in the sixteenth century that it was the basic argument of the partisans of Henri IV between 1589 and 1598. D'Aubray in his *Satyre Ménippée* declares: 'We want a king and a natural, not an artificial, leader, a king ready made and not to be made. . . . The king we want is ready made by nature, sprung from the true garden of the fleurs-de-lis of France, a straight and verdant shoot from the stem of St Louis.'

from the political thinkers of antiquity (in particular Aristotle) and from the influence of the conciliary theory, there remained, at least in scholastic debates and in the works of the *juristes*, the idea of legitimacy. The distinction between the lawful king, chosen for the good of the people, and his opposite, the tyrant who had seized the crown against the will of the people, was a notion that was familiar to the Schoolmen. Similarly, casuists debated the question of lawful deposition, selecting certain instances, including heresy. In their view, the only authority with the right to remove the lawful but heretical heir from the throne was the pope. At the end of the Middle Ages, such scholastic debates had scarcely been heard outside legal and clerical circles.[5] Between 1560 and 1600 they became the common property of the most outspoken subjects of the king of France. Both Protestants rebelling against persecution and Leaguers indignant at the agreements between Henri III and the future Henri IV raised once again to their own advantage the distinction between the tyrant and the lawful king,[6] while the Leaguers added to it the doctrine of tyrannicide. A little later, after the assassination of Henri III, the same Leaguers were to appeal to Rome, demanding the expulsion of the king of Navarre from the throne of France.

Reading through the works of theorists and preachers in those impassioned years, one would be tempted to believe that the French monarchy ceased to possess the characteristics of revered, hallowed sovereignty which it had had at the beginning of the century. Moreover, it would be vain to deny that the institution had been shaken. Henri III and Henri IV both paid with their lives for the popular success encountered by the doctrine of tyrannicide. Yet despite so many inflamed publications and verbal excesses, despite two assassinations, the hallowed nature of the monarchy was not only reasserted by a great many reputable authors with or without connections at court, but also very quickly restored as a self-evident truth, which was repeatedly demonstrated by the miraculous powers of the kings. Remaining faithful to Catholicism, the kings of France kept the semi-sacerdotal distinction which was theirs: 'though the kings of France are not priests like the pagan kings, yet they share in the priesthood, and are not just laymen', we find written in 1645. They quickly recovered their prestige as healing kings. In the seventeenth century, the healing of scrofula took its place once and for all among the rites surrounding the king on the great religious festivals. Behind the ceremony, it was the reality of the miracle and the sanctity of the royal personage that were reaffirmed.[7] In the midst of the civil wars, the

[5] The only problems debated publicly were the very different ones concerning relations with the papacy, in the time of Philip the Fair. The representation of the people at court was mooted from time to time in the States-General, in particular in 1355 and 1484, but always in a relatively discreet manner.

[6] On the 'horrible impudence' of this development, cf. Montaigne, *Essays* II, 12.

[7] Controversy about the royal authority was merely lulled, however. During the *Fronde*, notably, a new spate of pamphlets emerged (not to mention the lampoons on Cardinal

loyal Parisian, l'Estoile, had already lost his temper with the preachers who jeered at Henri of Navarre. On 22nd March 1592, he cried: 'All these marks were the first signs of God's watchfulness over the person of his anointed, whom he safeguards miraculously on this occasion as on many others.' So too later, when Jansenius, as part of the polemic he levelled against the king of France (in his *Mars Gallicus* in 1636) wished to attack the royal miracle, he did not deny it (any more than the Protestants had done in the middle of the sixteenth century); rather, he asserted that the gift of performing miracles was widespread even among the pagans (like Pyrrhus or Vespasian) upon whom God had bestowed it out of compassion for the sufferings of mankind. He added that these powers were proof neither of sanctity nor of superiority: the she-ass of Balaam had been a good prophet, but this did not give her supremacy over all other asses; a subtle and irreverent argument, but one lacking in true weight in face of the reality of the cures acknowledged all over Europe.

The State and the nation

As far as the French people were concerned, this august royal authority expressed itself in two other ways: it was responsible for both the enforced, constraining solidarity of the State, which administered justice and finance, and the spontaneous emotional solidarity of the nation and the homeland.

Throughout the provinces, many officials acting in the king's name ensured the day-to-day administration of the kingdom. Struggling against nobles who clung to what was left of their regalities and against towns which abused their privileges, they strove, not without a certain personal independence, to see the sovereign's authority respected. But fiscal receivers, councillors in the *Parlements* and presidial judges were not civil servants; as officials in absolute control of their posts, they did not consider themselves simply as executives. Many provinces, when they were annexed, retained the right to summon their States to decide the amount and the basis of royal taxation (*pays d'Etats*). All *Parlements* had the right to register royal edicts and to remonstrate with the king whenever he requested the application of a new ordinance. All this, which forms a very full chapter in the history of French institutions under the *ancien régime*, is common knowledge, as too is the independence of the bodies of office-holders, the whole story of the emergence of the *noblesse de robe*, as we have seen. But the most clear-cut consequence of all this for the king's subjects was the way in which his authority was both distant and irksome. It was distant because there could be no question of having recourse to the sovereign himself. He was too elusive, everlastingly up hill and down dale, at least until the beginning of the seventeenth century. François I, Henri II and the kings during the civil wars left Paris and the

---

Mazarin, known as *mazarinades*). On this occasion, the Protestants were the defenders of royal authority (cf. Moïse Amyraut).

departments which were fixed there, to roam the Val de Loire from Amboise to Blois, Saumur and Sully, or to visit Normandy or Brittany.[8] To pay court to the sovereign or make a direct appeal to him meant, therefore, joining the large army of hunting companions, of merchants responsible for supplying the needs of the entourage, and of poets, who ceaselessly lamented the enormous discomforts of this nomadic existence.[9] Furthermore, royal authority was distant because, thwarted by so many exemptions and exceptions which provincial particularism had managed to preserve over the centuries, it was exercised in the most desultory fashion imaginable. As Montaigne quite rightly says, a member of the lesser nobility could lead his life in peace, without having any dealings with it. 'He hears speak of his master once in a year, as of the king of Persia, and only acknowledges him by some ancient cousinship, of which his secretary keeps a note. In truth, our laws are free enough, and the weight of sovereignty is felt by a French nobleman barely twice in a lifetime.'[10]

At the same time, this administrative system was irksome and ponderous; it carried the combined weight of complexity and the law's delays on the one hand, of fiscal oppression through the method of collection and assessment on the other, and finally of the prestige attached to being in the king's service once such offices became hereditary. It would be easy to compile a book of the laments and recriminations provoked by the inefficiency of this administrative machine, which had been empirically adapted to run an ever-growing kingdom. It is equally significant that the myths of the good kings, like St Louis and Louis XI, grew up in these connections and flourished until a late date. Louis XI was the

[8] E.g. François I in 1532: *January*, Abbeville, Dieppe, Rouen; *February*, Rouen; *March*, Argentan; *April*, Caen, Saint-Lô, Coutances; *May-June*, Châteaubriant; *July*, Brittany; *August*, Nantes; *September*, the Val de Loire and Fontainebleau; *October*, Paris, Chantilly, Amiens, Boulogne, Calais; *November*, Amiens, Compiègne, Chantilly; *December*, Paris, where he stayed until February 1533; then, off again—*March*, Rheims. . . .

[9] Marot echoes Claude Chappuys:

Peut-être ce jour
Prendrons d'assaut quelque rural séjour,
Où les plus grands logeront en greniers
De toutes parts percés comme paniers. (Marot)
(Perhaps today
We shall storm some country residence
Where the most important people will be sleeping in lofts
Which are holed on all sides like baskets.)

M'ont fait coucher dedans des draps sans toile
Dessuz un banc, quelque foys suz la terre
Sans adviser a esclairs ny tonnaire . . . (Chappuys)
(I have been made to sleep inside without bed-linen
On a bench, sometimes on the ground
Without regard to thunder or lightning.)

[10] *Essays* I, 42.

king who managed to choose good, upright judges by sending trustworthy agents into the provinces to inquire after men of ability. When a vacancy arose, King Louis appointed one of these candidates, disregarding all recommendations or complaints. The contrast between the good, saintly king and the bad representatives of his authority, in itself beneficient, may appear to us to be extremely naïve, or indeed hypocritical, but the French accepted it and endorsed it for centuries.

*

It is helpful to understand how the patriotism of the French rested upon royal authority, and was inseparable from it. No doubt the memory of invasions in the distant and more recent past and the fear of foreign powers played a big part. Normandy constantly dreaded the return of the English, and the militia of Rouen was called out to man the walls whenever the least disturbance led to the fear of an English landing.[11] But France, the 'fertile mother', the new homeland of the humanists who were proud to be able to use the everyday French language to translate Latin, Greek, Hebrew or Italian,[12] the nation in whose name the *politiques* begged for peace at the end of the century, also constituted a fully-accepted, assumed force for solidarity. Ronsard constantly appeals to it:

> Si j'ai jamais dès mon enfance
> Abreuvé de mes vers la France.[13]

and sings its praises, feeling that his own land is without equal:

> Le Grec vanteur la Grèce vantera
> Et l'Espagnol l'Espagne chantera,
> L'Italien, les Italies fertiles
> Mais moy, Françoys, la France aux belles villes.[14]

At the end of the century the *Satyre Ménippée* was in its entirety a long and beautiful expression of this patriotism, which placed the French nation above

[11] On the national feeling of the peasants of Provence, cf. the article by G. Procacci, 'La Provence à la veille des guerres de religion', *Revue d'histoire moderne et contemporaine* (Oct.—Dec. 1958), p. 246.

[12] 'The French nation can today proudly boast that the present translation of the Decameron is a most sure token and good proof of the richness and wealth of our vulgar tongue, French.' Foreword by G. Rouillé to his edition of the *Decameron* (Lyons 1558).

[13] Ronsard (112), *Odes* I, 15:

> If I have always, since my childhood
> Heaped my verses upon France. . . .

[14] Ronsard, *Premières poésies*, ed. Laumonier, I, 25:

> The boastful Greek will vaunt his Greece,
> And the Spaniard sing of Spain,
> The Italian, the fertile Italian lands,
> But I, a Frenchman, France with its fair towns.

orders or individuals.[15] The same sentiment prompted Henri IV himself when he drove the Spanish out of France and signed the Edict of Nantes.

The Edict of Nantes

The pacification achieved in 1598 through a settlement between two inexpugnable parties was so original and brought into the religious and political notions of France such long- and short-term innovations that it is necessary to examine it here in its overall context.

We do not know precisely how many Protestants there were at the end of the sixteenth century. An eighteenth-century manuscript suggests figures which are probable, but cannot be taken as definite:[16] Henri IV is alleged to have taken a census which listed 694 public churches, 257 fief churches, 800 ministers (a corrected figure; the manuscript reads 2,800 !), and 274,000 families (including some 2,468 noble families); in all, about 1,250,000 Protestants. One Frenchman in 10 or 12 belonged to the new faith—an impressive figure, even if it does mask the uneven distribution of the Huguenots over the country, for they were strongest in Aquitaine, the Val de Loire, lower Normandy, the Dauphiné and the Languedoc (cf. map 6). This proportion alone is sufficient to explain the impossibility of re-establishing unity by force. There were some on both sides who may still have dreamed of doing so, even after thirty years of war, but these were fanatics. A German-style territorial solution, modelled on the Interim of Augsburg, conflicted with the principle of political unity and with the patriotism of both sides. A division into provinces—or into even smaller fiefs—some Catholic, others Protestant, was not even envisaged, perhaps because the Protestant population was so widely scattered as to form a majority in only a very few towns. They had not converted whole regions or even created homogeneous cantons. Finally, a system of equality—which would imply an act of toleration—whereby the two faiths existed on the same footing, the worship of both faiths being freely practised everywhere side by side, with everyone being guaranteed participation in public life—this solution could no longer be achieved since it was both emotionally and rationally unacceptable. This is the main explanation of the difficulties encountered by Henri IV in his attempts to restore peace within his kingdom.

Ostensibly, the road he travelled ran quite straight. France, remaining predominantly Catholic, adopted Henri of Bourbon from the day he became a Catholic. On 25th July 1593, he recanted at Saint-Denis; on 25th February 1594,

[15] The royal delegates addressed the envoys of the duc de Mayenne on 23rd June 1593, at Saint-Denis, demanding an end to the war which was ruining the Catholic religion, ruining likewise all the orders, and spreading all manner of vices among the nation. And they affirmed their 'extreme compassion for the poor people of the fields, wholly innocent of what is happening in these wars'.

[16] *Bulletin de la société d'histoire du protestantisme français* XXXVIII, p. 551.

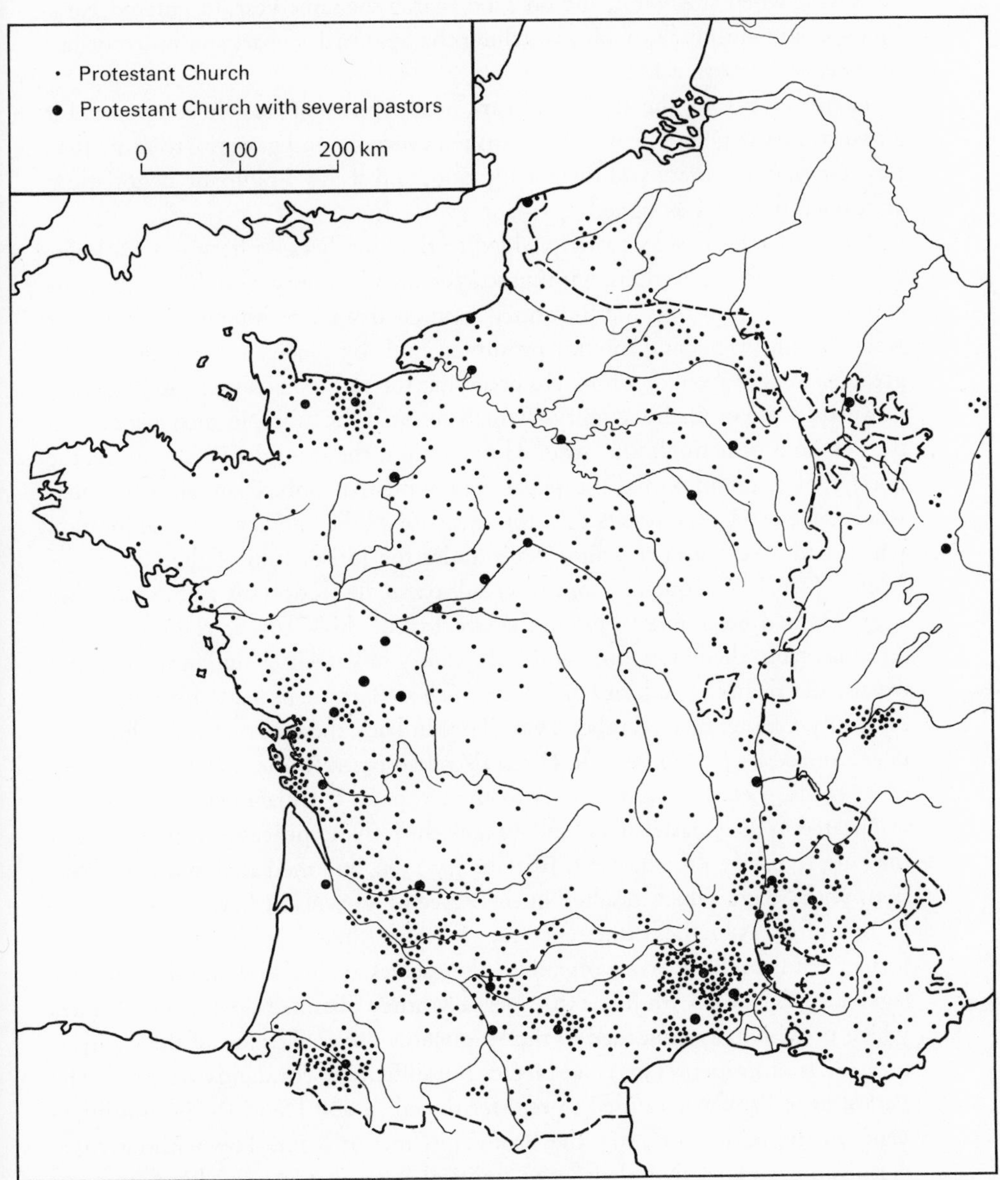

Map 6 Protestant churches, as listed in 1562 by Pastor S. Mours.

he was crowned at Rheims, and on 22nd March the same year, he entered Paris. Epinal colour-prints show him watching the Spaniards depart and murmuring: 'Paris is well worth a Mass.'

However, it took the king four years, until April 1598, to win acceptance for a peaceful settlement, one which dissatisfied everyone and gave rise to more than just reservations: there was further fighting, and secret diplomatic negotiations continued until it was signed.

On the Catholic side, towns yielded to the king because he was a Catholic, but they set their conditions, wishing to keep the autonomy won during the wars and above all to forbid the Reformed Church from worshipping within their walls. Parish priests and monks, prompted both by plebeian anger against the great (such as Mayenne) who were betraying the righteous cause, and by a very powerful sense of Catholic unity—which counted for more, in their view, than the demands of nationhood—wanted to continue the struggle. Furthermore, the Society of Jesus supported the papal viewpoint that only Clement VIII could absolve Henri IV; the Jesuits therefore questioned the validity of the abjuration which had taken place at Saint-Denis under the jurisdiction of the Church of France. Henri IV requested, and received, papal absolution on 17th September 1595. He had been able to judge the strength of this Catholic resistance from sermons, from the unrest fostered by the clergy in Paris itself and in many other towns, and from the audacity of fanatics such as Barrière in September 1593 and especially Chastel in December 1594. To win back these adversaries who were unconvinced by his conversion, Henri IV relied upon Rome, which gave freely of its confidence. It closed its eyes to the temporary banishment of the Jesuits implicated in the Chastel affair, encouraged the rallying processes which allowed the king to pacify Provence and Brittany by 1596, and mediated in the negotiations with Spain, which resulted in the Peace of Vervins in May 1598.

But after 1589 the Protestants too revealed their hostility towards their former companion in arms, organized themselves against him and demanded a legal statute. First on 7th July 1591, Plessis Mornay obtained the Edict of Mantes which provisionally conceded to the Huguenots the application of the pacificatory edicts of Poitiers (1577) and Nérac. But difficulties constantly recurred. The *Parlement* of Provence refused to register the edict, and Henri IV did not intervene. In the middle of 1595, the Protestants met at Sainte-Foy without royal permission, and created their own political organization: the kingdom was divided into nine provinces, with a council at the head of each; every year a general assembly of the delegates from the nine provinces was to consider the general interests of the Protestants. At the same time, they renewed their demands for a statute and called for admission to offices and professions, the creation of mixed chambers (*chambres mi-parties*) in the *Parlements*, and the concession of guarantee towns. In face of further hesitation on the king's part, the party leaders deserted the royal army while it was fighting against Spain and began to negotiate with Elizabeth of England and the States-General of Holland. In 1597, these 3,000 noblemen were on the brink of open rebellion when the king had the Edict of Nantes drawn up.

In essence, the Edict gave satisfaction to the Protestants, granting them the right to worship in carefully specified places (on the outskirts of towns and in the châteaux of *seigneurs hauts justiciers*), access to public offices, representation in certain *Parlements*, and the concession of fortified towns, whose garrisons and governors were to be paid for by the Royal Treasury. The National Synod of Montepellier, in a statement made on 22nd April, expressed its satisfaction with this 'edict which, while it does not wholly provide for all the essential requirements of the Churches, nevertheless seems adequate to place them in some security'. But the policy of enforcement which the king followed from 1598 to 1610 is no less significant than the document itself. Henri no doubt had to compel several hostile *Parlements* to register the Edict. But he employed a policy of vacillation which did not conciliate the malcontents of either party.

To begin with, the Huguenots did not see the creation in the *Parlement* of Paris of the special chamber, which was to consist of ten Catholic councillors, a President of the same persuasion and six Protestant councillors. The six Protestants were distributed among all the chambers and only sat in the 'chamber of the Edict' singly and in turn. Moreover, this chamber had within its jurisdiction not only the *Parlement* of Paris but also the *Parlements* of Rennes and of Rouen. On the other hand, at Toulouse, Bordeaux and Grenoble (acting for Aix and Dijon) the mixed chambers were properly set up. However, this first setback was hard felt by those who still adhered to the outdated view of Henri of Navarre as the protector of the Huguenots.

On their side, the Catholics, dissatisfied with the enormous privileges granted to the Protestants, speculated for a short period that the *Parlements*, upon which the king had imposed registration without discussion, would resist. A further source of indignation—perhaps an even greater one than that authoritarian act—was the granting of freedom of worship at the town gates. The Protestant Church at Charenton aroused the anger of the Parisians, who called for its demolition upon the death of the king. Thus the maintenance of peace between the two persuasions was repeatedly and dangerously challenged.

Henri IV was thus obliged to defend this expedient upon which internal peace was founded. He did so convinced that it was an acceptable solution, as is proved by his efforts to bring about agreements based upon the same principles abroad, both in England, between Elizabeth and the English Catholics, and in Holland, where President Jeannin was negotiating the status of the Dutch Catholics. But while pursuing this policy of pacification he did not lose sight of another enterprise—that of re-establishing the religious unity of the nation. Increasingly he came to admit that, according to the innermost feelings of his subjects, this was the very basis of the monarchy. Henri IV could not have failed to be struck by the fact that the humble people in town and countryside had been the last to rally to his side. In a region which had remained Catholic, such as the Comminges, where the Huguenots were confined to a few fortified towns, the great majority of the lower classes remained mistrustful of the king even after his abjuration and coronation. The States of the province had submitted, but the consuls of small towns such as Saint-Girons resisted for two years, refusing to recognize the new king, until the *Parlement* of Toulouse had to intervene to end this state of affairs.

And so Henri did all he could to restore royal traditions in their entirety, and thus to re-establish the religion of the monarchy. Shortly after his coronation, on Easter Sunday, 10th April 1594, eighteen days after his Entry, Henri IV touched for the king's evil. Paris had not seen this ceremony since 1588, and on that occasion it had been performed by Henri III, about whom the League had let it be rumoured that his impiety would cause the power of the touch to be lost. Henri IV was entirely successful in re-establishing this tradition which formed the most authentic proof of the legitimacy of his rule, and subsequently in 1609 he had his doctor, André de Laurens, publish a treatise on this miraculous power, acknowledged as belonging only to the Most Christian Kings.

But at the same time, the king encouraged debates with the most uncompromising of the Protestants, in the avowed hope of bringing the 'separated brethren'[17] back to the Church. He organized huge gatherings of several hundreds of people where Jesuits, monks, *Parlementaires* and porters humping vast tomes were assembled to debate with the Protestant noblemen, whom the king urged to take part in these confrontations. Similarly, he encouraged publications likely to 'end the religious disagreement'.[18] But these efforts, which were in any case little appreciated by the clergy and the Sorbonne, led nowhere. Discussions always broke down on two points over which opposition proved adamant: the Mass, considered as a sacrifice (with the doctrine of transubstantiation), and the authority of the pope. By comparison with these two points, many others, such as the celibacy of the priesthood, the cult of the Virgin and the Saints, and even the sacraments, seemed of quite minor importance. Moreover, the Council of Trent had defined and developed the Catholic position on these particular issues along with the rest, sanctioning both transubstantiation and papal authority. The result was that, if in the course of these debates organized by the king the two parties came to know their opponents' arguments better, on the whole the meetings actually deepened the rift, and made reunification appear even more unattainable in 1610 than in 1598. Each group became entrenched in

[17] Letter to d'Epernon, 5th May 1600 (*Lettres missives* V, p. 230).

[18] Jean Gontier, *La vraie procédure pour terminer le différend de religion* (1607); Rabier, *Discours au roi* (1607); a new edition of Melanchthon's *De Pace Ecclesiae* (1607); L. Turquet de Mayerne, *Advis sur le synode* (1608) etc.

its convictions and recognized how irreconcilable was the disagreement on fundamental issues.

The precarious peace of Nantes thus allowed the restoration of royal authority. It remained itself seriously threatened, and immediately after the assassination of Henri IV it was challenged by both Catholics and Protestants.

Only the political discernment of Richelieu—immediately after the siege of La Rochelle—and later of Mazarin ensured its survival for half a century. The provisional toleration granted to the Protestant minority after the civil wars maintained the unitarian principles of the kingdom through a compromise which doubtless lasted longer than its promoter thought it would.

Chapter 9
Temporary forces for solidarity: youth societies and feast days

The restrictive environments of family, parish or indeed of social group and nation, together comprised the essential forces for solidarity. They were felt or experienced in a far different way from today, and bound all men—of all ages. But they obviously did not entirely cover the real social experience of people in those troubled times. The merchant in Rouen or Marseilles had daily contact with foreign traders settled in the town and with his distant correspondents and agents in the great centres of European trade. In many respects, primarily in terms of professional background, he felt a far greater affinity with these representatives and travellers who led the same life as himself than with his own fellow-citizens.

Similarly, men like E. Pascal, Fermat, Mersenne and Descartes in the 1630s revealed their close attachment to people throughout Europe who shared the same passion as they did for mathematics, astronomy and music—a bond which reached beyond frontiers thanks to Latin, the international language. *A fortiori*, the Capuchin monk and the Jesuit father must have recognized, beyond these necessary bands of solidarity connected with their blood or home or language, the much wider one of their order stretching throughout Christendom.

These are examples of what one might call professional solidarity, and we shall return to the subject later when we explore the mentalities associated with various forms of activity. Brief mention has been made of them here only to avoid distorting the point at issue.

But they all represented ties which endured for a lifetime or a generation, not to say from generation to generation. Besides such lasting associations, one can observe other social phenomena which are noteworthy even though they were all temporary, as it were, and of limited duration. Although little is known of them and they are more difficult to apprehend, precisely because they were so ephemeral, they cannot be overlooked, if only because they involved the disruption of some group relationships and the formation of others. In a period which knew nothing of conscription and the conscript, age-groups made themselves felt through youth societies, which brought together young men—and sometimes even girls—by villages or towns, mostly without class distinction. Such gatherings were of a temporary nature, lasting only a few years, though it is not easy to specify at what age one joined or left them. In addition, throughout the country patronal festivals and other feast days and immovable public celebrations formed, in a still more episodic way, a social rite of exceptional importance. As moments of frequently exuberant relaxation, feast days often gathered together crowds from parishes and towns near or far, creating between their participants a familiarity of a few hours' duration in an atmosphere of exceptional licence of speech and behaviour. By these very conditions, they represented a social highlight outside everyday relationships.

Youth societies

Little is known of this institution, which seems to have existed in many different forms from one end of France to the other. As free associations of the young people from a town or a village, these societies usually chose a leader who took the title of Boy Lieutenant, Captain or *Abbé*. Under his orders, all sorts of enterprises could be launched, from a gingerbread race or a savage brawl with their opposite numbers from the neighbouring village, to the solemn reception of some important visiting personage.

In the Midi, the institution was a firmly-established tradition. The Boy Abbot figured, so to speak, among the dignitaries of southern towns. At weddings and *charivaris*, he levied dues directly on their inhabitants. In return, he was required to hold a ball with a string band for young people on 1st May, on St Lawrence's Day and during Carnival time, and equally to provide a banquet for the magistrates, and aubades and serenades for the young people according to a fixed calendar. The number of his duties implies that the Boy Abbot could scarcely have been of slender means, for the honour of stepping the maypole on May Day and of cavorting at the head of the young men outside the town gates seems to have been an expensive one; he could indeed have been a nobleman in those towns where the nobility had long been settled. In Auvergne, at the time of the *Grands Jours*, Fléchier records a custom still in existence in the province:

> On the occasion of a solemn festival, or a public celebration or the Entry of a personage of rank, all the young people assemble, and, bearing arms, parade around the town in fine array to honour the festival. Each of them seeks the noisiest weapons, and they regard it as a distinction to have fired the largest musket and made the loudest noise. . . .[1]

Boy Captains and *abbés* also existed in towns in the North. At Amiens, in 1574, it was the Boy Captain who was responsible for the reception of the Prince de Condé in the town. But besides this official institution, we find references to gangs of twenty or so young men which formed, each with its own leader, and engaged in all kinds of games and entertainments, not always appreciated

[1] Fléchier, *Mémoires sur les Grands Jours d'Auvergne* (1865 edn), p. 136.

by their elders. One can imagine them, for example, after a race repairing to a tavern for refreshment, then setting off in search of another similar band. In the towns these 'joyful seignories' bore the name of a parish, and the nickname of their leader; they made a great deal of noise, indulging in mutual provocation, shouting and creating as many opportunities as possible for making an uproar. Thus magistrates were not always very patient and forbade them to meet and stir up trouble amongst themselves, notably at Carnival time when, dressed in animal hides, and disguised as wolves and bears, they spread terror around them, bursting into houses, pawing the girls and jostling the women according to long-established rituals of wild abandon, the distant survivals of age-old traditions. But such adolescent sports already herald the feast days.

Among these young people's societies, special consideration must be given to student groups, to the assemblies of merry schoolboys, the heirs of the medieval 'nations' or merely gatherings of young people who frequented the same college or lodging-house. These professional associations, in which young men and adolescents mingled, were institutions for both work and play. They certainly played an important part in university towns, but one which was comparable enough to the ordinary youth society.

However, these merry 'abbeys' were not simply gatherings of young people in search of noisy entertainments on the occasion of feast days, receptions and other solemnities.[2] In certain provinces at least—notably in Savoy—they helped to spread the Reformation. Was this due to the shrewdness of the early Protestants, who infiltrated these youth groups to spread the faith, or to a conflict between generations, which produced Catholic fathers and Protestant sons? Certainly, Protestants sometimes so successfully took control that the societies were formally banned. In 1538, François I ordered 'that henceforth in this and neighbouring lands . . . whether in the guise of the abbeys that the young people of towns and villages are wont to form, or in respect of any fraternities or otherwise, there shall be no gatherings, companies or congregations; which abbeys and fraternities . . . we hereby abolish and suppress. . . .'[3] The tradition of youth societies was not to be suppressed so easily. It survived all condemnations and prohibitions until the Revolution, when conscription gave it both a new lease of life and definition by age groups and recruitment boards. But associations of conscripts did not flourish as the former abbeys had done; like the feast days, they gradually lost ground from then until the present day.

Feast days

In the sixteenth and seventeenth centuries, feast days were firm manifestations

[2] Gargantua's Abbey of Thélème is surely an idealized youth 'abbey'.

[3] *Bulletin de la société du protestantisme français* XLIII (1894), p. 594. Cf. also Herminjard, *Correspondance des réformateurs dans les pays de langue française* . . . (Geneva 1866–97), IV, pp. 33, 34, 52.

of solidarity, and the community gatherings which punctuated urban and rural life had a vitality we find difficult to imagine today. They were, in effect, a kind of momentary escape, a paroxysm of life among a gathering of people freed for a few hours or days from the work and cares of every day. It was a time for elation, which found expression in noise and exuberant activity, singing and dancing, and readily ended in orgy and violence. As a legitimate excuse for all kinds of excesses, for conduct and actions normally forbidden, the feast day unveiled a world without constraint, in which the myth of the Golden Age and of Chaos was revived, though doubtless only in the group subconscious, and despite christianization. These festivities, which opened to everyone the gates of a different world, were occasions for unusually close contact with the rest of the group. They left lasting memories, and were often recalled later, in everyday life, as good times never to be forgotten.

Spread over the whole year according to a great variety of calendars, the feast days varied somewhat in their pattern and themes, though the important, well-known feasts of the Holy Innocents and St John were doubtless celebrated everywhere. But in accordance with local dedications and traditions, considerable latitude prevailed in each region. Even the most modest of fairs would invariably end with some festivity or ball held in the same great square where the commercial business had been transacted. The patron saints of the parish and of fraternities and guilds added their own ceremonies to the calendar, when a mass of thanksgiving was followed by entertainments organized by the parishioners or members of the fraternity. But whether it was a parish festival or a weavers' festival, the celebrations were open to inhabitants of neighbouring villages and journeymen from other trades.

The exuberance of some of the principal solemn feast days is well known. The Feast of the Holy Innocents, in January, gave rise to downright eccentricities in some towns. At Tournay, the choirboys and the cathedral vicars chose a Fools' Bishop, led him to the tavern where he was baptized with buckets of water, and then paraded him through the streets escorted by torchbearers and the vicars in fancy dress. The masquerade lasted two or three days. For the Feast of the Ass, the day of the Adoration of the Magi, *soule* was played and there was dancing and singing in the church nave. The Feast of Fools was celebrated even in religious communities. The Cordeliers of Antibes, as Naudé tells us, invariably marked the occasion:

> Neither the priests nor the guardian go into the choir that day. Their places in church are taken by the lay brothers, the menial brothers who collect alms, those who work in the kitchen, the scullery lads, and those who tend the garden. They put on any old torn vestments they can find and wear them inside out. They hold their books back to front and upside down, and pretend to read them with glasses whose lenses they have removed and replaced with orange peel. In this attire, they sing neither

> the usual hymns nor psalms nor masses, but mumble certain jumbled words and shout. . . .[4]

Fancy dress and masquerades were also a prominent feature of such celebrations. Not only during Carnival time but on many other occasions individuals or groups changed their appearance with masks, make-up and animal hides to portray saints or demons: in December, St Nicholas in his priestly garb; St Lucy in the guise of a she-goat; or the werewolves which reappeared on certain winter nights, notably between Christmas and Epiphany—the same nights when the Sabbath assembled sorcerers and witches around Satan in some remote clearing in the forest, far from the village.

Finally, it is certain that many of these feast days represented in part a survival of old pagan beliefs and practices which had managed to persist in the guise of Christian ceremony. This was undoubtedly true of the bonfires on Midsummer's Day, and indeed of the custom of *Aguilanneuf*, which survived throughout the seventeenth century in the Angers diocese, despite being repeatedly forbidden by the Synods. In the long term, the christianization of pagan rites was profitable. In the case of the New Year mistletoe, the young people were reproached above all, in 1595, with spending the money which the collections brought in 'for banqueting, drunkenness and other debauchery'. But since the memory of the distant origins of these practices persisted, from the end of the Middle Ages ecclesiastical authorities were concerned to purify these feast days, to forbid them access to the churches—or indeed to abolish them altogether. As early as 1444, the University of Paris demanded the suppression of the Festival of Fools. 'The Feast of the Subdeacons, or Fools, was a relic of paganism, a damnable and pernicious corruption, which tended towards open contempt of God, of divine services and episocopal dignity. And those who observed it were imitating pagans and violating the canons of the Councils.' After the attacks launched by the Protestants, the Council of Trent stepped up this process. Even before the Council's decrees reached France, revised synodal statutes and provincial councils introduced many more prohibitions, forbidding the Carnival masquerades, the Feast of Fools and the holding of balls, theatrical performances and games on Sundays and religious festivals.[5]

This purification achieved by what is usually called the Counter-Reformation above all modified such festivities as took place in church, and reduced the number and the exuberance of these annual celebrations. In both town and countryside, feast days remained none the less moments of fraternal and collective liberation necessary to the life of the community, fleeting moments of effective solidarity in joy, after which the heavy burdens of everyday life again took control of hearts and minds.

[4] Quoted in Thiers (254), p. 450.

[5] Notably the provincial councils of Bordeaux (1583), Tours (1583), Rheims (1583), Bourges (1584) and Aix (1585).

Conclusion to Part II

In concluding this examination of the social categories in which the modern Frenchman found himself involved, we wish to stress once more the importance of collective constraints. From childhood, a French boy born in 1510 or 1603 not only came under the formative influence of the nuclear family, which today strives essentially to avoid making its authority felt; he was also subject to an extended family circle, where the experience of his grandparents counted for at least as much as that of his immediate elders. Later, whatever his calling—from a military career for the young nobleman to the most routine trade or craft—his apprenticeship was a lengthy initiation into a way of life and social relationships which were to play a decisive role in his existence. There is no doubt that this professional training was hard and exacting. We are familiar with the laments of apprentice humanists like Rabelais and Montaigne, because they could readily express themselves; but we are not so well informed on apprenticeships in the manual trades. However, the *livres de raison* sometimes reveal worried fathers who were anxious to find for their children a master whose methods were not too harsh—a rarity at this time. A few years later, our subject, now a man, became a member of a guild or a village community, a parishioner, the villein of some lord, or a bourgeois of a free town; and also a subject of the king of France. It is pointless to dwell at length upon the fiscal and spiritual constraints implied by these manifold dependencies.

It is equally certain that, from childhood, by means of the family circle the whole gamut of social requirements was imposed upon him, through the accepted notions, taboos and prescriptions hallowed by tradition. In the evenings, the sleepy child heard from his grandmother stories of the fantastic misdeeds of Merlin the Wizard, and of how the Prince of Hell rode the world. From his earliest years, he learned the *Benedicite* which his father said before breaking bread, and could recognize all the mythical values attached to this important act. The social order was imposed upon him through the thousand and one features of an upbringing which did not have much in common with that given to twentieth-century children, but still comprised its prescriptions and taboos.

The counterpart of such constraint lies entirely in the existence of 'forces for solidarity', under which heading we have placed the whole social environment. We are certainly very much alive to the weight of these manifold social categories, and to the aggressiveness they encouraged. A citizen enters into the life of his town in as many different ways today as at that period, and possibly in more ways, but has the impression of doing so in complete freedom, even when he is content to conform to some family or professional tradition. For the sixteenth century Frenchman, this was not the case; collective life was essential to him at each moment of his existence, every day of his life. Thus the constraint was less of a burden to him than we might believe, for he was in the first place aware of the mutual aid involved in belonging to a group, corporation, parish, town or youth society. This awareness derived from reasons which varied, of course, from group to group, and this is the point that must be stressed at the end of this section of our work. For the peasantry, cooperation was an integral part of their job, of joint enterprise. The gatherings of the nobility for a hunt or tournament stemmed from class feelings which actuated the petty squires as well as Henri III's courtiers. The meetings of the fraternities, which were at once religious and corporative gatherings, when, after a mass and procession, relief was distributed to unemployed journeymen, comprised another form of mutual assistance, more complex than a simple Friendly Society.

The modern social groupings, both stable and unstable, thus formed the basic elements of a full collective life in which each personality was formed and asserted itself. The recluse in his ivory tower could not be imagined at a time when everyone was well aware that he was caught up in and determined by the options of his group. This is obviously true of the dissenters of all kinds—the Protestants of the Cévennes and of Brie, or the *noblesse de robe* which broke away from the bourgoisie in the time of Henri IV and Louis XIII. It was also true wherever group conformity reigned uncontested—at court, in town, at the château or in the village assembly. The social categories provided the essential groundplan of the age, as a study of the different types of activity will prove once again, if further proof be necessary. The pattern they make up constantly overlaps with the one already revealed by our study of the social groups.

Part III
Forms of activity

The third stage of this systematic inquiry into the major components of the modern mentality is devoted to the various activities or occupations which day by day absorbed most of human life, and left a deep imprint on heart and mind. Hence, this section is no doubt the most important, and equally the most complex, so vital is it to consider fully all the different forms of activity. To this end, it is necessary to divide up, for clarity's sake at least, features which were often combined in the same man: everyone had a main everyday occupation—and at the same time practised some form of religion; and on Sunday afternoon, everyone sought pleasure in innocent sports or pastimes. The bourgeois who hung a handsome oil-painting of his father over the dresser in his living-room, and the artisan who liked to admire in his workshop one of the early biblical illustrations which wood-engraving made available in France from the fifteenth century onwards, were both in a sense artists—as consumers. To examine human activities thus means both taking account of the complexities which are inevitable in any personality, and picking out the main types, with regard to normal practice (thus in the religious sphere we shall treat separately the clergy and the mere faithful), professions, major occupations and preoccupations, by comparison with which hobbies are of less interest. For example, under the heading of sports and pastimes, we shall have to distinguish between the Sunday recreation of the vast majority and the daily diversions of those who could do nothing other than amuse themselves for fear of derogation.

Thus our treatment of this aspect of the modern period would seem to fall under three headings, corresponding to different attitudes of mind. The first comprises the routine professional activities and occupations on the most humdrum level of existence: the manual trades, positions in the world of small-scale and international trade, the sports and pastimes of the taverns and gaming-houses, or the great hunting expeditions. Already three types of men are involved, to which the humanists gave the fine sounding Latin names of *homo faber*, *homo lucrans*, *homo ludens*. Then on a higher plane than these everyday activities—by virtue of the accepted notions of the period—lay cultural and spiritual activities, a field which was so vast and fruitful in the sixteenth century. Artists, humanists, scholars and philosophers had certainly not remained anonymous in France before the Renaissance, but the Middle Ages never ascribed to them the importance they acquired at this period. Artists and humanists took their place alongside—and on equal terms with—the clergy in promoting spiritual life; for the intelligentsia became more numerous and more diverse, and likewise grew in social standing, a factor which was not without influence on this universally accepted hierarchy of occupations.

Finally, in a different vein from either routine occupations or the world of culture there are the escapist pursuits of those who in one way or another rejected the world in which they lived and the place they had been given in it: the real or imaginary voyages of men obsessed with unknown and attractive new worlds, or of those who haunted the forest glades in search of the witches' sabbath; the easy dreams of the drunkard in the tavern; and, lastly, the leap into the beyond of those who gave up: the most extreme form of such rejections was, of course, suicide, which was condemned by both God and man.

Does such an analysis exhaust the field of human activities? As far as its general categories are concerned, it undoubtedly does. But it certainly does not cover the infinite variety of occupations and the characters that these moulded. However, given the material at present available, a detailed examination of the subject is inconceivable for such distant times.[1]

[1] No collective psychology of man at work has yet appeared. Such works might well be undertaken on an experimental basis for our own period. They would be of immense help to historians studying the attitudes of former times.

Chapter 10
Routine activities: manual techniques

It may seem dangerous to class all manual workers together under the same heading. The peasant who each morning scanned the heavens, sniffed the fresh air and made contact with nature, and the artisan crouched over his bench in his dusty shop seem so very different. However, this classification is reasonably justifiable if one considers not so much their surroundings as their actual working conditions. In both cases the basis was collective organization. In the fields, as in the workshops, a few men and women worked together and passed on their methods to their successors—their children or their apprentices. Secondly, with the exception of mills, equipment consisted essentially of hand tools, of implements which acted as an extension of the hand ensuring its efficiency as an instrument of work adopted for the job, without there being any difference in structure between the tools of the peasant (e.g. the flail) and of the journeyman (e.g. the cobbler's knife). Finally, the versatility of the peasantry, which made many of its own implements during the winter's leisure, lends further support to the argument. Each peasant acted as mason, carpenter and joiner. Each village had its peasant artisans—weavers, blacksmiths, cartwrights and curriers—who continued to work a few plots of land while supplying their neighbours with the products of their workshops, often for payment in kind. This was the 'agricultural industry', to use the expression still current at the beginning of the nineteenth century.[1] No doubt, these three factors would not have carried the same weight at the end of the seventeenth century, once the factory system had regrouped artisans in large workshops, bringing dozens of journeymen into daily contact, setting up chains of manual production, and creating a new type of working man. At the beginning of the seventeenth century, the factory system was of virtually no consequence.

However, one feature which was common to all the manual trades, and which forms the strongest justification for our grouping them in this way, was the empirical nature of technical progress. Change in this sector was so largely

[1] Abel Hugo in *La France pittoresque* (1835) contrasted agricultural industry and commercial industry.

restricted to minor improvements to detail that stagnation appears to have been the general rule. In this respect the modern period prolonged without any appreciable change the fruitful tradition of the Middle Ages. Here again three factors were decisive.

Working conditions rested upon manual skill backed by the craftsman's capacity for observation and experiment. New inventions were invariably the work of the craftsman, and were quite unconnected with scientific speculation. The most complicated instruments that were produced, the clock movements of the automatons which had aroused such great enthusiasm in the medieval towns, show the degree of refinement which his ingenuity had been able to attain. But in fact, few tools were machines in the modern sense, working independently under the supervision of the workman. The predominance of this empirical approach is most clearly revealed by the apprenticeship, a lengthy process whatever the trade, since it called for the patience to learn the many physical skills. It meant mastering tools which the more primitive they were made the greater demand on the user.

The artisan's 'craft' thus saw its importance emphasized by the absence of highly productive sources of energy. Windmills tapped an unreliable force, and only for milling. Watermills, which were dotted along rivers and even brooks, could indeed turn millstones and work hammers; but their field of application remained limited because their water-power was ill-domesticated, despite the headraces and dams which more or less compensated for drought, though not for frost. On the other hand, the only source of the fuel required by blacksmiths, glassmakers and potters was the forests, where small furnaces, foundries and forges were established, as in the Jura, the Langres plateau and throughout Normandy. Thus, at the end of the sixteenth century, there were constant complaints throughout France about the shortage of wood.[2] In consequence, though improvements had been made in their manufacturing processes, the metal industries were incapable of large-scale production. This is undoubtedly the main reason why the use of metal tools remained restricted—and why the development of the tool into the machine was impossible. Everywhere, wood remained the basic raw material *par excellence*, certainly for the peasant's implements, including spades, harrows and rakes, which were hardened by fire. But many other spheres of operation had equally to manage without metal parts: Monconys, while visiting London in the mid-seventeenth century, notes that all the carriage wheels were made of wood, and did not have iron felloes.

Finally, the manual occupations formed the lower grade in the hierarchy of professional activities.[3] Despite the attention given to the 'mechanical trades' and

[2] In 1610 Claude Caire, the general manager of the Minières de France, claimed to have a secret process for ovens and furnaces which allowed the saving of about half the wood 'that the bakers, pastry-cooks, dyers and brewers normally burnt'.

[3] Artisans and farm-workers 'are considered base persons,' said Loyseau in 1613.

their progress by some 'masters' in various guilds, and despite the predilection of certain religious orders like the Cistercians for manual work,[4] such activity was nevertheless treated with humiliating contempt. On the one hand, aristocratic prejudice no doubt implied the inferiority of those who had to work with their hands to support themselves; on the other, the humanists—doubtless influenced by the same deep-rooted prejudice—gave a favourable reception to the writings of antiquity, by Aristotle and others, which asserted that work was for the slave and relegated anyone who engaged in it to the lowest rank in society. Equally they welcomed such writings as separated science from mechanical skill. Thus the manual occupations were unable to attract the interest even of people like the noblemen who benefited by some of them. The isolation of the mechanical trades and their lack of contact with the scientist in the age when Leonardo da Vinci was filling whole notebooks with designs for machines, none of which was ever built, is all too obvious.

All these circumstances combined meant that manual workers led a hidebound existence, confined within a basic empiricism which nevertheless allowed of some fine achievements. A smith could make a bombard as well as a straightforward wrought-iron gate. It was common to see the *échevins* ordering their artillery from the town's artisans, the same workshops producing both arms and ammunition. But the important fact here is that progress in the manual sector was sporadic and confined to improvements to detail, and tips, whose diffusion depended upon the random expeditions of journeymen, or the seasonal migrations which were the rule in some jobs. This technical stagnation was, psychologically speaking, highly significant. It revealed itself in a close dependence upon practices handed down from generation to generation, and severe restraint in imitating styles and methods. From a psychological viewpoint, this restraint was responsible for an endless routine, making up a closed world of forms and rules, whatever may have been in other respects the joy derived from the masterpiece or from the finish achieved on some patiently-wrought article.

However, if it is true that manual work in general, dominated as it was by the strict constraint of a routine which changed slowly and imperceptibly, produced men whose lives were bounded by the very horizons of their trade, one ought still to draw a distinction between the peasant artisan of the countryside and the town artisan. Both were slaves to these traditional practices, but as regards innovation, agriculture seems to have been even more handicapped than the town crafts. One has only to think how slowly the plants from the New World were adapted, between the sixteenth and the eighteenth centuries, and compare this with the spread of printing in the fifteenth and sixteenth centuries.

[4] In the sixteenth century, the monk 'shunned by and shunning the world' and concerned mainly with contemplation was not held in good odour: cf. Rabelais. But the regular clergy as a whole was then discredited.

Peasant methods

'Country lore' would seem to have been the most rigid of all restrictive forces, making the 'poor people of the fields'—the vast majority of the French—into a kind of agricultural robot. This rigidity stemmed, in our view, from three main causes.

Work on the land was always carried out jointly,[5] hence obedience to the rule of the group was total and inescapable. This communal life displayed several forms of constraint, which were cumulative in their effect. The division of the farm-land into strips, and compulsory participation in the common scheme, removed all scope for initiative in the choice of crop rotation. Only the kitchen garden at home offered the peasant the opportunity for such experiments, though only on a small scale and without any means of generally extending the experiment until he had first convinced the whole community. The poor results obtained by their implements—the swing-plough, the sickle and the flail—as well as the lack of sufficient livestock necessitated the cooperation between farmers which tradition had hallowed for centuries. Thus all the routine operations, from the sowing to the corn and grape harvests, were performed in accordance with an immutable norm: the height of the cocks, the use to be made of the seed, the maintenance of equipment—nothing could escape it. Moreover, to make this collective constraint complete, the stability of the joint family helped to strengthen tradition with the prestige enjoyed by family elders. Parents—and especially grandparents—instilled in the young peasant a respect for tried methods and the correct use of his implements, as well as a knowledge of men. Agricultural methods were thus of necessity absolutely stereotyped, since they were based upon empirical ancestral knowledge of the soil, plants and animals, and were handed down in a most rigid fashion from generation to generation.

In a sense the seignorial regime contributed to this technical stagnation. The great advance made by the Middle Ages—the use of hydraulic power—had been skilfully monopolized by the nobility. This they had achieved by virtue of owning the rivers or merely by building the mills, fulling-mills and presses with the help of the forced labour of their peasants; for such schemes were clearly beyond the means of the small farmer, even if they did not call for participation by a whole community. The lords thus 'banalized' this equipment. Increases in *banalités*, and the heavy burden of dues in kind attached to these services[6] inevitably encouraged the preservation and use by families of equipment which was more ancient, but was owned by the individual and thus escaped taxation by the lord: one can think, for example, of such items as mortars for crushing grain, and hand-presses.

[5] Except for the vine, for part of its annual cycle.

[6] Not to mention fraudulent levies: Gouberville does not hide his mistrust of the miller, and had his corn ground in his presence.

Lastly, having to contend with changeable weather conditions and haunted by fear of the different calamities which could come year after year to endanger the crops, the peasantry warded off these threats by observing what amounted to agricultural rites, which combined unerring empirical observation of the local micro-climate with an enormous number of superstitions in the form of predictions (such as, 'if it thunders in April, prepare your casks') and religious rites of conjuration, with processions, prayers and masses designed to help bring rain or sunshine, and to prevent frost and thunderstorms. This anxious watch upon the heavens and submission to the seasons contrives to give to their daily life an appearance of unrelieved constraint.[7] Ill-equipped to achieve mastery over nature, the most difficult technique of all, the peasant of those times thus found himself subjected to a very heavy burden of tradition.

Evidence of his dependence is to be found on all sides. The early almanacs[8] from the seventeenth century, like the one from Troyes, give us the repertoire, month by month, of prescriptions and obligations. When the first enlightened amateurs came to publish their 'Theatres of Agriculture' in the early seventeenth century, they inevitably gave considerable attention to this lore, and preserved both the good advice ('to make good butter, use only the cleanest utensils') and the most dubious practices ('if the butter takes a long time to set in the churn, put in a piece of silver'). Similarly there are the many precepts given in the *livres de raison*.

No doubt during the winter months, when the wood had been cut and the threshing done, the peasant became a carpenter, mason, weaver or potter. But this additional activity with its equally straightforward techniques did not really lessen his dependence, for many of these secondary tasks which complemented his agricultural work (everything to do with the maintenance of his house or equipment) were carried out solely with the village community in mind, and formed yet another piece of routine. To encounter a different type of manual worker, one must turn one's attention to the town and examine the artisan in his workshop.

The urban crafts

The town artisans were subject to fewer constraining influences than the peasantry. Though hampered by drought and frost, they were not decisively affected by climatic changes. Only the corporations of masters, which codified the careers of apprentices and journeymen and regulated production and marketing,

[7] To a certain extent, this constraint also accounts for the zeal for litigation displayed by countrymen, referred to in the often-quoted saying: 'There is not a *journal* of land in France which is not brought before the courts and disputed once a year.'

[8] The best known is no doubt *Le grant kalendrier et compost des Bergiers avec leur astrologie, et plusieurs aultres choses*, published at Troyes by Nicolas Le Rouge, n.d. (in fact 1529), of which a new edition appeared in Paris in 1925.

played a role roughly similar to that of the peasant community. Thus it is easy to establish that the tools of the smith or the weaver scarcely changed from the end of the Middle Ages to the eighteenth century. But access to the wider markets of international trade gave urban craftsmen greater scope for initiative. The best illustration of this is the opening of the first factories in the sixteenth and seventeenth centuries.

At the end of the fifteenth century, the town artisans worked either in small family workshops, which gathered at most about ten journeymen and apprentices around a master-craftsman, or at home, to the order of manufacturers who sometimes provided some of their equipment. The former system was used for metal work and trades using fire, while the cloth trade was better suited to the latter. Moreover, both shops and cottage industry perpetuated, with the same rigidity, the technical processes handed down from journeymen to apprentices on the shop floor.

No doubt this rigidity was not absolute. Progress in marketing in the sixteenth century encouraged the building of new looms, in the cloth trade especially, where cloth and silk merchants organized production networks to their advantage and helped to spread technical processes. The latter sometimes imported from abroad, in particular from Italy. A cloth merchant made his fortune the day he introduced some minor technical innovation—a new width of cloth or a dyeing or bleaching process. This happened to the Danse family from Beauvais[9] in the seventeenth century. Even in the cloth trade, where innovation seems to have been easier, the invention of a new tool was an achievement which it was proposed to protect at the end of the sixteenth century by regulations heralding the modern letters patent.[10]

But it was printing (not to mention the other new industries such as gunpowder etc.) which caused a certain amount of upheaval in this system in the fifteenth and sixteenth centuries, by introducing out of technical necessity a workshop where the various processes were linked in the right order, using a whole range of expensive equipment, from the preparation of the type to the binding of the printed book. Each printer thus directed a chain of production, whereas the traditional crafts entrusted the manufacture of a wheelbarrow, a saddle or a piece of cloth to a single workman.

Modelled on these workshops, the first factories, set up notably in the cloth trade, comprised the regrouping by bold entrepreneurs of artisans belonging to different trades (basically spinners, weavers and dyers) within a single shop. The trades involved were brought together but in no way changed their methods.

[9] Cf. the monograph by P. Goubert, *Familles de marchands de Beauvais sous l'Ancien Régime* (Paris 1958), pp. 45–8.

[10] The few historians who have worked in this largely neglected field do not have much to offer on working methods: no doubt scope for initiative varied according to the nature of the craft in question (glassblowers, curriers, potters, tapestry-weavers, dyers, etc.).

The advantage lay in the coordination of processes and the concentration of successive operations under the same roof. But until the arrival of new sources of power—in other words, until steam began to be used in the nineteenth century—working methods did not undergo any fundamental change.[11] The horizontal concentration of artisan industry was not a factor of technical progress, but primarily a commercial operation.

Certainly, the diffusion of skills and technical processes which, ever since the high Middle Ages, had been the work of migrant craftsmen who took them from town to town, heedless of frontiers, was restricted and impeded wherever factories were established. The latter brought with them industrial secrecy, which for a long time applied to details such as the composition of dyes. Montchrestien, who extolled the factory system, also saw in it the advantage of training labour more efficiently.

Nevertheless, the urban crafts did have a window open on the business world, which afforded their masters and journeymen active participation in economic developments. It is indeed most remarkable that access to new markets in the sixteenth century and an increasing influx of orders did not prove the stimulus to technical progress one might have expected. The increased demand for linen and cloth meant building more looms, engaging extra journeymen—and, above all, a rise in prices. The 'laws of market economy' could operate all the more easily because artisan production had practically no technological flexibility. To put it the other way round, the price increases in the sixteenth century bear witness by their severity to the absence of technical flexibility in the artisan sector.[12]

Nevertheless, what the great economic stimulus of the sixteenth century as a whole did provide in these trades (which in practice worked to order—day-to-day sales from the shop being insignificant, even in the cloth trade) was the opportunity for substantial profits, which were more often hoarded or spent on consumer goods than reinvested. For journeymen, an increase in wages accompanied, with some delay, the financial consolidation of their masters and the first manufacturers. But here again we encounter, and this time in the professional context, the very marked contrast which existed at that period between town and country.

Thus technical stagnation is ultimately the dominant feature of all the manual trades: to ply them—irrespective of one's specialization—was to submit to a whole code of practices strictly laid down by guild custom, and to be bound

[11] Thus, a factory could be moved without great expense. When Montchrestien, a native of Rouen, was sent to Châtillon-sur-Loire by the king, he moved his knife, lancet and scissor factory there.

[12] The only answer of the artisan to increased demand was to build new units. In the Conflent, the number of forges and sawmills doubled in the sixteenth century. This method had its limitations.

by a stringent unwritten law. The manual skills taught to apprentices over a period of several years are the best illustration of this. It was impossible to be a good journeyman without this training of hand and eye, which was achieved through imitation of one's elders. Finally, even for many of these people, such absolute submission to the trade tended to suggest the 'stamp of servility', to judge from the hostile contempt in which manual workers in the towns were held from the fourteenth century onwards.

Chapter 11
Routine activities: money and the capitalist spirit

The men whose livelihood was money—that small group, which prepared and foreshadowed the most brilliant achievements of the eighteenth and nineteenth centuries and was endowed with an outlook which was largely new—is not an easy subject for study. Contemporaries were still too attached to the medieval centres of interest and consequently were far more heedful of the lavish displays of the nobility and the religious life than of the fortunes of bankers and merchants. Thus the vocabulary was lacking, and its absence is too obvious to escape mention. Neither 'capitalism,' the twentieth-century term, nor 'capitalist', which appeared in the eighteenth century, could help in defining the new notions created by the growth of movable wealth. During the sixteenth and seventeenth centuries, the concrete terms alone gradually became more clearly defined: in 1595, Henri IV created exchange brokers, who in 1639 became *agents de banque et de change*, and in 1723 received their present title of *agents de change*. Similarly, *actions* (shares) *billets de banque* (banknotes), *valeurs* (securities) and capital slowly made their appearance, passing from the realm of specialist vocabulary—in other words from business documents—into general use. Moreover, another sign of how slow the ordinary mentality was to adapt can be observed in the way in which the idea of wealth remained at the time essentially connected with land, with real wealth. No doubt this was partly because it was a source of income or natural produce; but the main reason was that it gave power over men, and thereby secured a position in society. There is not one example of a sixteenth-century banker or merchant who was not concerned to convert at least part of the fortune he had amassed in overseas trade into land. It was not simply a case of lack of interest but rather one of positive mistrust: a whole series of accepted notions and a general hostility based upon a strong religious tradition, still worked to promote such an attitude at the time when the treasures of America gave European commerce an unprecedented stimulus.

It is therefore essentially in the commercial and banking achievements of the period that we must look for signs of this new outlook; it had not yet had time to become established as a school of thought, to mould the average mentality and instil into it its concepts. Quite the reverse: it would seem to have been in some respects inhibited and thwarted by the curbs which deep-rooted traditional attitudes brought to bear upon it. To make a fortune by buying spices in Lisbon and reselling them in Rouen or Paris was a normal commercial achievement. But to invest this money in purchasing a château which had been heavily mortgaged by its noble owner was to submit to just such a pre-capitalistic temptation. Similarly, another curb can be seen in the familiar pattern whereby a generation of 'entrepreneurs', international merchants well-placed in Medina del Campo, Seville or Lyons, were succeeded by sons who renounced trade and its handsome profits and were content to devour the accumulated wealth. Nor is it a sign of the capitalist spirit to earn money to hoard, to collect silver and gold coins. To a capitalist, making money is only meaningful for the purpose of immediately reinvesting his returns to make them yield further profit, without delay, if not without risk. Wealth creates more wealth with the accumulation of capital constantly providing new incentive to his spirit of enterprise.

Such concepts as these certainly do not date from the sixteenth century: it was the 'price revolution' which helped to spread them. A remarkable example of how slowly attitudes change, the restraints largely counterbalanced the stimulus given to capitalist initiative by the rapid expansion of trade. For one work like the *Discours œconomique* of M. Le Choyselat, 'showing how from a single investment of five hundred *livres* one can make a fair annual profit of four thousand, five hundred *livres*'[1] and expressing a completely modern capitalist spirit, many more were mere treatises on traditional domanial economy, praising the safe profits of ground rent. However, it should be stressed that the distinction between movable and immovable wealth is a good criterion, provided one realizes that profits from land were not negligible. But reinvestment in land, which would denote the accumulation of profits and capitalism, was all the more difficult because the social and technical structures were opposed to it, as we have just seen.

Signs of mistrust and anomalies

The growth of international trade would have been impossible without trust in the plighted word, in the letter or bill passed on by an agent. Mentally this was a new world, in the face of which the old securities of economic self-sufficiency continually upheld their superiority as values which were universally recognized

[1] The formula is simple and quite remarkable: rent a house, a cattle-shed and a few acres of land near Paris, and build some hen-houses; buy 1,200 hens and 120 cockerels (at a cost of 348 *livres*); the 1,200 hens produce 800 eggs a day, to be sold in Paris with the help of hucksters and doctors. At 6 *deniers* each, the gross receipts would be 7,300 *livres* per year or, minus expenses, 4,500 *livres*. Moreover, the big problem in the eyes of the author was not that of obtaining 800 eggs per day, but of finding the retailers and doctors who would provide the right addresses to guarantee this rapid disposal of the goods.

and everywhere accepted. To give a wedding present or make an endowment in kind remained a common practice in all classes of society. For example, at Toulon in the mid-sixteenth century, a nobleman settled on his youngest son, who was destined for the clergy, a strip of garden, a vineyard, a small olive-grove for his oil, and a dilapidated house which the eldest brother was to renovate. The father's will had provided in every way for making his son a recluse.[2] Charity was dispensed in the same way: the compassionate bourgeois took the pauper into his own home and fed, clothed and supported him, sometimes until his death. Such practices are by implication an expression of repugnance at the regular handling of cash, the basis of commerce.[3]

The same seems to be true of the practice of using a lawyer to deal with any important economic transaction. Even the bourgeois, who kept his *livre de raison* and had a good knowledge of the law and statutes, did not dispense with a lawyer. Obviously he called upon him to make a will; but equally he resorted to him if he wanted to buy a pair of mules or to engage a servant, and his doing so reflects a certain prudent timidity with regard to business transactions, the gateway to a dangerous and insecure world.

The frequency with which the *livres de raison* express astonishment at the great and rapid fluctuations in prices is yet another indication of the same phenomenon. Speculators in foodstuffs took advantage of the least break in the weather with an audacity which quite rightly caused concern. 'In Holy Week (1538),' writes a bourgeois of Paris, 'the North wind blew so strong and cold that it completely froze the vines, which were already well advanced . . . whereupon wine worth only 8 francs a *queue* was sold the next day for 15, and soon after for 20.'

Assuredly, it might be thought that these many signs of repugnance with regard to commercial life were the work of the only groups remaining attached to the primitive practices of exchanging goods and services: in other words, by and large, peasants and landowners. That they were displayed by townsmen and, in the last analysis, by all social classes shows that there is something more in this than the actual predominance of a localized exchange economy upon which the vital forces of world economy were able to make only a slight impact.

But to force of habit were added certain prejudices against commercial life which were religious in origin: the rich man is condemned by the Gospel.[4] In particular, for centuries, since the revival of trade in Europe, theologians had

[2] C. de Ribbe, *La Société provençale à la fin du moyen âge* (Paris 1898), p. 151.

[3] The *livre de raison* of Fazy de Rame (44), a lesser nobleman and native of Embrun, is one long example of the worries associated with the handling of cash at the beginning of the sixteenth century.

[4] Everyone knows the gloss: 'By expelling from the Temple those who were buying and selling, Our Lord indicated clearly that the merchant can rarely, if ever, be pleasing to God.'

persisted in condemning the loan at interest. *Pecunia pecuniam non parit* was the current maxim, which covered many a more violent formula, as for example: 'Not only ordinary laymen, but clerics and even doctors of divinity defile themselves with so flagrant a vice, and in their blindness shamelessly excuse and defend loathsome usury.'

St Thomas had already sought a compromise by recommending that commercial activities should be pursued only in moderation, by restricting the merchant's profit to what was necessary for the upkeep of his household and for almsgiving, and by authorizing the loan at interest in so far as the interest was justified by the actual injustice caused to the creditor. But the theologians' maxims and complaints, peppered with biblical quotations,[5] did not prevent the practice of lending money at exorbitant rates of interest, in other words usury, from being a common one. This was one of the main sources of wealth in the sixteenth and seventeenth centuries, enriching the lord who loaned a barrel of corn to one of his peasants after a bad crop no less than the bourgeois who sought good investments for his capital. Thus in 1559–60 we find the *échevins* of Amiens refusing two Piedmont bankers the right to set up in the town and 'lend and advance money and finance for some fair gain and reasonable profit'. Such alarming competition might have reduced the profits of the more wealthy bourgeois in the town.

Thus moneylending was unauthorized[6] but was practised on a large scale.[7] The occupation of merchant continued to be discredited on basically religious grounds, even though the merchants formed the economic and social backbone of urban life. In this respect, the beginnings of the modern period brought scarely any change, for the forces hostile to capitalism were indeed still very much alive. After the economic growth in the sixteenth century had promoted movable wealth to an unprecedented degree, the religious revival between 1580 and 1640 took place largely at the instance of the different branches of the Franciscan order—Cordeliers, Capuchins, Minims, and the order of St Clare—which glorified poverty, the old ideal of St Francis of Assisi, the merchant who renounced trade and riches. Reawakening the scruples of the rich, encouraging donations and religious foundations, the disciples of St Francis upheld the ideal tradition of a Church made by and for the poor, who were satisfied with their daily bread.

[5] In particular *Exodus* XXII, 25; *Leviticus* XXV, 35; *Deuteronomy* XXIII, 19.

[6] In French law, the first official authorization of interest is the law of 12 October 1789.

[7] It is difficult to distinguish between cases where it was practised unscrupulously, those where it was practised with the permission of the Church (*damnum emergens*), and finally, those where it was evaded in a purely formalistic manner, as in the case of royal usury by the creation of *rentes*. De Roover is quite right when he says of the exchange contracts studied by Scholastic theologians in the sixteenth century: 'The quibbles ill succeed in concealing the weakness of a system of classification which, basically, rests only on sophisms and contradictions.'

Capitalist methods

In reconstructing the life of the contemporary merchant, who was a great lover of travel, and of the risks he took, one is certainly presented overall with a marked contrast to, say, the life of the peasantry. It is very interesting to follow him from one market-place to another, to watch him coming to terms with a banker over a disputed bill of exchange, struggling to transport 1,500 *livres* by cart to make some urgent settlement, or negotiating a *rente sur l'hôtel de ville* in his own town. But it can also be misleading.[8] For many pitfalls await anyone who attempts to define a given turn of mind. Thus the desire for gain is no explanation, for it was not peculiar to that period when such enormous profits were so common. To judge from certain ordinances which attack foreign financial adventurers, Italian or German bankers, the picture risks being coloured by dubious religious or political shades: Jews and Protestants, we are told, were not bound by the usual scruples. The splendour of international trade also introduces us to the cosmopolitan world of merchants who were united by the countless successes of their manifold operations at Seville, Antwerp, Augsburg and Genoa. These vast European networks of many-sided business relationships, the powerful solidarities and rivalries of their agents and subsidiaries, represent the triumphant aspect of the new capitalism. But this was the *avant-garde*, the 'pole of development' which cannot be understood without reference to more ordinary enterprises and attitudes.

Bankers and moneychangers, specialists in the money trade and in bills of exchange, form a first type of businessman—though they were not necessarily distinguishable from dealers in merchandise. Every merchant could weigh a coin in his hand, assay it or even clip it. But the former were experts in the techniques of exchange, skills which were all the more indispensable in that the capital market remained somewhat restricted. These bankers had to have reliable connections in all the European centres: to lack a correspondent in Constantinople or Venice was to find oneself in difficulties with a bill for several thousands of *livres* which had to be paid there. Banking and exchange were thus always international: the needs of the Roman Curia and of the princes had favoured their growth in the Middle Ages at least as much as the requirements of Florentine trade. In the sixteenth century, when Sevillian commerce and the policies of Philip II created new trade channels, Florentine, Genoan and German bankers constantly extended their networks across Europe and France. Thus, by the end of the fifteenth century the bank at Lyons was a reservoir of capital and a place of arbitrage which financed the Italian Wars. These masters of international operations knew no fixed rules of conduct apart from honouring signatures. As they found the variety of French currency and its fluctuations with each

[8] It is not necessary, however, to point out the minimum aptitudes of any merchant. He could count, read and write . . . and use a bill of exchange, obviously.

royal manipulation inconvenient, they invented a new money of account, the *écu de marc*, with 65 *écus* to the *marc*, for use in calculating the Lyons exchange in the principal centres of Europe, and for settling arbitrage. If they were foreigners, they became naturalized as it suited them: the German Kleberger, a former agent of the Imhofs, became a citizen of Berne. A little later, if circumstances favoured it, they might equally well change to French nationality. It was thus not by chance that in 1547 the city of Rouen asked the king for an 'exchange, *estrade* or money-market' with 'privileges similar to those customarily enjoyed by the merchants frequenting the city of Lyons'.[9] Even if these financiers and dealers in bills of exchange spent most of their time speculating on 'news', on the differences in currency rates between Antwerp and Lyons, their presence was of great help to the ordinary merchant, and a great asset to the town which gave them shelter. What with loans, insurance, *rentes* and even lotteries, these pioneers of modern capitalism exploited every available resource of the market in money and letters of credit, often in addition to having some specialized business interest, or sometimes even a monopoly like the du Peyrat family in Lyons.

★

But alongside the financiers in the town itself there existed a great many less daring practices, including not only the laborious carriage of money by cart or on horseback, but even barter (wool for fish, or wine for silk). This contrast has often been pointed out. The merchant who went from one fair to another, and bought a *quartaut* of Malmsey as readily as a piece of cloth, was no prince of international commerce, but he was a great traveller, always on the road, a lover of adventure, of the handsome profits he made and the risks he took. He dealt in whatever chance placed in his way, or whatever offered the best returns, switching from hides, butter and corn filched from some granary or other to linen, cloth and spices. Dealing in all kinds of commodities, the average merchant was essentially a speculator. He gambled on foodstuffs increasing in value after a bad harvest, or took advantage of an influx of orders into one of the great ports, such as Rouen and Marseilles, to take a chance on exporting the linens, salt and French wines which were in great demand abroad. Finally, between two big commercial operations, notably during the winter recess, he speculated in the money market and lent to other merchants—in particular, to shipowners who were always short of capital—to artisans, to husbandmen, or even to the king himself, who was continually borrowing at high rates of interest. Undoubtedly, the risks involved in all transactions of this kind were huge. What with royal bankruptcies, currency conversions, and shipwrecks, with roads

[9] Throughout the period in question, Lyons was the great 'capitalist' centre of France. It was, in fact, the only town to publish books on commercial methods: reckoning (Pierre Savonne, Jean Tranchant), usury (Juan Azor, Gabriel Biel, V. Candido, L. Caspensis, V. Figliucci, Juan de Lugo, Fernao Rebelo, Valère Regnault, Juan de Salas, G. Scorza). Apart from Lyons, the lists of R. de Roover mention Paris (twice) and Douai.

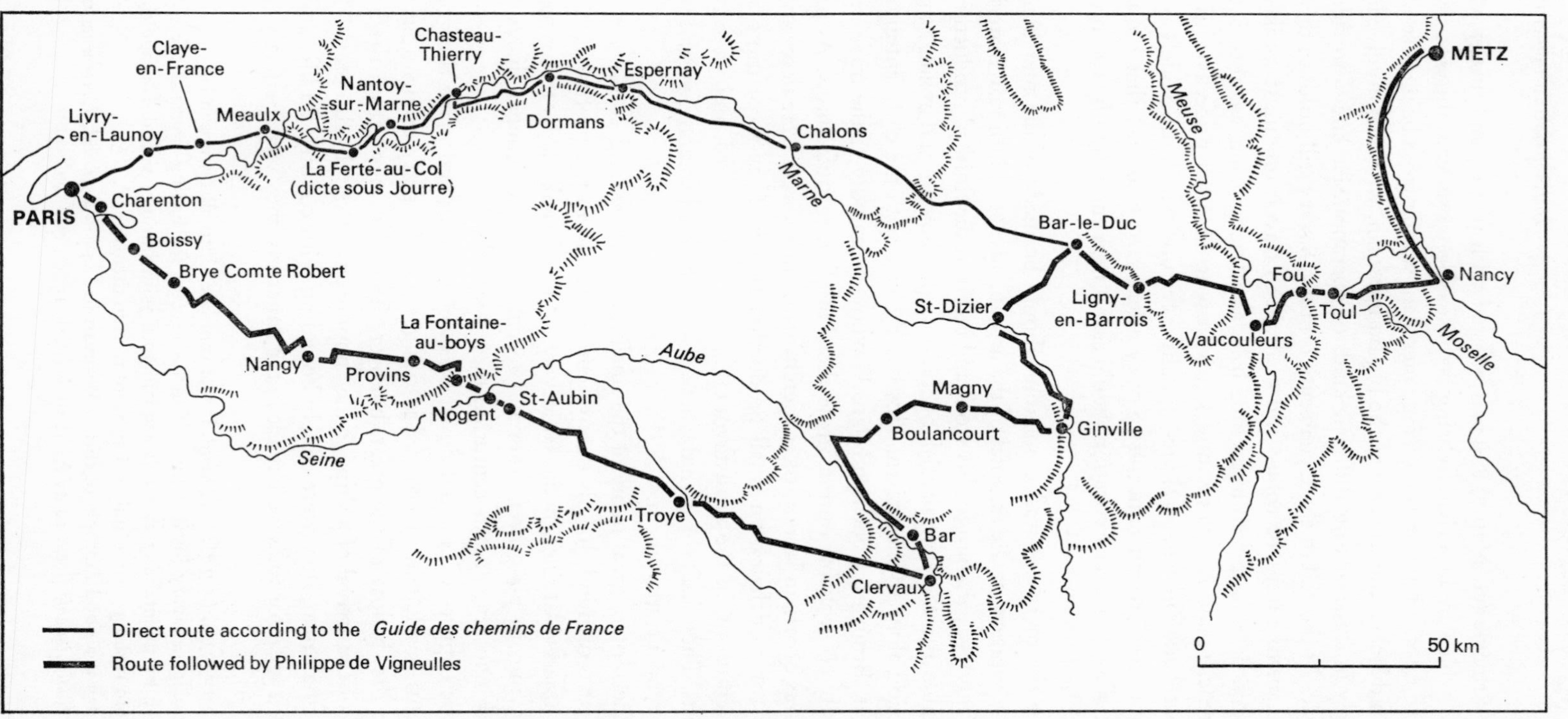

Map 7 The cautious route followed by a minor merchant: Philippe de Vigneulle's detour.

beset by thieves (cf. Map 7) and seas infested with pirates, and finally with the lawsuits which creditors had to bring because of losses suffered through charging excessive rates of interest, the average merchant was far from being certain of his profit and lacked the security of the big businessman, who was involved simultaneously in three or four different kinds of operation. He knew his role to be a gamble. At the end of the seventeenth century, Savary still holds to this: to be a merchant one must be robust and unafraid to travel; one must speak several languages, be as proficient in packing bales as in recognizing weights, measures or currencies; and lastly one must know how to fix a fair price. For his *Perfect Merchant*[10] does in fact reveal pre-capitalistic features which still widely persisted alongside more recent concepts: Savary asserts, for example, that the regular pursuit of a commercial vocation should earn a man enough to live according to his rank and no more.[11]

After the merchant-trader, mention should be made of the merchant who placed equipment at the disposal of the artisan, advanced him raw materials, or indeed money, paid him for his work and received the finished product. He was responsible for the commercial operations, the buying and selling, and left production alone to the artisan. This was the case with the cloth entrepreneurs in Lyons, Beauvais, Rouen and Paris,[12] whose monopoly of the trade in a safe and easily controllable output made them the first manufacturers. As prudent organizers of artisan labour, these merchant-manufacturers were necessarily tied to their town or their own small production region. They were more settled, less adventurous, in the most favourable sense of the word, and were narrow specialists. They dealt through the networks of the big businessmen, and were in part dependent upon them.

Furthermore a great many of the small fry in finance and commerce shared in this turn of mind, in this state of enterprise and in the profits which were boldly amassed—rather in the same way as many bank clerks today use their small savings to play the market and speculate in oil or copper shares. In the sixteenth and seventeenth centuries, these were the hucksters, the merchants' touts, the clippers who pared down overweight coins and made the gold and silver thus fraudulently recovered into ingots, all the petty occupations which lived in the shadow of the great, but were heedful of news from the business world: of the arrival of a ship, or the announcement of a bankruptcy. Though clearly small men, they were closely bound up with commercial life, and in an age when great fortunes were made in the Americas, they were perfectly capable

[10] Savary (236), *Le parfait négociant*. It was translated into all European languages.

[11] Similarly, Savary justifies himself in his preface for having revealed the secrets of commerce by maintaining that this acquaintance with business will discourage the foolhardy from rushing into it 'unless they want to ruin themselves'.

[12] There is a good example of this at Beauvais in 1548 in Leblond, *Documents relatifs à l'histoire économique de Beauvais au XVIe siècle* (Paris 1925), no. 222.

of taking their place in turn among the great merchants and later among the financiers—at the risk of ending up like Semblançay. For this was one feature peculiar to the world of commerce: despite what Savary said, everyone could at least entertain vague hopes of one day being in the front rank.

However, freedom of movement, international connections, material independence, a spirit of enterprise and continual advancement alone do not adequately characterize these capitalist groups. Added to their daily successes—which sometimes bordered on the scandalous—there was a new feeling of superiority, which was heightened by the economic circumstances in the sixteenth century. The big names, such as the Briçonnets, du Peyrats and Assézats, were not the only ones concerned here. An average merchant who had amassed an annual income of some 10,000 *livres* was henceforth the equal of the nobility in his province and was financially on a par with the commendator of an average diocese or of a large abbey. Obviously, he was aware of this social advancement. It little mattered whether he was a lover of fine books or paintings, or whether he bought ruined châteaux, or founded monasteries; his more or less capitalistic wealth found only one mode of asserting itself: insolence. In the seventeenth century, the well-known indignation of the big land-owning families against fortunes made in finance formed as it were, the counterpart of this.

The economic situation and economic thought

This is not the place to describe how France took advantage of the treasures from America—or rather how these spread from Seville throughout Europe. Contemporaries like Bodin, and Montchrestien too, were themselves struck by the methods used to bring doubloons and *reals* pouring into France. Spain cannot do without us, they repeated constantly: she buys from us linen, corn, joinery, paper, cloth and wood; every year she borrows some thousands of our peasants who go to work on the harvest as far afield as Castile. And so on. Rising prices and a more rapid circulation of money in more than plentiful supply struck the dominant economic note for over a century. These two factors largely account for the particular state of mind of businessmen—and also administrators—which has been called Mercantilism. The economic and political preponderance of Spain in the second half of the sixteenth century, if not later, accredited among close observers of this supremacy a theory which was to be widely held until the eighteenth century: namely, that the strength of a country lay in its stock of precious metals, and that this was the only means of pursuing a policy of greatness. In 1664 Colbert said, 'I believe that one will readily remain in agreement with this principle, that it is solely the monetary wealth of a State that determines its greatness and power.'[13]

[13] For his part, Montchrestien says: 'Anyone called to the government of a State must have as his main aim its reputation, its extension, and its *increased wealth*' (Montchrestien (235), p. 11).

If wealth was to be equated with money—despite the objections of those who remained attached to the values represented by land—the only way of acquiring it open to a country such as France, which was not rich in mines,[14] was to take it from her neighbours; partly, no doubt, by forced contributions and ransoms, but also by trade abroad, including smuggling, which the privateers of Elizabeth I of England practised with the greatest success along the Spanish coasts. Observers and rulers, struck by the wide range of French assets, saw France as admirably endowed for this undertaking. Her natural resources saved her from the necessity of buying abroad, thereby avoiding any loss of precious metals, while allowing her to sell to Spain and other countries linen, furniture, cloth, wine, vinegar, spirits, iron, ironmongery, paper and so on. 'There is only a fixed amount of money in circulation in Europe, which is from time to time increased by what is brought in from the West Indies. It is certain that in order to increase the 150 millions in circulation among the population by 20, 30, or 50 millions, we must take this from neighbouring States . . . and only trade and all that is dependent upon it can produce this momentous effect.'

Hence the prohibition of foreign goods and the efforts made to increase sales abroad. Hence too the fitting out of fleets necessary for overseas trade, and the establishing of factories to make the 'craft and industrial commodities' likely to find a ready market. This was the policy followed by Henri IV and Laffemas, by Louis XIII and Richelieu, by Fouquet and later Colbert. But, coherent though this policy may have been, these measures did not make up a system comparable to nineteenth-century liberalism. Rather it was a method, derived from observation and practical experiment, of appropriating for king and country the abundant wealth of the age of the Americas. In the same period, the English and Dutch used exactly the same methods, only more effectively. Economic thought remained similar, dominated in the same way by the astonishing experience of the century of Spanish gold.

In conclusion, must we follow distinguished predecessors in describing the beginnings and the various stages of capitalism? Such was not our intention. Must we outline a new definition of the capitalist spirit? In fact, there was no single spirit, but a series of mental trends—and processes—which varied according to the specialization and the social and geographical situation of the businessmen concerned. The latter did not embody a new spirit, but adopted a whole range of psychological innovations, which we have only attempted to outline in this preliminary survey. Such an inquiry is only meaningful by reference to the restraints, to the customary ways of thought inherited from other ways of life.

[14] Despite a lot of prospecting in the fifteenth century in Berry, Auvergne, Lyonnais and Brittany, and renewed efforts by Henri IV and Sully in 1597, 1601 and 1604.

Chapter 12
Routine activities: sports and pastimes

After manual work and commercial activities, it remains for us to consider sports and pastimes under the same heading. Theologians, who were strict with regard to those pleasures which could so easily 'lead man astray', allowed sports and pastimes as rest and legitimate relaxation, provided this was indulged in moderation, as recreation. Doubtless, the notion of leisure had not yet become as sacred as Rousseau and the eighteenth century sought to make it. Yet such modest recreation was becoming more and more prominent in life during the modern period. One wonders whether some connection should be established between the growth of an exchange economy, with its risks, calculations and gambles, and the taste for games of chance, lotteries and gaming-houses, which were a constant source of concern to moralists and the judiciary in the sixteenth and seventeenth centuries. It would be wrong to make such a bold claim without evidence, but it is impossible to avoid noticing the coincidence.

As mere moments of respite from work—which were not to be abused but were so liable to develop into passions—such recreational activities are not to be confused with feast-day celebrations. However numerous the latter may have been, they were not a daily occurrence in human life. Rather, as we have already seen, they represented the very reverse of daily recreation—a collective celebration which was indeed out of the ordinary. They could comprise sporting activities, indeed sporting activities on a grand scale, but they were more than an ordinary pastime.

Nor shall we include under this heading all the 'lusory' activities of the period. It is only too obvious that work can turn into play, that the artisan and the artist who were absolute masters of their media could delight in working some fine example of their craft; just as Rabelais played when he poured forth his living streams of words and exercised his verbal fantasy like a juggler. The line between a diversion, which is a form of relaxation, a momentary change of activity, and artistic expression is as easy to draw as the one between sports and festivities. Even if the one sometimes merges into the other, this does not justify such confusion as would place all human pursuits under the heading of play.[1]

[1] A temptation to which Johan Huizinga succumbed in his essay *Homo ludens* (260).

Even strictly defined according to the above criteria, the field remains singularly vast, and moralists laboured to class all these pastimes as word-games, games of skill and games of chance, to which must be added the more complex variety which combined skill and chance. Their range and number undoubtedly indicate the attraction which they held for the people of the sixteenth and seventeenth centuries, and the vehemence with which the resultant passions were denounced, particularly in the case of those who spent the whole day long at such pleasures, reveals the importance of these activities in everyday life. Long before Pascal, certainly, entertainment was one way of forgetting the hardships of the human condition.

We shall not attempt either to list or to give a new classification of the many different forms of recreation which were current. Taking account of contemporary habit, or of relative popularity, so to speak, we shall deal only with the most important of them and set aside the long lists destined for confessors. It would certainly not be without interest to clarify why a team ball game like *soule* seems to have been on the decline during the sixteenth century,[2] or why skittles and tennis, which seem very innocent to us, were repeatedly banned and lost favour. Assuredly, these games were not all interchangeable, either socially or psychologically; but the field is still too new for us to be able to make much progress along these lines. So we must confine ourselves to essentials—hunting, dancing and games of chance.[3]

A sport restricted to the nobility: hunting

Hunting, the passion of the ruling class, was doubtless more than a sport. Few noblemen heeded preachers and theologians and were indeed willing to make of it only a very occasional pastime. Too many reasons combined against this: hunting was the monopoly of their group;[4] their life of idleness offered few other possibilities of activity; not to mention a position to be kept up in mounting these great hunting and fowling expeditions.

[2] In Cotentin (Gouberville), it remained very popular, however. It was played every Sunday, parish versus parish, married men versus bachelors, and the parish priests also 'wielded a stick at *soule*'.

[3] This means omitting many very common, popular games like bowls, quoits, tennis, hopscotch, fights between animals, and the theatre, which was a feature of the carefully-organized solemn festivals, as well as a form of impromptu entertainment, thanks to the mountebanks who set up their stage in a different square each afternoon. The success of the theatre, especially in the sixteenth and seventeenth centuries, is undeniable. Everyone flocked to see it, and contemporary synodal statutes constantly reminded the clergy that these performances were forbidden them. (Similarly, they were forbidden from playing tennis, for example, because of the requisite dress: shirt and shorts.) For the theatre, see below, ch. 18.

[4] Poachers existed, certainly, but these were peasants out to protect their crops as best they could; and, above all, they did not ride to hounds.

And so we find the great and the not so great, princes and barons, ceaselessly preoccupied with such ventures, often more so than with their own positions. It was for this purpose that châteaux sprang up all along the Loire valley, for each of these great residences was initially a hunting lodge. But, as the participants themselves confessed, this passion was the best remedy for their cares. If the king was displeased with them, they left court and went hunting on their estates. If their sons ran into debt, they went off to forget these cares in the company of their dogs and horses. Or if they themselves were ruined, they preserved the necessary minimum—two horses and a small pack—to maintain the possibility of hunting with more fortunate neighbours.

That the sport was worth all these sacrifices, none could ever have doubted. Beribboned horsemen galloping through the forest, taking hedges and ditches at full speed, and sweeping through villages; the baying of the pack, the fanfares which were echoed and re-echoed, the mort and the currie—this long chase, ordered down to the last detail like a ceremony,[5] was a distraction fit for a king—and a very expensive one. What with famous huntsmen whose lives seemed one long halloo, old whippers-in on familiar terms with their masters, packs of hounds and game-keepers, a considerable amount of capital was immobilized in it, and few nobles could really afford it. The big packs of 90 hounds were in the minority. Yet even the most impoverished nobleman, who lacked money for his daughters' dowries, kept a few acres of woodland where his keeper addressed him hat in hand.

In the still largely wooded countryside of France, hunting thus remained the pastime *par excellence* of the nobility (cf. Plate 5). It was not simply a diversion but a veritable passion, just like the tournaments which formed the highlight of aristocratic festivities. Both activities exalted courage and recalled in more ways than one the intoxicating pleasures of war, and the traditional virtues of men of the sword, endurance and bravery.[6]

A pastime common to all: dancing

Dancing and balls were universally appreciated and had never ceased to be one of the most widespread of all forms of entertainment, despite many condemnations. When Fléchier went to Auvergne for the *Grands Jours* in the mid-seventeenth century, he noted without surprise the custom of dancing the *bourrée*. 'With the arrival of spring, the lower classes as a whole spend every evening in this pursuit and no street or public square can be found which is not crowded with dancers.'[7]

[5] In learned treatises: cf. Jacques du Fouilloux, *La Vénerie* (Paris 1635); and for fowling, cf. Jean de Franchières, *La Fauconnerie* (Paris 1618).

[6] Thus we are told that wolves and lynxes 'are cruel beasts and require men of great courage to overcome them'.

[7] Fléchier, *Mémoires sur les Grands Jours d'Auvergne* (1856 edn), p. 243.

For centuries—for so long, in fact, that it would be difficult to presume to establish its date of origin—this diversion had occupied leisure time and worried Churchmen. Dancing is not wrong in itself, medieval preachers had already stated, since it is a public activity, but it can lead to temptation. In his *Introduction à la vie dévote*, François de Sales recommends his protégée to be most prudent. 'Balls and dances are indifferent in nature, but in the way in which one normally pursues the activity it is greatly disposed and inclined to be wrong.' So that, in the end, he grudgingly allows that 'to play and dance in a permissible manner, it must be for recreation and not out of a liking for it; briefly, and not until one becomes tired and dizzy; and only on rare occasions.'[8] Protestant synods in the late sixteenth century, notably those at Figeac (1579) and La Rochelle (1581), were not so generous: they totally forbade dancing to the faithful on pain of the most severe punishment.

However, despite mere reproaches or strict prohibitions, this pastime continued to be popular among all classes of society, so much so that at the end of the seventeenth century there were some theologians who deplored the indulgent attitude of François de Sales, which was doubtless invoked by many an unrepentant sinner. Thus, synodal statutes and provincial councils from 1550 to 1650 constantly reminded secular priests that they must not attend balls (nor *a fortiori* take part in them). Each French province already had its own particular dances (which were then little known outside their native region) and this fact too bears witness to the resistance of this custom to religious prohibitions.

As a popular diversion, but one which was enjoyed in all social circles, including balls at court, dancing was equally an important element in certain of the great festivals. There were, for example, the masked balls of Carnival time, as also the balls held in the public squares when kings or princes of the realm made an Entry. As a public entertainment which was open to all, it was then, in a sense, one of the modes of expression of the solidarity we have studied above. Yet at the same time it was the most common form of relaxation, at least for the young. In this capacity, given an organization to suit the conditions of modern life, it has flourished until the present day (cf. Plate 6).

Increasingly popular games: dice, cards, gaming-houses

All gambling, whether in games of pure chance like cards and dice, or in those where chance and skill combined, such as *le triquetrac*, *l'oie*, *la chouette*, *le jardin militaire* or *les quatre fins de l'homme*, was both strictly condemned by the Church and becoming more and more widespread. Noblemen, bourgeois and lower classes spent their time after supper in endless gambling sessions for coppers or gold, as was repeatedly recorded by travellers like Thomas Platter, who

[8] *Introduction à la vie dévote*, Part III, chs. 33 and 34.

encountered gaming everywhere he went. Moreover, in the towns, gaming-houses were set up and found no lack of customers. Centuries earlier, St Louis had already condemned dicing schools. But in the sixteenth century, the vice proliferated: 'academies' or gambling-dens sprang up everywhere; innkeepers provided dice or cards for their customers; specialized establishments were open to all and charged their regular clients a subscription; and there were also types of private clubs to which only the guests of the proprietor were admitted, in this case free of charge. Everywhere, 'huge piles of gold' on the tables explained the frenzied application of the players and the disturbances which often accompanied these interminable sessions.

Thus, if the civil authorities were not concerned to confirm ecclesiastical prohibitions on dancing, they did on the other hand prove most vigilant where gaming was concerned. Royal ordinances (in 1577, 1611 and 1629) and decrees of the *Parlement* constantly renewed prohibitions together with heavy penalties for all offenders, the owners of the gaming-houses as well as their clients. Even exemplary prosecutions such as the case of the *tripotier* (keeper of the gambling den) of Angers, 'master of the *jeu de paume* at the Pelican in the suburb of St Michel', who was sentenced to a fine of 240 *livres* plus costs, do not seem to have been very effective! The details specified in these laws, and the reasons adduced, reveal the extent of this passion: every document specifies that the ban applies to everyone 'of whatever rank he may be'; the ordinance of 1577 stresses the 'corruption of minors', and a decree of the *Parlement* of Paris dated 23rd June 1611 in particular forbade 'all goldsmiths, lapidaries, jewellers, tapestry-makers and others to attend such games, or to keep the score or the reckoning at them, or to aid or abet them, or to take or send to them, or to lend by promissory note, sums specified or unspecified, directly or indirectly; or to provide gold or silver bullion, money, rings, jewels, precious stones, furniture and other goods'. The ordinance of 1629 was even more severe, prescribing expulsion from the town for anyone organizing 'gaming sessions' and 'declaring from this moment all those . . . who prostitute themselves in so pernicious a pursuit, vile, intestable and barred from ever holding royal offices'.

Here again, gaming was more than a pastime; it was a passion which devoured whole fortunes. There is no doubt that this pursuit met with continuing favour, despite condemnations and repressive measures.[9] In the last instance, to play was not to spend a moment in recreation, to amuse oneself, but to gamble, to pledge one's fortune—or at least a part of it—to speculate for financial gain without work or effort. Gaming then ceases to be a mere diversion. Certainly, the popularity enjoyed by dice and cards at the beginning of the modern period must have covered both types of activity: the frenzied pursuit of a few addicts, and

[9] Until the eighteenth century, at least, when every drawing-room had its gaming table continually prepared.

an exciting pastime for the majority, for whom an hour's card-playing each evening represented a most pleasant way of passing the time.[10]

★

It is not easy to assess the place occupied by such forms of relaxation in daily life. We can see the excesses, the passion for sport which took hold of certain groups, or certain prominent individuals. But we have a much less clear picture of the daily recreation of the husbandman, the artisan or even the bourgeois. This gap is important, for it is the rhythm of their lives which eludes us, together with all the phenomena of psychological fatigue to which doctors and sociologists today attach such great importance.

[10] Unfortunately, the 'players' of the time have left us little information on their motivation, and the fulminations of preachers cannot compensate for their silence.

Chapter 13
Cultural and spiritual activities: art and the artist

To leave the activities of everyday life, the humble realities of even the most successful business, the workshop or the gambling den, for the works of art destined to endure for the delight and glory of mankind, is to move on to a form of activity which was recognized as being superior. At least, this was so in the modern period. If it is virtually true that during the Middle Ages it was impossible to distinguish the artisan from the artist, clearly in the sixteenth century the artist who was on familiar terms with kings and princes was no longer to be confused with the journeyman working on his masterpiece in his shop. This is the clearest possible case of the creation of a brutal hierarchical distinction. In the same way, the clerical groups which had formerly monopolized the functions of intellectual and spiritual life were transformed—as it were, devalued—not only as a result of the breach caused by the Reformation, but also, as was obvious at the beginning of the seventeenth century, because of the increased participation of the faithful, the laity, in spiritual life. The clergy found itself confronted by an increasingly large body of non-clerical intellectuals who, as humanists, scientists and scholars, embarked independently upon the conquest of the world. Even if progress was uneven, with the humanists advancing more rapidly than the scientists, they were all conscious of being to some extent superior to the ordinary mortal who spent his time on manual or merely lucrative pursuits. The arrogance of these men of the Renaissance, who could sense better than many of their contemporaries the approach of a new age and of a great triumph for Western man, is apparent from their whole demeanour: the poets believed themselves to be *vates*, the great were their equals, the study of the humanities was the best possible title to nobility. To their own advantage, they created images and myths which were resoundingly re-echoed by the Romantics and have long served as accepted notions until the present day. The images, such as Leonardo da Vinci dying in the arms of François I and Charles V picking up one of Titian's brushes, are striking, but the myths go much further. Poetic—or artistic—predestination followed on Calvinist predestination; the opposition, dialectic or otherwise, between thought and action resulted from the isolation into which these superior souls retreated, soon to address themselves only to an élite of initiates. By a cruel paradox, at the very moment when printing was able to guarantee the man of letters as wide an audience as the erudite monk, who was wholly dependent upon manuscript, would ever have dared to dream of, many modern writers such as the 'college Apollos' multiplied the obstacles which restricted their public to a small group of connoisseurs. On the other hand, these limited groups of intellectuals and artists, clerks and scientists, whatever their audience—obviously an enormous one for devotional works, and very limited in the case of science—shared in a changing and fruitful life whose trends it is not always easy to define precisely, but which must be considered here. It is common knowledge that for artists and humanists the 1520s were years of success and exhilaration such as were scarcely recaptured later. To judge only from the rate at which they worked the scientists cannot possibly be confused with the humanists, so far do the former appear to lag behind, still searching for their tools, while the latter already possessed a method by the time of Erasmus and Lefèvre. On the other hand, the plastic arts, pioneering the way, were passing through a complex phase in their development which cannot be adequately summed up by the two textbook labels, 'Renaissance' and 'Baroque'. This complexity stems from several equally important factors: firstly, the social advancement of the artist who, immediately after the Italian Wars, became the eminent personage at court and in town that he was long to remain; secondly, the technical changes which are well known where painting is concerned, even if the explanations we can give of these phenomena are not always satisfactory; finally, and above all, changing attitudes, of which the various artistic phases are a distant echo. The years of expansion and world domination mentioned a moment ago, the interminable wars in the second half of the sixteenth century and finally the troubled years which were marked by economic crisis and the social disorder between 1620 and 1640 made up at least three phases of sensibility which can be seen through the evidence of poets and artists. The first and the last, christened 'Renaissance' and 'Baroque' respectively, have caused more ink to flow than all the anonymous though monumental artistic activity of the Middle Ages. Our sole aim here is to bring out the attitudes which characterized this change.

The birth of the artist

This apparently naive heading requires immediate qualification. To begin with, it should be remembered that we are dealing only with France, for in Italy the artist had long since been awarded his true place in the city-states of Florence, Lucca or Venice. But, above all, it would be wrong to separate the rise of the artist from the humanist movement of the time. If the artist came to the forefront of social life, it was not only through the good offices of generous patrons who could refuse nothing to their painters and architects. By receiving them at their tables and showering honours and presents upon them they certainly did much to make them prominent among their fellows. It must even be allowed that an important factor in this was the development of the family portrait: the patron himself was 'portrayed' half length or full length or on horseback, while the painter responsible won the kind of fame that the subject commissioning the picture already possessed in abundance—otherwise kings, emperors and even lesser-known princes would never have found so many painters ready to commit them to canvas. But the advancement of the artist was, above all, an expression of the modern 'humanism'. In a world whose true proportions had for some years been realized, the artist foresaw the domination that was imminent. Excited by the great discoveries, he shared in a new pride. The humble creature which the teaching of the Church had in daily worship made out to be a weak being, constantly threatened, suddenly stood erect before this unexpected proof of human stature. The whole section of mankind which was aware of these achievements was easily convinced of this re-evaluation of human nature, and identified itself with the success of the pioneers.

It was altogether natural, then, that this rise of individualism should be felt and extolled by the artist. Remaining an artisan in the organization of his studio and in his techniques, he first changed his title, the image-carver becoming the sculptor, the master of works, the architect, the (all-purpose) painter, the artist. At the same time, schools were founded—or at least studios bearing the name of the best known of them, whose reputation attracted commissions and provided work for a whole team. This is obvious in the field of architecture, but the same is also true in painting, the French being quick to imitate the Italians in this. Beyond these stages, which rescued artistic activity from anonymity, lay the exceptional achievements of the contemporaries of Leo X, the companions of kings and emperors, of whom Leonardo da Vinci is the best known example.

This obviously does not mean that every mason, painter or stonecarver signed everything he produced. Seventeenth-century baroque ornamentation, notably altarpieces in country churches, continued to be the work of anonymous artists, for whom the modest title of artisan was still apt, whatever the quality of the workmanship or especially of its testimony. This new circle of modern artists thus broke away from an older, more numerous company. It was an élite that was noisy—everyone knows the tales of Benvenuto Cellini—importunate and cosmopolitan, for there were many Italians[1] who came to wed their methods to France's own, as the châteaux of the Loire and royal portraits constantly reveal. This élite was certainly small in number, and had only one word on its lips—

[1] But the Italians were not the only nationality involved. The studios of Dijon brought together Flemish, Dutch and Spanish painters, as well as others from Lyons. The same was true of Avignon, Paris, etc.

beauty.[2] For this reason, we can justifiably add that the birth of the artist was at the same time that of art as we understand it today: a function no less basic to man than the most material one, but a function which then recovered its self-awareness once again after the anonymity of the Middle Ages, when the work of art had been primarily for instruction and edification. Even though restricted to a very small group, the promotion of the creators of beauty into the foremost ranks of a society which was itself in process of transformation was an essential element of artistic life.

New concepts in the plastic arts

However, as regards the very techniques of their trade the artists of this new age were aware of far-reaching changes which led them away from earlier styles. Stained-glass and the miniature were outdated media, not only because of the development of civil architecture in the one case and printing in the other, but because of new preoccupations.

Foremost among these must be counted the discovery of anatomy. The exact portrayal of the human body was then characterized by an almost clinical desire to understand better the joints and how they worked—at least as far as the muscles were concerned. The anatomy lesson was not the monopoly of medical students in the time of Rembrandt; Vesalius (cf. Plate 8) had already practised it and catered for many of the artist's preoccupations. But this same interest—which comprised a large measure of admiration for the human machine—was to be found even in works by architects, who presented the symmetry of their buildings, from châteaux to mere urban dwellings, as reflections of bodily symmetry.[3] *A fortiori*, the increasing proportion of portraits among works under commission and the emphasis given to the plastic art of Antiquity, in which the nude is so prominent, encouraged the same trend: the Fountain of the Innocents by Jean Goujon (1549), like many studies and sketches by painters, shows the importance of this preoccupation.[4]

What has been called the revolution of perspective was doubtless of even greater importance.[5] At the end of the Middle Ages there occurred the transition from a piecemeal to a unitary portrayal of space, that is to say a new concept originating in Italy with Brunelleschi and Donatello, Alberti and Piero della Francesca. This introduction of depth into the representation of space was, in fact, an attempt at pictorial geometry, the addition of an extra dimension which had become vital. In this respect, Renaissance painters were ahead of science

[2] Which had very precise canons: for example, the most beautiful creation of God is the nude male (or female) in his divine, natural perfection.

[3] Such a comparison was the rule in all the architectural treatises of the time.

[4] A preoccupation shared by poets: d'Aubigné mentions his 'panting heart', his 'ravaged stomach' and his 'entrails'. Cf. *Les Tragiques*, Sonnets 3, 6, 7.

[5] We shall omit the extremely technical problem of the use of oil for painting.

itself, for although Euclid's geometry had already been known and studied for a long time, scientists were still far from using it to reconstruct reality. Obviously, this did not amount to a new code of rules for representing reality which was imposed upon all artists around 1480 or 1500. Each individual temperament and studio training intervened to bring its own variations on the adoption of any given practice, which by no means ruled out the survival of earlier concepts. Some were fascinated, obsessed by three-dimensional portrayal, others were slow to adopt it.

This exploration of space was, in one respect, a discovery of the void and of its value as a means of expression. Whereas in the stained-glass window, where all the figures existed on the same plane, there was no empty space, and the medieval cathedral, hemmed in by houses and shops in a maze of narrow streets, had no expansive splendour, modern artists knew how to leave a space round their monuments (for example, all the châteaux of the period) or around their human subjects. By sharply outlining a figure in a halo of space against a background of distant Roman remains or bare rock, the artists bathed it in atmosphere, made it stand out from this very setting and gave it a new depth, which was further accentuated by the effects of light and shade.

How did three-dimensional perspective become established in modern painting? Studies on these basic facts of artistic expression are still too rare for its progress to be traced. In particular, the part played in this development by new concepts of the earth, from Magellan's voyage round the world to the systems of Copernicus and Galileo, as well as by the spread of mathematics since the High Middle Ages, is largely unknown. By all appearances, the artist was in advance of the mathematician, who was still dallying with scholastic exercises and discussions on the properties of numbers. The new art[6] was not only a more faithful figurative representation of reality; on a different plane, it announced the scientific progress of the seventeenth century, from Descartes to Newton.

From Renaissance to Baroque

Once these basic changes have been recognized, it is easier to point out that the Renaissance—so highly acclaimed for a century since Michelet first launched the notion—did not consist simply of a return to antiquity. Whatever the part played by journeys to Rome, or such vestiges of antiquity as survived through the Middle Ages,[7] or the infatuation with Rome and Athens, the early sixteenth century remains much more clearly characterized by that liberation of man discerned by Michelet. The new artistic and literary spirit went together with

[6] Pierre Francastel has clearly described this transformation in *Peinture et société*. The explanations that he gives of it by resorting to child psychology and the work of ethnologists would require further proof. Such research is still incomplete.

[7] Cf. the book by Jean Seznec, *La survivance des dieux antiques* (London 1939 and 1954), reviewed by L. Febvre in *Annales* (1965), p. 280.

the widening of world horizons and with social and economic change. The maritime expansion of Europe across three oceans, which were virtually uncharted a hundred years before, counted as much as the reading of Cicero by the contemporaries of Lefèvre d'Etaples. And the religious audacity of Luther and Calvin was itself part of a veritable spiritual revival, for the small group of artists was alive to all these upheavals, to the implications of the retreat of Islam as well as of the conquest of the West Indies.

There is no doubt that this thirst for knowledge, this desire to discover all that the wide world was in process of revealing to the dazzled Europeans, extended to antiquity. All Renaissance painters handled mythological subjects, just as all writers imitated Virgil and Martial and invoked the immortals without thereby becoming pagans.[8] The Renaissance nevertheless remains a time of unprecedented glorification of the forces of individual liberation, a time of exhilaration at the prospect of a new life. From Italy to the Low Countries, from Spain to Germany, the same breath of freedom and human grandeur was carried to every corner of France. Italy undoubtedly exerted the greatest influence, since her subjects flooded into the land—not only artists showered with honours and financial rewards, of whom Leonardo da Vinci is a characteristic example, but also clerics holding many of the important benefices, who took up residence and brought with them the new taste[9]—not to mention servants and craftsmen. From this hub of world activity, which continued to play such an important role, there came into France, along with these emigrants, the most enterprising of her subjects, those most imbued with the precocity of the Quattrocento—not ancient Romans disguised as modern men.

Thus the Renaissance in the arts must have appeared as a joyful time of release—and conquest. This was the moment—which barely extended beyond 1540—when hopes were at their highest. For this small group which lived in the luxurious ease of kings, princes and rich merchants and saw Europe establish footholds throughout the world, regulate its life to the tempo of Atlantic traffic and revitalize the abused faith, the early years of the sixteenth century were years of joy and hope and of new creations in every sphere.

Intense religious fervour combined with political ambition brought about a brusque change of atmosphere in the 1540s. After the warning in 1534 came the persecution of the Protestants between 1545 and 1560, when the accusation of Lutheranism or Calvinism literally envenomed life in the humanist and artistic milieux which had been the glory of the previous period. Then came the religious wars, from 1560 to 1598: they doubtless did not stamp out all artistic activity, but it is important to see a new mental climate afterwards pervading

[8] However, a statistical survey of the works of these painters is quite revealing, even outside France: Titian painted 23 pagan subjects, as against 114 Christian.

[9] E.g. at Dijon, the *abbé* of Sainte-Etienne in 1511 was an Italian, as was the *abbé* of Sainte-Bénigne in 1525.

such activity. If there is any justification for using the term 'Baroque' to describe the architectural and especially the sculptural output between 1600 and 1640, it is this: a century after the Renaissance, the feelings and needs expressed were no longer the same.[10] The hopes of a religious regeneration—and above all of world conquest—were replaced by a falling back upon the division of Western Christendom and of France, by disappointment and, principally, by a desire to re-establish Catholicism. At the same time, in the political sphere a more authoritarian monarchy than that of François I was asserting itself. But most important, the economic recession between 1620 and 1640 led to an intensification throughout France of the social crisis that the rise of the bourgeoisie in the previous century had already brought to a high point. Spiritual resurgence and social upheaval went hand in hand and certainly favoured the decorative exuberance which is one of the dominant characteristics of Baroque architecture—which was itself so largely religious. Certainly, the methods, the techniques, remained the same as a century before; but the artists of the early seventeenth century no longer sought to express exhilaration and hope for a better world, but rather their anxiety, or even their anguish, along with their nostalgia for lost hopes.

Without any doubt, our presentation of the two principal artistic phases of the period claims to be nothing more than a stylization, and it would be wrong to see it in any other way. Each artist, in so far as he experienced and expressed his times with his own particular genius, set his own stamp upon this expression, remaining a representative either of the Renaissance or of this post-Renaissance with which the Baroque eventually became fused, especially in France. This is the dual climate which we have tried to bring out. To go further would involve analysing individual works of art.

[10] Suffice to say that we do not subscribe to the theories of the baroque published over the last fifty years in Germany and elsewhere by Wölfflin, Reymond and many others. In a recent work, V. Tapié has reviewed this literature. *Baroque et Classicisme* (270); cf. also my article in *Annales E.S.C.* 5 (1960).

Chapter 14
Cultural and spiritual activities: the humanists and intellectual life

Alongside the artists, the creators of beauty, came the scholars who were not yet called humanists, but were fired with enthusiasm for human knowledge. They were destined to live on for centuries thanks to those successors who knew and taught the 'humanities', the product of sixteenth-century scholarship. The word 'humanism', like the term 'Renaissance', has been so perverted and so many interpretations have been put upon it that it scarcely seems worthwhile using it here.[1] Suffice to say that we shall call 'humanists' those writers and scholars who, caught up in the wave of optimism between 1500 and 1530 along with painters, architects and monks who dreamed of reforming the Catholic Church, worked as philologists, poets and editors for the glory of the new man, whose future role they foresaw and whose advent they laboured to bring about. Here again, one must certainly consider in the first instance the generation covering the first third of the sixteenth century, which, led by Erasmus and Lefèvre d'Etaples, established the tradition and raised high hopes. Later poets and scholars, the members of the Pléiade and companions of the Gryphe and Estienne families, already represented a more sombre brand of humanism, which was fully expressed in the discretion and misgivings of a man like Montaigne. But by the second half of the century, the academic tradition was established, and humanism began to be confused with the 'humanities' which the Jesuits taught in their colleges—which meant primarily the Latin of Cicero and the Greek of Demosthenes. Soon the only people called humanists were the pedagogues who taught the rudiments of the dead languages. Amid the devoutness of the early seventeenth century, humanism lost some of its faith in humanity, some of the passion for knowledge which had fired its promoters a century before. Instead, it became the first stage of a spiritual journey—as it were, the intellectual stage. This can be seen with Camus and Bérulle. At that point, humanism as it had been in its heyday was almost dead, and the academically-accepted traditions which

[1] How many arguments would have to be quoted—and immediately disposed of—confronting, defining or discussing old and new humanism, Dantesque humanism, Christian humanism, Marxist humanism, etc.

perpetuated it retained neither the enthusiasm of the associates of Guillaume Budé, nor even, perhaps, their unbridled aspirations to encyclopedic knowledge. But the initial impulse remains; the greatest scholars of the early period, such as Budé and Erasmus, remain as models of human exploration—through all the humanities. It is with them that must be sought the principal definitions of this spirit, which was only partly new, and of which they were henceforth the standard-bearers.[2]

The humanist and social preferment

The intellectuals who lived in the first thirty or forty years of the sixteenth century embodied an ideal of human progress. They were able to communicate to others their faith and hopes and this is too rare an occurrence, even in the history of the would-be Athenian civilizations, to avoid being emphasized. Of course, their dreams were not shared by the whole population, but at least men of letters were able to achieve some fame and find an enthusiastic audience among the urban classes.

Castiglione was certainly exaggerating when he declared in the *Courtier* in 1528, 'the French recognize only nobility of arms and reckon all else as naught and thus not only do they not esteem, but they abhor letters. . . .'[3] The Italian, steeped in the refined culture of Florence in the Quattrocento, was no doubt scandalized; on the other hand he was unstinting in his admiration of François I, who did so much for his humanist friends. However, the contrast remains and allows us to appreciate better how in a few years the fellow scholars of Erasmus, Lefèvre and Budé were able to rise to such heights and win for their works the recognition that they possessed a dignity comparable to that of the knight-at-arms and the most skilful jousting champion.

The part played by François I is too well known to require description. At most, one might indicate how far his preoccupations confirm the Italian's criticisms. The urge to edify and educate his subjects, particularly the nobility, explains the favours bestowed upon translators of Greek and Latin texts, the printers' privileges, pensions and rewards of every kind. On 16th October 1527, in granting his secretary the privilege to print and sell French translations of Greek and Latin works, left by Claude de Seyssel, he declared, 'As we have

[2] Together with the humanists, special consideration should be given to other 'intellectuals' of the time—jurists, lawyers and magistrates, who formed rather one section (the most important) of the humanists' audience, but who were also their continuators. Little is known about the members of the legal profession. Treatises on jurisprudence tell us little about the outlook of those who applied the laws. The (political) agitation by the *Parlementaires* in the seventeenth century is only one aspect of it. One must admit that this whole field still requires clarification.

[3] Castiglione, *The book of the courtier*, translated by Charles S. Singleton (New York 1959), p. 67.

always particularly desired the instruction and edification of all our good subjects, and especially those of noble rank. . . .'[4]

As educators of the kingdom, the humanists of this great age saw themselves provided with all the resources they requested to carry out their task: royal presses for Latin, Greek and French, and in 1530 the *Collège royal*, granted to Guillaume Budé to teach the three basic languages—Hebrew, Greek and Latin. These innovators disquieted the somnolent universities by their eagerness to discard the traditional methods of Scholasticism in favour of a detailed study of ancient manuscripts, wherein they discovered a complete view of man and the world—and also the Old and New Testaments in their original versions. But though they were certainly regarded as disruptive elements by the established forces in the university and the Church, the humanists received the support of the king during the decisive years when they pursued their immense task of publishing, editing and translating the medieval manuscripts which preserved the treasures of ancient thought.

No doubt after 1534 and 1536 they came under suspicion of having Protestant sympathies, and royal favour was less readily forthcoming at the end of the reign, when on the other hand we have the onset of religious persecution. After all, Calvin had been a keen student of Guillaume Budé. And the same Calvin protested against the 'nicodemical' timidity of these philologers who were the first to discover in their reading of the New Testament a view of Christ which was somewhat misunderstood by Church tradition. Even more significantly, Etienne Dolet, who brought out so many great classical works, perished at the stake in the Place Maubert in 1544.[5] The 'contaminations' or 'amalgams', by which the reputations of these scholars have long suffered,[6] are of little account; what matters is the position their studies assumed in the social and intellectual life of the times.

On this score there can be no possible hesitation. The intellectual backbone of the Middle Ages in their heyday—as it were, in the thirteenth century—the canons of the chapter schools and the masters in the universities, were supplanted by this new generation of humanists who, outside the traditional Schools, and using any available accommodation—to begin with the Collège de France was without its own premises—taught philology and a love of the humanities to audiences as large as they were enthusiastic. Literature, from Ronsard to Rabelais, shows the effects of their teaching, and was unhesitatingly committed to the same cause. And at the same time, these men of action, who were simultaneously

[4] *Catalogue des Actes* I, p. 527. At the end of the translation of Thucydides, it is even mentioned that the work was published 'at the command of the Most Christian King François, the first of that name, for the profit and education of the nobility and subjects of his kingdom'.

[5] Cf. Febvre (334): the case of Dolet.

[6] After the period under consideration, this is only too obvious.

research-workers, editors, printers and teachers, acquired a social standing incomparably superior to that of the intellectual in the Middle Ages. One need only recall the Estienne family in Paris and the Gryphe family in Lyons.

Humanist erudition and the printed book

Every learned humanist was, if not an editor—though there was no editor at this date who was not learned—at least a great bibliophile. The Estiennes and Budé, the Péliciers, Scaliger and later de Mesmes and Nicolas Colin all had impressive libraries.[7] It is well known that it was through the printed word that the humanist movement was able to win the audience in question; it was the book, and the necessities of printing, which determined the humanist method and set limits to the open-mindedness characteristic of these scholars.

One must credit the printed book with the two basic elements of this generation's turn of mind, their critical and historical senses—though the historical was more pronounced, more apparent, so to speak, than the critical. Criticism of manuscripts to establish a 'definitive' text was their common pursuit for half a century. From texts corrupted by scribal errors and by degrees rendered unintelligible, they gradually unearthed the authentic reading. At the same time, restoring the exact idiom of Aristotle, Cicero and Plutarch, they replaced the barbaric Latin of the Schools with the refined language of the best Roman and Greek authors. As the work of philologists in the modern sense of the word, this task of restoration led them to reconstruct all aspects of the ancient civilizations; in this way textual criticism automatically led to historical research proper. But to present thus the two main facets of the work of Budé, Dolet and Estienne is to pass too quickly over the most exciting aspects of their critical quest. All were involved in collecting and collating manuscripts, in discovering in monasteries or cathedral schools throughout Europe a few fragments of Pliny, Herodotus or Thucydides. Renaissance scholars too were great travellers and engaged upon a quest which was as enthusiastic and ardent as that for relics in earlier times. This passion for manuscripts persisted for a long time: in 1653, the innocent Mersenne could not resist the attraction of a Chinese manuscript, even if it was obscene.[8] Then, as editions of the great works of Antiquity in the original language or in French or Latin translations became more numerous, the more strictly historical work developed, resulting in the gradual emergence of a sense of the different ages and civilizations making up mankind's past. This sense is apparent from the time of Erasmus, whose letters reveal a most finely graduated attention to

[7] It is not proposed, at this point, to give a history of books or of libraries. Our knowledge of the reading public of the humanists is not insignificant, though the question has scarcely been broached as yet. Cf. Febvre and Martin (286).

[8] He writes to Peiresc (15th September 1635): 'Monsieur Haultin writes to say that he has a Chinese manuscript containing all the postures of Aretino, which he has promised to show me.'

ancient history, and Budé—who undertook a methodical study of Rome in addition to his work of editing and translating—right through to Montaigne in the seclusion of his library or on his travels across southern Germany and Italy. But with Montaigne it was no longer simply the history of mankind before and after Christ, the history of the peoples of the Old and New Testaments, which was brought out to become part of the accustomed modes of thought—but also the diversity of existing human societies inside and outside Europe.[9]

These two basic attitudes of the humanist mind were displayed by the scholars as they edited and translated texts and confronted interpretations and reconstructions of the distant past. Were they also typical of their many readers, who delighted in commerce with 'these good, dumb hosts, who never grow angry'? Certainly, the output in the sixteenth century was such that printed books became available to all who could read—artisans and noblemen, lawyers (an insatiable audience) and apothecaries, barbers or mere clerks. It is clear also that the scholar's thirst for knowledge was to a certain extent shared by many bibliophiles. E. Pasquier was proud of his library and, comparing himself to a nobleman going the rounds of his estate, he maintained that he hunted 'more in a quarter of an hour in his study' than the nobleman did in a day in the country. But it seems right to assume that what the reading public retained of the scholar's work was the discovery of new worlds and historical perspectives. 'Philology' remained the exclusive asset of the scholars who formulated the discipline and its rules. The new and wider sense of the history of man was the common asset of their vast public, whose curiosity, as one must again emphasize, extended to both the human and Christian past. In this respect, the historical bent of both the scholars and their reading public led to encyclopedism.

Humanist encyclopedism

The debt of this first generation of humanists to antiquity is common knowledge. Speaking and writing the three ancient languages, they communicated their love of the literature of Greece and Rome to the creative writers, so that Ronsard, who read the Iliad in three days in the original version, could proclaim, somewhat conceitedly:

> Les Français qui mes vers liront
> S'ils ne sont et Grecs et Romains
> Au lieu de ce livre, ils n'auront
> Qu'un pesant faix entre les mains.[10]

[9] Not without suspicion: cf. Plate 7.

[10] The French who will read my verse
Unless they be Greeks or Romans
Instead of this book will have
Only a heavy burden on their hands.

However, men of letters were not constantly steeped in Greek and Latin. Montaigne

Yet it must be pointed out that the legacy of the ancient civilizations was not everything for the companions of Erasmus and Lefèvre. Undoubtedly, they drew freely upon these rehabilitated works, which were studied in their own right—and no longer, as had been the practice among the Church Fathers and medieval clerks, as a preparation for Christianity. Among the ideas of the Greek and Latin authors they found above all the notion of human destiny, forged to a large extent by man himself: *fabrum suae quemque esse fortunae*. In this sense, the heroes of Plutarch who were soon universally known even outside the circle of scholars, thanks to Amyot's translations, provided them with an extraordinary selection of human examples in which all the great problems of man were solved: for suicide, take Cato or Seneca; for the conflict between civic duty and filial piety, take Brutus: *Tu quoque, mi fili*. Each maxim, each scene bore with it, like a medallion, its weight of human experience, which was readily applicable to the present.[11]

It is quite true that pedants like the 'college Apollos' studied by Lucien Febvre in his *Rabelais* became intoxicated with this ancient culture, and seized the opportunity to stand out from the common herd by speaking and writing Latin exclusively and parodying Martial, Ovid and Horace. In any case, they were not the great humanists—and barely counted, even in their own day, by comparison with the Estiennes and Rabelais. But they filled the air and whole tomes with their *nugae*, their puns on proper names, their jeremiads and their squabbles about which of them would be the Virgil of the day:

Hoc saeclum genuit duos Marones. . . .[12]

These were mere pedantries of no consequence except that they reveal this mania for antiquity which took hold of some contemporary men of letters.

A more accurate impression of the importance of antiquity in the humanists' preoccupations can in fact be gained from the varying flow of publications. In Paris,[13] works by Latin and Greek authors and studies devoted to antiquity remained fewer in number than religious works until 1525 (when the figures were 37 and 56 respectively). But in the years following, the humanist output leaped forward—134 works, compared with 93 religious works in 1528, 204 compared with 56 in 1549.[14]

However, the humanist scholar's thirst for knowledge was not limited to

---

in his time confesses that he knows only Virgil and cannot compare him to Homer. Later, Corneille, Pascal, the great Arnauld and Molière were not familiar with Greek.

[11] Rabelais has preserved the two themes which would allow one to distinguish between humanists and Protestants; Pantagruel shows us man incapable of doing anything by himself, and in God's hands; but, in Thélème, he forges man anew.

[12] Cf. Febvre (284), p. 20.

[13] Figures published by Febvre and Martin (286), p. 400.

[14] Out of the 204, 33 were in Greek and 40 in Latin; the others consisted of translations and studies.

antiquity, but extended to the whole body of knowledge available at the time. Doubtless, antiquity partly slaked their thirst, with the rediscovery of the works of Pliny the Elder, Ptolemy, Pythagoras and Aristotle himself. But the encyclopedic curiosity of Lefèvre, Rabelais or, a little later, of Ramus, was without bounds. Ramus is perhaps the most striking example of this—a master of arts (like Lefèvre) who wrote on philosophy, the liberal arts, mathematics, geometry, dialectic.[15] Works of natural history and geography—dealing, moreover, with the known worlds (the Mediterranean and Near East) rather than with the newly-discovered continents—and mathematical treatises are thus to be found in booksellers' catalogues. And to appreciate fully the boundless curiosity of the humanist, we must doubtless further add the editions of legendaries, which perpetuated both traditional hagiography and pagan legend, and the many legal publications. The importance of the custom provided by the legal profession[16] to a certain extent explains the popularity of legal works, at a time when important traditional concepts—in particular, that of natural law preached by St Thomas—were called into question as a result of a more precise knowledge of ancient history—and of the mystical concepts originating in the Reform movement.[17] In fact, the humanist was a scholar interested in knowledge of every kind, an encyclopedist, though in no sense a dilettante, who found in scholarship, especially in the compilations of antiquity, the primary but not the only source wherein to satisfy his thirst for knowledge.

★

Not all these features are to be found in the humanist tradition as it was later perpetuated. The type of scholar who deciphered manuscripts, triumphantly fixing upon the correct reading for the most corrupt of texts, inevitably became less common once the process of cataloguing and collating the manuscripts rescued from oblivion was over. But many other features no longer applied by the end of the sixteenth century. The scholar-publisher-printer of the kind common in literary circles in the fifteenth and sixteenth centuries, from Johannes Amerbach to Robert Estienne, became rare and virtually disappeared in the seventeenth century—however cultivated Molière's or Pascal's publisher may have been. So too, without any doubt, the enthusiasm that had fired the generation of Erasmus and Lefèvre, impelling so many people, rich and poor, towards

[15] Cf. Hooykaas (304); on the scientific movement, cf. below, ch. 14.

[16] Presidents and councillors in the *Parlements*, in Paris and elsewhere, commonly had libraries of between 700 and 1,000 volumes. Cf. Febvre and Martin (286).

[17] The development of positive law—including the notion of the social contract which was developing in the last decades of the 16th century—occurred under the influence of two factors: a better knowledge of the history of Roman law, and the mystical concept fostered by Luther, Machiavelli and Bodin according to which the world is basically evil.

Plate 5 Hunting: an aristocratic privilege.

APRILVS.

C'est en Auril que le soleil s'aduance
D'herbes produire, & faire les châps beaux,
Et lors chacun se met en diligence
Apres le Cerf, ou au vol des Oyseaux:

On voit aussi sortir à grans troupeaux,
Beufz, & Moutons, pour aux châps pasturer,
L'hôme est trop plus expert a telz trauaux,
Qu'à son salut ou il doit aspirer.

Plate 6 A country dance.

Plate 7 The dream of St Jerome the Ciceronian. St Jerome dreamed that he was suddenly brought before God in judgement and scourged for his attachment to pagan literature: 'Who are you?' 'I am a Christian.' 'You lie, you are not a Christian but a Ciceronian, for where your treasure is, there also is your heart.'

ANDREAE VESALII
BRVXELLENSIS, SCHOLAE
medicorum Patauinæ profeſſoris, de
Humani corporis fabrica
Libri ſeptem.
CVM CAESAREAE
Maieſt. Galliarum Regis, ac Senatus Veneti gra-
tia & priuilegio, ut in diplomatis eorundem continetur.

Plate 8 The anatomy lesson.

learning, was lost in the second half of the century. Whereas before 1550 towns strove to provide the instruments of learning, founding liberally-endowed libraries and establishing municipal colleges which would provide a secular education like the Collège de France, at the end of the sixteenth century, as a result of the acute suspicion provoked by the Reformation and of the ravages of war—and soon because of shortage of funds—municipalities relinquished their colleges, which were resumed by the clergy. At Amiens, for example, the college was abandoned by its principal and staff, who were no longer paid, and in November 1599 it passed into the hands of an archdeacon who accepted half-salary.

Thus one can judge the extent to which the religious humanism of the early seventeenth century differed from the humanism which immortalized Erasmus and Guillaume Budé. The former, professed by the Jesuits and reputable authors like Camus, Bishop of Belley, curbed the humanist yearning for knowledge. Man and the world are certainly admirable and worthy of study, but only because they allow one to rise to knowledge of the Creator, man being the masterpiece of the Universe because he is the very image of God. Thus, in classical studies, preference was given to those works and figures which in some way announced and prepared the coming of God's Church. This was a different attitude wherein religious preoccupations dammed up the hopes and conquering fervour alive in the first third of the sixteenth century.

Chapter 15
Cultural and spiritual activities: scientists and philosophers

It may seem questionable to include scientists and philosophers here, among those engaging in what were considered to be superior forms of activity. Despite a few very famous names, such as Leonardo da Vinci (whose treatises were not in any case read by his contemporaries), Copernicus, Kepler, Vieta and Galileo, sixteenth-century science is held in disrepute by historians of science. Both the scientists of the Renaissance and those of the late sixteenth century are usually scornfully dismissed as mere compilators, accumulating the rediscovered wealth of classical knowledge—until Descartes. As for the philosophers, they are better left unmentioned. For the great majority of contemporary thinkers, Thomism, which confused philosophy and theology, remained the rule, to be broken occasionally by a few foolhardy figures like Petrus Ramus. Historians of philosophy condemn them irrevocably, as it were, on the same charge of eclectic misuse of antiquity. Here again Descartes played the part that Boileau ascribed to Malherbe in the field of literature.

However, provided one attempts a relatively close reconstruction of the intellectual climate in which these scientists lived, the situation does not seem so gloomy. Even before Descartes, modern France had its scientists—who were also its philosophers—and who, famous or not, tried to understand nature and, to do so, looked everywhere for support, precedents and *auctores* to help them in their task.

But before examining the attitude of mind expressed in these endeavours, one must briefly underline the social prestige of the scientist. He was not, as he is today, a professional, engaged full-time in research or teaching. The universities, it is true, did admit mathematical, legal and medical studies, and there certainly existed a numerically very small social group of teaching scientists, whose influence did not extend far beyond the student body. These lawyers, theologians, medical professors and 'physicists' of the quadrivium regurgitated the stereotyped lessons of the Schoolmen, into which the Renaissance movement did not immediately introduce new life. Hippocrates, Aristotle and the Code of Justinian remained the authorities which were followed with a formalism that was faithfully reflected by the university ceremonies themselves, the *disputationes* in which were debated important points of currently-accepted doctrine. To declare against Aristotle or Galen, inside or outside the university, was to expose oneself to downright condemnation, as happened to Petrus Ramus in 1544. Even doctors and jurists, contending with the inevitable innovations brought by the passage of time—the new diseases of the sixteenth century, or the royal ordinances of a great legislator like François I—could not escape this constraint, which was modelled upon the strictness with which theologians in their field had for centuries protected orthodoxy against heresiarchs and heretics of all kinds.[1]

Thus, it was not the professional teachers who provided the natural sciences, once they were brought to life by the great discoveries, with their exponents and their prestige. It is well known that the important figures even in the view of the traditional history of science were, so to speak, amateurs with a passion for research. The example which immediately springs to mind is Bernard Palissy, the self-educated artisan who was not afraid to confront theory with practice. But Vieta and later Fermat and Pascal's father were magistrates, whose professional activities no doubt left them ample freedom for exercising their curiosity outside their main occupations. Many doctors also played a big part—not academics, but practitioners contending with life. For this passion for science was widespread. From the early years of the sixteenth century, printed translations of classical works placed at everyone's disposal Euclid's geometry, Archimedes' mechanics, Ptolemy's geography, Aristotle's physics and Pliny's natural history. Rabelais was himself fascinated by the rediscovery of ancient science, and steeped his Gargantua in it. In this respect, he was neither an exception nor a precursor; by the late sixteenth century all men of culture were already collectors. This was the heyday of the curio collections in which, beside books, were piled astrolabes, portolans and maps of the world 'on wooden rollers', seashells, fish-skins from the South Seas and ancient medallions.[2] At the beginning of the seventeenth century Father Garasse, in his campaign against dissembling atheists and free-thinkers, observes that everyone in Paris wanted to be able to call himself a scientist: 'To be called a worthy fellow costs nothing; to be called a scientist is much more expensive.' Doubtless, as we see every day, to have pretensions to knowledge and to be learned are not the same thing. But this infatuation clearly reflects the prestige of the scientist at the beginning of the modern period. Indeed, the confusion inherent in the science of the time may

[1] A strictness which, in the case of the jurists, is not to be confused with the authority of jurisprudence, the fundamental principle of our legal practice today. Despite royal sovereignty, the judge had enormous freedom at that time. The *disputatio* was an academic exercise, and nothing more.

[2] At Amiens, probate inventories from 1587 onwards reveal quantities of such curios in the homes not only of doctors and magistrates, but also of ordinary bourgeois and merchants. This lesser manifestation of scientific curiosity continued to develop until the eighteenth century, when it assumed the proportions of a veritable collectors' passion.

have added to this prestige, however paradoxical this may seem. Only later did methodological precision and clarity of explanation become the criteria for success.

Scientific confusion and foretastes of the future

Here we shall omit the question of scientific apparatus, language and conceptualization. Nothing has yet appeared to replace or even to supplement the treatment Lucien Febvre gave to these aspects in his *Rabelais*.

Possessed of insatiable curiosity, the contemporary scientist also sought utilitarian knowledge. His most common beliefs channelled his interest in this direction, as the connection between astronomy and astrology well illustrates. 'If,' says Kepler, 'the confident hope of reading the future in the heavens had not existed, would men have been wise enough to study astronomy itself?' This is even more true of medicine, or magic, which was included among the sciences in the same way as alchemy and occultism. To establish a hierarchy among the sciences, or to classify them as sciences and false sciences—as we can today—would be meaningless; we must follow the contemporary mentality in admitting occultism along with Vieta's algebra. Relying upon experience—but not experimentation—and upon tradition, the scientist first devoted himself, for the most part, to collecting the countless 'facts' which had increased in number as a result of the diffusion of ancient science and the widening of world horizons following the great discoveries. He was not an encyclopedist insofar as he did not introduce order into these facts, but his turn of mind was encyclopedic. From this point of view, there was no difference between the humble Rheims bourgeois, who collected stuffed birds from the West Indies, and the more famous scientist who had visited the Indies and described at greater length the fauna unknown to Europeans. The medieval *Speculum naturale* was suddenly considerably enlarged by collections of plants, and by plates or engravings which faithfully reproduced the original down to the last detail.

But as a traditionalist the scientist accepted everything which bore the stamp of authority. The most striking example here is Ambroise Paré on the subject of the powder of the unicorn's horn,[3] which protected against plague: he does not deny the monster's existence, since this was affirmed by the Church; but after listing all the reasons he has for not believing in it, he concludes that he does believe in it. In any case, in medicine, notice had to be taken of current beliefs, for if a patient died of plague without having had this remedy prescribed for him, his relatives would hound the doctor. Thus, among their data they welcomed all the descriptions—monsters included—found in the Natural Histories of Pliny and Aristotle. The authority of the predecessor, a principle contested by twentieth-century science, where achievement constantly supersedes achieve-

[3] *Discours de la Licorne* (1579).

ment, was, conversely, the fundamental axiom of the sixteenth-century scientist.

The same is true of experience, if by this one understands not the art of proving a fact by repeating it, but the mere recording or enthusiastic observation of a phenomenon. An apparition, a shooting star, a fiery sword in the sky or a dream which was deemed to be prophetic were facts of experience. They provided the material for the art of 'prognostication', which was so prominent among the preoccupations of the times that, in fact, almanacs of prognostications, more or less astrological in tenor, can be seen as the most common means of popularizing contemporary scientific knowledge. Actions that were remote in time, coincidences or successions of events between which a causality was spontaneously established, were constantly exploited by the scientist as facts derived from experience and observation.[4] This receptive frame of mind, open to any and every 'experience', was certainly another characteristic feature.

Thus, one can understand the confusion between astronomy and astrology. To measure the heavens, map and count the stars and determine the size of each of them, and the distance between them, was basic astronomy; but to do this was also to determine the signs which influenced everyone's destiny. It was less important to know one's date of birth according to the calendar than to know the figure and disposition of the stars, by which a man's whole life could be foretold. In this respect, astrology was a difficult art in which the most gifted took an interest without feeling in the least that it was a failing.[5]

Alchemy, which remained the most glamorous of the sciences, reveals a similar ambiguity. At times, the alchemist sought a panacea, to provide medicine with the sovereign remedy against plague and other diseases; at other times he sought the secret of making gold out of common substances—stone and base metals; on the one hand health, on the other wealth. In approach, this ambitious scientist was an empirical chemist, the essence of his ability residing in the fusion and distillation of elements. The slow, tedious processes involved in heating and alloying metals, using varying proportions, had not been altogether wasted in this science's past history. Certainly, no Doctor Faustus ever successfully completed his research into either transmutation or the all too famous philosopher's stone. No alchemist ever concluded his exploration of the microcosm and the macrocosm. But alcoholic spirits were discovered by the alchemist, and many metals and common alloys were developed in his laboratories, where the rarest—and in our eyes, the most preposterous—powders, which were very often imported from the East, stood alongside the well-tried products of medieval metallurgy.[6]

[4] With varying degrees of success.

[5] As L. Romier indicates in the case of the wife of Henri II: *Le royaume de Catherine de Médicis* (1922), I, p. 73.

[6] Paracelsus and his numerous disciples were alchemist-pharmacists, who pioneered the way for present-day biochemistry.

Lastly, the exponent of the occult sciences and magic itself also remained a scientist, one who sought to determine and guide the invisible forces present in nature, which were more difficult to master than those directly perceived by the senses. But the 'panpsychism' implied in magic—not to mention the theological aspect of the latter in the case of black magic—was wholly acceptable to the contemporary mentality; this is what Febvre, in his *Rabelais*, called the lack of a sense of the impossible. Only a few rare spirits such as Charron and Montaigne were able, on occasion, to denounce superstition and irrationality in experiments with magic. Not only did their contemporaries wholly accept such preoccupations; they even ascribed to them a sort of pre-eminence over other forms of knowledge.

Thus, in the scientific mentality there was, in our view, a constant intermingling of rational elements, obtained by deductive method and observation too, and of irrational elements, derived from tradition or from uncontrolled experiments. One essential consideration overrides the temptation to separate the wheat from the chaff—the unity of the mental process involved. Vieta's mathematics were at the same time the good and bad numbers of Pythagoras. The first telescopes, which allowed the verification of Galileo's observations and Copernicus's theories, and which led Kepler to his theories of optics, were praised by Porta of Naples in his *Magia Naturalis* as objects endowed with a power that was as beneficial as it was occult.[7] Progress in medicine and the natural sciences was achieved through the accumulation of a great mass of information and definitions derived from a wide variety of sources and accepted without order or method. From this variety there sometimes emerge unexpected foretastes of the scientific progress which the eighteenth century began to achieve. In the midst of astrological fancies, of a host of descriptions of monsters (see, for example, Ambroise Paré) and 'prognostications', we find the drawings of Leonardo da Vinci and the patient experiments of Bernard Palissy. But a score or so premonitions of this kind do not make for Science, as the mid-seventeenth century was to begin to understand it.

Scientific method and philosophy

To say today that scientific progress was closely bound up with advances in mathematics and early attempts at experimentation certainly seems rather naïve. We are well aware that mathematics and the experimental method were behind the most outstanding successes in the centuries which followed, and the conclusion is an easy one. Yet it is certainly true that such progress as the beginnings of modern science can boast came in these spheres. Descartes puts it well: recalling in the *Discours de la méthode* his intellectual development in the early years of the seventeenth century, he emphasizes how delighted he was with mathematics

[7] Porta (298), XVII, ch. 10.

whose 'foundations (are) so firm and strong', while expressing astonishment that no-one had 'built any loftier edifice upon them' than technical applications such as surveying, cartography or fortification.

Mathematics and astronomy, aided by their wholly formal nature, have always had a solidity and manifestness to which sciences dealing more with material phenomena were unable to aspire. They were equally aided by the reappearance of the ancient treatises, from Archimedes to Ptolemy, including Apollonius, whose fragments continued to elicit attempts at reconstruction until the mid-seventeenth century, when Fermat was still working upon them.[8] Ptolemy pioneered the way for Copernicus and Galileo. The *Conics* of Apollonius were carefully studied by Kepler. Moreover, the need for precision introduced by the study of mathematics had its effect even upon everyday life. The words 'architect' and 'geometer' date from the sixteenth century and reveal the influence of Greek science. A city like Amiens employed for a whole year a painter and 'architector' who, compass in hand, drew up a map of the town, portrayed its suburbs and fortifications, and even drew a street plan, including such abutments as might exist. Applying measurement and number to all forms of knowledge was still an ill-formulated ambition; all we have, as yet, is the basis of seventeenth-century mechanicalism.

More apparent, however, is the progress made by experimentation, the deliberate and rational exploration of nature—at least in the closing years of the sixteenth-century. If a figure like Descartes later remained attached to mathematics, and sought to submit nature to laws of number, others like Ambroise Paré and Bernard Palissy were not afraid to entrust the advancement of their knowledge to experiments.[9] Hippocrates' medical writings encouraged this approach, which was still tentative, by their positive descriptions of diseases and living beings, which never resorted to explanations founded on magic. The post-mortem, which became more and more common, was a stage in the progress of experimentation.[10] Similarly, a man of inquiring mind like Claude Haton, anxious to understand the celestial phenomena which greatly increased in the skies of 1575 and 1576, speculated as to whether these lights which suddenly burst forth were not comparable to the 'elemental fire in flax on the distaff', which travelled without glowing until it burst into flames.[11] Certainly, these are mere indications. The same Bernard Palissy who opposed his practice as an artisan to the theories of Cardan is often content to make assertions or draw mere

[8] The correspondence of Father Mersenne, which has been part-published by Tannery, provides a fine example of the passion for mathematics which fired all scientists at the beginning of the seventeenth century.

[9] Palissy puts it well: 'The mistakes I have made in mixing my enamels have taught me more than my successes.'

[10] Cf. Vesalius' Anatomy Lesson, Plate 8. [11] Haton (7), II, p. 823.

commonsense comparisons, or occasionally to do even worse. In his *Traité des pierres*, he deduces from the presence of marble in the Pyrenees a relation of cause and effect between the abundance of water and the hardness of the stone. No-one had yet arrived at systematic experimentation.

*

The value of the sciences in the form they took during the pre-Cartesian period has not failed to encounter its detractors. At the beginning of the seventeenth century, Mersenne and Bacon wrote attacking the sceptics who were baffled by the contradictions and uncertainties inherent in many explanations. By the end of the sixteenth century, the Aristotelian edifice on which the late Middle Ages had lived had been dismantled. The naturalism of the sixteenth century attributed the value of a natural element to every piece of evidence, every recorded experience vouched for in time and space. Everything was possible because everything was natural, including what we today call the miraculous or supernatural event.

Philosophy thus defined itself within the scientific attitude. The fervent polemics between Aristotelians and Ramists in mid-sixteenth-century Paris formed an important stage in the renewal of thought. The starting-point for the scientific revival was in fact the discussion on 'physics' or astronomy without hypotheses. Three-quarters of a century later, Mersenne and Descartes came to grips over problems in mathematics,[12] and brought in a whole system of physics: Descartes' readers thought at least as highly of his mechanical system as of his methodical doubt.

A change in philosophical and scientific thought in fact took place in the early years of the seventeenth century. From the compilations and methodological uncertainties of the preceding period there gradually emerged the notion of a rational method necessary to ensure scientific progress. The day of the collectors—and the metaphysicians—was over. The hundred and fifty or so correspondents and visitors of Father Mersenne, whom one of his biographers has carefully listed, were all passionately fond of mathematics and obsessed with logical thought. The young Pascal, who knew these gatherings in the Place des Vosges, is most explicit on this point: no-one was better than he at helping one to rid oneself of the 'tyranny of accepted opinions', for 'he had a very special gift for formulating good questions . . . although he did not have the same good fortune in resolving them'. Today, we would call it the art of posing problems. The passion for science which fired all the companions of the Minim, both clerical and lay, derived certainly from their premonition of an important step forward: one which would lead to clearer understanding and would ensure for

[12] To use the word in the broad contemporary sense, which allowed a lodestone or a telescope to be considered as a mathematical instrument.

them knowledge as indisputable as Euclid's geometry.[13] The moment was at hand when the 'Truth of Science' would blaze forth.

The atmosphere of this period, which culminated in 1637 in the *Discours de la Méthode*, was that of a struggle in which the champions of medieval Aristotelianism and the exponents of all traditional formulae already appeared as defenders of a lost cause, an outdated rearguard, which was stigmatized by Guy Patin in his advice to his son, a doctor like himself:

> a doctor who opposes the superstition and bigotry of the people of Paris will immediately be decried by the ignorant populace and the bigoted bourgeoisie, by the Jesuit faction, by the canters and cowled hypocrites who look at the world through a veil, by a host of ignorant priests, and even by the very highest in the land, who owe allegiance to the cabal of the hypocrites.[14]

Though violent and unjust,[15] this warning has the virtue of sending us an echo of the conflicts in which scientists were engaged in the early decades of that century, a reflection of the progressive secularization of philosophy and science. New concepts of the natural—and human—worlds were swiftly taking shape, at the cost of revisions which either disquieted or fired with enthusiasm all who were involved. But, whereas the Jesuit theologians appropriated the pagan humanism of the Renaissance, absorbing it and integrating it into their own thought in the form of religious humanism, the same process was impossible in the case of science—at least in the seventeenth century. The triumphant impetus of mathematics, astronomy and physics contradicted too many traditionally-accepted truths which were considered immutable, as Copernicus and Galileo reveal. Scientific progress had necessarily to assume the appearance of a contentious innovation, cheerfully denying many a 'Gospel truth'; such, indeed, was the tenor of scientific life in the time of the Encyclopedists. In this sense, Descartes was both the culmination of all sixteenth-century effort—and a fresh starting-point.

[13] In their opinion, of course. Such an expression would not be valid today.

[14] Published by Pintard, in his study *La Mothe le Vayer, Gassendi, Guy Patin* (Paris 1942).

[15] There were almost as many bishops, priests and monks as laymen in Mersenne's circle; and some of Loyola's disciples were also prominent.

Chapter 16
Cultural and spiritual activities: the religious life

In France under Henri IV or François I, the three types of men we have just encountered, humanists, artists and scientists, formed a small minority. Engaged in the pursuit of learning or creating things of beauty, they laboured for a somewhat restricted audience. The humanists addressed themselves to those, inquisitive if not learned, who were interested in the rediscovery of classical antiquity, in pagan reason and in the disturbing pre-Christian civilizations, with which the medieval Church had allowed only its own clerics to become familiar. The artists, architects, painters and sculptors could perhaps be said to offer their works to the gaze of all their contemporaries: one would think this to be the case with the architects at least. But the time had not yet come when the Louvre, Fontainebleau and the châteaux of the Loire would be known to everyone, when everyone who was French would wish to visit them once at least. Finally, the scientists were unrecognized in so far as their sciences had as yet no real grasp of nature and man. Thus the small body of scholars, scientists and artists did not widely influence contemporary society.

On the other hand, religion was of universal concern. As Lucien Febvre has shown in his *Problème de l'incroyance*, religion was present at every moment of human life, sanctifying all the important events from birth to death. It gave everyone a redeeming hope for his journey on earth and especially for the after-life. At that time, it would not have occurred to anyone to harbour feelings of indifference towards it, even carefully concealed in his heart of hearts. Universality of belief was doubtless not an original feature of the dawn of modern times; it was a tradition which was not immediately undermined by the distressing disputes in the midst of which the religious unity of France and of western Europe foundered.

However, we do not propose to recount the vicissitudes of the social and dogmatic conflicts which rent the country and the hearts of its people for almost a century. This long episode, whose roots lie in the metaphysical qualms of the fifteenth century with its fears of Death and Hell, and which did not end either with the Edict of Nantes or the Peace of Alais, or even with the Revocation of the Edict of Nantes, is as much a part of social, political and even demographic history as of historical psychology.[1] What we aim to discover here is the meaning of faith—or, let us say, of the modes of belief—for the people who were caught up in the turbulent destiny of the Reformation and the Counter-Reformation—if one must use this stereotyped terminology.

To believe, to doubt, to worship: these words and notions are meaningful when used to describe the religious attitudes of our contemporaries. Helped by the monumental work of analysis by philosophers exploring all the nuances between simple faith and critical agnosticism, and guided by the methodical inventory of worship compiled by the French school of religious sociology,[2] which has for twenty years been assiduously recording, indexing and charting churchgoers, both regular and intermittent, we can with some success substantiate these expressions with valid definitions of faith, lukewarmness or unbelief. The same is not true for the sixteenth and seventeenth centuries, in the first place because they did not possess the conceptual apparatus we have at our disposal today, a factor which indisputably limits their range of possible alternatives, and above all prevents us from automatically employing our own analytical methods to define their religious experience. To take what is, in appearance, the most straightforward of cases, that of the monk praying in his cell, no-one would think of treating the Benedictine of 1530 in the same way as his 1960 counterpart. Very often it was the way they reacted to the life of their times which led them to the cloister. But quite apart from that, when this sixteenth-century monk addressed his prayers to Christ or Mary or one of the Saints, he was surely appealing to a God or an intercessor who held a rather different significance for him from the one it has for us today. There is certainly no one, eternal way of believing—or of doubting. We know, of course, that modern man 'wanted to believe'; but it is also obvious that the contemporaries of Erasmus and Calvin,[3] or later of Bérulle and d'Aubigné, did not 'experience' their faith in the same way.

If we wished to explore in detail the religious attitudes of the period, which were made particularly complex by a perpetual anxiety about the future, one would no doubt have to proceed step by step through the different phases of the spiritual life of the times. Although they had many features in common, the peaceable reformers of 1510–20 certainly bore little resemblance to the fierce

[1] A work devoted to the religions of the sixteenth century, for which Lucien Febvre had done the groundwork, is contemplated in the collection *Evolution de l'humanité.*

[2] Under the direction of Gabriel Le Bras.

[3] Perhaps one should indicate that these names figure here as landmarks, not as types. The personality of Erasmus lies beyond the bounds of research into group psychology: a man who refused a cardinal's hat and declared that he had adopted the Socratic motto 'I only know one thing, that I know nothing' is a special case. For him, even more than for Rabelais, there arises the problem of a precursor. Cf. the preface by Henri Berr to the book by Lucien Febvre, *La religion de Rabelais.*

champions of the Wars of Religion. Moreover, if there is no doubt that important dates like the breach of 15 June 1520, or the end of the Council of Trent, were decisive for the spiritual life of the times, it is equally true that their repercussions were not felt by everyone in the same way at the same time. Luther's expulsion from the Church meant, or so Rome believed, that within a few years it would rid itself of the canker, now that the monk was isolated, marooned in a hostile Germany. Some ten or twenty years later the Protestant Churches were proliferating. The Council of Trent restored the dogma, and, above all, the discipline of Catholicism, but as we know, the Church did not revert to solemn austerity within a year. In France, the application of the Council's decisions was long delayed by the Gallican resistance of the *Parlements*, which were opposed even to the publication of its decrees. There then followed the delays necessary for the prohibition of the popular festivals, the saturnalia to which the humbler classes were very attached. At the end of the seventeenth century, some were surprised to find that the Festival of Fools still survived in places. In a more positive vein, the campaign to stimulate worship, which was seen by the Council as one way of effectively combating the spread of heresy, began to have an effect in France in the first decades of the seventeenth century.[4] A history of religious life based upon these great traditional phases would once again amount to a history of its leading figures. All that interests us here is the diffusion of its essential acts, the inflexion it gave in its time to worship and to spiritual life.

By way of further clarification, let it be said that the acts of cruelty perpetrated during the Wars of Religion are of interest in themselves as evidence of the insensitivity of the combatants, which scandalized many an observer like Claude Haton: 'The Catholics stole and robbed other people's property as much as the Huguenots—except that they did not pillage and ransack churches, and did not kill clergymen. Otherwise, they were as bad as the Huguenots.'[5] But we shall have to bear in mind this new climate in which for thirty years religious disputes took place when we come to examine the different forms of spiritual life; it is not a decisive factor nor even a major element in this topic.

In this investigation into the characteristics of each religious attitude, one fact dominates all those we have just mentioned. For the Catholics in the first place, there was a wide gulf separating the clergy, whom we may term the professionals, from the ordinary laity, the faithful worshippers of a religion whose rites, fixed by centuries of codification, made up for any deficiencies in an inner life. On the other hand, the new religious edifice established by the Protestants

[4] Similarly, the theologians at Trent extinguished for some time the taste for and sense of the dialogue, which so prevailed amongst the humanists brought up on Plato. However, throughout Europe there were many Catholic and Protestant pacifists who were keen to continue the debate immediately after the Edict of Nantes.

[5] Haton (7), II, p. 597.

set the pastors and their flocks on equal terms. The new Christianity was an individualistic rather than a hierarchical religion. No doubt it is true that at the beginning of the seventeenth century, laymen occupied a more prominent position in the Gallican Church than before. More than before, in fact, they demanded and obtained a place in the temporal administration of the parish, through the 'church councils' (*fabriques*), an institution which took root everywhere in the seventeenth century. In addition, much of the revival movement between 1600 and 1640 was the work of the laity, and especially of devout women. However, this was only a special moment of participation by the faithful in the sacred life of the Church, whereas among the Protestant sects the laity traditionally played the major part.

The Catholic 'professionals': the clergy

The bishops and princes of the Church, abbots and priors of religious houses, heads of regular orders, masters and students in the universities—and parish priests and monks, the countless rank and file of this hierarchy—comprised the clergy, which histories of the Church, when they claim to cover the field of religious activities, usually take as their subject matter. And it was indeed within the orders of the visible Church that were undoubtedly to be found those who instigated movements for reform, and promoted the most austere moral and spiritual practices: the founders of orders, monastic reformers, and masters of discipline—all the leading figures of ecclesiastical history came from their ranks. Nor is this in any way surprising if one considers what differences in dogmatic and liturgical training the Church brought about between the clergy and the faithful in the sixteenth century. A priest who was anxious to deepen his faith, or a monk who was curious to discover the intellectual bases of his mystical experiences, had at his disposal not only the resources of his own private library which, given the wealth of theological publications since 1450, could be monumental (provided he had the means), but also the enlightened services of the universities which were open to him. The theology of the Fathers and Doctors of the Church and the Canon Law of the conciliary and pontifical collections could be studied in Paris, as at Orléans or Bourges. The works of the Church Fathers, with St Augustine and St Paul prominent amongst them, were an inexhaustible source of meditation and inspiration.

In this way, both seculars and regulars were aware of perpetuating the most ancient of traditions, the very one which had made the Church. The stamp of this tradition was surely to be found on every attitude of the priest, even though he might shock the faithful. Many examples were already apparent in the sixteenth century at the time when important issues were being reconsidered: for example, there was the theology of marriage[6] which had been laid down by

[6] To take one example among many: in northern France, at the beginning of the seventeenth century, the burial of a very young child was followed by a celebration to mark the

ascetics living in expectation of the Day of Judgement. St Thomas had already combated the Immaculate Conception with arguments drawn from common morality.[7] Similarly the rite of churching implied that all sexual union, even when legitimate, was a sin of which one should be cleansed. Such rigid austerity largely helped to separate the priest from the great mass of the faithful.

Finally, the very variety of the orders which comprised the regular clergy, living in seclusion in the house of God, was a further element of spiritual enrichment. The Franciscans, Dominicans and Benedictines were the most numerous and popular of the regulars—until the Society of Jesus (from about 1540) and then the many seventeenth-century orders came along to modify this hierarchy. Assuredly, holy orders were not, and never had been, a career in the modern sense of the word; but they lay open to all who were fired by an exacting faith as the only road—though divided into many different pathways—leading to an intense spiritual life and to the mystical life. This point was constantly repeated by all the books of spiritual exercises of the period.

An ascetic, a scholar, a spiritual guide: the clerk did not always correspond to this definition, as we know. Between it and everyday reality there were discrepancies, which necessitate our differentiating according to function and training.

Positions in the upper ranks of the secular clergy, archbishoprics and bishoprics, were filled in accordance with an agreement between the king and Rome which gave the king a considerable *de facto* privilege. The Concordat (of Bologna) of 1516 in practice left the king free to appoint whomsoever he wished as his bishops, from the younger son of an impoverished family to some zealous confessor. And despite the observations of the Council of Trent concerning the residence of bishops or the holding of *commendams*, appointments in the upper clergy continued to depend upon the hazards of royal favour. Henri IV was himself responsible for some well-known examples of this at the beginning of the seventeenth century.[8] It meant that episcopal duties were often carried out by coadjutors lacking in authority, or by incompetents who were often not equal to conducting a theological discussion. Hence the unevenness of diocesan life. Depending upon the incumbent, the result could be either absenteeism, laxity among the regular clergy, and quarrels and law-suits between canons; or conversely a bishop devoted to his duties, who visited his diocese at least in part each year, silencing capitular rivalries, encouraging foundations and building projects and, after Trent, trying to establish a seminary. These 'reforming' bishops, as they were called by contemporaries, were more common than one is led to suppose by the traditional works of history, which dwell interminably on the abuses in the Church in the sixteenth century.

---

arrival of a new angel in heaven. A systematic investigation of these disparities between the standards of the theologians and popular morality would be a worthwhile subject of research.

[7] Cf. also Marot (111), following Erasmus, *Colloque de la Vierge méprisant mariage*.

[8] One need only recall the case of the Bishop of Lodève.

Another group, with a different outlook, was formed by the monks and nuns of the regular orders. Here again, royal nomination and the practice of *commendams* doubtless played their part in the appointment of abbots and priors. But whereas absenteeism on the part of commendatory bishops, which left the administration in the hands of incompetent chapters, always appreciably harmed the faithful and disrupted the smooth running of the diocese, the same fault in the case of commendatory abbots was less serious. The religious house pursued its work along the lines laid down by the founder of the order and continued to administer its own affairs under the authority of a prior drawn from the ranks. Not that one can paint a blameless picture of monastic life. Rabelais and many others with him repeatedly asserted that many abbeys may have harboured companies lacking in zeal, and that many nunneries, open to all comers, led an unseemly existence. Yet fifty years after the indignant mockery of the Protestants and of Rabelais, monastic life had recovered an astonishing degree of prestige. Monastic reforms were even more common than diocesan reforms between 1600 and 1630, when monasteries were being founded by the dozen all over France. Such a startling recovery would be inexplicable but for exaggeration on the part of Rabelais's contemporaries. But the Wars of Religion provide further proof of the vitality of the orders and of the fervour with which studies were pursued in their houses. In 1567, when a royal mandate and a papal brief authorized Churchmen to bear arms to protect themselves against Huguenot attacks, the monks were the first to abandon their breviaries for the sword or the blunderbuss. Doubtless, this was an indication of their eagerness to defend their faith; but it was also the 'blunderbuss' monks who preached against the heretics, and who, in the time of the League, did not hesitate to preach against the king. Capuchins and Jesuits led this army which roused the urban masses to the pitch of fanaticism between 1589 and 1598. Once peace returned, the regulars in the reformed monasteries and in the newly founded orders—Oratorians, Visitandines etc.—were among the most effective artisans of the Catholic revival in the seventeenth century. The monk 'shunned by and shunning the world' had given way to the effective servant of the Church in the world. Traditionally filling almost all the positions in the universities, devoting themselves more than ever to preaching, education and charitable works, these regulars formed the vanguard of the Church.

There remain the least clerical of the clerics, despite ordination—the parish priests. The lower clergy, which maintained daily contact with the faithful in parish life and permanently combined pastoral and administrative duties, were certainly members of the clerical world. But the lower clergy received practically no doctrinal and liturgical training and instruction;[9] and this applied even to those destined for town parishes, where, in addition, the holding of *commendams* had its effect. They were mostly recruited locally from candidates

[9] A situation which caused concern long before the Council of Trent. But the short

whose sense of vocation, though often doubtful, was rapidly strengthened by what we today would call periods of probation with elders of good repute. The parish priests were above all close to their flock.

Teaching and perpetually regurgitating a brief catechism, the whole year round—a fact which explains by contrast the success of the regulars who travelled round the dioceses preaching during Advent and Lent—the lower clergy, whose material needs were in many cases ill-assured, did not enjoy much prestige over their congregations. A lord like Gouberville employed the local parish priests as agricultural day-labourers for carting, waxing and milling. Everywhere, the priest shared in all the major tasks of the peasantry—the corn and grape harvests and the ploughing. Thus, even if he wanted to, he scarcely had time for reading, for improving his knowledge of dogma or liturgy or studying points of conscience. Even in the mid-seventeenth century, when the diocesan seminaries demanded by the Council of Trent were gradually endeavouring to provide each diocese with priests who had received a less summary training and were capable of giving moral and spiritual guidance to their flocks, it was still exceptional to find the records of pastoral visitations mentioning a presbytery whose occupant owned more than three or four books: a breviary, a copy of the *Golden Legend* and one of the *Imitation of Christ* were, in effect, the usual assets.

Moreover, it is certainly true that the lower country clergy, who were all too often uneducated, did not lead a life in accordance with the requirements of their estate. Memoirs and *livres de raison* abound in stories of drunkards and concubines, and even mention—before and after Trent—priests who married in open contempt of celibacy. Here, the priest's frock did not adorn a rigorous ascetic existence; it was the insignia of a little-respected profession, which was plied like a routine trade, retaining nothing of apostleship save its poverty.[10]

However, as the sole repository of that erudite and complex culture, Catholic tradition, which had been formed by 1500 years of meditation on the mysteries and doctrinal evidences of the Church, the clergy as a whole were wedded to modes of thought whose essential characteristic was to evolve slowly. The cleric was behind the times out of a sort of intrinsic necessity, which his university education with its scholastic methods further confirmed. Since the *Summa Theologiae* of St Thomas Aquinas, which contained all the teachings

---

treatises published at the end of the fifteenth century and the beginning of the sixteenth with an eye to parish priests (*Manipulus curatorum*, *Instructio sacerdotum*) with their simplified version of theology, insist above all on ritual. These meagre works of instruction undoubtedly failed to achieve their aim.

[10] The vow of chastity is best left unmentioned. As for obedience, its significance was greatly reduced by the fact that the superiors of the parish priests were generally little concerned with their subordinates.

of the Church, Christian thought seemed petrified with regard to the problems which the secular world had to solve, with regard to the discovery of the solar system from Copernicus to Galileo and the thorny and much-debated questions of interest and usury. In this sense, one must see in the efforts of the Jesuits to understand ancient humanism, and to integrate it with Christian thought in the religious versions that flourished in the seventeenth century, a form of modernism, the only one to be successful at the time. The companions of Loyola, who ardently defended tradition in its entirety, and who triumphed at the Council of Trent, were daring innovators in their attempts at reintegration. In this respect, the Oratorians, though even more radical in their educational methods, were, whether they intended it or not, their continuators in the seventeenth century. Nevertheless, on the whole the theologians who were the moving spirit of the regular orders and the universities, who inspired those bishops possessing a sense of vocation, and defended a dogma which in the mid-sixteenth century was pronounced intangible in its formidable complexity, remained in part strangers to the problems of the laity, their contemporaries. A gulf separated the mentality of the cleric from that of the layman. Faith, Hope and Charity did not mean the same to both.

The Catholic laity

In contrast to the clergy who were not very numerous—perhaps some hundred thousand people—stood the great mass of practising believers which, at ten to twelve million, was a hundred times greater. In contrast to these men (and women) whose active concern was the spiritual life and to whom we have perhaps generously ascribed a good knowledge of their faith, the capacity to encompass the most abstruse mysteries of the Trinity or of transubstantiation, and the ability to live in accordance with a carefully-considered and orthodox interpretation of the law of Christ, we have the multitude for whom the ancestral religion provided not only the solemn setting for every important event, but the viaticum whereby the individual could rise above his everyday material concerns. Townsmen and countrymen formed in this respect two basic types of believers, the former harder to please, the latter easily satisfied—to use, by way of analogy, epithets from the business world.

In trying to investigate the spiritual life of the faithful, we encounter formidable problems which were not posed by the clergy, the repository, as of right, of the living and eternal thought of the Church. The faithful, on the other hand, though they did indeed belong to the Catholic Church from the moment they were baptized, were destined to know this thought only through what the clergy could itself teach them. Printing developed the habit of freer private reading, but it did not give rise to compulsory education, so that for the masses it was still the word of the priest that taught and guided the sinner.[11]

[11] Cf. the meaning of the layman's prayer in 1527—Plate 9.

The religion of the faithful thus comprised in the first instance customary worship. The house of God, whether a village or town parish church or the chapel of one of the regular orders, was where the community gathered every Sunday morning, at least in so far as the Lord's day of rest was kept by peasants handicapped by the existence of only a single service and by bad roads. The church was the setting for all—or almost all—the solemn acts upon which the Church had set its sacramental seal. Doubtless midwives authorized by the priest could hurriedly baptize weakly, new-born infants at home, and extreme unction was also administered outside the church. But all the other sacraments took place within its walls, in accordance with a solemn ceremonial which was known and valued by the faithful, who in particular extolled the splendour and pomp of ceremonies in the towns.

This worship consisted of a rigorous observance of the sacraments, with Easter communion, preceded by confession, remaining the solemn act *par excellence*. Baptism, communion, confirmation (which sometimes waited years for a visit by the bishop or an archpriest delegated by him), marriage and extreme unction served in addition as the most permanent of landmarks along the Christian's path through life. But it is difficult to know what lay behind these acts for the people of the sixteenth and seventeenth centuries; to ascertain, for example, how far this was due to social conformity—necessarily a major factor, even after the possibility of choice offered by the spread of the Reformation—or to intimate participation in the sacred mystery implied in all communion. We are well aware today that any mystery, to be fully understood as such, needs first of all to be defined. First-hand evidence concerning these essential acts of Christian life is too rare to allow of more than mere hypotheses. The almost total absence of catechistic training in rural areas—in almost all dioceses, it was only during the seventeenth century that catechism classes were established—and the lack of education from which the rural clergy suffered leads one to believe that for country parishioners worship was very 'socialized', though this did not exclude a simple faith in God's goodness and in the wickedness of the devil; a crude and diffuse Manicheism which had long been given rein in the pursuit of witches and sorcerers, and which found a new target once heresy spread throughout France. In the towns, on the other hand, there was certainly no lack of devout believers for whom a knowledge of the liturgy and the traditional thought of the Church helped to instil profound significance into the receiving of the sacraments. It was not only in 1643 that the problem of Frequent Communion was raised. Weekly or even more frequent communion had long been common in the towns—in particular at the instigation of the Jesuits, who were concerned with spiritual guidance—when the Jansenists attacked this practice, albeit while drawing distinctions.[12] Certainly, in the

[12] Arnauld continued to recommend frequent communion, but exclusively for the devout.

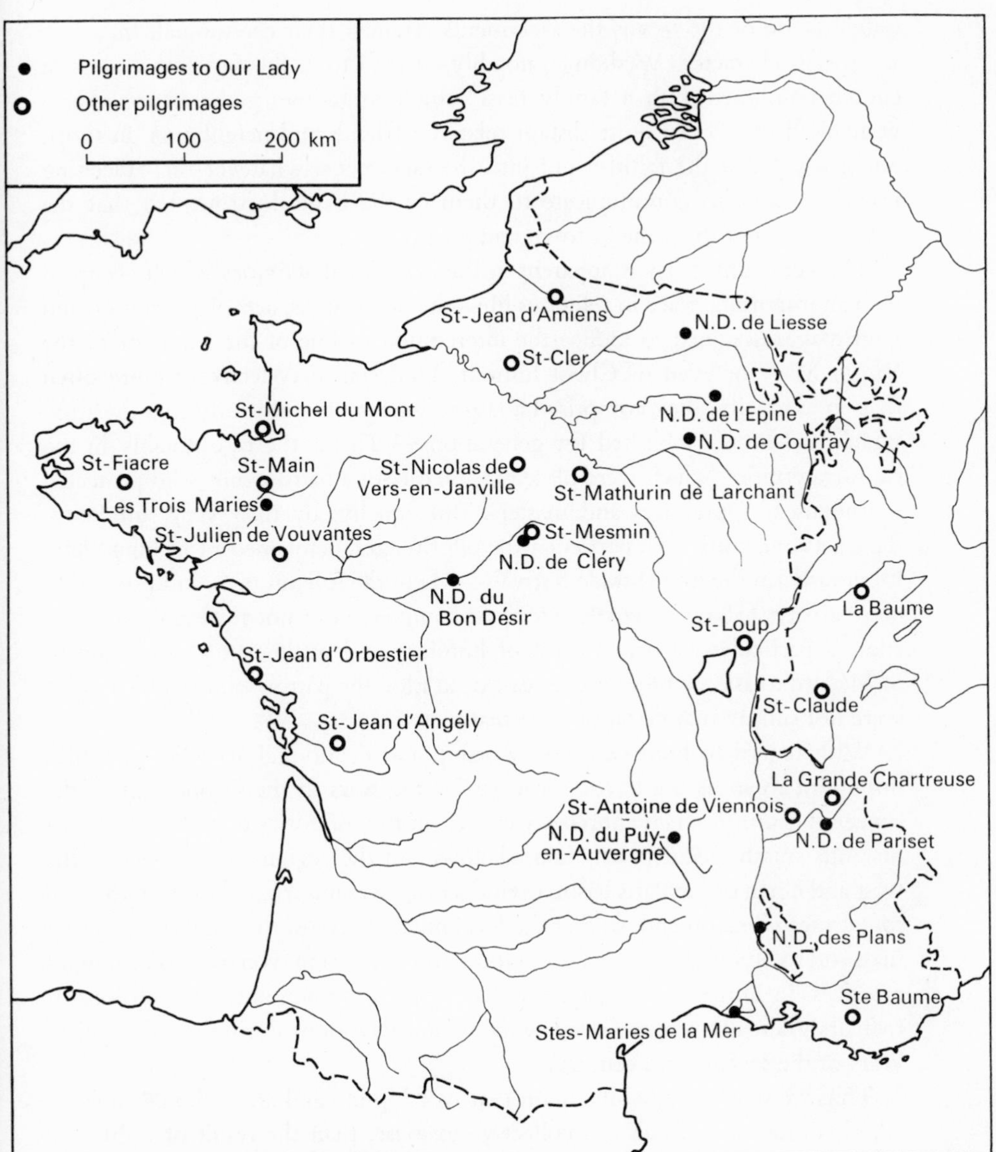

Map 8 Pilgrimages of national repute in the mid-sixteenth century.

religious life of the towns the sacraments retained their ceremonial, that is to say social, character. Weddings, notably, always took the form of a mass in church combined with a family feast which sometimes gathered together a veritable host of even quite distant relatives, friends and neighbours. In short, one can say that the faithful put into the sacraments whatever the officiating priest was able to communicate to them of the basic doctrine, but that the tonality was not the same in town and country.

The same ambiguity is apparent in the devotional activities which occupied such an important place in religious life—the processions, acts of veneration and pilgrimages designed to induce the intercession of one of the Saints or of the Virgin Mary or even of Christ himself. Undertaken collectively more often than individually, they comprised a large element of conformity to a tradition which had been established for generations.[13] This is the case notably in the trade fraternities, which were placed in the care of a patron saint who protected journeymen, apprentices and masters. But equally, by their very simplicity, these acts of devotion, in particular the pilgrimages, betokened a touching piety. Obviously, in the event, trade festivals—where the solemn mass and procession were always followed by receptions or banquets—did not invariably demonstrate a particularly marked spirit of humility and penitence: a procession to St Médard to ask for rain, or the Feast of St Éloi, the patron saint of goldsmiths, were not simply manifestations of great piety.

With regard to both common worship and devotional activities, it is also important to stress the havoc wrought by the wars in the second half of the sixteenth century, when churches were set on fire, oratories demolished, statues of saints smashed and priests hunted down. In the regions most affected, the west and north of the Paris basin, divine service was interrupted for months, and sometimes years, on end, so that the local inhabitants lost the habit of attending mass and receiving the sacraments, without thereby being won over to Protestant practices. In Poitou, Champagne and Picardy, what amounted to missions of regulars gradually re-established worship and devotions during the first thirty years of the seventeenth century.

Thus we would readily maintain that worship in rural areas, though universal, was more a social fact, a collective exercise, than the result of individual meditation. It represented a family and social routine, inherited from one's ancestors, in which the rites solemnizing the important stages in human life predominated: the habitual expression of a simple faith, in which theology was reduced to a straightforward conception of the twin formulae of good and evil—the Devil and the good God, Hell and Paradise—and in which the complexity of Catholic dogma was surmised rather than truly perceived. On the other hand, worship in the towns which was equally universal but more

[13] Cf. Map 8. This should not lead us to forget, however, that each diocese contained some tens of 'minor' pilgrimages.

diligent, can allow one to suppose a more active participation in the intellectual life of the Church and a relatively widespread knowledge of essential sacred literature—the Gospels, St Paul and some of the Church Fathers. Without any doubt, the presence in the towns of active and devoted members of the regular clergy, who were quick to preach and, after 1540, to dispute stoutly the heretical propositions of the Protestants, was no little help in creating among town parishioners demands which were revealed not only on the devotional but also on the moral plane.

★

For apart from these acts of worship, which give little indication of the intellectual quality of their faith, the religious life of the faithful comprised essentially a moral code. The concept of sin, which is basic to the dogma, also determined the moral life of each believer—and, moreover, provides us with a fine example of the variety of meanings which the same word or article of faith can imply according to the spiritual context in which it is understood. Undoubtedly, to a theologian, sin was primarily destruction of the divine order, the sinner losing his righteousness of will, a grace granted him by God, the sinner offending God, the infinite being; it was also a wound inflicted upon the being by the sinner himself. To a village parishioner this concept was certainly not endowed with the same wealth of significance. It meant an offence or wrong-doing in defiance of a moral code which was certainly demanding, but which, at best, was known by the enumeration of the Ten Commandments. Moreover, to make of the laws of Moses the breviary of normal Christian moral standards is not to minimize their sense or their moral significance: to respect another's property, not to kill, etc.

With Christian morality were doubtless combined—though to what extent it is difficult to say—the remnants of a very ancient popular wisdom. Sometimes this took the form of a utilitarian philosophy, at others of a kind of idealistic view of life which ascribed a precise significance to duty, happiness, work, gain and justice. In the form of dictums which had survived for centuries and which are to be found intact in their proverbial form from Pibrac's quatrains to the nineteenth century almanacs,[14] this morality modified and also supplemented the commandments of the Church.

To appreciate how far the morality preached and administered[15] by the Church was that of French society in the sixteenth and seventeenth centuries,

[14] Of the kind 'Like father, like son', 'Money doesn't bring happiness'.

[15] This supervision formed the object of the only publications which the clergy willingly entrusted to educated parishioners at the beginning of the sixteenth century: the many manuals of confession and penitence (*Manuale confessorum*, *De Modo poenitendi et confitendi*, *Examens de conscience*, or again the *Arts de bien mourir*).

one would have to be able to estimate a norm of conduct, express this statistically and gauge it by the scale of social and economic constraints; in other words, to arrive at a better knowledge of the rules and above all of their application. Consideration of conjugal morality alone would presuppose a knowledge of rates of adultery, of how marriages worked under normal conditions, of how long they lasted on average and of the respective ages of spouses. On this topic, as on all those which a methodical exploration of criminal records would allow us to clarify, we are far from having sufficient information even to be able to advance hypotheses. For the moment we must omit any attempt to describe and explain the average morality of the French at that period, with a view to making a wholesale comparison with the standards of the Church.

All we can do is to stress two aspects which indicate obvious variance between Church morality and lay morality. The first of these concerns the use made by the Church of the whole apparatus of ritual sanctions to protect moral laws. Assuredly, bishops' courts varied greatly in their severity. A precept which frequently occupied church tribunals was the one concerning the protection of other people's property. Lucien Febvre has conclusively demonstrated this for Franche-Comté,[16] but the dioceses beyond the Saône do not seem exceptional in this respect. From a twentieth-century viewpoint, one is tempted to say that the severity of the punishment seems disproportionate to the offence committed. Moreover, the temporal practices of the upper clergy, the quarrels and lawsuits between canons over prebends, incited the faithful at the very least to disrespect. Without any doubt, the strict jurisprudence of the theologians who inspired the ecclesiastical courts could not fail to discredit at bottom the morality of the Church: the 'social climate' probably explains the pressure exerted by the courts; the 'abuse'—to use the term hallowed by traditional historiography—clarifies the relative discredit of the clergy in this sphere.

They were thus discredited in the eyes of the humbler classes, who were crushed by an economic system which made the peasant farmer, or even the day-labourer who owned his own plot, a prey to the ambitions of land speculators and moneylenders of all kinds. To this popular form of discredit must be added another of humanist origin, which involved more particularly the educated. Pagan antiquity provided the readers of Cicero, Seneca, Aristotle and Plato with admirable models of good philosophers whose every deed was virtuous though they had been under no Christian influence. Thus there was formed—in Italy and then in France—among those who were conversant with the best of the pre-Christian texts, a notion of moral perfection, or virtue, which related to a man endowed with physical strength, wisdom and liberality. The

[16] Cf. 'L'excommunication pour dettes en Franche-Comté' in Febvre (334), p. 225, and the short work *Notes et documents pour servir à l'histoire de la Réforme et de l'Inquisition en Franche-Comté* (Paris 1912).

humanists thus separated virtue and religion. It was not by chance that at the end of the sixteenth century a sharp mind like Charron drew such a clear distinction between religion, 'a special and particular virtue, distinct from all other virtues and able to exist without them and without probity, as has been said of the Pharisees, who were both religious and wicked', and virtue, which can exist 'without religion, as in the case of several good and virtuous philosophers who were nevertheless irreligious'.[17] For a small number of Christians at least, another morality, which was mostly Stoic in inspiration, acquired full status alongside Christian morality—or else was allied with it by means of a kind of intellectual alchemy which it is difficult to analyse.

The Council of Trent did not pay particular attention to the dangers which were in the long term inherent in such a dissociation of lay morality from the morality of the theologians (a dissociation already apparent on many other questions: moneylending is the best known, or rather the most often quoted, example). Humanist morality, which was destined for a glorious future thanks to the place given to the 'humanities' in the new educational programmes of the Jesuits and the Oratorians, was an essential factor in maintaining, or indeed in developing, the fundamental differences in religious mentality which separated the clergy from the laity in the Catholic Church.[18] The Protestants, who were more aware than anyone else of this divorce, sought to remedy it: this is one of the most outstanding, original features of the new Churches.

The new Protestant edifice: a lay movement

In the face of Catholic traditionalism, of a form of belief and a discipline which were staunchly reaffirmed at Trent and in the movement known as the Counter-Reformation, the Protestant Churches inaugurated a new kind of faith and a new understanding of Christianity.

To be a Protestant in the sixteenth and seventeenth centuries was to be possessed of a desire for renewal which was strong enough to lead to an actual break with the Catholic Church. This is the important distinction between the Protestants and those who sought to promote reform within the Church: men life Lefèvre d'Étaples, Briçonnet and many others who, at the end of the fifteenth century and the beginning of the sixteenth, dreamed of a religion which would be simplified in its doctrines and rites by an invigorating return to the Word.

[17] *Toutes les œuvres de P. Charron, Parisien* (Paris 1635), II, pp. 64 and 65. Cf. on the same theme, Montaigne's *Essays*.

[18] However, spiritual guidance, which was practised so assiduously by the Society of Jesus, was one means of bringing clergy and faithful closer together, by raising the believer to a spiritual life which was nearer that of the clerk. The inadequacy of their efforts, in practice restricted to an urban elite, is obvious: it was so even to contemporaries. Later, the Jansenists were very preoccupied with this problem.

The many admirers of Erasmus of Rotterdam and the loyal disciples of Lefèvre, who translated and annotated the Scriptures and embodied the great reforming hopes of the first twenty years of the sixteenth century, were not Protestants. After the final breach between Luther and Rome, they toned down their ambitions and fell back into line within the Catholic Church. If necessary, they fell silent altogether; but at all events they remained Catholics.[19] The Protestants, on the other hand, accepted the breach, vehemently stressing their points of disagreement and soon lamenting the sorry plight of the vast Catholic flock which was heading for damnation.

But these condemnations, lamentations and affirmations of the evangelical credo were the work of individuals. Certainly they knew what they were talking about, and had read the French translation of the four Gospels which was disseminated throughout France from 1523 by Lefèvre himself. Very often, especially in the beginning, they were monks, Franciscans and others who had pored over St Paul and found therein support for their yearning for a faith which found fulfilment in each individual, without either the human intercession of priests, bishops or confessors, or the paradivine intercession of the saints and the Holy Virgin. The French Protestant lived out his faith as an individual. At most he nurtured it with the help of the guides whom Geneva sent across France in their hundreds from 1550 onwards.[20] As the logical conclusion to the Protestant attitude with its refusal of the Catholic celestial and terrestrial hierarchies, one must admit of a completely individualized form of religion, and contemporaries of Calvin noted without undue surprise a few incidental cases of 'individual heresies which were neither clearly Calvinist nor clearly Lutheran'.[21] The extent of this individual initiative can be judged from its outward manifestations, from the aggressiveness shown by the Protestants towards Catholic symbols. Statues in porches were smashed, windows broken, and altar paintings defaced with great frequency on the eve of the Wars of Religion. Everyone has heard of Jacques Le Clerc, the wool-carder from Meaux, who was banished from France by the *Parlement* of Paris for having torn up the notices of a papal jubilee, and who in 1525 ended his short life of rebellion at Metz where, armed with a tibia, he broke all the statues of the Virgin and the saints in a cemetery. Even at the stake this eloquent little carder preached his faith to the whole town which had gathered to watch; he still debated resolutely with his Inquisitors, refusing in his last moments to say an *Ave*, and died singing *Benedictus Dominus Deus*. These outward forms of revolt are a poor indication

[19] Very much to the indignation of Calvin or Bucer, who saw this as mere discretion or even cowardice.

[20] This would obviously apply less to Lutherans. But Lutheran groups formed before the *Institutes of the Christian Religion* were drawn towards Calvinism, at least within the frontiers of France as they existed at that time.

[21] An example (from 1567) is to be found in Haton (7), I, p. 509.

of the superhuman effort involved in this complete break with the socio-religious environment from which the 'evangelicals' succeeded in escaping. Here again, the evidence of contemporaries carries great weight when they note with some admiration the fervour and dignity with which the condemned Protestant faced the stake. The thousands of Frenchmen who left their families and belongings for exile in Geneva when persecution first broke out also demonstrate in a different way the quality and individualistic nature of their spiritual needs.

As laymen who wished to commune directly with their God, the Protestants restricted the organization of their church to the egalitarian fellowship of believers, whence the only ones to stand out were the elders, whose age and experience entitled them to advise the younger members, and the pastors, the men of learning, the members of the community who were most conversant with the Word. For the communion of the Protestant with his God was not the mystical ecstasy of the devout believer, who had risen to contemplation of Christ through private prayer and thanks to the mysterious intervention of the Holy Spirit. This communion consisted in the first place in reading the Bible. At both the beginning and the end of the *Institutes of the Christian religion*, one finds direct contact with the Scriptures—minus the necessity of translating from Latin into French, minus also the selections and commentaries of the traditional theologians. Morning and evening, the Protestant opened his Bible and gave his own clear and simple commentary in plain French on the parable of the lamp or the denials of Peter. The role of the pastor, who had studied in the Academies at Sedan, Saumur—and Geneva—was quite clear: he was above all the best educated, the most learned of the brethren, who Sunday by Sunday helped the faithful to a better understanding of the difficult passages in the Gospels and the Epistles of St Paul. He was a guide who acknowledged the complete autonomy of the faith of those around him. The representative of God on earth was here replaced by the wise man of the community: as one might say, *primus inter pares*.

To a certain extent, the same characteristic explains the Protestant innovations in doctrine and worship. The monks who went over to the new religion, and initially formed its backbone, had been overtaken by the very logic underlying the whole approach. In the case of the sacraments, as also with regard to salvation by faith and by works, grace and predestination, the simplifications introduced by the Protestants were based upon the New Testament. This is not to say that the doctrine of predestination, when it was not understood in this egalitarian context, did not become a difficult concept—and ultimately almost as impenetrable as many of the Catholic mysteries, which the Protestants had reduced to the status of symbols. But exclusive reference to the Old Testament, the Gospels and the Epistles of St Paul remained the guiding line of this return to a 'pure' form of religion, which the growing mass of Catholic tradition had caused to be forgotten.[22] As Calvin says at the beginning of the *Institutes*, it is a question of respecting and honouring the truth.

Assuredly, this definition of the doctrines of the 'true faith' was not achieved without heart-searching, doubts and second thoughts. How many sacraments should there be? What should be their significance? What should be the place in the liturgy of psalms sung in French? The replies given by Calvin and his followers, in Strasburg and then Geneva, are well known.[23] They gradually won acceptance from the moment when Geneva—more so than Strasburg—was able to provide the pastors, the organization and a résumé of doctrine in the confession of faith of the Protestant Churches of France in 1559. Scruples associated with a stock of the old beliefs inherited from ancestral custom are apparent in contemporary accounts. In 1567 some Huguenots destroyed the decoration of the Church of St Loup de Naud, but left untouched the 'image' of the Patron saint himself, St Loup, who protected against epilepsy. According to Claude Haton,[24] they spared it for fear that God might allow them to be afflicted with epilepsy. Similarly, the Protestants refrained from attacking the healing power of the kings of France, even at the height of the Wars of Religion, thereby demonstrating more discretion than the Leaguers. In his *Les Rois thaumaturges*, Marc Bloch has carefully analysed these attitudes, which from a straightforward conception of the respective orthodoxies one would be tempted to call aberrant. It would be wrong to imagine the followers of the new faith as being wholly consistent, like Calvin, that prophet of inexorable logic.

Similarly, it would doubtless be wrong to exaggerate the moralism of Protestantism, which is all too well known, and rarely seen in its true perspective. On the one hand, the moral standards of Calvin were those of the Apostles themselves, and he based this morality on the particularly exacting, not to say inhuman, doctrine of predestination. On the other hand, the population of Geneva, upon whom this discipline was in the first place imposed, was not particularly prepared to receive it. Thus, as early as the sixteenth century, the Protestant moral code acquired its reputation. According to some memorialists, the Evangelicals stood out even in everyday life on account of their modest and reserved demeanour. But the Reformed Churches, made by and for the laity, did not systematically disparage man's earthly vocation, as certain Catholics had done. In a sense, they even rehabilitated it.[25]

[22] Thus the Catholic Church, in self-defence, could do no other than to join in. The decrees and canons of the Council of Trent refuted 'erroneous' doctrines with many references to sources invoked by the Protestants, which were open to debate (in addition, obviously, to the texts of Catholic tradition).

[23] The interpretation of these choices by the theologians of each orthodoxy obviously does not matter here.

[24] Haton (7), I, p. 442.

[25] This does not justify speculation like that of Max Weber on the predetermined harmony between Protestantism and capitalism.

Thus a new type of Christian arose in the sixteenth century. A million or more French men and women were following the new faith on the eve of the Wars of Religion. Afterwards there were fewer of them, but still enough for their conversion to be postponed and their presence within French society provisionally accepted by the Edict of Nantes in 1598. A new mode of Christian life and experience was imposed by persuasion and force of arms.

Freethinkers

In contrast to the religious hope of the after-life there remains the negative attitude, the most difficult one to grasp for the people of the time. For if it is plausible enough to see laymen and clerks, through meditating upon their reading, upon the Scriptures and the abuses of the century, conceive a new faith, a new doctrine of salvation, it must indeed be observed that these innovators remained Christians, no less attached to first truths (the existence of God and of His Son etc.) than the Catholics. Three centuries of Catholic historiography of the Reformation have instilled into us the stubborn prejudice that, as from the sixteenth century, the daring Protestants were all harbingers of unbelief and atheism. But Lucien Febvre in his *Rabelais* and René Pintard in his *Libertinage érudit* have sufficiently clarified this question to eliminate the need to reopen it at length. If the garrulous Jesuit, Father Garasse, and Father Mersenne —who was more considered in his views—saw freethinkers proliferating in early seventeenth-century France, one can only try to give a more accurate notion of the numbers of these proud spirits, who maintained that they were complete unbelievers, but allowed nothing of this to be seen in their outward behaviour.

In fact, today we can ill appreciate the difficulties into which even the sharpest minds could then be cast by their basic inability to refute wholesale, as being false and valueless, what were universally-accepted truths. There was nothing unusual in preaching the inadequacies of the Church in 1530, since the Vaudois had been doing just that throughout the Midi for two centuries; but to assert that the God of the Bible did not exist was altogether a different matter.

Doubtless, students of antiquity might have found in their reading of the pagan philosophers, in the praises of Stoicism or Epicureanism, a basis for ideas which departed from Christian doctrine. Some of them, indeed, through reading Lucian or the rare (preserved) controversies which marked the beginnings of Christianity, might have found in these works disturbing polemics concerning the most delicate points of doctrine or the most unfathomable of mysteries. This was the case with Des Périers, who could not accept the divinity of Christ, a case which has already been studied at length by Lucien Febvre.[26] Still others might have been tempted by the enigma posed by the discovery of new worlds

[26] Febvre (285).

peopled by nations with no knowledge of the Christian religion—and, by all appearances, unknown to Christ, his Apostles and their successors. However, the crucial step was not taken, despite the possibilities offered by ancient mythology, rich in poetic imagery allowing a great degree of licence, or by literary forms such as the dialogue, which was cherished by Erasmus and detested by the theologians, who fully appreciated the ambiguity and dangers inherent in it.

The 'century which wanted to believe' doubtless did not produce freethinkers who denied God and confessed this even confidentially to a diary or a trustworthy friend. Neither Des Périers nor Rabelais nor Montaigne were of this order, whatever they have been made to say since. On the other hand, at the beginning of the seventeenth century—and this is where the evidence of Father Garasse is not wholly to be dismissed—a small group of *esprits forts* lived in Paris, lying and dissembling, the group which Pintard has tracked down and brought out into the daylight. Garasse accuses men like Cardan, Charron and Vanini of believing in God only 'out of propriety and political expediency', and of secretly professing total scepticism which allowed them to lead an unprincipled life. What is true in the denunciations of the Jesuit, and what Pintard has amply shown, is that the freethinkers in the early seventeenth century were scientists,[27] who were well-versed in the classics and steeped in ancient philosophy and in the scientific knowledge of their day. La Mothe le Vayer, Gassendi and Patin were men of great culture, and were definitely isolated from the vast majority of their fellow-citizens. They were certainly known as scientists, which explains the attention given to them by such men as the Minim, Mersenne, himself a scientist, or even by the Jesuit Father, Garasse.

But one can safely suggest that the freethinkers in the early seventeenth century, whatever they may have developed into later, whatever their 'standing' even in Pascal's day, were no more than hesitant precursors, whose attitudes were not as yet widely shared. They certainly existed, but merely serve to indicate the radical opportunities missed by the age of humanism.

★

Indifferent, intermittent and devout, the categories used by modern French religious sociologists, are therefore not valid to describe the religious attitudes of the sixteenth and seventeenth centuries. The 'model' which Gabriel Le Bras has devised for a time of widespread dechristianization is inapplicable to former times. Yet some typology deserves to be created, to allow an accurate reconstruction of these different attitudes. Universality of worship scarcely masks a disparity in beliefs as great as in our own day. The devout and the freethinkers still doubtless represented the two extreme standpoints, but they were both minority groups, the one having pride of place while the other lingered in

[27] Their scientific daring in some respects counts for more than their religious scepticism.

obscurity. The attitudes in between, which involved the great majority, are however the most interesting. Not until these original standpoints, which closely allied superstition, pagan survivals and articles of orthodox faith, have been fully explored and explained, shall we be able to form a valid impression of the spiritual life of the modern period.

Chapter 17
Escapism: nomadism

Above the routine activities which were devoted to achieving some degree of mastery over the world and men, but on a lower plane than the superior creative activities of artists and scholars and the transcendency of the religious life, lay a third—and no less significant— attitude of mind. It was escapism or flight into another world, seen as a means of eluding the cumbersome, tiresome or simply monotonous realities of everyday life. This is a common attitude in a world where social and even natural constraints weigh so heavily upon the vast majority of mankind. To escape, temporarily or permanently, thus appears as a form of compensatory activity, which has its skilled practitioners in every society; and the society of modern France was certainly no exception.

The variety of escapist pursuits practised in the sixteenth and seventeenth centuries is some indication of the strength of this feeling, of this desire to flee, if only momentarily, from a hard life. The evidence of this almost universal aspiration serves as a fitting rejoinder to those who would see only the splendours of the Renaissance or the Counter-Reformation. Almost every profession had its travellers who, while no doubt perpetuating medieval guild traditions, were also satisfying a need to elude their routine existence in a very real way for a few years. Pilgrims and soldiers also sought a positive escape far from their own parish and traditional environment. But even more numerous, perhaps, were those who took refuge in the world of the imagination and found in exotic accounts, in the festivals or in commemorative dramatic presentations an even more fleeting and ephemeral liberation from their everyday circumstances. Their dream world knew no bounds once the details of the recent great discoveries became widely known. Lastly, there were others who, more demanding and perhaps also more disillusioned, despite appearances, invoked the Devil, hoping thus to obtain at the cost of eternal damnation a mastery over the world and men which no-one at that time could expect from science or from human capabilities. The logical conclusion of this search for escape was, in our view, a complete rejection of life with its mediocre hopes and its overwhelming strictures: suicide, the last resort and literal act of renunciation, was doubtless the most real form of evasion practised by modern man—though it was no more prevalent than at other periods. Whether their escape was real or imaginary, temporary or permanent, whether they were satisfied with a momentary change of element or dealt in stronger emotions, all who sought elsewhere what their everyday life did not offer bore witness in their respective ways to a common attitude of mind which it is essential to take into account in attempting to understand this difficult period.

★

Foremost among such types of escapism came nomadism, the wanderlust that would not be denied. Students, peasants, artisans, soldiers and, above all, the dreaded vagabonds who made a profession of roaming the roads, all thronged the highways and found undisguised joy in spending years wandering across Europe. This mobility, for which some have sought distant parallels in a history steeped in racial primitivism, was one of the great social features of the time. Braudel has demonstrated this for the Mediterranean area in particular, but there is no doubt that it was a European phenomenon, with northern France sharing in it just as much as the Midi. Dole, a small university town in Franche-Comté, welcomed students from all over Europe; Besançon witnessed the passage within its walls of journeymen of all trades, along with pilgrims visiting the shrine of St Claude and merchants drawn to Lyons. Many human destinies were ruled by this constant urge to travel the world. We read for example of a native of Autun, who was arrested at Dijon at the beginning of the sixteenth century for stealing a horse. A dyer by trade in his native town, he had been prompted by a disease of the legs to make a pilgrimage to St Antoine de Viennois. There he met a galleymaster who took him to Avignon, and then off to sea for two years. Thence he returned to Lyons in the service of a man-at-arms, who dragged him off to fight in Brittany, then in Picardy where he gave up soldiering and made his way alone to Provence, then to Southern Italy. He was still in Naples when the French king arrived; he entered his service and returned to France as a bombardier, only to desert at Dijon.

This is perhaps an extreme case; but it is certainly true that such wanderings held no terrors—despite the well-known discomfort of travel on foot or on horseback. After all, Noël du Fail's Eutrapel recommended, as a means of improving the administration of the kingdom, the appointment of itinerant judges, bishops and priests who might move on every three or six months. Peripatetic officials to deal with a shifting population: the formula is significant.

Equally extreme is the case of the sailors who went to sea avidly seeking adventure (cf. Map 9). They were attracted by the discovery of new worlds and by the life of danger led by those who sailed the seas. At the beginning of the seventeenth century, it was no longer the Mediterranean but the Atlantic which provided the opening for this major form of escapism.[1]

[1] Which knew no frontiers, either: Magellan's crew included ten French sailors.

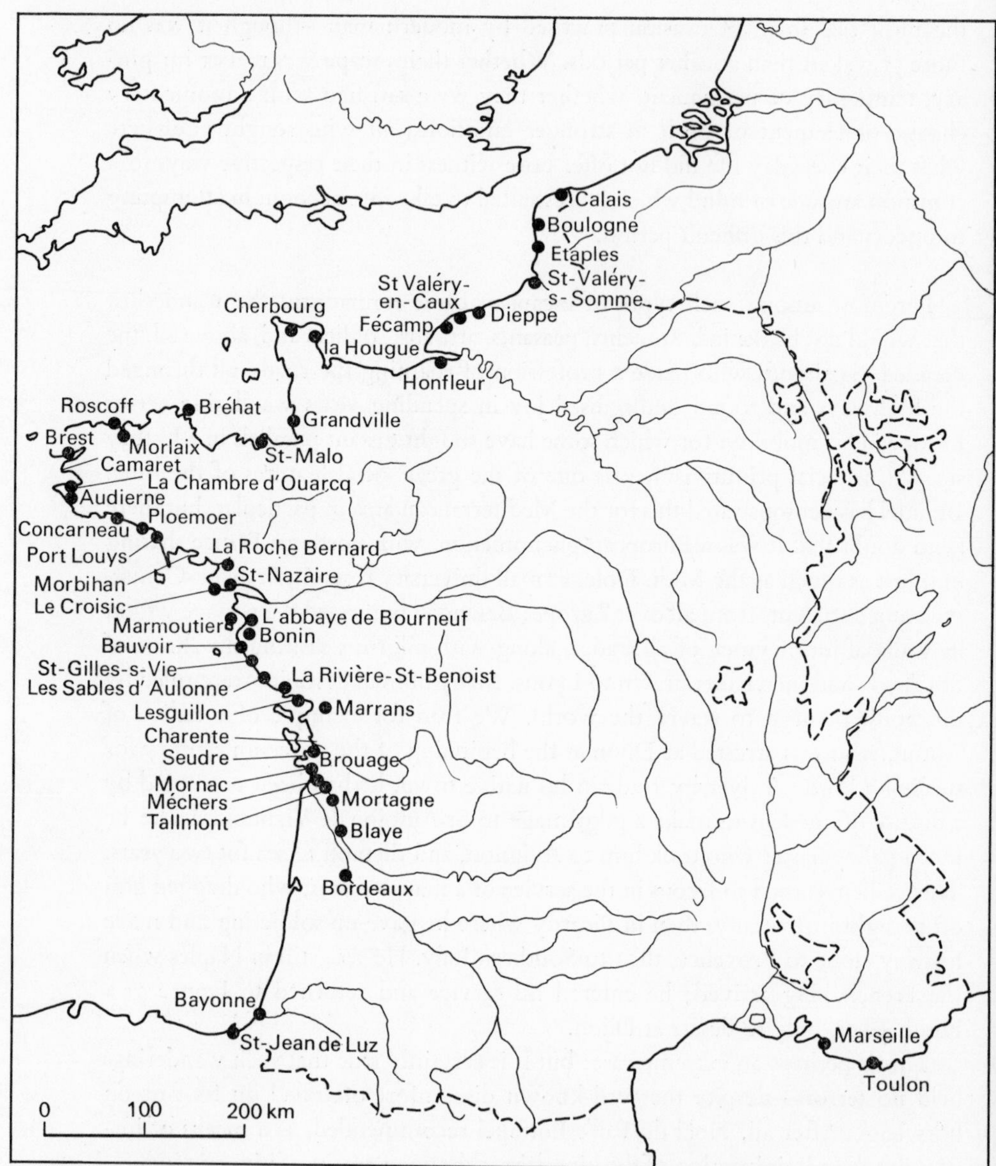

Map 9 The great escape overseas: the main ports at the beginning of the seventeenth century, according to Isaac de Razilly.

Plate 9 The layman's prayer (1527), or the difference between this and the seventeenth-century orison.

Plate 10 Stimulants and drugs: a drinking song.

Plate 11 The Devil at the cradle of a newborn child.

DESPERATIO
QVISQVIS EST HANC FVGITO
DIRA AD SVSPENDIA COGIT

Plate 12 Desperatio: a woman hanging herself.

Moreover, it was the men who travelled. Apart from ladies of high nobility, who took some part in royal expeditions, womenfolk clearly stayed at home. And in many cases the woman proved incapable of holding the nomad, for whom leaving home might be a wrench or, quite simply, a flight. The thousands of Protestants[2] threatened with persecution who sought refuge in Geneva between 1549 and 1560 were almost all men: of 6,000 refugees less than 200 were women. It was common to leave one's family, even a large family, for several years—and to do so was certainly not regarded as outrageous.

Nevertheless, there was more than one form of nomadism. The vagabonds who terrorized the roads and the soldiers who ravaged the countryside, two groups who immediately spring to mind, were what one might call the most extreme cases. But pilgrims, artisans or mere travellers like Montaigne, though less dangerous and less committed to a life of vagabondage, were nevertheless 'nomads' who were more or less consciously fired by a thirst for adventure.

The nomadic professions

To examine the occupations which allowed of—or presupposed—some measure of travel for those who pursued them, would ultimately involve our mentioning them all, since, for a variety of reasons, they all implied, or sometimes facilitated, absences for which work could act as a pretext.

Not even the peasant was exempt from this, despite his attachment to the land. In his case it was famine or freak weather conditions that made it necessary. In the spring of 1531, famine brought 8,000 poor peasants to the gates of Lyons on one occasion alone; they had been driven from their villages by lack of food. During the two months from 19th May to 9th July, 12,000 paupers found food and shelter with the Franciscan and Dominican friars in the same town. In 1533–4 a new wave of paupers descended upon Lyons, ill and infirm, young and old, and all clamouring night and day. Completely destitute, they wandered aimlessly and upon a chance encounter joined some band of soldiers or a caravan of gypsies and roamed Spain or Italy—perhaps to settle again months later, after many misfortunes, in some village which had been abandoned by its inhabitants seasons before under the same circumstances. Alongside these mass migrations necessitated by natural disasters and the temporary and as yet little known migrations of the inhabitants of mountain regions into the plains in the south to profit by the differing times for harvesting, there also existed a floating rural population of agricultural day-labourers, semi-vagabonds who roamed the roads in search of odd jobs between providing seasonal labour for the corn and grape harvests and the sowing. They formed a sizeable group,

[2] However, they were not exactly nomads: religious persecution gave rise to migrations which were lasting rather than temporary. But this does not weaken our argument. Cf. Map 5, p. 80.

which it is difficult to distinguish from the professional vagabonds, the criminals who infested the notorious forests.

The case of the artisans, who went from town to town learning their trade and the skills and processes peculiar to each region—before settling in some pleasant spot—already seems more orthodox. Thus, braziers from Auvergne went as far afield as Spain and ironfounders from Lorraine and Parisian cabinetmakers offered their services all over France. There was a certain logic in this: it seemed easier to bring a Parisian cabinetmaker to Touraine than to transport a fragile piece of furniture over bad roads and run a thousand and one risks. Similarly, bellfounders went from church to church, and printers from town to town, while artillerymen and saltpetre-men were in great demand everywhere. Moreover, tradesmen such as these did not merely travel round France: heedless of frontiers, they wandered throughout Europe. Very often, these lengthy tours led them to mix with the brigands who held the highways. Many such trades were held in disrepute and their noisy bands were not always well-received—whatever services they rendered. In 1527, the French braziers who were robbing the poor in Spain found the streets forbidden to them!

The 'intellectuals' of the time were no less mobile than the 'mechanics'. Everyone has heard of the students who went from university to university to study under the best masters. The Italian schools were at a premium in the sixteenth-century market, but all the French universities, from the smallest like Dole to the most famous like Montpellier had their 'nations' of foreigners. Young Germans and Swiss came in a constant stream to Montpellier, to stay a few months and then move on, as Felix Platter notes. But the masters were just as mobile as their students. To have a 'visiting professor' in a Faculty was by no means unusual, and each university would have several who were attached to it for varying periods, after which they returned to their house of origin, or moved on farther afield. Paris sent teachers to places all over Europe, but so too did Salamanca and Coimbra. Also on the move were the monks who were charged with a mission for their order or were at the disposal of their provincial or prior—or again, those who had already moved onto the fringes of monastic life, having virtually abandoned the cloister, and who lived on the roads as tutors or surgeons, saying mass on occasion and from time to time rejoining a house of their order or some university. Artists too travelled round the country in response to their commissions and the hospitality of generous patrons; they were accompanied by a whole *familia* of apprentices, assistants and young relatives, who worked under their direction until they in turn had their own studios. For all who pursued these occupations, the desire to see strange lands was no doubt less important than their wish to learn or to pass on their own knowledge. In 1553, we find the lord of Gouberville taking into his home 'a young man from Touraine . . . who . . . dabbled in philosophy and wanted to go to the Indies to practise his art', whom he kept for two years. The boy was fed and kept in clean linen, and taught the master of the house the Greek alphabet and the art of constructing stills 'to distil spirits'.

In the case of the merchant, travelling seems to have been more in keeping with the requirements of his profession. From the petty hawkers who roamed towns and villages after trade fairs to the bankers and big traders of international commerce, they all had to take to the road, often for months on end. Lyons and Paris were invaded by Genoese and Lucchese, who were easily recognizable by their different costumes. The inns of the big commercial centres formed a vast network of commercial rendezvous, where all languages were spoken and a thousand and one business deals transacted. And if it is true that the princes of international trade could afford to do business at long range, it was thanks to a host of agents and couriers who travelled post-haste to bring them news, quotations and offers in time, and to pass on orders to buy and sell. A prey to attack by vagabonds, the merchants certainly formed the largest group among the nomads who thronged the roads. They protected themselves to the best of their ability, travelling in convoys and under escort. The frequency with which their risks and misfortunes are recalled indicates how numerous were the professional nomads, to whom we shall return in a moment.

Pilgrims and 'tourists'

The countless pilgrims who, staff in hand, took the road to St James Compostella, Our Lady of Loretto, Rome, or even Jerusalem were also escaping from their everyday way of life. These long-distance travellers must not lead us to forget the pilgrims who were more modest in their aims and were content with some relic or shrine of local or barely national repute; such were St Jean d'Angely or Notre Dame de Cléry and many others, which were often dedicated to healers, like St Marcoul de Corbeny or St Amable de Riom. These pilgrims were often sick and in need of the intercession of a 'specialist', each sanctuary having its vocation clearly defined by tradition. Others were fulfilling a vow made during some time of trial or, more prosaically, after a bout of feasting. They were thus making a journey of devotion which they would doubtless not have the opportunity of repeating in their lifetime.

We know the most popular pilgrimage centres and their access routes well enough to be able to imagine the usual procedure. When embarking on a pilgrimage to Notre Dame du Puy or to the Mont Saint Michel, the penitents modelled their journey on the way of the Cross. Placing themselves under the protection of the patron saints of travel (St Christopher and St Anthony), they went from sanctuary to chapel, taking care to worship on the way all the saints along their route. When they had the means, they even founded churches or chapels in the name of the patron saints of their native region who were watching over them. Thus, in Oisans there were chapels to St Julien (of Brioude) and

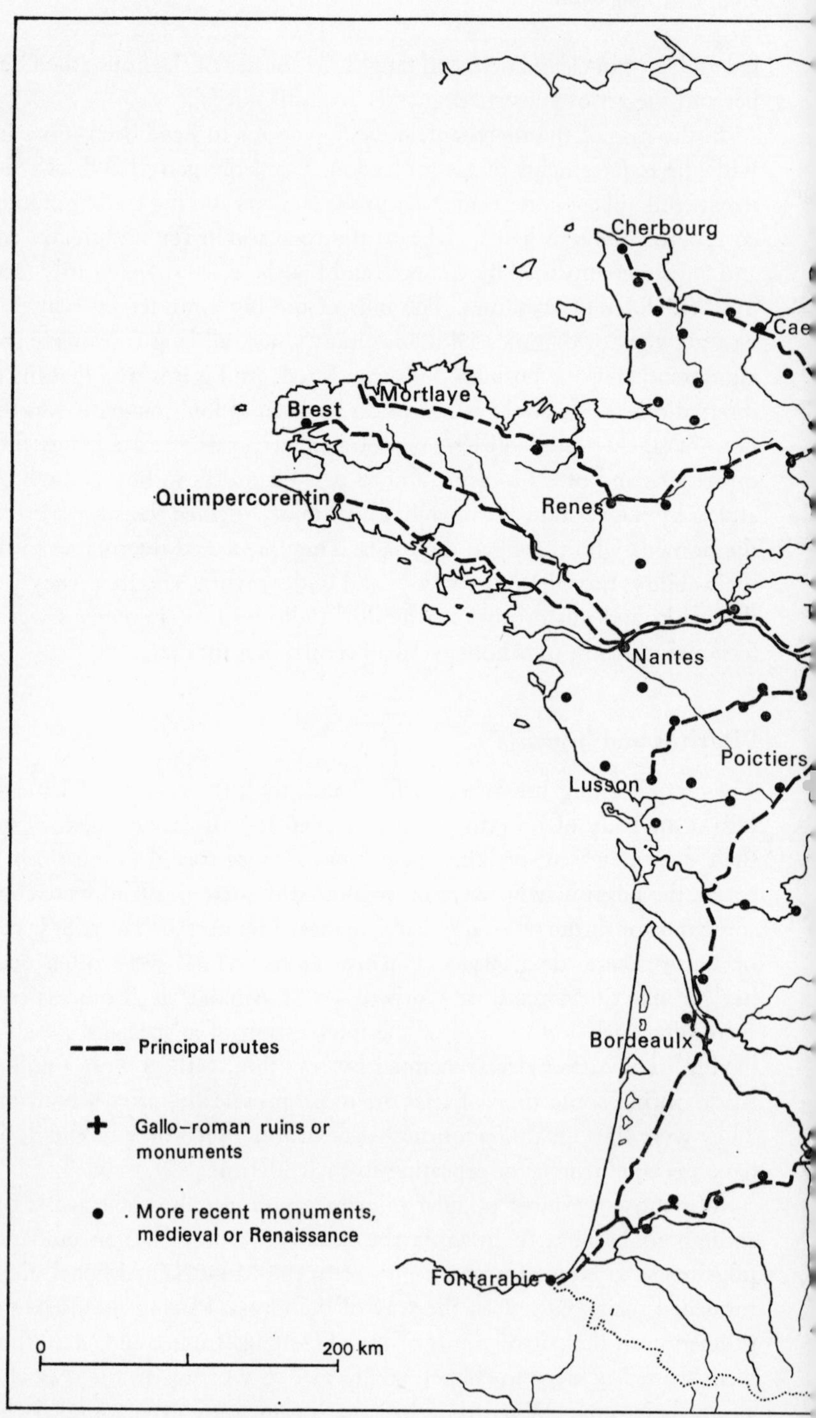

Map 10 Travel and places of interest in the mid-sixteenth century, according to C

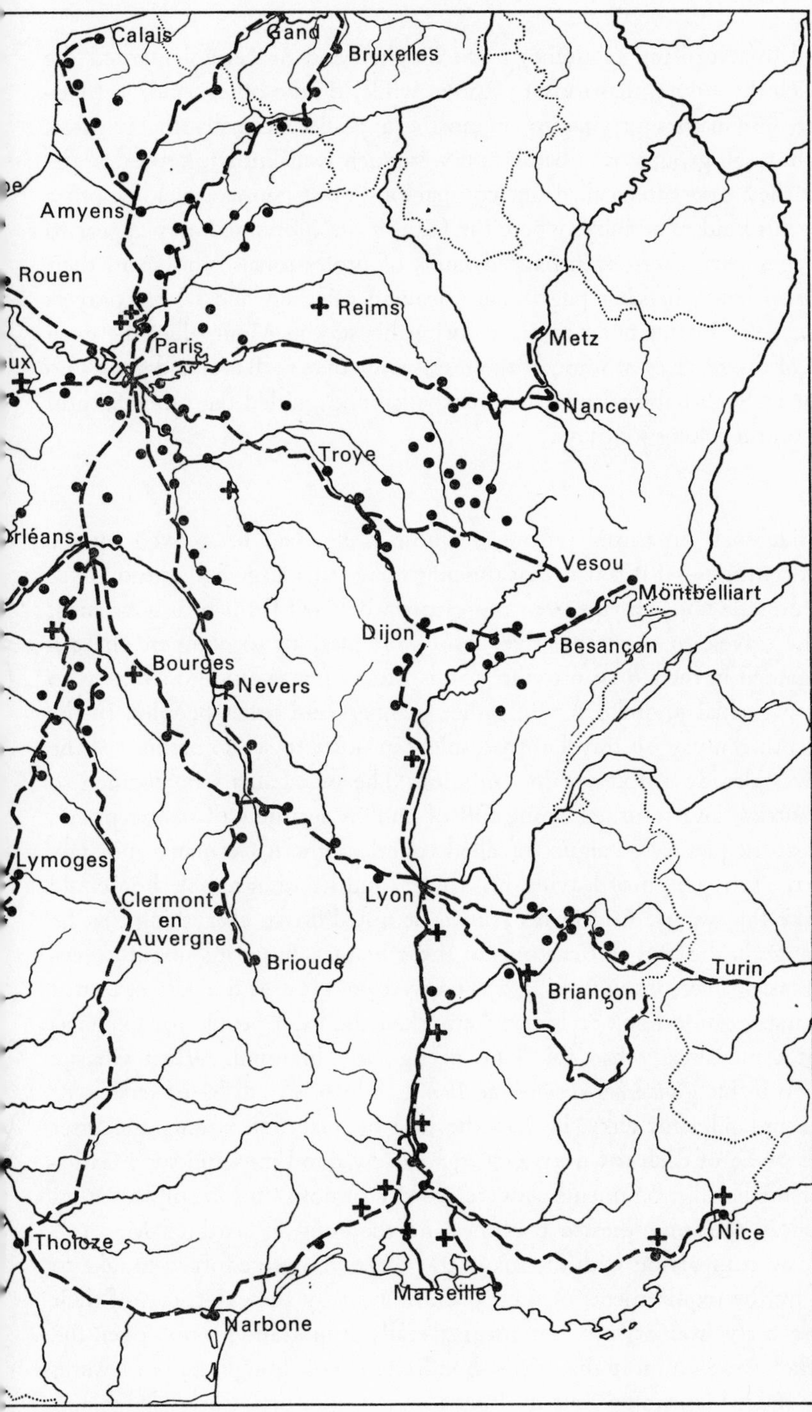

Calais
Gand
Bruxelles
Amyens
Rouen
Reims
Paris
Metz
Nancey
Troye
Vesou
Montbelliart
Dijon
Besançon
Bourges
Nevers
Lymoges
Clermont en Auvergne
Brioude
Lyon
Turin
Briançon
Nice
Tholoze
Marseille
Narbone

ne.

St Géraud (of Aurillac). Churches to St Stephen and St Ferréol marked the route which the Auvergnats took to Rome, while, on the other hand, in Maurienne we find names originating in northern France. Usually the pilgrims travelled in small groups or in bands and were such well-known figures on the roads that they were often called the 'companions' of St James or of some other shrine. In this kind of activity, where the faith of the individual may appear to play a bigger part, there even existed kinds of professionals who spent their lives, staff in hand, making pilgrimages, leaving offerings and saying prayers for others. Felix Platter notes the fact during his stay in Montpellier (he even made use of the services of some of them to send letters to Basle) and shows no surprise at it. Such habitual pilgrims marshalled and guided the other faithful travellers on their long journeys.

*

Alongside such organized journeys, whose routes had been fixed by the custom of centuries—if it is true that the pilgrimage to a large extent took over from the crusade and perhaps even represents a debased form of it—we must include the travels of the inquisitive, who were anxious to compare the experience gained in their own province (or as Montaigne would go so far as to say, their parochial prejudices) with other manners and other peoples. In the mid-sixteenth century, to travel abroad solely in order to see something of the country was already a noteworthy ambition. The merchants who roamed so many countries, and returned home full of endless accounts of exotic places, found their disciples. Montaigne travelled round southern Germany and Italy more for the satisfaction of leaving his 'tower' and his disagreeable household than to take the waters. And in his *Journal* he noted down everything that he found strange in the uses and customs of those he met, inquiring about everything and taking pleasure in visiting and conversing. He was the perfect tourist who, lacking a guide-book in his pocket, asked the local people for explanations. But some already had this kind of sightseer in mind. When Charles Estienne wrote his *Guide des chemins de France*, which was to be of service to merchants and pilgrims alike, he had the idea of including among the brief particulars given of each town or each stage a few good inns and such Gallo-Roman or medieval monuments as were worthy of note—for example, cathedrals, basilicas, the amphitheatre at Nîmes and the Pont du Gard (cf. Map 10). Certainly, by comparison with the many travellers who were forced to take to the roads by the requirements of their profession or by the exigencies of their faith, these early 'tourists' do not form a really important group: over the century, they were no more than a few hundred men of thought and of leisure, who were indeed 'escaping', but in order to arrive at a better knowledge and understanding of the world in which they lived. In short, one can say that tourism at its outset was more serious in intention than it is today.

Pilgrims and tourists were temporary nomads. Apart from the few who risked the journey to Jerusalem, they did not remain on the road for long—a few months, or a year at most. This feature alone is enough to distinguish them from the 'professionals'.

Soldiers and professional nomads

There was little difference between the soldier and the brigand. If a troop was disbanded, the soldiers without ties or resources became brigands for a time, though they still kept in touch and served again when recalled. Thus no one was misled. From Jean Bodin to Montchrestien, it was generally considered that soldiers were recruited among the 'hotbloods' of the population—the thieves, idlers, rebels, murderers and vagrants who corrupted loyal subjects, and of whom one ought to 'purge the country as of phlegm'. Bodin was even of the opinion that, if the State lacked enemies, some ought to be created to ensure that these 'corrupt humours' were put to use.[3]

No reference is intended here to the military vocation of the nobility or the local town militia. By soldiers we mean the mercenaries recruited by officers to meet the needs of current campaigns, who season by season acted as fighting men on the frontiers, abroad, or between 1560 and 1600 in the civil wars. The ravaging troops and their train of hangers-on, carts for booty, and loose women were the most dreaded of the professional nomads. Nothing could resist them, except towns which were protected by strong walls and were able to use artillery against their ranks—and which at all events could negotiate about the billeting of officers and men. Military life certainly did not lack prestige. If the kings of France readily called upon foreign troops from Switzerland and Germany, it was so as to control more effectively their perennially disobedient troops. There was no lack of volunteers in France itself, so highly was the fighting man valued in this period of continual war. Montluc puts it well when he says at the end of the century: 'I have seen soldiers, the sons of husbandmen, who lived and were buried with the reputation of being the sons of great lords because of their worth and the store that kings and their lieutenants set by them.' This itinerant life of brigandage, of musket-shot and swordplay, combined the charms of vagabondage with security and the glory of feats of arms. It was the most glamorous form of professional nomadism, of life outside the law.

With the arrival of a period of calm or a general peace these companies were almost entirely disbanded, but continued to lead the life of 'outlaws'. Retaining some of their weapons, they headed for the forests and hills and formed

[3] Half a century later, Montchrestien added another outlet—the conquest of New France. He wanted to send soldiers over there to do the fighting, then respectable family men to occupy the land.

the bands of vagabonds which terrorized villages—just as much as the gypsies, those bands of aliens that were continually being driven out of the kingdom, yet were ever-present. These highway robbers, formed into well-organized bands, roamed the open countryside, occupied the 'prosperous' approaches to towns like Lyons and Rouen, and even infiltrated a great city like Paris, where they were a law unto themselves, at least at night, without the king and his agents being able to combat them very effectively. A few notable arrests from time to time[4] were a poor remedy against a way of life which was assured of an indefinite supply of recruits by social pressure. The town and highway robbers were the professional nomads; they were in contact with the nomadic artisans, monks and peasants, and obviously also drew fresh recruits from amongst their ranks given the right circumstances. A kind of solidarity of the poor means that it is difficult to separate these various groups. But this very fact helps us to understand the importance of nomadism in the group psychology of the period.

[4] 'On Thursday 3rd September 1609, one of the principal officers of the court that their Honours the robbers and pickpockets of Paris had set up and were holding near the hay-docks, sentencing some to fines, some to flogging and some to death . . . was discovered and caught . . . then hanged. Some said he was their president, others their general.' A N, AD, III, 2, 86.

Chapter 18
Escapism: imaginary worlds

The second expedient of those who rejected the iron age in which they lived was to take refuge in the creations of their own imagination, where the possibilities were endless. Anyone who was unable to travel across Europe or the world had at his disposal travel books written by missionaries and soon afterwards by geographers. Anyone who lacked either the rank or the means to aspire to the privileged classes of the day could always resort to identifying himself with them, if only momentarily, during festivities or theatrical performances. Anyone who lacked the strength of will to shut himself off from the world and lead the monastic life, spent in contemplating God's mysteries, could also seek escape in mysticism if his prayers for grace were only answered. All these forms of mental escapism were constantly practised by large numbers of people, especially at the end of the sixteenth and the beginning of the seventeenth centuries. In this respect, a change of climate is particularly noticeable between the years 1500–1540 and the following period.

A characteristic of all these 'mental constructions' is that they were wholly conscious, and must be defined as such. Unlike our contemporaries in the twentieth century, modern man did not have at his disposal the varied and effective range of stimulants and narcotics which make it possible to harness physiological processes to the workings of the imagination, or indeed to increase the power of the latter tenfold. We must first assign a place to this deficiency.

Lack of stimulants and narcotics

As we have already indicated in the chapter on food,[1] the French in the sixteenth century did not drink coffee, tea or cocoa, which at that time had only just reached Europe by way of the Mediterranean and were still curiosities. The same is true of tobacco, although this spread much more rapidly. Taken as snuff or in quids as often as in cigars of rolled leaves, it was sufficiently popular

[1] Cf. Part I, ch. 1, p. 22.

at the end of the sixteenth century to be planted in gardens more or less everywhere. Olivier de Serres included it in his *Théâtre d'agriculture*: 'that exquisite Nicotine plant which easily grows in every corner of France, though it came from Portugal and was brought there from America'.[2] At the end of the period in question, the consumption of tobacco in the towns began to worry municipal authorities, who blamed it in some places for encouraging tavern crawling and causing an increase in drinking. In 1628, the procurator fiscal of Amiens deplored 'the use of tobacco or *petun*' which he wished to have prohibited. In 1630, an ordinance asserted that 'several artisans and tradesmen . . . partake of the said spirits and tobacco unnecessarily, only in order to make themselves thirsty and give themselves cause to drink. . . .' In short, the two went together; though one should point out that spirits, which had been known to apothecaries for a very long time, seem to have become popular well before the spread of the tobacco plant.

From the middle of the sixteenth century, it would seem, the custom spread of borrowing from apothecaries the 'vessels' which they used for making spirits (ardent spirits) to distil all kinds of ordinary drinks—wine, beer, cider and *lye de bière*. Often, indeed, the apothecaries accompanied their equipment and themselves undertook to make the liquor, which thus ceased to be one of the remedies used in the learned preparations of alchemistic pharmacy and instead became a drink, essentially a tavern drink. In the seventeenth century, spirits by far surpassed wine or cider as the main resource of the drunkard, and some towns did not hesitate to forbid their sale in taverns, and even by private individuals.

However, it is very difficult to judge the consequent increase in drunkenness. Police regulations accuse the humbler classes, the artisans and the poor, who are alleged to have found in such oblivion ready satisfaction which was dangerous for their health and families. The lord of Gouberville, who quite frequently made spirits for his own use, mentions country lads who went round the village with bottles in their pockets. Assuredly, the new drink spread quickly, and before 'ardent spirits' became popular, wine, cider and beer served the same purpose in all classes of society.[3]

The range of physiological aids to escapism was thus relatively restricted. In fact, there was almost nothing apart from mere crude drunkenness induced by wine or alcohol—and, at all events, none of the sweet dreams of the drugs from the Orient. The 'artificial paradises' were not yet open.

Music and the theatre

Music and the theatre, being more than mere entertainments like dancing or playing bowls,[4] introduced performers and audiences into an unreal world,

[2] De Serres (217), p. 572.
[3] Drinking songs—cf. Plate 10.
[4] Cf. above, Part III, ch. 12.

and thus gave all their participants far more than the most popular of games. A small stage in a public square, or a few drapes in the choir of a church, and without much effort everyone was transported back to Judea in the time of the Passion, or simply into a society without orders or rites, where the villein spoke his mind to the lord, where animals remonstrated with men, or where the fantasy of comedy and song was allowed free rein.

At the beginning of the sixteenth century, great religious festivals and important political events (the signing of a peace-treaty or the birth of a dauphin) were the usual occasions for these theatrical performances, which took place, following the procession across the town, either in the parvis or the choir of the church—or cathedral. Derived as they were from medieval mystery plays, these festivities were for a long time—certainly for as long as they were held on sacred ground—devoted to illustrating some event of Church history. The Passion obviously headed the list, but mysteries drawn from the Acts of the Apostles, the Old Testament and the Apocalypse were also very commonly performed.

Alongside these historical and apologetic productions, mountebanks offered at random, wherever fairs, royal Entries, or their regular tours led them, topical presentations, farces, *sotties*, morality plays and songs, which the inhabitants flocked to see. Their little plays often did not last half an hour, were performed by two or three characters, and had as their only scenery a brief preliminary statement by the prologue which located the action. However, this theatre was no less popular than the solemn presentations.[5]

In the second half of the century, college presentations were added to the traditional forms at the instigation of the Jesuits. The towns which founded colleges were just as keen as the Fathers on this form of activity, and many foundation charters stipulate the organization of such spectacles which, in addition, allowed the pupils to acquire 'ease and confidence'. These performances were sometimes given in the public square, in the courtyard of the bishop's palace, under the market-hall—or more often, in the establishment's own chapel or in a hall specially built for declamations, a sort of hall for festive occasions which in the seventeenth century was often the only hall of its kind in the town. Pont-à-Mousson, Chaumont, Besançon, Autun, Nevers, Moulins, Roanne, Lyons and Chambéry—to take examples from the eastern half of the country alone—had just such an 'auditorium' in 1630.

The success of these different kinds of theatre (accompanied by music) cannot be doubted. The whole town flocked to see them and returned for each performance. For example, in 1609, the bourgeois of Le Puy were treated to 'the story of Daniel in a French verse adaptation by Brother Jacques Mondoct,

[5] Mountebanks, moreover, did not feel precluded from performing the Passion or the Old Testament. Often the *échevins*, in giving them permission to perform, asked them to stage mystery plays and not only 'undesirable and unseemly' farces.

prior of St Pierre le Monestier'. Everyone returned on each of the three days of Whitsun when the play was presented; and for long after they talked about Daniel, Nebuchadnezzar and Susanna. But for the mountebanks it was better still; it was necessary to prohibit their performing during sermons and vespers, to limit the length of their stay and the number of their performances in each town, and to forbid candlelight performances. Through the miracle of theatrical communion, everyone could feel for a few instants freed from his miseries and transformed into Alexander.

In other companies and in other places—although dramatic performances of all kinds were regularly accompanied by songs and *vielles*—the music of Josquin des Prés, Jannequin and Lasso undoubtedly served the same purpose, and perhaps with even greater ease than rhetorical drama or broad farces on the stage. There is no doubt that through this polyphonic music, which gave such direct expression to gladness and lamentation, grief and joy, contemporaries, to whom hearing remained all-important, were irresistibly borne far away from their preoccupations and habitual surroundings. Great noblemen and prelates had amongst their retinues one or more musicians who played and sang to them several times a day to soothe them. But the bourgeoisie and the lower classes, who took greater delight in songs than in more elaborate works, expected as much from this art which the still too turgid, wordy and heavy-handed literature of the period could not equal. The 'sweet strains of instruments', of which Ronsard loves to sing, were surely one of the passions of the age.

Imaginary journeys

However, especially from about the mid-sixteenth century, reading provided an endless fund of inspiration for anyone tempted by armchair travel. During the Renaissance, it was above all the works of the ancient geographers that were published; but with the development of voyages of exploration in the new worlds, and especially with the growth of the missionary spirit, a whole new type of literature sprang up, which reached its peak at the beginning of the seventeenth century. Between 1600 and 1640, accounts of voyages of exploration and missions numbered almost 300 titles.

We have no means of judging the success of these literary *genres* other than the volume of published works and new editions. Descriptions of new lands and accounts of missionary activity fell into more or less equal groups, with the Middle East and Far East occupying a far higher place than America in this strange order of merit, thanks to works written by missionaries. There can be no doubt that these hundreds and thousands of books found readers. But it is also possible to note how far a taste for exotic accounts pervaded the world of literature. Novels, which became more and more popular in the seventeenth century, readily adopted an important geographical theme. As the unknown author of the *Histoire africaine* pompously declared in his preface: 'I have paid attention to details with which very few others have been concerned, in particular to geographical accuracy.'[6] Similarly, the *Mercure français* from its outset took care to offer its readers detailed descriptions of little-known lands, sometimes accompanied by plans or maps.[7] The great travellers like Razilly, Lejeune, Dutertre, Lescarbot and du Jarnic, who have left their names in this exotic literature, doubtless provided the *Mercure* with much of its information. Finally, a last indication of this acknowledged favour, of this desire to know distant lands, may be found at the end of the period (from 1633 to 1642) in the place occupied by geography in the lectures of Renaudot's *Bureau d'adresses*. Once a week, a session was devoted to history and geography and attracted many of the intelligentsia.

The fact that the accounts given by Jesuit or Capuchin missionaries or even travellers' reminiscences were not particularly accurate is of minor importance here. To encourage vocations, the good Fathers had no scruples about colouring the picture somewhat. Their audience was obviously interested in the picturesqueness of their accounts, in the descriptions of localities and their flora and fauna (including the monsters, which led to a revision of the medieval monster bestiaries) and of their pagan, though often virtuous, natives, for the myth of the noble savage was already present in these early accounts by missionaries. Exoticism was a sense of wonder which the reader obtained cheaply, and in respect of which authors were never sparing in their efforts.[8]

Mysticism

The path of mysticism lay open to those who were revolted by the brutality of a world which from 1560 seemed committed to butchery, or who pursued with unrelenting and heroic energy the attainment of a moral ideal of human and divine charity.[9] Divine Grace, say the many books of Spiritual Exercises, makes God visible to the souls of such men. With the help of the imagination, it acts upon their senses and gives them a perceptible impression of Him. They then begin to break away from all creatures and become accustomed to going to God, the only true good to which they aspire. They thus achieve happiness by rejoicing in God, and like to rejoice only in Him.

The way to mystical escape was gradually determined during the second half of the century, when the custom of private prayer, of the orison in all its forms, spread among the laity. This is perhaps the main trend of the Counter-

[6] Cf. de Dainville (351), p. 370.

[7] In its first year (1605), it dealt with Muscovy.

[8] The Jesuits even transposed exoticism into their college theatrical presentations: cf. de Dainville (351), p. 393.

[9] This is the mystical impulse of the lay believer rather than of the clerk, to return to the distinction made above.

Reformation: not the reform of secular abuses, which resisted stubbornly, but the extension of the use of private prayer, with a view to meditation and ecstasy before God. Men and women who practised this exalted form of prayer withdrew from the world, completely disregarding both 'the filth of creatures' and even the disputes which ceaselessly divided the Church itself.[10] Quite naturally, moreover, the conclusion to such an effort was the aspiration to saintliness. The mother of Pierre de Bérulle directed her son towards this end from infancy, and so convinced him of it that at the age of seven the future cardinal himself formed 'a keen desire to achieve saintliness'.

This growth of mysticism at the end of the sixteenth century is reflected in the published works of the period. Between 1570 and 1610, priests, monks and laymen too translated almost all the great mystics of the Church, up to and including St Theresa.[11] But in addition to licensed publications, one ought to take account of the vast quantities of notebooks and tracts which were recopied by spiritual advisers or penitent women and passed from hand to hand, thereby helping to spread the *exercitationes* and descriptions of ecstasies. Through inspired preachers, these tracts could reach even simple village women, leading to the series of retreats which took place at the end of the seventeenth century.

We referred to penitent women and village women, for this exaltation affected women more than men, as far as one can judge from contemporary evidence. Possessing a naturally keener sensibility which was constantly bruised by endless years of war, they turned to prayer and to the love of God as a refuge.[12] This was certainly the most spiritual form of escapism from this earthly life, but it was still escapism.

Assuredly, these different forms of escape into the world of the imagination cannot be evaluated. Even if they could, we should still lack a valid assessment of the numbers who practised them. We can establish without difficulty the enormous success of the theatre and of travel books; but for all that we do not have any exact, statistical notion of the importance of this form of escapism. Here again, a whole area of research remains to be done.

[10] It is indeed in this sense also that the author of the *Introduction à la vie dévote* writes in 1612: 'If the prelates, the Sorbonne and the monks were fully united in France, heresy would disappear within ten years.'

[11] Brémond (330), beginning of vol. I.

[12] Cf. the article by L. Febvre in *Annales E.S.C.* 4 (1958).

Chapter 19
Escapism: witchcraft and death

To dream or to go in search of adventure: for all who were dissatisfied with their daily lives, the remedy was at hand, as we have seen. Travel could be a necessity for someone like the peasant whose land did not support him; but it was also the most exciting form of escape for anyone who was not afraid of distances. Great ports like Saint Malo, Dieppe, La Rochelle and Nantes catered for adventure as well as trade. And many French contemporaries of Catherine de' Medici travelled right across Spain to embark at Seville, where demand long exceeded supply. For those who were held back by love of home or country, or by fear of shipwreck, the widening of horizons made possible by the great discoveries remained a significant outlet. Strange new lands and peoples which were curious in many respects haunted even the most home-loving imagination—the *folle du logis*, as it was called by one *philosophe*, who nevertheless took it into account.

But there were other, more dangerous ways of making good the shortcomings of everyday life. The Prince of Darkness offered formidable compensations to anyone who was not afraid to call upon his services. Of course it meant pledging one's eternal life; no-one could entertain any false hopes on this score. From a twentieth-century viewpoint, it also meant invoking the world of the imagination in the broadest possible sense, but belief in and recourse to magic were too widespread, and as indisputably real as the existence of God the Father Himself, for us to be able to dismiss them as mere illusory escapades. To invoke the Devil implied a denial, a negation of the human and divine order, as was apparent to even the lowliest of men—who were often prominent among the exponents of satanism. Witches' sabbaths, charms and evil spells made up, in essence, the stock of magic incantations by which anyone could instantly transform the world and those around him. But for the fear of hell, Satan's disciples would undoubtedly have been even more numerous, so multifarious and effective was the power of Black Magic acknowledged to be. The sixteenth and seventeenth centuries saw the culmination of a tradition which, since the High Middle Ages, had continually asserted the omnipotence of the Devil in opposition to Christ. However, we readily acknowledge that witchcraft comprised a large element of disillusionment, though this is difficult to detect since its practices as a whole are known to us through the writings of judges responsible for repressing the crime of treating with the Devil. The very extent of this disillusionment is perhaps indicated by the relatively high suicide rate. For anyone who renounced the last drastic step of incurring eternal damnation through dealings with the Devil, there remained no other means of escape save to take one's own life, the other, though seemingly less agreeable, road to damnation, since it did not even bring the minor earthly advantage of the pact with Satan.

Invoking the Devil

It is certainly not easy to identify with any precision the exponents of satanism. All the misfits who lived more or less on the fringes of society and its moral code could be numbered amongst them. But one ought to discount the sick, the persecuted, the perverted, and the mentally deranged, all of whom were given to self-incrimination and were capable of using reminiscences to tell and to persist in the most astounding lies. Among these problem personalities should be included the sexual perverts who preyed upon young boys and girls, dragging them off into the woods, or who assumed the guise of animals (lycanthropes) or again, exhumed corpses (necrophiles).

However, to understand fully the extent of these dealings with the Devil—some indication of which is given by the epidemic of witch trials between 1560 and 1640[1]—one should once more recall that even the most balanced of men, those who were most endowed with the famous, evenly-distributed 'common sense', lived daily in a phantasmagoria, in a universe inhabited by spirits and semi-divine or para-divine demons, who controlled natural forces and produced interrelated phenomena. According to Ronsard, the air is peopled by 'demons', just as the 'depths of the waves' are by fish, the heavens by angels and the earth by men.[2] Pico della Mirandola and Paracelsus make similar assertions. And the

[1] It is not proposed to determine the causes of this epidemic, but simply to mention it as an expression of this frequent—though imaginary—recourse to the Devil. There is no need to 'expound' the legal aspects of the question, which later works will clarify.

[2] Ronsard, *Hymnes* I, 'Les Daimons'—Ronsard is inexhaustible in his descriptions of demons, both good (the angels) and bad. The latter, he says,

> apportent sur la Terre
> Pestes, fiebvres, langueurs, orages et tonnerre.
> Ils font des sons en l'air pour nous espoüanter.
> Ils font aux yeux humains deux soleils présenter,
> Ils font noircir la Lune horriblement hydeuse
> Et font pleurer le ciel d'une pluye saigneuse. . . .
> (bring to earth
> Plagues, fevers, languors, storms and thunder.

same Ronsard long remembered how one night, when on his way to see Marie, he saw the wild hunt, the infernal, hallooing hunt to which he would have fallen victim had he not drawn his sword and hacked the air all around him. This was the headlong flight of the battalions of Hell, whirling in full cry under the orders of the demon Hellequin, their only hope of relief being the prayers of the living.

Those who could resist such fantasies were reminded even by religious plays of the existence and also the power of the demons. Included as an integral part of medieval mystery plays for the purpose of edification, with a series of attributes and actions which quickly became traditional—the mouth of hell, the *diables à quatre*, the clanging of cauldrons—Satan and his attendants continued to figure in this context for as long as mystery plays were performed in the church close—in other words, at least until the mid-sixteenth century. At the end of the next century, some towns were still presenting *diableries*, which were much appreciated by audiences with whom such devilry still proved very popular, as representing the exemplar of attractive anarchy in a moment of triumph.

Finally, to grasp the extent of these dealing with the Devil, one must equally allow for the ingenuity of a few shrewd individuals whose exploitation of the state of credulity was made so much easier because all accepted notions and the whole teaching of the Church took account of the presence and the power of the Devil. To speak of credulity is always to misuse the word in a way which the progress of scientific attitudes in our own day scarcely justifies.[3]

★

Thus, anyone who wished momentarily to feel master of his village or town had at his disposal that magnificent form of hallucination, the witches' sabbath. It seems incredible that a man could daydream, recount his exploits to a trustworthy neighbour and convince himself of it by sheer repetition, even though hundreds of thousands of confessions exist to vouch for the fact. To mount a broomstick and fly off to the witches' sabbath, to kiss the goat on the buttocks, dance the saraband, say counterfeit prayers and have before one's eyes for just a few seconds the entire wealth of the earth—gold, silver, precious stones, cloths and carpets—these were intangible pleasures which disappeared at dawn

---

They make noises in the air to frighten us.
They make two suns appear to human eyes.
They make the Moon darken, horribly hideous,
And rain down from the sky a shower of blood. . . .)

[3] One can only allow of the 'credulity' of the sixteenth and seventeenth centuries provided that one does not forget that of the twentieth: the frequency with which legal records mention haunted houses and black masses, and the large numbers of lawyers, high officials and politicians who frequent the consulting-rooms of clairvoyants, etc.

with the painful awakenings from nights that were all too short. They were complemented by an endless fund of evil spells; for if the Devil's disciple could scarcely prove to his fidgeting, or downright disbelieving, crony that deep in the clearing he had held in his arms the most beautiful woman 'in France or Italy', evil spells were very much in evidence. Sick animals, neighbours aching from their work in the fields and infants found dead in their cradles or seized by convulsions were accidents that were customarily blamed upon the spell-binder who had made a pact with the Devil. But as a fair return for their faith, Satan allowed his bondsmen to do good—or rather to repair the *maleficia* which they or others were responsible for. Whoever cast a spell could lift it; whoever had dealings with the world of magic knew a thousand and one cures. The Master of Hell did not go so far as to grant them the power of manufacturing wealth, but he readily allowed them lesser achievements. When Blaise Pascal was born in 1623 into a household dominated by the dignified figure of Etienne Pascal, a magistrate and physician of repute, it is said that a witch cast a spell on the newborn child. The father immediately undertook to treat with the shrew to rid him of it, offering a horse but finding a cat to be sufficient. A magic cataplasm thus cured Blaise on the stroke of midnight, after a terrible convulsion which almost killed him. This famous example allows one to suspect the frequency of similar happenings in other circles.

The tragic end met by thousands of witches, particularly in eastern France, and the epidemics which invaded villages and sometimes whole provinces in a relentless onslaught which affected even religious houses (notably in the seventeenth century) give an impression (legally biased) of the sorcerer as an evildoer who was charged with many real crimes as well as with betraying God. It seems, however, that between these feverish outbursts, these furious 'purges' carried out by the secular arm, the art of witchcraft could be of a much more acceptable nature. For years on end, the village sorcerer could be considered a local worthy—one who was able to commune with the Devil and who, as a result, had power in excess of the ordinary mortal. He healed and helped—perhaps above all with kind words, but this form of assistance was not insignificant, psychologically speaking—and even protected the whole community against the activities of other less well-inspired disciples of the Devil. The flames of persecution often interfered with long-standing practices which no-one would have dreamt of disturbing until the legal authorities intervened and led off to the stake not only the so-called sorcerer or witch, but also all his 'customers', who were all accomplices or beneficiaries to some degree. Thus, the collective hallucination was definitely substantiated at the very moment when the practice of witchcraft was temporarily halted.

Such petty witchcraft[4] is only mentioned incidentally in court records, for

[4] The Devil was seen as being present everywhere, beginning with the child's cradle: cf. Plate 11.

release of ligature and murrain were of little interest to judges mainly concerned with accounts of the witches' sabbath and with demoniacal possessions which resisted all exorcisms. It reflects not only a universal and firmly-rooted belief in the earthly powers of the Devil, but also this permanent need for a superior presence which could intervene in everyday life and completely upset its course. Nevertheless, just as to invoke a God of love seems in accordance with Christian tradition, so to have recourse to infernal powers was to gamble dangerously. Hell was as sure a reality of the eternal life as purgatory or paradise. The witch and her associates, however ignorant of theology, knew perfectly well what they were risking by invoking the aid of the infernal spirits to obtain some favour or other: they were compromising their eternal lives without the hope of remission permitted in the case of 'ordinary' sins. Does the high incidence of magical practices justify our thinking that their consequences were not clearly perceived by the 'demoniacs'? Burnings at the stake, exhibition of the victims and public descriptions of their crimes would also lead one to admit that many reminders of these first truths were necessary. Perhaps some sort of 'usury' was established, as with the use of excommunication for debt, as a result of the apparent disproportion between the extent to which witchcraft and natural magic were commonly practised,[5] and the sanctions which attended dealings with Satan. At least, sorcerers and their associates knew that they were risking the stake if ever denunciation or mere indisretion revealed their activities to an enterprising judge. This certainty alone is enough to reveal the extent of their temerity. Diabolical escapism was certainly the greatest temptation of the period.

Suicide

There remain the many who, in despair, gave up the difficult business of living and finally decided to bring about their own death, 'horrible death' (cf. Plate 12), despite all the revulsion it inspired and the perils it involved.

The revulsion was the result of the entire tradition of the late Middle Ages. Everywhere, death was portrayed as a grimacing, grinning skeleton to which small pieces of flesh still clung, and whose gaping belly swarmed with worms. It took hold of men and women in their prime and dragged them off towards the decay of the flesh. The artistic heritage of the previous century,[6] with its

[5] Reputable authors, theologians and jurists, who studied the possessed, the witches and their practices, were most careful to distinguish between 'natural' magic, consisting of philtres and a wide variety of superstitious practices which were commonly used, and witchcraft or Black Magic, which entailed the invocation of Satan, the sabbath and the pact. But the average mentality tended to confuse the one with the other, and the very word 'witch' denoted a person who practised either.

[6] Cf. in A. Tenenti, *La vie et la mort à travers l'art du XVe siècle* (Paris 1952), pp. 90–91, a list of the *danses macabres* for the whole of western Europe. For France, we find: Paris (Church

danses macabres and frescos portraying the Triumph of Death, still impinged heavily upon man's sensibility. Erasmus's *Colloquies* and his treatise *Praeparatio ad mortem* would show this to be so, despite the serene discourses on the immortality of the soul and the separation of body and soul. Death continued to be a source of terror, to stifle the religious significance which the Church sought to give it and popularized in so many versions of the *Ars moriendi*. Between death and judgement too many souls went astray, too many unpredictable vital forces were at play for the Christian to resign himself to taking this step equably.

Moreover, from the Christian viewpoint, fear of purgatory and hell was added to such anguish, Purgatory was readily portrayed as a lukewarm hell which was ultimately almost as painful. Hell was promised to all who did not have an easy conscience, or only half believed in the generous remission of their sins, or neglected, even if they were spared the time, to call monks and priests to their bedside to help them with their prayers. Thus, even in the most Christian death, fear remained in a different form.

On the whole, death continued to hold some measure of terror. Yet, as Erasmus records in his *Funus*, there were many suicides; what would be the case if death held no horrors: *Etenim, cum videamus et hodie tam multos sibi manus adferre, quid censes futurum, si mors nihil haberet horribile?*

The high incidence of suicide was lamented throughout the sixteenth century, though more so in other countries than in France itself.[7] Montaigne devotes a long chapter (the third) in his second book to refuting the ancients who sang the praises of voluntary death. In his view, nothing can justify it, and he approves of its being condemned by human and divine law.

However, to give some idea of the relative proportions of suicides and natural deaths, one would have to be able to quote figures, as one can for the nineteenth and twentieth centuries. Unfortunately, our only sources of information are legal and parish records, where the evidence is widely scattered and has not yet been systematically collated. When a man committed suicide, the law condemned him posthumously and his corpse was subjected to public punishment similar to that prescribed for condemned criminals, the publicity given to the affair being supposed, in this case as in so many others, to deter the living from

---

of the Holy Innocents), Dijon (ducal chapel), Amiens (cathedral), Saint Omer (abbey), Strasburg (Dominican chapel), Kermaria, La Chaise Dieu, La Ferté Loupière (Yonne), Rouen (St Maclou), Montvilliers (Somme), Fécamp, Lisieux (Ste Marie des Anglais), Angers (St Maurice).

[7] Germany seems to have been particularly affected, to judge from the extremely 'subjective' evidence of the Bishop of Mainz in 1548 and of Luther in 1542. Both make this outbreak of despair the work of the Devil. Cf. Luther, *Lettre à Lauterbach*, 25, VII (1542); Michael Helding, *Funfzehn Predige* (Ingolstadt 1548). In 1569, there were fourteen suicides in three weeks at Nuremburg.

imitating his action. The body of a man who had hanged himself in his attic was hanged again on the town gallows; that of a woman who had cut her throat was dragged round the town on a hurdle and finally thrown to the dogs. Ecclesiastical penalties were added to these civil sanctions, since the Church refused the Office for the Dead and burial to those who were responsible for their own 'homicide'. But since the necessary evidence has not been collected, we must abandon any attempt to measure or even to suggest approximate numbers of suicides.

A fortiori, we must abandon any attempt to analyse the reasons for such despair. Despondency, 'melancholy' and anguish, the words used by contemporaries in deploring the acts that they had witnessed—some mention of which is to be found in most of the *livres de raison*—do not give us the key to this attitude. Certainly, it was a case of a final rejection of the world, of a 'cowardly and effeminate' escape, to quote Montaigne once more. It is scarcely possible to say more, until suicide has been the subject of a systematic investigation.

Conclusion to Part III

The professional 'environment'—to use this sociological expression in its broadest possible sense—was certainly the one which most influenced individual and group psychology. Whatever traumatic experiences were suffered in childhood, whatever habits and ideas were acquired within the family circle at the most impressionable age, the entire heritage of upbringing underwent the test of adult activity. The thirty-year-old man and, *a fortiori*, the forty- or fifty-year-old man (though we should not think too often in terms of such advanced ages for the sixteenth and seventeenth centuries) was in the first place a man of his trade. At the beginning of the modern period, the wearing of distinctive dress (or items of dress) further accentuated such differences: the long gowns of the legal profession, the peasant's smock and the large cloaks worn by travellers—to which was added the overt carrying of one's trade tools, notably by guild journeymen. The latter are an obvious example. The length of the working day lawfully imposed upon them a prolonged period of constraint, a daily 'conditioning' into which only feast-days brought a measure of relaxation. But the frequency with which guild meetings were held in the confraternities, the trade assemblies, on such holidays shows the strength of this hold over them.

Thus, the socio-professional groups which we have just described briefly—and which one would have to be able to enumerate town by town and province by province to arrive at a valid description of the working Frenchman during the period—in some respects form the most important element of the typology we are seeking: to take only one particularly illuminating example, it was surely at this period that the lasting opposition between manual workers and intellectuals developed as a real, effective force. The job made both the man and the group. And each form of work was responsible for a large element of the personality, whatever hierarchies were established, here and there, between the different forms of activity. It is in this direction that the underlying significance of the peasant revolts at the beginning of the seventeenth century lies: they were a protest by an oppressed group which was at least vaguely conscious of its effective and essential role in the society which it fed. The aspirations of countless monks for Church reform at the beginning of the sixteenth century were in the first place the expression of a need for improvement peculiar to clergymen forming the Church militant and making apostleship the purpose of their existence.

We have dealt at length with other activities, everyday pastimes and real or imaginary forms of escape, which were closely linked with these professional factors. Though they were secondary—at least if one considers only the time most people devoted to them—and less 'formative', as one might say, such pastimes and forms of escape are nevertheless a source of revealing actions and habits. Dancing, reading, travel and the arts of magic were the pursuits of those who were not really satisfied with their daily work, their circumstances. And this search for compensation in itself undoubtedly deserves close attention from historians concerned to understand the mental processes of both individuals and groups. 'The human condition', to use the words of Montaigne, perhaps does not imply throughout all time this propensity for 'entertainment' which so angered Pascal in the middle of the seventeenth century; in their turn, then, these pastimes reveal original temperaments. From the moralist's viewpoint, to dance in the mall every night was not wrong in itself. In our view, to do this was to reveal that one was of a different frame of mind from those who skulked in their cottages and invoked the Devil to spread terror around themselves; which is different again from simply believing in the high incidence of these magical arts. This field, like many others, is still far from being systematically explored. One must be content with blazing a trail, with indicating avenues of research. The infinite variety of human activities at that period cannot easily be reduced to a few essential types; but these do at least allow us to approach the great diversity of attitudes which creative, cultural and escapist activities helped to determine and define.

General conclusion

The psychological portrait of the modern Frenchman as completed in Part III is too analytical to satisfy fully the historian; though in using the word 'analytical' we do not mean to oppose analysis and synthesis using the simple approach of conventional logic. Rather we are anxious to stress once more that this investigation conducted successively on three planes—human dimensions, the social context and forms of activity—is far from being a list or inventory. On the contrary, it is based on the preponderance (in the etymological sense of the word) of the group, of the socio-professional environment, in the collective psychology of this *ancien régime* society. Yet this examination, which seeks to provide the main lines of explanation rather than a descriptive catalogue, does not exhaust the issues implied in reconstructing the group mentalities of the period. The huge simplifications that are permissible when one seeks to define constants and large-scale conjunctional trends, here as in economic or political history, do not, in our opinion, allow one to dissemble either the infinite variety of individual mentalities or the great complexity of group mentalities. Without doubt, the persistence of great myths common to a people as a whole, such as the healing powers of the French kings, which only figures incidentally within the narrow chronological limits of this work, forms a unifying element of considerable importance. However, it seems more appropriate to end by stressing the dissimilarities and the complexity of these psychological reconstructions, of which this book is intended to provide one 'model'[1] among the many that social psychologists, historians and sociologists may be tempted to propose.

We can measure this complexity by quickly retracing our steps and suggesting the number of possible combinations which can follow from the aspects we have already described. By moving, as it were, from one keyboard to another, from human dimensions to social groups or to forms of activity, we can give some idea of the performance which must come out of such an investigation.

Take as the first example the concepts of time and space, the bases of every mentality. In Part I, we dwelt upon the general difficulty which all French

[1] In the sense in which the economist uses the word.

people at that time experienced in measuring and imagining these dimensions. Thus it has been possible to suggest, though doubtless only too briefly, the elements of uncertainty involved in the vistas of time and space. Yet it is quite clear that a man's notion of time and space varied according to his activities. The merchant from Lyons or Rheims who lived from one fair to the next, waiting for his bills to fall due, speculating on corn being scarce in springtime or on money being in ample supply, successfully concluding a deal on St Martin's Day which the Feast of St John 'compensated for' with some misfortune, did not have the same notion of the calendar or of time in general as the monk, who led within the cloister an earthly existence remote from any pattern of time other than the daily round of prayers and chants which made up his life.[2] The peasant and the humanist can be similarly contrasted. The peasant's only horizons, physically speaking, were his village, its farmland and the black line of the common woodlands, while the humanist, with his passion for geography, collected treatises on 'cosmography' and pored over descriptions of America and the East Indies. These distinctions are obvious; and nothing would be gained by describing them at greater length.

For a more conclusive example in a different register, we should confront briefly the chronically underfed (mentioned in Part I) with popular celebrations such as the town or country parish festivals or the Entry of a king or prince into a loyal town (which were dealt with in Part II). These occasions, when the whole village or town (including the prisoners in the governor's *château*) made merry, sang and feasted to their hearts' content, were indeed times when the two companions of everyday life, fear and famine, allowed some respite. As regards the feelings and emotions fostered by a precarious material existence, these feast-days formed a kind of interlude, which was repeated several times during the year, and even more often in the towns than in the country.

But we do not propose to compile, using such methods, a descriptive catalogue of the attitudes we have suggested above. It is better to use these final pages to stress the present state of our resources and indicate the future lines of development implied in this kind of analysis. Under the first heading come the characteristics which all contemporaries had in common—as it were, the mental background which is overlaid with the differences which strike us initially and are often better known than the underlying realities. Under the second we shall include two methods of approach which are an essential part of our scheme: first, the use of the notion of the 'view of the world', an essential component in anyone's psychological make-up; second, the pursuit, over and above the mental structures already described, of mental conjunctures which are more delicate but which are so much more accessible because they mask the structural constants.

[2] Cf. on this subject the article of J. Le Goff in *Annales E.S.C.* 3 (1960), 'Au Moyen Age: temps de l'église et temps du marchant'.

Common features

To pick out the elements prevailing throughout French society as a whole does not mean invoking some average mentality (which is meaningless) but suggesting the basic features common to every mentality at the time.

Foremost among these general characteristics of modern group psychology we will readily place hypersensitivity of temperament. This was a result not only of the chronic malnutrition, from which most people suffered, and the inadequate technical and intellectual means available for mastering a preponderantly hostile environment, but equally of oral traditions, in part legendary, which fostered violence, fear (in so many different forms) and emotional instability. This hypersensitivity, or emotivity,[3] was a permanent and universal trait, so rare were the individuals or groups who apparently escaped it.[4] To describe it one has only to invoke the many indications which reveal how immediately and violently contemporaries reacted to the least emotional shock with extreme displays of emotion: of pity at the sight of a slow-moving column of galley slaves, weighed down by their fetters; or violent demonstrations with wringing of hands in token of grief or mourning. But this does not mean such emotivity was mere sentimentality. The taste for strong emotions was sufficiently a part of their make-up for them deliberately to pursue such emotions on occasions, hence the (in a sense) disconcerting mixture of fervent expressions of pity or grief and obvious cruelty. In hunting, the quarry was slaughtered with zest. In the towns, an execution was a choice spectacle and drew the crowds, whatever its form. This particularly keen receptivity, in short, implies an inclination for such emotional shocks.

However, the best evidence in favour of this first feature doubtless consists in the existence everywhere of fear, in countless different forms, so much so that merely to list the occasions and pretexts for fright in daily life would run to pages. A few examples must suffice. Night, as we know,[5] gave innumerable grounds for fear because of its darkness. But in addition there was the fear of wolves and of brigands on the roads, and especially in the woods. Again, comets and eclipses of all kinds bewildered and frightened, since it was thought that they inevitably heralded some misfortune, for the good reason that man did not understand such phenomena. Even the learned astrological predictions of the almanacs could cause panic. Daily, moreover, man lived in fear of the mad dogs which roamed the countryside and the town streets, and dreaded

[3] The two words are certainly not synonymous, but the truth falls between them. The physical conditions of this were demonstrated in Part I.

[4] Montaigne and Descartes, both of whom took refuge in the safety of retirement, far from the passions of the world in general, would appear at first glimpse to escape through sheer willpower and lucidity. Yet even these exceptions would require further examination, if one were to pursue the investigation from the point of view of the individual.

[5] Cf. Part I, ch. 20.

plague and all the other contagious diseases which constantly recurred from epidemic to epidemic and were never stamped out by the medical profession. Everything combined, as it were, to produce fear: the material conditions of life, the precarious nature of the food supply, the inadequacies of the environment, and above all the intellectual climate. Approximate knowledge was responsible for its own brand of terror, adding to the fear of wolves the fear of werewolves, or men changed into wolves by the hand of the Devil. All the fantastic products of the imagination here played their part.

This partly explains, in our opinion, the force of the collective waves of fear—the panics caused by epidemics and wars, the peasant revolts and urban riots. Perhaps one ought finally to include under this heading, at least as regards its primitive causes, the fear of the Devil aroused by epidemics of witchcraft. When, through the efforts of some distinguished judge, satanic terror descended upon a village or a region, no one, to be sure, escaped its influence which enveloped everyone and everything in the most sordid suspicion, prompting whole communities to denunciation and ritual crime. On the other hand, in this atmosphere of perpetual threats, one can understand the significance of the times of relaxation amid fleeting security, the joy of the moments of liberation. The best of the peasant festivals was undoubtedly the harvest festival, when nights were short and granaries were temporarily well stocked.

★

The second feature is the social antagonism or, more accurately, the social aggressiveness, which forms the reverse of the fabric of solidarity, of which we have already analysed the various strands. This aspect, which terminology as hallowed as it is inadequate would have us call negative, was in the context of corporate life an integral part of such solidarity. The social groups of parish, class and youth society were formed to a large extent as a result of vital feelings of hostility which they had to meet: solidarity was a means of defence and protection, and also a collective weapon. This is all too obvious in the case of the family, where biological necessity supported and promoted (even as far as the concept of the 'blood') the ideal of a cell which put its internal solidarity to the test each time it came into contact with others. Marriage, partition and inheritance were all practices which give evidence, even down to the specific legal traditions which were invariably respected, of the suspicion which attended relations between families. The parish or village deliberately set out to be a community which was closely united against all who were 'strangers'[6] to the small group as it was geographically defined by the village land. One thinks

[6] This attitude has still not entirely disappeared in French rural areas where traditional ways of life have been preserved to the greatest degree. Less than half a century ago, strangers were still treated with systematic hostility in villages in the Auvergne.

immediately of soldiers, vagabonds, and plague-carriers, who were certainly a dreaded brood. The same reception awaited peaceful travellers, merchants or tourists, who were also suspect. But this automatic reflex even operated, to a lesser extent it is true, against the peasants of neighbouring villages, even though they were to some extent acquaintances; as also against townspeople, who were only too often tax-farmers, owners of lands or privileges—which was another, different reason for keeping them whenever possible at a distance.

This aggressiveness is again apparent among those larger groups, the social classes. Not that we intend to reopen the bulky file of the class struggle. If the Marxist pattern is not strictly applicable to the many different kinds of social conflict which studded the modern period, no one could honestly deny the existence of social antagonism which brought into conflict noblemen, bourgeois, peasants and artisans, to quote only these examples.

The political solidarity which is expressed in the modern State fostered national feeling through conflicts with foreign powers. For centuries, the English in the west (from Normandy to Guyenne) and the Germans in the east had provided well-established models of hostility. To them the sixteenth century added a choice recruit—the Spaniards, who were cursed with admirable eloquence by the *Satyre ménippée*. We need not go into the strength of the religious antagonism aroused by the lightning spread of the Reformation in France under François I and Henri II, since forty years of fighting tell their own tale. Nevertheless, the Wars of Religion, where the specifically political and religious aspects were the conditioning factor, offer further evidence, in minor details of attacks upon châteaux, towns, villages and isolated companies, of the virulence of these conflicts between social groups, which are again apparent in the thick of war: noblemen fighting peasants, noblemen fighting bourgeois, etc. This aggressiveness can even be identified in the temporary social settings, which seem by definition the least apt to assume the vital protection of a group. The youth societies, those groups of youths who liked to cavort at the town gates, illustrate in their own way the same feature: they reveal the weight of the parental supervision exercised by elders, parents and grandparents. To a large extent, this was the current expression of the strained relations which always exist between fathers and sons.

*

Illustrating these social tensions by a catalogue of conflicts does not entirely dispose of the identification of this aggressiveness. It may perhaps be seen in a different form in the tendency to imitate the ruling class. The *noblesse d'épée*—whatever its real position—continued to represent for all other groups a mode of behaviour to be copied. It was not simply a question of its original justification, its military function, though certainly this still found expression in jousting, duelling, and hunting (not to mention its taste for pillage and disorder). But it would be wrong to claim that such imitation made the tournament or the curry the model of all kinds of conflicts, including, say, those between Catholics and Protestants. At most one might suggest that this was true of the parades held by youth societies or the rough contests which brought to grips champions from neighbouring villages.

However, this tendency to imitate can be seen in a more subtle fashion in the most important group attitudes. During the Middle Ages, an equivalent of feudal honour, the emotional 'reflex' of the aristocratic moral code, was gradually evolved by the other social classes. The group's notion of honour—whatever the group—informs both written constitutions and customary practices. It is unworthy of a nobleman, Lesdiguières once said, to butcher peasants who are in revolt against a salt-tax collector; it is unworthy of a bourgeois, said an *intendant*, to abet an urban revolt. Thus the rights and duties of each group were defined progressively in imitation of the nobility. And paradoxical though it may seem at first sight, this process extended even to highwaymen, who did not rob just anyone or indiscriminately spare the life of monk or bishop, but half the time took it upon themselves, with some success, to dispense justice, redress wrongs, avenge the oppressed and protect the weak. It is in reading guild statutes and memoirs that one finds this notion of a code of honour peculiar to each group and suited to its function. A host of nuances combine to express this manifold sense of a moral hierarchy: to quote just one particular example, one might recall the jurist who, in describing contemporary society, uses an expression which reveals both his social concepts and his own views by calling manual workers, artisans and husbandmen, 'base persons'.

★

The third general characteristic, which is no less obvious than the first two, is man's feeling of impotence in face of the natural world. This again is a result of the combination of two factors: from an intellectual standpoint, physical and biological nature was an unfathomable mystery; in addition, the equipment of the technicians who strove to master it was effective to a very limited degree. Thus sixteenth-century man could neither rationally comprehend nor actively control the world in which he lived.

One might almost suggest that, by comparison, social relationships with their occasional disputes over precedence and their often violent clashes reveal that man enjoyed a far greater degree of mastery over his fellows. Certainly the king, the bishop and the *hobereau* were not always obeyed to the letter, but at least in the form of ordinances or of customary practices they had been able to evolve laws (in the first sense of the word) to govern an organized society.

Established practices and written laws do indeed represent a relatively successful effort to order human relationships. On the other hand, there was not as yet any corpus of the laws of nature. What is more, the Copernican revolution had upset, at least in appearance, the only system in which the Middle Ages had thought it recognized perfect clarity and stability.

Faced with the inexhaustible wealth of nature, which had been extended by the great discoveries to include the new wonders of the tropics and of all the Indies, the sixteenth- and seventeenth-century Frenchman felt, as it were, disarmed. Even the monsters and prodigies which filled his bestiaries are unimportant. These 'phenomena', which were accepted as strange but viable products of nature with her unfathomable purposes, above all demonstrate their receptivity to the *supernatural-natural* and the miracle. More precisely, one should say receptivity through deference to the facts of personal experience: prophetic dreams which were alleged to have come true, instances of telepathy, haunted houses and the many other phenomena which were held to be authentic because they were confirmed by witnesses whose word could not be questioned. Nature, God's creation, could create or produce anything.

It is doubtless more important to dwell upon the slender means at their disposal for changing the natural world and using it to advantage. Not that we shall waste time listing the scientific techniques of the twentieth century which were not even suspected then; it is quicker to review contemporary resources. Basically these were limited to agricultural methods which extracted the entire supply of food from the soil, and its flora and fauna. Assuredly, the empirical application of these techniques achieved significant results. The lord of Gouberville made tree-grafting his hobby and successfully produced twenty to thirty varieties of apple-tree, thereby benefiting a whole region. Similarly, the art of training wild animals for the needs of the 'domestic economy' was most remarkably advanced. These agricultural methods, the legacy of age-old traditions, appear inadequate to us, in view of the progress made in botany and zoology over the last two centuries. Despite the successes they achieved, some of which have been mentioned, they also appeared inadequate to contemporaries. At the time, agriculture was barely able to support the urban and rural communities. A bad frost in March or a storm in July could destroy not only the hopes of the peasant, but the vital resources of a whole region. Without any doubt, one factor in this agricultural inadequacy was a social system which accentuated in distribution the technical deficiencies in production. The feeling of natural insecurity was thereby further strengthened.

Husbandry apart, the other techniques which man brought to bear upon nature (the artisan crafts and, a little later, the factory system) reveal the same contrast between remarkable perfection in their empirical achievements and age-old stagnation which was incapable of complex change and especially of increased productivity. The techniques of working in wood or stone, of spinning, weaving and dyeing wool, silk or linen, and of tanning leather were all firmly established by strictly controlled trade guilds. Technical progress came within the framework of these guilds, which set more store by the end product, the 'masterpieces' reproduced many times, than by methods allowing increased productivity and output. Oral and written customs in a sense perpetuated the technical tradition, so that nothing provoked or encouraged the introduction of new ideas.

Thus the overall result was a very restricted degree of mastery over the natural world, which those concerned found to be no more satisfactory than current scientific knowledge. The accumulation of a nomenclature which was all the more shapeless in that it welcomed every piece of evidence, and the impossibility of distinguishing between the natural and the supernatural, made these sciences, whose only method of approach was compilatory, an uneasy tool of investigation. Not even the greatest minds possessed a method for purifying the astonishing mixture of halftruths, inherited errors and accepted fancies revealed by every branch of science. No-one had the kind of panoramic view of things and of the infinite and mysterious world which would allow the fragmentary solutions of isolated problems to be woven together. Thus the fear shown by the sailors at the end of the fifteenth century as they were on the point of reaching the new continent was a reflection, hardly symbolic, of this confusion, while the alchemist, searching for the secret of secrets in his retorts and furnaces, represents even more clearly the impotence of the scientist.

★

Being unable to master and explain the world, or rather creation, man turned to the Creator with all the greater fervour. Explanations, aid and favours were asked of God who made everything—and if not of God himself, of his saints—and of his fallen angels. This is certainly not the only explanation of the religious fervour displayed by the modern period, which wanted to believe. Without any doubt there were many other reasons—and emotional impulses—which urged man along the difficult path of faith. In another respect, a close relationship might also be established between the resistance which the natural environment offered to human endeavour and man's passion for dominating his fellows. However, the influence of the supernatural element found in nature supports the argument: it was an essential mental step to have recourse to an omnipotent God, upon whom the lot of man and of all creation constantly depended. It allowed one to ask God or some intercessor for the favours, the 'blessings', which human genius was not sure to obtain. The approach was the same when Satan or one of his evil, seductive agents was petitioned.

The Christian awareness which was constantly in everyone's mind—and heart—thus provided (not to mention the real social pattern, the framework 'from birth to death') a mode of thought characterized by the predominance of this divine order which, constantly solicited and ever-present, intervened at every moment at the heart of the affairs of men. The Christian religion also provided a moral code, as we all know. But perhaps most of all, at a time when the long doctrinal disputes[7] between champions of orthodoxy and heretics eventually succeeded in muddling even the simplest of tenets, Christianity was responsible for a form of sensitivity—or perhaps one ought to say of 'sensitization'—to the precariousness of human destiny, played out on a little-known earth as rich in banes as in blessings. Certainly, this sensitization was a long process which had developed throughout the Middle Ages ever since Christianity had become widely established in the Merovingian period, and which achieved its aim in the fourteenth and fifteenth centuries, when religion itself became more human than dogmatic. After the age of doctrinal definition, after St Thomas and St Bernard, it was precisely the trust which mankind in deep humility placed in a God who took pity on the miseries of this world which was expressed in the countless representations of the Passion, the Pietà, the stigmata of St Francis, the Holy Sepulchre, and the Crucifixion. To all, both Catholics and Protestants—and even the rare freethinkers of the period 1610–40—they meant a regard for human suffering, piety, and religious sincerity which had come to be regarded as 'natural' and which consisted primarily of confidence in the supranatural omnipotence of God. And the Frenchman of the time found in this religious awareness not only the hope of eternal salvation but also a sense of humanity which informed his whole life, however tormented it may have been.

Views of the world: mental structures

If one considers them fully with all their implications, these factors—emotivity, social aggressiveness, inability to master the world of nature, and spiritual and intellectual confidence in divine omnipotence—already comprise a complex psychological climate. Next one must go on to define differential mental structures.

This second approach, though in our view a necessary one in conclusion to such a work, is not easy to describe. It would lead, it might be said, to a reconstruction of individual and group personalities, to a restoration of the ego, which is all the more justifiable in that the sixteenth century had more a sense of the individual than previous ages. To rediscover the consistencies—and sometimes the profound logic underlying certain inconsistencies—behind the themes we have just called up is to formulate the fruitful notion, *the view of the world* (which recalls the German *Weltanschauung*) indicating in what sense (for we can see at least two) the historian can employ it most meaningfully.

[7] Disputes in which not every Frenchman took part to the same degree.

The contemporaries of François I, Henri IV or Louis XIII, who lived through part of this period which produced innovations in every field, certainly carried within them a very different mental universe from the companions of St Louis: for many of them at least, the view of the world even in the literal, geographical sense had been renewed, at once by the discovery of the West Indies, the voyages of Vasco da Gama and Magellan, and the revelations of Copernicus and Galileo. But by 'view of the world' we understand many other concepts as well: social relationships, the place of man in creation, knowledge of man's past and present, the concept of human development. *Weltanschauung* covers all the notions—intellectual as well as ethical—within which individuals and groups daily developed their thoughts and actions.

*

Where the individual is concerned, this kind of research is not strictly speaking new. With varying degrees of method and continuity in their investigations, literary historians, who have been traditionally concerned to trace the antecedents, the 'sources' of their authors—major or minor—have often striven to reconstruct in this way the mental horizons within which the personalities they were studying were formed and lived. Thus for the period in question we have a whole gallery of portraits which are only too often stereotypes, but which are interesting for their value in helping greatly to clarify what scanty biographical evidence leaves in obscurity. Ronsard, du Bellay, Montaigne, d'Aubigné, Jodelle, Marot, etc. all had their own destinies and characters—and equally their own notions of the world. Though they were exceptional, precisely because of the quality of their sensibilities and temperaments, these great literary figures cannot on this account be excluded from our investigations. To use the conventional expression, they were often far more perceptive than their contemporaries. At least so far as their works allow one to discover the actual man—not only Ronsard the courtier and gallant, but also the Ronsard who wrote the *Discours des Misères de ce temps* and the *Responce aux injures et calomnies de je ne sçai quels Prédicans et Ministres de Genève;* the Tahureau of the *Sonnets, Odes et Mignardises amoureuses de l'Admirée* and of the *Dialogues*—the psychological portraits of literary history are a valuable source of material for reconstruction, and often reveal more than one kind of individual view of the world.

However, it should be pointed out that in this respect those who wrote *livres de raison* hold out the possibility of equally important research. Men like Gouberville, Claude Haton or Jacmon, who for years recorded their doings and their reflections on what they saw around them, offer an impressive fund of precious, if scattered, evidence, which will inevitably help in reconstructing their particular mental horizons. Gouberville, the Norman nobleman with a passion for pomiculture, had precise notions of Europe, if not of the new worlds. He knew the locations of Canada, the Caribbean Islands and Africa. He kept abreast of the political life of the kingdom, while at the same time conducting himself like a *hobereau* on his estates, proving a hard lord to his peasants and an exacting 'master' to his servants. Jacmon was a petty artisan of Le Puy, who was proud of his town and its processions, and of the small urban society in which the college and the cathedral formed the only real highlights. Equally he was filled with compassion for the sufferings of the poor peasants who came to beg in the moat outside the walls in times of famine. He never really speaks of anything other than the plain of Le Puy, the town and its immediate dependencies. His horizons seem as limited mentally as they were geographically by the volcanic peaks and the plateaux which enclose the depression of Le Puy.

However, the scope for this kind of research is in our view endless, so that to obtain valid results one would have to resort to a methodical analysis of the whole range of individual case studies. By way of example, take the following revealing documents: they are two probate inventories from Amiens in 1617, one relating to a squire, the other to a lawyer. By their descriptions of the house and land outside the town, the furniture and the servants, these documents reveal the kind of life the two men led. To begin with, they give quite a good idea of their financial status; but equally, they convey a reasonable impression of their tastes, their preoccupations and their activities. The attention given to the wine-cellar in one case and to the maintenance of the carriage and stables in the other are essential elements in their social outlooks—or at the very least form a good introduction to their social choices: to keep up one's position, to strive more or less skilfully for promotion. This is no more than an intimation of the process. Their libraries, however, are an even better illustration of this than such social details; for both left a few books. The squire possessed some works of Erasmus, a Rabelais, the *Satyre ménippée* and the printed text of the Edict of Nantes. But he had doubtless also read, and in any case he kept by him, the *Guide des chemins de France*, and various histories of America, Florida and the Indies. The lawyer for his part was content with religious works: the *Spiritual Works* of Louis of Granada, a Life of the Saints, the Breviary of Amiens, and the works of Pellevé, the Leaguer cardinal. Already we have in outline two portraits, as one might say, two types of Frenchmen: the one a Gallican, a loyalist, open to the novelties of the past century, the other a disciple of the 'blunderbuss' monks who took up arms against Henry of Navarre, and never forgave him for the Edict of Nantes: two types of Frenchmen at the beginning of the seventeenth century. But this expression, which springs to mind so readily, is significant too: in defining views of the world one encounters not only original men in the Pascalian sense of the term, but models, with the view of the group underlying the personal view. Without any doubt, the tangible richness of the individual personality remains precious, especially here, where the flavour of some human trait compensates for unavoidably arid abstractions. But the study of the individual is only the first stage.

*

This reconstruction of individual views of the world is of full value in so far as it leads to a typology and allows one to reconstruct corporate views. It was the group that was important, for it brought the whole weight of social conformity constantly to bear on the individual. Each social class—as also each profession or even religious group—had its characteristic outlook. Here again, one must extract and order the many indications of these perennially complex attitudes which are to be found on every page of the most varied literature. One might recall the example of the cobbler and the financier in La Fontaine. The first task is simply to describe the mental horizons characteristic of the different social groups—a task which has never yet been attempted. Throughout this work we have, we believe, made apparent the necessity of recognizing all that distinguishes the peasant, tenant-farmer or landowner, who was attached to his land and had never left his small *pays* (in the old sense), from the day-labourer who roamed the roads, begging and on occasion resorting to brigandage, but who also provided the manpower for the harvest from June to August, from the Languedoc to Picardy. In conclusion, each of the socio-professional groups deserves perhaps to receive a summary of its main features. Moreover this would once more involve our correlating the three sections which form the body of this work: thus one would bring together, for example, as regards Protestants versus Catholics, everything to do with the intellectual conditioning of the faith, and the general life of the Church; or in the case of the merchant bourgeoisie, the conditions favouring safety in the towns and the hazards of large-scale international trade, etc. Fifteen or twenty tables with all the necessary gradations and subdivisions could thus be both mathematically and subtly deduced from the discussions which precede this conclusion. For the time being we shall ignore this project.

What must be stressed is that the sociological factors were the most weighty. Our own investigations confirm this, having concentrated largely on social groups and professions. But these factors alone are not enough. They give neither a full description nor a full explanation of all the mental structures of a group; by which we mean that the view of the world held by a group cannot be defined from too restricted a standpoint. In particular, it must not be studied exclusively in terms of the social factors which can be inferred from a sociological pattern of class struggle and class consciousness.[8] To reduce the mental horizons of the *noblesse d'épée* between 1600 and 1630 to its dual conflict with the bourgeoisie and the *noblesse de robe* is to fall short of reality and of the historical evidence. Ways of life, hunting, duelling, jousting, the demesne and

[8] The reference here is to the analyses of false consciousness, of possible consciousness, which are much used by certain Marxists. The recent French translation of the unobtainable work by Lukacs, *Histoire et conscience de classe* (which appeared after this work was written) will allow this question to be debated afresh as fully as is required.

its cultivation and the undercover campaign against encroaching royal authority all come into consideration, whatever the practical historical function of class consciousness, whatever the role of the growing awareness of socio-economic antagonism. The latter being what they were—or more precisely being such as we can reconstruct them—it is certain that they do not form the whole of the group's view of the world.[9]

Certainly all historical psychology, all history of mentalities is social history; but it is also cultural history, the modern period being characterized by the enormous variety of views of the world which the intellectual and religious crises of the sixteenth century had implanted in the fabric of French society. Printing and the spread of books, increased numbers of colleges and the uneven dissemination of devotional works are the main facts which can most readily be adduced to explain these glaring disparities.

*

But let us take this point a little further. We shall then discover from this point of view the kind of feature which, since it influences the whole of a given society, deserves to be emphasized in this conclusion. To compile and catalogue a group's views of the world is, as we have just said, to discover the original characteristics of its culture, the scope of its knowledge of man and of nature, the tenor of its beliefs and of the instruments of its faith, and the stock of accepted ideas and prejudices which were acquired through family and social upbringing. In short, it is to discover a notion of the world and of man with its consistencies and contradictions, and also to compare this with other similar notions, which are more or less complex or comprehensive. In this respect, the modern period was the decisive moment in French—or indeed Western—history when there occurred an upheaval whose consequences have not always been accurately measured by the historian. It was the moment when the regular, if not the secular, clergy as a group ceased to bear the most elaborate and complex view of the world, one which derived its character from a combination of Scripture and the lessons handed down by pagan antiquity.

Doubtless, the twelfth and thirteenth centuries in France had known a cultured aristocracy which in its castles—the meeting-place for the troubadours—led a decidedly rich intellectual and artistic life. Even then, however, secular culture did not have the range and breadth of vision demonstrated by the upper clergy and the monks, who were steeped in the Church Fathers and a large part of the traditions of the ancient world. With the modern period, the clergy lost its supremacy to new groups of intellectuals, who may indeed have been educated by the universities and colleges run by the Church, but who were indebted to them for only part of their knowledge: first humanists and a little

[9] In this sense Goldmann (335) wrongly reduces the Jansenist view of the world between 1640 and 1660 to the *possible* class consciousness of one class, the *noblesse de robe*.

later scientists. To become aware of this change, one has only to examine the Parisian scientific scene at the end of the period in question and to analyse, for example, the circle of Father Mersenne. Certainly, clergymen were still present, since sixty of his correspondents and friends were Churchmen (including four archbishops, eight bishops, and six Sorbonne theologians). But one hundred and ten laymen form the majority, among whom the legal profession (led by the *Parlementaires*) were the most numerous with forty or so members.

This intellectual renewal, which also marked the beginning of a process of secularization which was to go on spreading in the following centuries, is certainly linked with the economic and social developments and political changes which are much better known (from the influx of American gold and silver to the growth of absolutism)—and from which the widening and redistribution of mental horizons is inseparable, as has been stressed above. A lasting trend was thus outlined during the Renaissance and confirmed, after the interlude of the Wars of Religion, in the first thirty years of the seventeenth century, thus following the traditional historical divisions. This correlation is obviously not accidental but the result of two essential causes which still remain to be discussed. On the one hand—and there will be no need to dwell on this—any attempt to reconstruct views of the world takes into consideration the actions and conduct of men, not only their words. It thus quite naturally rejoins the main patterns of a general history embracing all human activities. On the other hand, when dealing with psychological make-up, as with any other subject, there are no changeless structures, but a constant interaction between structures and conjunctures.

⋆

All group psychology is also the psychology of behaviour. For a period when men were less expansive than now, when groups had not always acquired the tell-tale institutions which even the smallest organization has today (house journals, internal bulletins, circulars and confidential letters) actions make up for the lack of words and provide us with a valuable part of the structural concepts we are seeking to define.

This was certainly demonstrated in the third section of this book. But we should like to dwell for a moment on the importance of such behavioural analyses when one comes to define these mental structures, or views of the world. Take for a moment the obvious example of the French merchant bourgeoisie, which at the end of the sixteenth century turned from trade to careers of State, to public offices or to acquiring estates. Some historians have made of this change in interests the decisive event which explains how France let slip its opportunity for great economic power, while England and the United Provinces were exploiting the Spanish commercial decline. In fact, this change of direction has never been measured with the mathematical precision which is required of social history today,[10] to discover precisely how many merchant families abandoned trade year by year, here between 1580 and 1590, or there between 1610 and 1620. Instead we rely mainly upon the laments of contemporaries, whether of Richelieu himself in his *Testament politique* or merely of a nobleman such as Isaac de Razilly, whose concern was for trade and colonial expansion, and who despised his contemporaries. We can certainly follow the trend in the price of offices immediately before and after the introduction of the *paulette*, as Roland Mousnier has done for Normandy. The investigation must be pursued tirelessly and systematically through all available records. But the actual state of research does not affect the argument. What we wish to point out first of all is how far such research is basically an inquiry into attitudes. The choice made by a section of the merchant bourgeoisie to abandon a form of activity which had made its family fortunes does not merely reflect disappointment at a worsening economic situation. In the case of land purchases, it reveals the lasting attraction of the values represented by land, and through these of noble rank. At a time when it was still possible to become a nobleman without causing too great a scandal by buying estates which were thought to be noble, fiefs which lacked legal heirs or had been abandoned by descendants in desperate straits, the prestige of the ruling class appealed to the bourgeois for more reasons than one. To calculate how many noble estates were thus purchased is to measure this abiding prestige.

The same can be said of the shift towards royal offices. Even before the introduction of the *paulette* these posts, which conferred a certain social distinction, found no lack of candidates, who were necessarily of bourgeois origin. After 1604, and throughout the seventeenth century, the enthusiasm for posts in administration, which had now become hereditary, scarcely waned. The real appeal which they held for bankers and merchants can be judged from the number of such changes made; for it is obviously not altogether true, as Razilly maintains, that '*all* merchants finding themselves rich . . . have spent *all* their fortunes on offices for their children. . . .'[11] There is no doubt, however, that such research will provide the material for a conclusive answer to the question of the options and opinions of the merchant class.

Let us take this even a little further, since the problem which we have chosen by way of example clarifies the whole economic development of modern France. To discover how many merchants, proportionately speaking, abandoned trade for offices or real estate is not only to measure long-lasting social prestige —and therefore mental structures which were social in origin—but also to clarify the commercial vocation of France at the dawn of modern times, and

[10] With the exception of the major work on the offices by R. Mousnier, *La vénalité des offices au temps de Henri IV et de Richelieu*; cf. notably pp. 458–62.

[11] I. de Razilly, *Mémoire au Cardinal de Richelieu*, ed. Léon Deschamps, *Revue de géographie* (1886). The italics are my own.

to offer a more reliable and more acceptable answer to the problem than the studied writings, in which the literary cud has so often been chewed, even by reputable authors, on the natural inclination of the French to bureaucracy, the predetermined harmony between Calvinism and capitalism, and many similar false generalizations, which are primarily rhetorical exercises. In contrast to the ponderous workings of a form of sociology which bears no relation to reality, the historian employs the slow, painstaking and difficult process which succeeds in combining the investigation of reality with an effort at conceptualization.

It is in this spirit that the 'philosophical' notion of the view of the world is useful. It sums up in a phrase—as 'mental structure' would also do if only this term were in current use in the scientific vocabulary of our times—all the notions accepted by an individual or a group, and used by them daily in the course of their thoughts and activities. As all will realize, it is not easy to reconstruct these patterns, and this is shown by the mere fact that they must be approached from different viewpoints, as we have seen throughout this book. And one must add yet another difficulty: in the case of attitudes, even more than in the fields of economic or political history, it is not always easy to identify structures and conjunctures, and to give each its respective weight. In political history, for example, institutions form an important part of the structures. As scrupulously-observed customs or carefully-composed constitutions, they are always easy and precise subjects for analysis. Surely no-one would dispute the meaning of the law *Le Chapelier* of 17 June 1791. Here again, further remarks seem called for. They will be the last.

Climates of sensitivity: mental conjunctures

We have used mental conjunctures throughout the book without ever making them the basis of our study. The expression is a particularly fortunate one for referring to the successive climates in which crises arise, and in which develop the great problems which reflect gradual changes in outlooks. Doubtless, the relation which is thus established between structures which evolve slowly and conjunctural climates is a particularly subtle one. It would be wrong, for example, to see the latter simply as a mere tincture of pessimism for the bad years—and of confident optimism in human destiny for times which seem more fortunate. The mental climate of a period can never be reduced to so simple a formula. Though the period 1515–35 appears to be one of bold *joie de vivre*, the spread of Lutheran ideas itself introduced a particularly pessimistic view of the world and of man. But on the other hand—and this is even more important—we detect these changes in group sensitivity thanks to only one section of society—as it were, the most receptive and expressive elements. It is not the popular classes of the towns and countryside between 1515 and 1535 which justify one's speaking of an atmosphere of freedom and conquest, but rather the business world and most of all the intellectuals and artists, the many Frenchmen who witnessed and took part in a great renewal. In a sense, the mental conjuncture is the work of the *avant-garde*, of the cultural groups which set the tone—at least so long as there is not too great a disparity between the *avant-garde* and the majority. Thus, thanks to these elements which were endowed with a particularly keen sensibility, one can detect the atmosphere characteristic of each period.

We have repeatedly referred to the two principal trends of the sixteenth century—the bold hopes of the first third of the century, and the sombre decades of the civil and religious wars. In fact, a more subtle pattern (incorporating all the relevant data, whether political, religious, economic or social) can be laid down. The great hopes of the period 1515–35 were tinged with anxiety long before the Affair of the Placards (1534). Assuredly, the atmosphere worsened much more quickly afterwards, until the first spate of persecution from 1547 to 1560. But between 1525 and 1530, political difficulties resulting from the king's captivity, and Lutheran activities based upon the northern and eastern frontiers made many people uneasy and prepared for the subsequent stiffening of attitudes.

Similarly, during the long period of the civil wars from 1560 to 1598, one can pick out some periods of respite. For example, the beginning of the reign of Henri III, from 1574 to 1584, was a kind of interlude in which are rediscovered remnants of the times of hope. Equally, after 1598, one would take pains to lay special but varied emphasis upon the peaceful reign of Henri IV from 1598 to 1610, or to indicate the great epidemic of plague in 1630, which ravaged almost the whole country.

But one can pursue the notion of the conjuncture even further and link it with the shorter period representing a generation. Let us follow briefly the rise of French Protestantism, and chart its progress otherwise than by using the traditional landmarks: 1517 Luther, 1534 the Placards, 1537 the *Institutes of the Christian Religion*, etc. The heroic age of Protestantism was, in our opinion, from 1520 to 1540, when clergy and laity had to choose for or against a new faith and a new Church. The age of the founders ended once a man was born a Protestant. The choice had been made by the previous generation, and a family conformity—or indeed nonconformity—then appeared easier than the choice itself. Then from about 1547 to 1549 the first period of persecution began, creating another conjuncture since the persecuted did not belong to the generation of the founders. The latter had taken the decisive step without having to protect themselves immediately from physical attack. The former, when they were violently attacked, had other choices to make: to leave home, to conceal their sympathies, to resort to duplicity or to declare themselves. The problems were completely different, as all can see. Moreover, persecution takes on its full meaning for Catholics and Protestants alike when one can discover all its implications. If Protestants left France for Geneva in their thousands between

1549 and 1560, if they were butchered by the thousand in August 1572, it was because persecution and murder called into question more than rivalry between the two religious groups. What was at stake once the *chambre ardente* was established was the defence of a community whose basic principles were threatened. The executions were simultaneously a physical liquidation and an expiation offered to divine anger. In the Massacre of St Bartholomew there is doubtless an important element of ritual murder. The precariousness of the Edict of Nantes is surely to be understood in this context, which basically derives from age-old traditions that have not yet been identified clearly enough. Here again, what contrasts were to be found at each stage, from one generation to the next; from the generations which fought in the Wars to the one which grew up in peacetime, benefiting by the Edict.

And a little later, under the system set up by the Edict, how the atmosphere differed between the years of organisation and settlement which followed immediately upon the signature and registration of the royal Act, and the feverish anxiety with which the struggle was undertaken between 1620 and 1629 to maintain the liberties and privileges acquired in 1598. It is not a matter of the political wisdom of Henri IV or of Richelieu, but rather of the feelings entertained at a precise moment in time by the thousands of Frenchmen who were directly affected by the Edict of 1598 and the peace treaty of 1629. Obviously, whether they affect only a restricted group or society as a whole, conjunctural developments in attitude are of the same order: thus the French Protestants, those rebels who aspired to a purified and effective faith and were the bearers of a new form of Christian experience and Christian worship found themselves confronted from generation to generation by different political, social and spiritual circumstances. Their notions of religion and of the world—in particular of France and of Europe—were thereby certainly modified. This is precisely the close relation between structure and conjuncture.

The same is true of mental climates as of economic climates: they vary in duration. We have just seen this in the two examples quoted above: if one looks for the general historical pattern of French life between 1500 and 1640 one finds that it falls into three main periods, three successive climates which 'lasted' from forty to fifty years each: 1500–60; then 1560–98; and finally 1598–1640. A close examination of this new social group in French life, the Protestants, reveals a shorter cycle, in which the generation is the essential factor: 1520–45, the founders; 1545–60, the martyrs; 1560–98, the combatants; 1598–1615, those who benefited by legal status; 1615–29, the defenders of the Edict, etc. The links between the two patterns are obvious.

*

There are other aspects too which one would include under the heading of mental conjunctures, or climates of sensibility: to be precise, one might well also use the term 'mental epidemics'. To be sure, these are not very easy to identify, but they certainly existed, as extreme cases reveal. In the eastern provinces, from Lorraine to Franche-Comté, which were not then formally a part of France but were French-speaking and came under her influence, the struggles between Protestants and Catholics during the period 1560–90, which were closely connected with those which ravaged France proper, were succeeded by an epidemic of witchcraft. Witch-hunting took over from Protestant-hunting for some decades, from 1590 to about 1630. This was when Boguet, Rémy and their many lesser-known disciples flourished. But the writings of judges who were concerned zealously to apply age-old laws were not the only factors. As instruments of implacable justice, they helped to extend for ten or twenty years the repressive frenzy which hounded down even in the smallest villages all who could be suspected of being in league with the Devil. The atmosphere of denunciation and suspicion which was then rife among the whole population was certainly a passing phenomenon. In many villages in the Vosges, persecution flagged for want of victims—which was the most extreme case of all. The fury of the purge had been such that almost no one escaped. But more often the frenzy lapsed, as if of its own accord, after a long series of trials. Sometimes it was jerked into life, when the son or daughter of a witch was in turn accused of having dealings with the Devil; then the epidemic died out. No attempt will be made here to seek risky explanations of this phenomenon; one might simply note its cyclical nature, which fully justifies our use of terminology such as 'epidemic' and 'conjuncture'.

There is, in our view, an even more precise illustration of this state of hypersensitivity. The end of the sixteenth century, the time of the League and the years following the re-establishment of peace, was a period of lachrymose and cruel sensibility, which recalls in many respects the morbid sentimentality of the late fifteenth century. The exhibitionism of the Leaguer monks, and of their processions in which weeping, sobbing, wailing and fainting were so prominent, is one obvious symptom of this. At Marseilles in 1596, Thomas Platter witnessed a procession of the brotherhood of the *Battus* who scourged themselves publicly on certain days. Four thousand inhabitants of the town filed past dressed in sackcloth which revealed only their tear-filled eyes, their wailing mouths and their scarred backs. In Paris at the height of the League, not a week went by without flagellants rousing the population with their cries and their antics. Closely connected with this inclination to morbid sentimentality would seem to be the instances of cruelty in the same period, the long list of massacres, rapes, hatred and horror which characterized the civil wars. Perhaps even the sexual perverts, from the *mignons* of Henri III to those guilty of the widespread crime of bestiality, deserve to be included in the same emotional category. In reality, we are already dealing with the sensibility of the Baroque period.

Certainly, to analyse such conjunctures one must resort to all the methods of investigation which we have had to deal in so far. The emotional behaviour illustrated by the flagellations of the Leaguers, and the violence of the monks and of the urban lower classes at the end of the sixteenth century, involved urban society as a whole—not only the more cultured classes. This conjuncture affected all townsmen at least, whereas the apparent emotional and peaceful stability of the period 1515–30 is defined in terms of very restricted groups of humanists, artists and scholars representing a cultural elite—and exclusively in terms of these groups. To examine systematically a mental conjuncture from 1515 to 1598 thus also involves explaining why the popular urban classes were relatively silent[12] in 1515–30 when they were so violent and demonstrative in 1589–98.

To account for this state of exacerbated, exasperated emotionalism in the towns thus means launching into urban history, into a long and complex period of social history. Were the same popular groups involved in all cases? What about the economic situation, whose psychological repercussions were so apparent when excessive taxation increased market difficulties and caused trade riots, new taxes, increases in taxes and levies, and renewed controls? Did it not play its part in 1515–30, as also in 1589–98?

Certainly, in defining these emotional climates one must also take account of material circumstances: famines, good harvests, the shortage or abundance of money, epidemics and general health are obvious factors. Finally, one must also consider their geographical boundaries. Like Romanticism in the early nineteenth century, the Baroque in the first third of the seventeenth century was a European phenomenon, which did not concern France alone. Closely connected as it was with social and economic developments unprecedented in the history of western Europe, this state of hypersensitivity knew no frontiers, even if the legacy of the past and local circumstances meant that its precise character varied from one end of Europe to the other. This has been shown in the case of the late fifteenth century, in the magnificent account given by Huizinga.

There is a good illustration of it in the European pacifist trend in the years following the proclamation of the Edict of Nantes. In all countries where there was a division of convictions comparable to that in France, the act of 1598 appeared as the solution to be imitated. It seemed a better formula than the German one (of fragmentation on the basis of the German principalities) for ensuring the peaceful survival of the two communities. In the Swiss cantons and in Italy, Henri IV appeared momentarily as the peacemaker of the Church, and for several years his success served to promote a whole current of religious pacifism.

To define emotional and intellectual conjunctures as briefly as we have tried

[12] Or indeed why 'iconoclastic' attitudes were adopted by groups of artisans who were just as sympathetic to Protestant ideas as the flagellants in 1589–94 were devoted to the aims of the League.

to do here is thus primarily to show that psychological history, like all history which seeks to explain in depth, knows no frontiers. Above all, it is not distinct from other branches of history. To presume to isolate psychological history (even under the impressive title of the history of ideas and of feelings—or again, the social history of ideas)[13] is a wellnigh hopeless task. The history of mentalities is a permanent and inseparable part of total history, conceived not as the idealistic and Romantic dream of a Michelet, but as a continuous methodological requirement of research.

*

This is the point to stop. It is fitting that this examination of how our attempt to take bearings in the difficult field of the history of mentalities expands to take its place in the complex pattern of the historical revival should end by stressing the necessary interrelation between all the constituents of social history. Besides, we certainly do not claim to have exhausted the possibilities of description and explanation with this tableau of France at the beginning of the modern period. The work was deliberately subtitled *An essay in historical psychology*. It is nothing more than that; indeed, as we mean to state once again in conclusion, it is seen essentially as a starting-point for the fresh research which is indispensable if one is to respond to the appeal made by Lucien Febvre[14] in 1938 and 'integrate historical psychology. . . . (still to be written) in the main current of history in the making'.

[13] As. L. Trénard has done in *Lyon, de l'Encyclopédie au romantisme* (Paris 1958).

[14] 'Histoire et psychologie', *Encyclopédie française* VIII. Repeated in *Combtas pour l'histoire*, p. 207.

Bibliography

Obviously the bibliography for such a work is endless, at least on some aspects. A student of the Reformation should not look for an exhaustive bibliography of his subject here. We have mentioned only those works which we have used and which were able to help us clarify the concept of the history of group psychology.

However, it should also be pointed out that while some aspects are particularly well documented, and sometimes excessively so, others have little to offer. On Humanism, the Renaissance, the Reformation, institutions or court life we are presented with an impossibly wide choice, and in these instances we have omitted many excellent works so as not to emphasize the disproportions, and overload the bibliographical apparatus. On the other hand, on sports and entertainments, habitation and even food, documentary evidence and studies are much rarer.

This selective bibliography is divided into two main parts: firstly a list, on a regional basis, of printed *livres de raison* and memoirs[1] which in a sense have formed the basis of this study; secondly, the selection of texts, and especially of critical works, which we have just sought to justify, arranged in accordance with the general plan of the book, and observing its general sections.[2]

'Livres de raison' and memoirs

Paris region:

(1) Bourrilly, *Le Journal d'un bourgeois de Paris sous le règne de François Ier (1515–1536)* (Paris 1910).

(2) De l'Estoile, Pierre, *Journal* (for the reigns of Henri III and Henri IV), new edn by L. R. Lefèvre, 3 vols (Paris 1958).

(3) Dubuisson-Aubenay, *Journal des guerres civiles* (S.H.F.[3] 1883).

[1] We are aware that dozens of *livres de raison* in manuscript form lie unexplored in many archive collections.

[2] The second part of the bibliography is divided into: (1) texts and documents and (2) critical works.

[3] *Société d'Histoire de France.*

(4) De Campion, Henri, *Mémoires* (Paris, S.H.F. 1857).
(5) Du Fossé, *Mémoires sur MM. de Port-Royal* (Amsterdam, 1739 edn).
(6) Fagniez, *Livre de raison de Me Nicolas Versoles, avocat au Parlement de Paris 1519–1530* (*Mém. soc. hist. Paris* XII, 1885).
(7) Haton, C., *Mémoires*, 2 vols (Paris 1857).
(8) Pradel, C., *Un Marchand de Paris au XVIe siècle (1564–1588), after the papers of Simon Leconte* (Toulouse, *Mém. Acad. des Sciences* 1889).
(9) Rou, J., *Mémoires (1639–1711)* (Paris, S.H.F. 1857).
(10) *Mémoires du Marquis de Beauvais Nangis* (Paris, S.H.F. 1862).

Western France:

(11) Abbé Aubert, *Notes extraites de trois livres de raison de 1473 à 1550. Comptes d'une famille de gentilshommes campagnards normands* (*Bulletin historique et philologique du comité des travaux historiques* 1898).
(12) Chatenay, L., *Vie de Jacques Esprinchard, Rochelais, et Journal de ses voyages au XVIe siècle* (Paris 1957).
(13) Clouard, E., *Livre de raison de deux bourgeois de Vitré, 1490–1583* (*Rev. de Bretagne* 1914).
(14) *Journal du sire de Gouberville (1553–1564)* (Caen, *Mém. Soc. Ant. Normandie* XXXI, 1892).
(15) *Journal de Gilles de Gouberville pour les années 1549–1552.* (Caen, *Soc. Antiq. de Normandie*, 1895).
(16) Laigne, R. de, *Livre de comptes de Claude de la Landelle (1553–1556)* (Rennes, *Les bibliophiles bretons* 1906).

Central France:

(17) Guibert, L., *Livres de raison, registres de famille et journaux individuels limousins et marchois*, 2 vols (Limoges and Paris 1888).
(18) Guibert, L., *Nouveau recueil de registres domestiques limousins et marchois* (Limoges 1895–1903).
(19) Guibert, L., *Registre domestique des La Garde de Tulle (1569–1645)* (Brive, *Bull. soc. scient. de la Corrèze* 1892).
(20) Guibert, L., *Livre domestique de la famille de Burguet de Chauffailles (1602–1702)* (*Bull. soc. archéol. du Limousin* XXXVIII, 1891).
(21) Guibert, L., *Mémorial de Jean et Pierre Roques frères, bourgeois de Beaulieu (1478–1525)* (Brive, *Bull. soc. scient. de la Corrèze* 1890).
(22) Guibert, L., *Journal domestique de Martial de Guy de Nexon, lieutenant général à Limoges (1591–1603)* (Brive, *Bull. soc. scient. de la Corrèze* 1893).
(23) Guibert, L., *Notes d'Antoine Raymond, notaire de la Vicomté de Rochechouart 1572–1620* (Brive, *Bull. soc. scient. de la Corrèze* 1893).

(24) Guibert, L., *Journal historique d'Elie de Rouffignac (1588–1589)* (Brive, *Bull. soc. scient. de la Corrèze* 1893).

(25) Leroux, A., *Livre de raison et registre de famille des sieurs Terrade, notaires à Chaumeil (1548–1685)* (Brive, *Bull. soc. scient. de la Corrèze* 1892).

(26) Leroux, A., *Registre de la famille Salignac de Rochefort près Limoges 1571–1626* (Paris and Limoges 1888).

(27) Leroux, A., *Livre de raison et registre de la famille de Pierre de Sainte-Feyre (1497–1533)* (Brive, *Bull. soc. scient. de la Corrèze* 1890).

(28) Leroux, A., *Livre de raison et registre de famille d'Antoine de Sainte-Feyre (1570–1597)* (Brive, *Bull. soc scient. de la Corrèze* 1892).

(29) Leroux, A., *Journal de Vielbans, conseiller au présidial de Brive 1571–1598* (Brive, *Bull. soc. scient. de la Corrèze* 1893).

(30) *Mémoires de Jean Burel, bourgeois du Puy (1601–1629)* (Le Puy 1875).

(31) *Mémoires du comte de Souvigny (1618–1660)* (Paris, S.H.F. 1906).

(32) *Journal d'Antoine Jacmon (1627–1651)* (Le Puy 1885).

(33) *Le Livre de raison d'Ant. de Thales, seigneur des Farges et de Cornilhon (1514–1551)* (Saint-Etienne, *Bull. La Diana* 1895).

South-western France and the Languedoc:

(34) Fabre, E., *Deux livres de raison de l'Albigeois (1517–1550)* (Paris 1896).

(35) *Livre de raison des du Pouget, bourgeois de Cahors (1522–1598)* (*Bull. soc. des études du Lot* 1895–6).

(36) Forestié, *Les Livres de comptes des frères Boysset, marchands de S. Antonin de Rouergue (1520–1528)* (Montauban, *Bull. soc. archéol. du Tarn et Garonne* 1892).

(37) Tamizey de Larroque, *Livre de raison de la famille de Fontainemarie (1740–1774)*, with a general bibliography of *livres de raison* known to the author (Agen 1889).

(38) Tamizey de Larroque, *Deux livres de raison de l'Agenais* (Auch and Paris 1893).

(39) Tamizey de Larroque, *Le Livre de raison de la famille Dudrot de Capdebosc (1522–1675)* (Paris 1891).

(40) Tamizey de Larroque, *Livre journal de P. de Bessot (1609–1652)* (*Bull. soc. hist. du Périgord* 1893 and Paris 1893).

South-eastern France:

(41) Brun-Durand, *Mémoires d'Achille Gamon, avocat d'Annonay (1552–1586)* (Valence 1888).

(42) Guillaume, Paul, *Livre de raison de Martin de la Villette seigneur majeur des Crottes (1500–1525)* (*Annales des Alpes* IX, 1905–6).

(43) Lubac, J. de, *Le Journal d'un vieux gentilhomme (Guillaume de Chalendar de la Motte, 1583–1597)* (*Revue du Vivarais* V, 1897).

(44) Manteyer, G. de, *Le Livre journal tenu par Fazy de Rame en langage embrunais, 1471–1507* (Gap 1932).

(45) *La Vie de Thomas Platter écrite par lui-même*, translated from German into French (Geneva 1862).

(46) Ribbe, C. de, *La Famille et la société en France avant la Révolution, d'après des documents originaux*, 4th edn (Tours 1879), 2: *Les Livres de raison en Provence et dans l'ancienne France.*

(47) Teil, T. du, *Le Livre de raison de noble Honoré du Teil (1541–1586)* (*Annales des Basses-Alpes* 1893).

(48) Vachez, A., *Les Livres de raison dans le Lyonnais et les provinces voisines* (Lyons 1892).

Eastern France:

(49) Breneau, C., *La Chronique de Philippe de Vigneulles*, 4 vols (Metz 1933).

(50) Feuvrier, J., *Feuillets de garde: les Mairot (1535–1769)* (*Mém. soc. émul. du Jura* 1901).

(51) *Livre de raison de la famille Froissard de Broissia (1532–1701)* (*Mém. soc. émul. du Jura* 1886).

(52) Michelant, *Gedenkbuch der Metzer Burgers, Philippe von Vigneulles, 1471–1522* (*Bibl. des Literatur Vereins in Stuttgart* 1852).

(53) Prost, B., *Extraits d'un livre journal tenu par une famille bourgeoise de Bletterans (1542–1661)* (*Bull. soc. agric. de Poligny* 1877).

(54) Prost, B., *Journal de Guill. Durand, chirurgien à Poligny (1610–1623)* (*Bull. soc. agric. de Poligny* 1881–2).

Northern France:

(55) Jadart, H., *Mémoires de Jean Maillefer, bourgeois et marchand de Reims (1611–1684)* (Paris 1890).

(56) Ledieu, A., *Le Livre de raison d'un magistrat picard Philippe de Lavernot (1601–1602)* (Abbeville 1889).

Individual human dimensions (Part I)

I—FOOD

1—Texts and documents:

(57) Bruyerin-Champier, *De Re cibaria* (Lyons 1560).

(58) Curti, Matteo, *De Prandii de Caenae modo libellus* (Rome 1688).

(59) Durante, C., *Il Tesoro della sanita* (Venice 1588).
(60) Hageciøus, T., *De Cervisia ejusque conficiendi ratione natura, viribus et facultatibus opusculum* (Frankfurt 1585).
(61) Palmarii, J., *De Vino et pomaceo libri duo* (Paris 1588). The author was Julien Le Paulmier, a doctor in the Faculty of Medicine in Paris. (*Traité du vin et du cidre*, 2nd edn, Caen 1589; 3rd edn 1607).
(62) Platocomus, *De Natura et viribus carevisiarum et mulsurum opusculum* (Wittenberg 1554).
(63) Quercetani, J., *Diaeteticon polyhistoricon opus utique varium magnae utilitatis ac delectationis quod multa historica, philosophica et medica tam conservendae sanitari quam variis curandis morbis necessaria contineat* (Paris 1606).

2—Critical works:

(64) Ashley, Sir W., *The bread of our forefathers: an enquiry in economic history* (Oxford 1928).
(65) Bourdeau, L., *Histoire de l'Alimentation* (*Etudes d'histoire générale*) (Paris 1894).
(66) Castro, J. de, *Géographie de la faim, La faim au Brésil* (Paris 1949).
(67) Christoffel, K., *Durch die Zeiten strömt der Wein* (Hamburg 1957).
(68) Deniau, J., 'La Vigne et le vin à Lyon au XVe siècle', *Etudes Rhodaniennes* 3 (1930).
(69) Drummond, J. C., *The Englishman's food. An history of five centuries of English diet* (London 1955).
(70) Gibault, G., *Historie des légumes* (Paris 1912).
(71) Gottschalk, F., *Histoire de l'alimentation et de la gastronomie, depuis la pré-histoire jusqu'à nos jours* (Paris 1948).
(72) Habasque, F., *La Vie en province au XVIe siècle. Comment Agen mangeait au temps des derniers Valois* (Agen 1887).
(73) Jacob, H. E., *Histoire du pain depuis 6000 ans*, translated from German into French (Paris 1958).
(74) Lippmann, E. von, *Geschichte des Zuckers, seit den ältesten Zeiten bis zum Beginn der Rübenzucker—Fabrikation. Ein Betrag zur Kulturgeschichte* (Berlin 1928).
(75) Maurizo, A., *Histoire de l'alimentation végétale depuis la préhistoire jusqu'à nos jours*, French translation (Paris 1932).
(76) Schoellhorn, F., *Bibliographie des Brauwesens* (Berlin 1928).
(77) Soepper, D. K., *L'Alimentation de l'humanité. Son économie, sa répartition, ses possibilités* (Paris 1942).
(78) Sorre, M., *Les bases biologiques de la géographie humaine* I (Paris 1943).
(79) Weber, F., *Essai historique sur la brasserie française* (Soissons 1900).

II—ENVIRONMENT

1—Texts and documents:

(80) Besson, J., *Théâtre des instruments mathématiques et méchaniques* (Lyons 1578).

(81) Boudeau, N., *Principes de la science morale et politique sur le luxe et les lois somptuaires*, ed. A. Duboc (Paris 1912).

(82) Colyn, M., *Habits de diverses nations de l'Europe, Asie, Afrique et Amerique* (Antwerp 1581).

(83) Vecellio, C., *Degli habiti antichi e moderni di diverse parti del mundo, libri II* (Venice 1590).

2—Critical works:

(84) D'Allemagne, H. R., *Histoire du luminaire depuis l'époque romaine jusqu'au XIXe siècle* (Paris 1891).

(85) Aragon, H., *Les Lois somptuaires en France. De Louis XI à Louis XIV* (Perpignan 1921).

(86) Quenedey, R., *L'Habitation rouennaise* (Rouen 1926).

(87) Quicherat, J., *Histoire du costume en France, depuis les temps les plus reculés jusqu'à la fin du XVIIIe siècle* (Paris 1875).

III—HEALTH AND DISEASE

1—Documents:

There are innumerable treatises on diseases and remedies: since the Middle Ages, doctors had been producing small learned compendia of symptoms and the cures achieved by all kinds of methods. A scholar has recently begun an inventory of the medieval manuscripts preserved in the Latin collection of the *Bibliothèque Nationale.* This investigation must be extended to cover other periods—and above all it must be carried further than a mere cataloguing of texts. A systematic analysis of this vast body of literature, which combines a mixture of quack remedies, treatises by doctors and actual case-studies, is indispensable if we are to reconstruct the physical state of man in earlier times. In this respect, the great works which have achieved literary fame—for instance, the works of Ambroise Paré, which were constantly being republished (the 10th edition appeared in Lyons in 1641)—are less important than short accounts written on the occasion of some lethal epidemic, or in honour of some thermal spring or healing shrine.

The following are quoted as examples—and form merely a small sample:

(88) Abraham, Nicolas, sieur de la Framboisière, *Le Gouvernement nécessaire à chacun pour vivre longuement en santé* (Paris 1600).
(89) *Brevis facilisque methodus curandarum febrium, authore Jacobo Cahagnesio Cadomensi, medicinae regis professore* (Cadomi 1616).
(90) Brosse, Guy de la, *De la nature, vertu et utilité des plantes . . .* (Paris 1628).
(91) Capivaccio, J., *Methodus practicae medicinae omnium humani corporis affectum causas signas, et curationes exhibens* (Lyons 1596).
(92) Du Chesne (Quercetanus), *Pharmacopea dogmaticorum restitua* (Paris 1607; Frankfurt 1615; Geneva 1620.)
(93) Duval, Claude, *Libellus Alexiterius de peste precavenda et curanda* (Paris 1623).
(94) Joubert, Laurent, *Erreurs populaires au faict de la médicine et régime de santé* (Avignon 1586; 1st edn, Bordeaux 1578).
(95) Juliani Palmarii, *Medici Parisiensis, de morbis contagiosis libri septem, ad amplissimum Senatum Parisiensem* (Parisiis 1578; 2nd edn, Frankfurt 1601; 3rd edn, The Hague 1664).
(96) Le Paulmier, Julien, *Bref discours de la praeservation et curation de la peste* (Caen 1580; 2nd edn, Angers 1584).
(97) De Nancel, Nicolas, *Discours très ample de la peste, divisé en 3 parties, adressant à M.M. de Tours* (Paris 1581).
(98) Riolan, Jean, *Generalis methodus medendi* (Paris 1580).
(99) Riolant, Jean, *Les Œuvres anatomiques* (1626).
(100) Van der Heyden, *Du Trousse galant, dit choléra morbus* (Ghent 1645).

2—Critical works:

There is certainly no lack of general histories of medicine, but these vary in their use to the historian, except for:

(101) Laignel-Lavastine, M., *Histoire générale de la medecine*, 3 vols (Paris 1938–49).
(102) Cf. also P. Delaunay, *La Vie médicale aux XVIe, XVIIe, XVIIIe siècles* (Paris 1935).
(103) Levy-Valensi, J., *La Médecine et les médecins français au XVIIe siècle* (Paris 1933).
(104) Wickersheimer, E., *La Médecine et les médecins en France à l'époque de la Renaissance* (Paris 1906).

Cf. the beginnings of a major project:

(105) Quemada, B., *Introduction à l'étude du vocabulaire médical (1600–1710)* (Besançon 1955).

On the problem of demography, in addition to:

(106) Goubert, P., *Beauvais et le Beauvaisis de 1600 à 1730. Contribution à l'histoire sociale de la France du XVIIe siècle*, 2 pts, *Démographie et sociétés* 3 (1960).

there are a few studies to quote:

(107) Braudel, F., *La Méditerranée et le monde méditerranéan au temps de Philippe II* (Paris 1948), pp. 347ff.

(108) Meuvret, J., 'Les Crises de subsistance et la démographie de la France d'ancien régime', *Population* (Oct.–Dec. 1947).

(109) Reinhard, M., *Histoire de la population mondiale de 1700 à 1948* (Paris 1949).

(110) Roupnel, G., *La Ville et la campagne au XVIIe siècle. Etude sur les populations du pays dijonnais* (Paris 1956), pp. 109ff.

IV—MENTAL FACULTIES: PASSIONS, FEELINGS

1—Texts:

Contemporary documents, apart from the evidence one finds in the *livres de raison,* are of two kinds: on the one hand, poetical works designed to express emotion, and on the other the moralist tradition, which in the seventeenth century produced Descartes' *Traité des passions*, and the works of Pascal. We have thus drawn upon:

(111) Marot, C., in the Paris edition of 1554.

(112) Ronsard, P. de, in the Paris edition of 1571, and the edition by Blanchemain.

(113) Du Bellay, J., in the Paris edition of 1558.

(114) D'Aubigné, A., *Les Tragiques*, ed. Schuhmann (Paris 1911 etc.).

(115) Heroet, A., *Œuvres poétiques*, ed. Gohin (Paris 1909).

In addition, a few little-known treatises were used:

(116) Marande, Léonard, *Le Jugement des actions humaines* (Paris 1624).

(117) Lemoyne, R. P., *Les Peintures morales, où les passions sont représentées par tableaux, par charactères et par questions nouvelles et curieuses*, 2 vols (Paris 1640–43).

(118) Senault, R. P. J. F., *Traité de l'usage des passions* (Paris 1641).

2—Critical works:

No history of sensibility has yet been written. Lucien Febvre has alone outlined the plan for such a work in the last section of his *Rabelais et le problème de l'incroyance au XVIe siècle* (Paris 1942); cf. especially pp. 461–73. He also illustrated the monograph approach:

(119) Febvre, L., *Autour de l'Heptaméron: amour sacré, amour profane* (Paris 1944).

V—MENTAL FACULTIES: MENTAL EQUIPMENT

1—Texts and documents:

(120) Salomon de la Brosse, *Le Cavalier françois* (Paris 1602).
(121) Du Bellay, J., *Défense et illustration de langue française* (reprinted Paris 1904).
(122) Estienne, Robert, *Dictionnaire français-latin* (Paris 1539).
(123) Grison, Frédéric, *L'Ecurie du Saint-Frédéric Grisson*, translated from Italian into French (Paris 1579).
(124) Meigret, Louis, *Traité touchant le commun usage de l'escriture françoise, auquel est debattu des faultes et abus en la vraye et ancienne puissance des lettres* (Paris 1542).
(125) Paré, Ambroise, *Les Œuvres d'Ambroise Paré reveues et corrigées en plusieurs endroits et augmentées d'un fort ample traicté des fiebvres, nouvellement treuvé dans les manuscrits de l'auteur* (Paris 1628).
(126) Tory, Geoffroy, *Briesve doctrine pour deument escripre selon la propriété du langaige français* (Paris 1533).
(127) Vaugelas, *Remarques sur la langue française, utiles à tous ceux qui veulent bien parler et bien écrire* (Paris 1646).

2—Critical works:

(128) Audin, M., *Histoire de l'imprimerie par l'image*, 4 vols (Lyons 1930).
(129) Bilfinger, G., *Die mittelalterlichen Uhren und die modernen Stunden* (Stuttgart 1892).
(130) Berthoud, F., *Histoire de la mesure du temps par les horloges* (Paris, Imprimerie de la République, An. X, 1802).
(131) Brun, A., *Recherches historiques sur l'introduction du Français dans les provinces du Midi* (Paris 1923).
(132) Brunot, F., *Histoire de la langue française* II: *Le XVIe siècle* (Paris 1931); III: *La Formation de la langue classique* (Paris 1933).
(133) Callot, E., *La Renaissance des sciences de la vie au XVIe siècle* (Paris 1949).
(134) Couderc, *Etapes de l'astronomie* (Paris 1955).
(135) Cournot, A., *Considérations sur la marche des idées et des événements dans les temps modernes* (Paris 1934).
(136) *Encyclopédie française* I: *L'Outillage mental* (Paris 1935).
(137) Huguet, H., *La Syntaxe de Rabelais* (Paris 1894).
(138) Humboldt, A. de, *Cosmos, essai d'une description physique du monde*, 2 vols (Paris 1846).

The social context (Part II)

I—THE MARRIED COUPLE AND THE FAMILY

1—Texts and documents:

(139) Erasmus, D., *Le Mariage chrétien,* in the 1714 translation.

(140) *Petite instruction et manière de vivre pour une femme séculière* (Paris n.d., rue Neuve N. D., à l'écu de France).

(141) *Le Protocole des notaires . . . contenant la manière de rédiger par escript tous contractz, instrumens, partages, inventaires, comptes, commissions, rappors, demandes et autres actes et exploictz de justice. Avec le Guydon des secrétaires, contenant la manière d'escripre et adresser toutes lettres missives. Nouvellement composé à Lyon* (G. Rose) (1531).

(142) *Le Protocole des secretaires et aultres gens desirans scavoir l'art et manière de dicter en bon francoys toutes lettres missives et épistres en prose* (Lyons 1534).

(143) *L'Histoire d'Aurelio et Isabelle en italien et françoys en laquelle est disputé qui baille plus d'occasion d'aymer, l'homme à la femme ou la femme à l'homme* (Lyons 1555).

2—Critical works:

(144) Ariès, P., *L'Enfant et la vie familiale sous l'ancien régime* (Paris 1960).

(145) Auffroy, H., *Evolution des testaments en France des origines au XVIIIe siècle* (Paris 1899).

(146) Bremond, H., *Histoire littéraire du sentiment religieux en France, depuis la fin des guerres de religion jusqu'à nos jours* IX, (Paris 1932), see chapter on the mystique of marriage in the seventeenth century.

(147) Petot, P., 'La Famille en France sous l'ancien régime', in *Sociologie comparée de la famille contemporaine*, Colloques du C.N.R.S. (1955).

(148) Plessis de Grenedan, J. du, *Histoire de l'autorité paternelle et de la société familiale en France avant 1789* (Paris 1900).

(149) De Ribbe, C., *La Famille et la société en France avant la Révolution* (4th edn, Tours 1879).

(150) De Ribbe, C., *La Vie domestique, ses modèles et ses règles* (Paris 1877).

(151) Febvre, L., *Autour de l'Heptaméron: amour sacré, amour profane* (Paris 1943).

(152) Wendel, F., *Le Mariage à Strasbourg à l'époque de la Réforme* (Strasbourg 1928).

II—THE PARISH

1—There are no published documents entirely devoted to the subject.

2—Critical works:

(153) Febvre, L., *Philippe II et la Franche Comté* (Paris 1912).

(154) Huard, C., 'Sur l'histoire de la paroisse rurale des origines à la fin du moyen âge', *Revue d'histoire de l'Eglise de France* XXIV (1938).

(155) Roupnel, G., *La Ville et la campagne au XVIIe siècle, étude sur les populations du pays dijonnais* (Paris 1922; reprinted 1956).

(156) Vaissière, P. de, *Curés de campagne de l'ancienne France* (Paris 1933); deals in fact with the seventeenth and eighteenth centuries.

III—ORDERS AND SOCIAL CLASSES

1—*Texts and documents:*

(157) Bigot de Monville, (*Mémoires du Président*) *sur la sédition des Nu-pieds et l'interdiction du Parlement de Normandie* (Rouen 1876).

(158) Vulson de la Colombière, *Le Vray théâtre d'honneur et de chevalerie de la noblesse contenant les combats ou jeux sacrés des Grecs et des Romains, tournois, les armes . . .* (Paris 1648).

(159) Estienne, Charles and Liebault, J., *L'Agriculture et la maison rustique* (Paris 1583).

(160) Godefroy, D. and Godefroy, T., *Le Cérémonial français* (Paris 1649).

(161) Loyseau, C., *Traité des ordres et simples dignitez* (Paris 1613).

(162) Loyseau, C., *Traité des seigneuries* (Paris 1613).

(163) Loyseau, C., *Cinq livres du droict des offices* (Paris 1610).

(164) *Diaire ou journal du voyage du chancelier Seguier en Normandie après la sédition des Nu-pieds* (*1639–1640*), ed. A. Floquet (Rouen 1862).

(165) Tiraqueau, A., *Tractatus de nobilitate* (Paris 1579).

2—*Critical works:*

(166) Babeau, A., *Les Bourgeois d'autrefois* (Paris 1886).

(167) Bloch, M., 'Enquête sur le passé de la noblesse française', *Annales d'Histoire Economique et Sociale* (1937).

(168) Bloch, M., *Les Caractères originaux de l'histoire rurale française* (reprinted Paris 1952).

(169) Boissonnade, P., *Le Socialisme d'Etat, l'industrie et les classes industrielles en France* (*1453–1661*) (Paris 1927).

(170) Borkenau, F., *Der Ubergang von feudalen zum bürgerlichen Weltbild* (Paris 1934).

(171) Bouglé, C., 'Remarques sur le régime des castes', *Année Sociologique IV* (Paris 1900).

(172) Chassant, A., *Les Nobles et les vilains du temps passé ou recherches critiques sur la noblesse et les usurpations nobilaires* (Paris 1857).

(173) Coornaert, E., *Les Corporations en France avant 1789* (Paris 1941).

(174) Abbé Leclerc, 'Rôle du ban et arrière-ban des nobles du Haut Limousin en 1568', *Bulletin de la Société Archéologique du Limousin* (1894).
(175) Levasseur, E., *Histoire des classes ouvrières et de l'industrie en France avant 1789* (Paris 1900).
(176) Merle, L., *La Métairie et l'évolution agraire de la gâtine poitevine, de la fin du moyen âge à la Révolution* (Paris 1958).
(177) Mousnier, R., *La Vénalité des offices au temps de Henri IV et de Richelieu* (Rouen 1946).
(178) Normand, C., *La Bourgeoisie française au XVIIe siècle. La vie publique, les idées et les actions politiques, 1604–1661* (Paris 1908).
(179) Porchnev, B., *Les Soulèvements populaires en France, 1623–1648*, French translation (Paris 1961).
(180) Raveau, P., *L'Agriculture et les classes paysannes. La transformation de la propriété paysanne dans le Haut Poitou au XVIe siècle* (Paris 1926).
(181) Roupnel, G., *La Ville et la campagne au XVIIe siècle, étude sur les populations du pays dijonnais* (Paris 1922; reprinted 1956).
(182) Travers, E., *Rôle du ban et de l'arrière-ban du bailliage de Caen en 1552* (Rouen 1901).
(183) Vaissière, P. de, *Gentilshommes campagnards de l'ancienne France. Etude sur la condition, l'état social et les moeurs de la noblesse de province, du XVIe au XVIIe siècle* (Paris 1903).
(184) Venard, M., *Bourgeois et paysans dans la région au sud de Paris au XVIIe siècle* (Paris 1958).

IV—THE STATE, THE MONARCHY AND RELIGION

1—Texts and documents:

(185) Barclay, G., *De Regno et regali potestate, adversus Buchanum, Brutum, Boucherium et reliquos monarchomachos* (Paris 1600).
(186) Bèze, T. de, *Traité de l'autorité du magistrat en la punition des hérétiques, traité très nécessaire en ce temps pour advertir de leur devoir tant les magistrats que subjects* (1560).
(187) Bodin, Jean, *Les Six livres de la République* (Paris 1583).
(188) Calvin, J., *Institution de la religion chrétienne* (preface) (Geneva 1562).
(189) Coton, Pierre, *Lettre déclaratoire de la doctrine des Pères Jésuites conforme aux décrets du concile de Constance* (Paris 1610).
(190) Godefroy, Théodore, *Le Cérémonial de France, ou description des cérémonies, rangs et séances observées aux couronnements, entrées et enterrements des roys et roynes de France* (Paris 1619).
(191) Goulart, S., *Mémoires de l'Etat de France sous Charles IX* (Meidelburg 1577).

(192) Hotmann, F., *Franco Gallia* (Geneva 1573); French translation, *La Gaule française* (Cologne 1574).

(193) Jansenius, *Le Mars français, ou la guerre de France, en laquelle sont examinées les raisons de la justice prétendue des armes et des alliances du roi de France* (1637).

(194) Lebret, Cardin, *De la Souveraineté du Roy* (Paris 1632).

(195) Mariana, J. de, *De Rege et regis institutione libri III* (Toledo 1599).

(196) Plessis Mornay, P. du, *Vindiciae contra tyrannos* (*sive de principis in populum populique in principem legitima potestate*) (Edinburgh 1579).

(197) *Satyre Ménippée de la vertu du catholicon d'Espagne et de la tenue des Etats de Paris* (Tours 1593).

(198) Savaron, Jean, *Traité de la souveraineté du Roy et de son royaume* (Paris 1615).

(199) Sorbin, Arnauld, *Le Vray resveille-matin des calvinistes et publicains françois, où est amplement discouru de l'auctorité des princes et du devoir des sujets envers iceux* (Paris 1576).

2—Critical works:

(200) Aulard, A., *Le Patriotisme français de la Renaissance à la Révolution* (Paris 1921).

(201) Bloch, M., *Les Rois thaumaturges* (Strasburg 1924); includes a bibliography of older works on the subject, which has not been reproduced here.

(202) Buisson, F., *Sébastien Castellion, sa vie et son œuvre, 1515–1563* (Paris 1892).

(203) Febvre, L., *Un Destin, Martin Luther* (Paris 1928).

(204) Heyer, H., *Guillaume Farel. Essai sur le développement de ses ideés théologiques* (Geneva 1872).

(205) Imbart de la Tour, P., *Les Origines de la Réforme* (Paris 1905–35).

(206) Mercier, C., 'Les Théories politiques des calvinistes en France au cours des guerres de religion', *Bulletin de la Société de l'Histoire du Protestantisme français* (1934); also gives a bibliography of pamphlets and studies.

(207) Moore, W. G., *La Réforme allemande et la littérature française. Recherches sur la notoriété de Luther en France* (Strasburg 1930).

(208) Mours, S., 'Liste des églises réformées', *Bulletin de la Société d'Histoire du Protestantisme français* Year CIII (1957), nos. 1, 2, 3.

V—YOUTH SOCIETIES AND FEAST DAYS

1—Texts and documents:

There are not many documents devoted specially to the subject. One has to use scattered evidence from such works as:

(209) Thiers, J. B., *Traité des jeux et divertissements* (Paris 1686)

or consult the reproductions of triumphal arches and tableaux kept in the Print Room of the Bibliothèque Nationale.

2—Critical works:

(210) Adam, A., *Histoire de la littérature française au XVIIIe siècle* I.
(211) Lebegue, R., *Le Théâtre baroque en France* (Geneva 1942).
(212) Prunières, H., *L'Opéra en France avant Lulli* (Paris 1913).
(213) Rousset, J., *La Littérature de l'âge baroque en France: Circé et le Paon* (Paris 1954).
(214) Tapié, V. L., *Baroque et classicisme* (Paris 1957), especially II, ch. 2.

Forms of activity (Part III)

I—MANUAL TECHNIQUES

1—Texts and documents:

(215) Besson, J., *Théâtres des instruments mathématiques et méchaniques* (Lyon 1578).
(216) Choppin, R., *De Privilegiis rusticorum libri III* (4th edn, Paris 1606).
(217) De Serres, O., *Théâtres d'agriculture et mesnage des champs* (Paris 1600).
(218) Estienne, C. and Liebaut, J., *L'Agriculture et la maison rustique* (Paris 1564).
(219) Montchrestien, A. de, *Traicté de l'œconomie politique, dédié au Roy et à la Reyne mère du Roy* (n.d. [1615]).

2—Critical works:

(220) Bezard, Y., *La Vie rurale dans le sud de la région parisienne de 1450 à 1560* (Paris 1929).
(221) Bloch, M., 'Les Inventions médiévales', *Annales d'histoire économique et sociale* (1935).
(222) Bouvier Ajam, M., *Histoire du travail en France des origines à la Révolution* (Paris 1957).
(223) Coornaert, E., *Les Corporations en France avant 1789* (Paris 1941).
(224) Faucher, D., *Géographie agraire. Types de culture* (Paris 1949).
(225) Gille, B., *Les Développements technologiques en Europe de 1100 à 1400* (1955).
(226) Hauser, H., *Ouvriers du temps passé* (Paris 1927).
(227) Hauser, H., *Travailleurs et marchands de l'ancienne France* (Paris 1929).
(228) Nef, J., 'A Comparison of industrial growth in France and England from 1540 to 1640', *The Journal of Political Economy* (1936).
(229) Raveau, P., *L'Agriculture et les classes paysannes. La transformation de la propriété paysanne dans le Haut Poitou au XVIe siècle* (Paris 1926).

(230) Wolff, P. and Mauro F., *Histoire générale du travail: II, L'âge de l'artisanat* (fifth to eighteenth centuries) (Paris 1960).

II—THE CAPITALIST SPIRIT

1—*Texts and documents:*

(231) Bodin, J., *Les Six livres de la République* (Paris 1583).
(232) Einaudi, L. (ed.), *Paradoxes inédits du sieur de Malestroict touchant les monnoyes avec la réponse du Président de la Tourette* (Turin 1937).
(233) Laffemas, B. de, *Comme l'on doibt permettre la liberté du transport de l'or et de l'argent hors du royaume et par tel moyen conserver le nostre, et attirer celuy des estrangers. Avec le moyen infaillible de faire continuellement travailler les monnoyes de ce royaume, qui demeurent inutilles* (Paris 1602).
(234) Le Choyselat, Prudent, *Discours œconomique . . . monstrant comme de 5 cens livres pour une foys employées, l'on peult tirer par an 4 mil cinq cens livres de proffict honneste* . . . (Rouen 1612).
(235) Montchrestien, A. de, *Traicté de l'œconomie politique* (n.d. [1615]).
(236) Savary, J., *Le Parfait négociant* (Paris 1675).
(237) Savonne, P. de, *Brieve instruction de tenir livres de raison ou de comptes par parties doubles* (4th edn, Lyons 1608).

2—*Critical works:*

(238) Chaunu, P., *Séville et l'Atlantique,* 11 vols (Paris 1956–60).
(239) Ehrenberg, R., *Le siècle des Fugger,* translated into French (Paris 1955).
(240) Febvre, L., 'Types économiques et sociaux du XVIe siècle: le Marchand', *Revue des cours et conférences* (1921).
(241) Harsin, P., *Les Doctrines monétaires et financières en France du XVIe au XVIIIe siècle* (Paris 1928).
(242) Hauser, H., *Les Débuts du capitalisme moderne en France* (Paris 1902).
(243) Jeannin, P., *Les Marchands au XVIe siècle* (Paris 1957).
(244) Lapeyre, P., *Une Famille de marchands: les Ruiz* (Paris 1955).
(245) Roover, R. de, *L'Evolution de la lettre de change XIVe–XVIIIe siècles* (Paris 1953).
(246) Schnapper, B., *Les Rentes au XVIe siècle. Histoire d'un instrument de crédit* (Paris 1957).
(247) Sombart, W., *Der Bourgeois. Zur Geistesgeschichte des modernen Wirtschaftsmenschen* (Munich 1913).
(248) Tawney, R., *Religion and the rise of capitalism* (London 1926; reprinted 1936, 1938).

III—SPORTS AND PASTIMES

1—Texts and documents:

Question chrétienne touchant le jeu, adressée aux dames par Théotime, sçavoir si une personne adonnée au jeu se peut sauver, et principalement les femmes? (n.d.).

(249) St François de Sales, *Introduction à la vie dévote.*

(250) Daneau, Lambert, *Briève remonstrance sur les jeux de sort ou de hazard, et principalement de déz et de cartes, en laquelle le premier inventeur des dits jeux et maux infinis qui en adviennent sont déclarez, contre la dissolution de ce temps* (1591).

(251) Daneau, Lambert, *Traité des danses, auquel est amplement résolue la question, à savoir s'il est permis aux chrestiens de danser* (1580).

(252) Pasquier, E., *Recherches de la France* (Paris 1621).

(253) Sorel, C., *La Maison des jeux* (Paris 1642).

(254) Thiers, J. B., *Traité des jeux et divertissements* (Paris 1686).

2—Critical works:

(255) Allemagne, H. R. d', *Les Cartes à jouer du XIVe au XXe siècle . . .* (Paris 1906).

(256) Aragon, H., *Les Danses de la Provence et du Roussillon . . .* (Perpignan 1922).

(257) Ariès, P., *L'Enfant et la vie familiale . . .* (Paris 1960).

(258) Caillois, R., *Les Jeux et les hommes* (Paris 1958).

(259) Fournier, E., *Histoire des jouets et des jeux d'enfants* (Paris 1889).

(260) Huizinga, J., *Homo ludens, Versuch einer Bestimmung des Spiel-elements der Kultur* (Basle 1944).

IV—CULTURAL ACTIVITIES: ART AND THE ARTISTS

1—Texts and documents:

(261) Alberti, L. B., *L'Architecture et art de bien bastir* (Paris 1553).

(262) Cellini, B., *Opere*, French translation by L. Leclanché (2nd edn, Paris 1847).

(263) Fréart de Chambray, R., *Parallèle de l'architecture antique et de la moderne . . .* (Paris 1650).

2—Critical works:

(264) Faure, E., *Histoire de l'art: l'art renaissant* (1924).

(265) Febvre, L., 'Quatre leçons sur la première Renaissance française', *Revue des cours et conférences* (1925).

(266) Francastel, P., *Peinture et société* (Lyons 1942); makes use of the work of Panofsky, Kern, Oertel, etc.
(267) Lavedan, P., *Histoire de l'art: moyen âge et temps modernes* (Paris 1947).
(268) Male, E., *L'Art religieux de la fin du moyen âge en France* (Paris 1925).
(269) Seznec, Jean, *La Survivance des dieux antiques; essai sur le rôle de la tradition mythologique dans l'humanisme et dans l'art de la Renaissance* (London 1940).
(270) Tapié, V. L., *Baroque et classicisme* (Paris 1957); provides a good discussion of the question of the Baroque.

V—CULTURAL ACTIVITIES: THE HUMANISTS AND INTELLECTUAL LIFE

1—Texts and documents:

(271) Amyot, J. (tr.), Plutarque, *Les vies des hommes illustres* (Paris 1558).
(272) Budé, G., *Summaire ou epitome du livre de Asse, fait par le commandement du Roy* (Paris 1538).
(273) Budé, G., *De l'Institution du prince, livre contenant plusieurs histoires, enseignements et sages dicts des anciens, tant Grecs, que Latins* (Paris 1547).
(274) Des Periers, B., *Œuvres françaises* (1856 edn).
(275) Dolet, Etienne, *Commentarium linguae latinae* (Lyons 1538).
(276) Erasmus, D., *Epistolae familiares* (Antwerp 1545).
(277) Lefevre d'Etaples, J., *Commentarii initiatorii in quatuor Evangelia* (1521).
(278) Pasquier, E., *Œuvres* (1723 edn, Amsterdam).

2—Critical works:

(279) Bremond, H., *Histoire littéraire du sentiment religieux en France . . .*: I, *L'humanisme dévot* (Paris 1916).
(280) Brunot, F., *Histoire de la langue française*: II, *Le XVIe siècle* (Paris 1927).
(281) Dainville, R. P. F. de, *Les Jésuites et l'éducation de la société française, la naissance de l'humanisme moderne* (Paris 1940).
(282) Delaruelle, L., *Guillaume Budé, les origines, les débuts, les idées maîtresses* (Paris 1907).
(283) Doucet, R., *Les Bibliothèques parisiennes au XVIe siècle* (Paris 1956).
(284) Febvre, L., *Le Problème de l'incroyance au XVIe siècle, La religion de Rabelais* (Paris 1942).
(285) Febvre, L., *Origène et Des Périers, ou l'énigme du Cymbalum Mundi* (Paris 1942).
(286) Febvre, L. and Martin, H. J., *L'Apparition du livre* (Paris 1958).

(287) Renaudet, A., *Préréforme et humanisme à Paris pendant les premières guerres d'Italie* (Paris 1953).

(288) Renaudet, A., *Erasme, sa pensée religieuse et son action d'après sa correspondance (1518–1521)* (Paris 1926).

VI—SCIENTISTS AND PHILOSOPHERS

1—Texts and documents:

(289) Bacon, F., *Novum organum* (London 1620); English translation by W. Wood (London 1893).

(290) Cardan, J., *De propria vita liber* (Paris 1643); English translation by Jean Stoner, *The book of my life* (London 1931).

(291) Copernicus, N., *De Revolutionibus orbium coelestium libri VI* (Nuremberg 1543); French translation by A. Koyré (Paris 1934).

(292) Galileo, *Les Mechaniques de Galileo*, translated from Italian into French by Father Marin Mersenne (Paris 1634).

(293) Galileo, *Les Nouvelles pensées de Galilée*, translated from Italian into French by Father Mersenne.

(294) Mersenne, M., *Correspondance du P. Marin Mersenne religieux minime*, I and II, ed. P. Tannery and C. de Waard (Paris 1933, 1945); subsequent vols ed. C. de Waard, R. Lenoble and B. Rochot.

(295) Nicolas of Cusa, *De Docta ignorentia,* ed. Croce and Gentile (Bari 1913). vol. 19.

(296) Palissy, B., *Œuvres*, 2 vols (Niort 1888).

(297) Paré, A., *Œuvres complètes*, ed. J. F. Malgaigne, 3 vols (Paris 1840–41).

(298) Porta, J. B., *Magia naturalis* (Naples 1589).

(299) Ramée, Piette de la, *Dialectique* (Paris 1555).

2—Critical works:

(300) Bachelard, G., *La Formation de l'esprit scientifique* (Paris 1938).

(301) Busson, H., *Les Sources et le développement du rationalisme dans la littérature française de la Renaissance* (Paris 1922).

(302) Febvre, L., *Le Problème de l'incroyance . . . au XVIe siècle. La religion de Rabelais* (Paris 1942): the chapter on science.

(303) Gundel, *Dekane und Dekanesternbilder, ein Beitrag zur Geschichte der Sternbilder der Kulturvölker* (Hamburg 1936).

(304) Hooykaas, R., *Humanisme, science et Réforme* (Leyden 1958).

(305) Koyré, A. *et al.*, *La Science au XVIe siècle, colloque de Royaumont* (Paris 1960).

(306) *Léonard de Vinci et l'expérience scientifique au XVIe siècle,* Colloque du C.N.R.S. (Paris 1953).

(307) Lenoble, R., *Mersenne ou la naissance du mécanisme* (Paris 1943).
(308) Prowe, Léopold, *Nicolaus Coppernicus*, 3 vols (Berlin 1883–4).
(309) Schmidt, A. M., *La Poésie scientifique au XVIe siècle* (Paris 1939).
(310) Taton, R., *Histoire générale des sciences:* II, *La science moderne de 1450 à 1800* (Paris 1958).

VII—THE RELIGIOUS LIFE

No subject has given rise to a greater wealth of literature: we shall mention only those works exploited from our own particular viewpoint upon which we drew in the preparation of this chapter. It is therefore a select bibliography along conventional lines.

1—Texts and documents:

(311) Calvin, J., *Traité des scandales,* in *Opera omnia* (Brunswick 1900), VII.
(312) Calvin, J., *L'Institution chrétienne,* the 1541 text reprinted by Jacques Pannier (Paris 1939).
(313) Charron, P., *Trois livres de la sagesse* (Bordeaux 1601).
(314) Erasmus, D., *Opus epistolarum,* ed. Allen (Oxford 1910), I and II.
(315) Erasmus, D., *Exomologesis, sive modus confitendi* (Basle 1524).
(316) Farel, G., *L'Ordre et manière qu'on tient en administrant les sainctz sacremens, assavoir le baptème et la cène de Nostre Seigneur* (Geneva 1538).
(317) Garasse, F., *La Doctrine curieuse des beaux esprits de ce temps ou prétendus tels* (Paris 1624).
(318) Gassendi, P., *Opera omnia . . .* (Lyons 1658).
(319) Mersenne, M., *L'Impiété des déistes, athées et libertins de ce temps* (Paris 1624).
(320) Montaigne, M. de, *Journal du voyage en Italie* (Paris 1774).
(321) Rabelais, F., *Œuvres complètes*, ed. Plattard (Paris 1929).
(322) Raemond, F. de, *L'Histoire de la naissance, progrès et décadence de l'hérésie de ce siècle* (Arras 1611).
(323) Thomassin, R. P. L., *Ancienne et nouvelle discipline de l'Eglise . . .* (Paris 1679).

2—Critical works:

(324) Adam, A., *Théophile de Viau et la libre pensée française en 1620* (Paris 1936).
(325) Bataillon, M., *Erasme et l'Espagne* (Paris 1935).
(326) Benichou, P., *Morales du Grand Siècle* (Paris 1948).
(327) Berr, H., *Du Scepticisme de Gassendi*, tr. B. Rochot (Paris 1960).
(328) Bloch, M., *Les Rois thaumaturges* (Strasburg 1924).
(329) Borkenau, F., *Der Ubergang vom feudalen zum bürgerlichen Weltbild* (Paris 1934).

(330) Bremond, H., *Histoire littéraire du sentiment religieux en France depuis la fin des guerres de religion . . .* (Paris 1920–36).

(331) Busson, H., *Les Sources et le développement du rationalisme dans la littérature française de la Renaissance, 1533–1601* (Paris 1922).

(332) Desjardins, *Sentiments moraux au XVIe siècle* (Paris 1887).

(333) Febvre, L., *Le problème de l'incroyance au XVIe siècle. La religion de Rabelais* (Paris 1942): cf. the classified bibliography it contains.

(334) Febvre, L., *Au Coeur religieux du XVIe siècle*, a collection of articles (Paris 1958).

(335) Goldmann, L., *Le Dieu caché* (Paris 1955).

(336) Hauser, H., *Etudes sur la Réforme française* (Paris 1909).

(337) Le Bras, G., *Introduction à l'histoire de la pratique religieuse en France* (Paris 1942).

(338) Léonard, E. G., *Le Protestant français* (Paris 1953).

(339) Orcibal, J., *Les Origines du jansénisme* (Paris 1948).

(340) Pintard, R., *Le Libertinage érudit dans la première moitié du XVIIe siècle*, 2 vols (Paris 1943).

(341) Romier, L., *Le Royaume de Catherine de Médicis* (1922).

(342) Suaudeau, R., *L'Evêque inspecteur administratif sous la monarchie absolue* (Paris 1940).

(343) Weber, M., *Die protestantische Ethnik und der Geist des Kapitalismus* (Leipzig 1905).

VIII—NOMADISM

1—Texts and documents:

(344) Bodin, J., *Les Six livres de la République* (Paris 1583).

(345) Estienne, C., *La Guide des chemins de France* (Paris 1552); facsimile with commentary, ed. J. Bonnerot (Paris 1935).

(346) Montaigne, M. de, *Journal de voyage en Italie* (Paris 1774).

(347) Montchrestien, A. de, *Traicté de l'œconomie politique* (n.d. [1615]).

2—Critical works:

(348) Allix, A., *Un pays de haute montagne. L'Oisans* (Grenoble and Paris 1930).

(349) Braudel, F., *La Méditerranée et le monde méditerranéen à l'époque de Philippe II* (Paris 1949); in particular pp. 33–44, 126–31, 357–60, 643–60.

IX—IMAGINARY WORLDS

1—Documents:

Nothing would be gained by providing here a bibliography of travel books and missionaries' accounts: it is the commercial success of these works which is important, not their titles, a list of which has in any case already been given in the works by F. de Dainville and L. Deschamps cited below.

2—Critical works:

(350) Cohen, G., *Recueil de farces françaises inédites du XVe siècle* (Cambridge 1949).
(351) Dainville, F. de, *La Géographie des humanistes* (Paris 1940).
(352) Deschamps, L., *Histoire de la question coloniale en France* (Paris 1891).
(353) Lebègue, R., *Les Ballets des Jésuites* (Paris 1936).
(354) Lebègue, R., *La Tragédie religieuse en France. Les débuts (1154–1573)* (Rennes and Paris 1929).
(355) *Musique et poésie au XVIe siècle*, Colloque du C.N.R.S. (Paris 1954).

X—BLACK MAGIC AND DEATH

1—Texts and documents:

There can be no question of including here a bibliography of contemporary literature on witchcraft and demonology: it would run to pages. On the other hand, on the subject of death, not to mention suicide, there are only a few rare works, following the vogue of the *Ars moriendi* in the fifteenth century, among them:

(356) Clichtove, Jossé, *Doctrina moriendi* (Paris 1520).
(357) *La Prognostication du Ciècle advenir contenant troys petits traictez. Le premier détermine comment la mort entra premièrement au monde. Le second parle des âmes des trépassez. Et de la différence des paradis. Le tiers de la dernière tribulation. Et de la résurrection des corps* (Lyons 1537; *BN, Rés.* D, 80054).

On the subject of magic, we shall mention only the classic studies:

(358) Boguet, H., *Discours exécrables des sorciers, ensemble leurs procez, faits depuis deux ans en ça* (Lyons 1603).
(359) Crespet, P., *Deux livres de la hayne de Sathan et malins esprits contre l'homme et de l'homme contre eux* (Paris 1590).
(360) Del Rio, M., *Les Controverses et recherches magiques de M. del Rio* (Paris 1611).
(361) Lancre, P. de, *Tableau de l'inconstance des Mauvais Anges et Démons, où il est amplement traicté des sorciers et de la Sorecelerie* (Paris 1612).
(362) Loyer, P. le, *Quatre livres des spectres ou apparitions et visions d'Esprits, Anges, et Démons* (Angers 1586).

(363) Nynauld, J. de, *De la Lycanthropie, transformation et extase de sorciers* (Paris 1615).

(364) Remy, N., *Demonolatriae libri tres* (Lyons 1595).

(365) Sprenger, J., *Malleus maleficarum. De Lamiis et Strigibus et Sagis* (Frankfurt 1588, Lyons 1604).

(366) Taillepied, F. N., *Traité de l'apparition des esprits . . .* (Rouen 1600).

2—Critical works:

Hitherto, few modern studies have been published on these two problems, and those that exist do not approach the subject from our point of view. On witchcraft, one might mention:

(367) Bavoux, F., *La Sorcellerie au pays de Quingey* (Besançon 1947).

(368) Bavoux, F., *Hantises et diableries dans la terre abbatiale de Luxeuil* (Paris 1956).

(369) Delcambre, E., *Le Concept de la sorcellerie dans le duché de Lorraine au XVIe et au XVIIe siècles*, 3 vols (Nancy 1948).

(370) Delcambre, E. and Lhermitte, I., *Un Cas énigmatique de possession diabolique en Lorraine au XVIIe siècle: Elisabeth de Ranfaing, l'énergumène de Nancy* (Nancy 1957).

(371) Pfister, C., *L'Energumène de Nancy: Elisabeth de Ranfaing et le Couvent du Refuge* (Nancy 1901).

(372) Pfister, C., 'Nicolas Rémy et la sorcellerie en Lorraine à la fin du XVIe siècle', *Revue historique* (1907).

(373) Wagner, R. L., *Sorcier et magicien* (Paris 1939).

On the subject of death:

(374) Bremond, H., *Histoire littéraire du sentiment religieux en France . . .*: IX, *La vie chrétienne sous l'ancien régime* (Paris 1936).

(375) Halbwachs, M., *Les Causes du suicide* (Paris 1931). Cf. the review by Marc Bloch in *Annales d'histoire économique et sociale* (1931), p. 590.

(376) Tenenti, A., *Il Senso della morte e l'amore della vita nel Rinascimento* (Turin 1957).

Index